HAWKWIND:
DAYS OF THE UNDERGROUND

First published by Strange Attractor Press 2020

CoverArtwork by John Coulthart
Book Design by Richard Wilkins / Layout by Maia Gaffney-Hyde

ISBN: 9781907222849

A CIP catalogue record for this book is available from the British Library.

Strange Attractor Press
BM SAP,
London, WC1N 3XX, UK
www.strangeattractor.co.uk

Distributed by The MIT Press, Cambridge, Massachusetts.
And London, England.

Printed and bound in Estonia by Tallinna Raamatutrükikoda.

# Hawkwind:
# Days Of The Underground

Radical Escapism In The Age of Paranoia

# Joe Banks

*To Rachel, Alexa and Catrin,*
*with love*

*Let the myth do the work*
Doug Smith

# Contents

# A Note On The Text

*Days Of The Underground* isn't a standard music biography, so a few words of explanation first.

Roughly speaking, there are four types of 'chapter' in the book:

[CHRONOLOGY] A year-by-year overview of and commentary on Hawkwind's progress through the 1970s, including analyses of every non-album and relevant solo recording released or broadcast at the time

[ALBUM] A track-by-track, in-depth look at each album, from *Hawkwind* to *Levitation*

[ESSAYS] A series of think pieces on Hawkwind's musical and cultural impact on the 1970s and beyond, from psychedelia to science fiction, myth-making to punk

[INTERVIEWS] Conducted 2016-19 with key members of the Hawkwind crew

The book moves in a chronological direction, though you may experience some sideways motion through time, particularly in the essays. It can be read from page one onwards or dipped into as the mood takes you. There are a lot of endnotes, but I'd encourage you to keep your finger in the relevant page (at the end of each chapter) as you read – even the most hardcore of Hawkfans will discover something new. Please also note that many of the images in the book are rare, archival material; we've chosen to include them even if they appear damaged or imperfect.

Joe Banks, March 2020

# In Visions Of Acid, We Saw Through Delusion

*Hawkwind is a movement, not just a group.*
Melody Maker, 1972[a]

Hawkwind were a one-band revolution in the 1970s. While the rest of the British rock scene was stuck in a dead end of pseudo-classicism and reheated versions of the recent past, Hawkwind tirelessly travelled the country to spread the good news of the counterculture – long after it had been declared dead by the supposed tastemakers of the media. They animated the provincial underground and became a rallying point for heads and freaks everywhere.

Aggressively flying in the face of music industry convention, Hawkwind valued raw energy over technical proficiency and displayed a bloody-minded desire to do things their own way, both qualities that would be taken up in the middle of the decade by punk – as far as Stephen Morris (Joy Division/ New Order) is concerned, "Punk rock started because in every small town there was somebody who liked Hawkwind".[b]

The story of Hawkwind's first decade reveals an alternative narrative for music in the 1970s. Figureheads of the free festival, avatars of the underground, and heralds of punk, it portrays a band offering an active means of resistance to both mainstream music and society. Yet it's a story that remains mostly unacknowledged. It's also been largely forgotten just how big Hawkwind were, particularly in the first half of the 70s.

At the height of their artistic and commercial powers, Hawkwind channelled and amplified the era's psychic tenor via a science fiction sensibility, mind-blowing visuals, and their unique brand of deep space psychedelia. For the young people of a planet seemingly on the brink of destruction, they offered a form of radical escapism and an alternative account of this strange new world.

As one of the few bands with a genuine cultural hinterland throughout the 1970s, Hawkwind demand a more considered evaluation, and that's what this book sets out to provide. As well as being an in-depth primer to the music of their classic years, *Days Of The Underground* explores the ideas and concepts that fuelled Hawkwind during this period, and speaks to the crew that manned the ship.

◇◇◇◇◇◇◇◇◇◇◇◇◇◇◇◇◇◇◇◇◇◇◇◇◇◇◇◇◇◇◇◇◇◇◇◇◇◇◇◇◇◇◇◇◇◇◇◇◇◇◇◇◇◇◇◇◇◇◇◇◇◇◇◇◇◇◇◇◇◇

a     'Hawkwind - The Joke Band That Made It' – Andrew Means, *Melody Maker*, 12/08/72

b     'Bakers Dozen: Joy Division & New Order's Stephen Morris On His Top 13 Albums' – Ben Hewitt, *The Quietus*, 7/12/10

DAYS OF THE UNDERGROUND

In visions of acid
we saw through delusion
and brain-box pollution
we knew we were right.
The streets were our oyster
we smoked Durban poison
and we turned our noise on
we knew how to fight
We dropped out and tuned in
we spoke secret jargon
and we would not bargain
for what we had found
in the days of the underground

We believed in Guevarra
we saw that head held up
and our anger welled up
but we kept it cool
no needx for machine guns
the system was crumbling
our leaders were fumbling
while we broke every rule
we saw them on Tv
they'd blown their cover
and we tried to smother
their voices with sound
in the days of the underground
whatever happened to those chromium heroes
are there none of them still left around
since the days of the underground.

Now we can look back
on the heroes we were then
we made quite a stir then
with our sonic attack
street fighting dancers
assassins of silence
with make-believe violence
on a hundred watt stack
they offered us contracts
we said we don't need em
we'll just take our freedom
we will not be bound
in the days of the underground

Some of us made it
but not smiling Michael
his black motorcycle
got eaten by rust
and John the Bog dreamt that
he slept at the wheel when he it was real
too late to have sussed
and Jeff was a poet who wrote
with a spray can on walls saying
hey man - I believe we have drowned
in the days of the underground.

Robert Calvert's typed lyrics to 'Days Of The Underground'
(source: Robert Calvert archive.)
All images from the Robert Calvert archive courtesy of Nick Calvert.

Brock and Turner, rehearsal circa 1972
(photo: Pennie Smith)

# Standing On The Runway

August–December 1969

All successful religions have an enduring creation myth, and Hawkwind are no exception.[1]

On 29 August 1969, the band – hurriedly billed as "Group X" – gatecrash a gig at the All Saints Hall in London's Notting Hill and persuade promoters Clearwater Productions to let them play a short set, a 20-minute jam based loosely on the riff from The Byrds' 'Eight Miles High'.[2] Yet rather than a reverential take on a psychedelic standard, it's an eruption of pounding drums, caveman guitars, primitive electronics and wailing sax.[3] It's the birth of a unique brand of sonic attack that would reverberate throughout the 1970s and beyond.

The gods are smiling on them that night. In the audience is influential DJ and doyen of the underground John Peel. As he leaves, he tells Clearwater's **Doug Smith** to "get involved", which Smith duly does, plugging the band into the alternative gig circuit that companies like Clearwater are helping to create. Almost exactly a year later, Hawkwind will release their debut album.

▾    ▾    ▾

Pre-Hawkwind, **Dave Brock** and **Mick Slattery** play a raucous, psychedelic-tinged version of the blues in their band The Famous Cure. When that breaks up, Brock takes to the streets of London and earns a successful living as a busker. He also forms an acoustic blues trio – Dave Brock & Friends – that supports groups including The Pretty Things and the Groundhogs, and blags a session on John Peel's *Night Ride*.

In January 1969, Brock plays the Albert Hall as part of a special 'Buskers' Concert' organised by Don Partridge, and records a version of Willie Dixon's 'Bring It On Home' for the accompanying album. And in May, he joins Partridge on 'The Buskers' tour, a nationwide travelling revue featuring other street musicians and itinerant acts.

But both Brock and Slattery are increasingly being turned on by the proto-electronic rock coming from underground clubs such as UFO, where Pink Floyd and Soft Machine are deconstructing R&B and jazz to create a spacier and more improvised strain of British psychedelia. Brock begins experimenting with tape loops, creating strange drones from old blues harmonica recordings, which he and Slattery play slide guitar to through a Binson echo unit. They discover this sounds particularly good under the influence of LSD.

It's the direction they want their next band to go in. Brock recruits bassist **John Harrison** – previously a player with popular dance band the Joe Loss Orchestra – while untutored but enthusiastic 17-year old drummer **Terry Ollis** is found via an ad in *Melody Maker*. Rehearsing over the summer, the two guitarists extend and jam blues standards and songs from Brock's busking repertoire into new, more abstract shapes while Harrison provides a low-end anchor.

But it's with the arrival of two new members that their sound really begins to evolve.

Brock and Slattery had first encountered Nick (subsequently **Nik**) **Turner** when The Famous Cure played Tent 67, a 'psychedelic circus' touring the Netherlands which Turner had helped to crew. Now living in Notting Hill, after a spell in Berlin's avant-rock and jazz scenes, Turner owns and drives a van, shifting stock and equipment for headshops and bands. Initially hired as road manager and driver, his rudimentary talent on the saxophone soon sees him inducted into the new band.

The final addition to the line-up is Richard Michael Davies aka **DikMik**, a mutual friend of both Turner and Brock/Slattery. Initially a roadie, he joins the band after being given a piece of electronic equipment, which turns out to be a signal generator for testing radio valves. DikMik discovers that by running this equipment through a tape delay system, he can produce the type of eerie tonalities that Brock has been experimenting with, but without the need for cumbersome tape loops.[4]

Turner and DikMik bring an elemental chaos to the band's sound that helps them break away from the blues-based structures that most rock music still pivots around. Turner has enthused about playing free jazz in a rock context ever since his time in Berlin, while the often violent electronic sounds produced by DikMik's primitive set-up become notorious for the physical effect they have on the audience.[5]

Turner will later describe the band as, "…a complete environmental thing, where all the senses are moved and used. We want people to get stoned on the show, not on acid and things. At the moment, we're rehearsing with the strobes turned on, and it really does get you high."[a] With pulsating lights and bowel-shuddering vibrations, they become a band not just heard, but *felt*.

▼        ▼        ▼

Now playing regular gigs in and around London, and re-named Hawkwind Zoo – partly in reference to Michael Moorcock's Dorian Hawkmoon character,[6] but mainly inspired by Turner's prodigious phlegm-hawking and wind-breaking – their next task is to record a demo. Brock taps up Don Paul, a producer at Essex Music and the man behind The Buskers tour, who arranges a recording session for the band at EMI Studios in Abbey Road.

Rather than attempt to reproduce the improvised excursions of their live shows, and perhaps wary of scaring off potential record companies, they record three relatively conventional tracks.

'**Hurry On Sundown**' will go on to become the band's first single, but there's a more melancholic vibe in this early take, the chiming intro slower and less sitar-like. However, Brock's confident and distinctive vocals, honed by years of playing on the streets, are clearly a major asset. Slattery's bluesy psychedelic vamping is pleasant enough if a little half-hearted – the subsequent version will replace electric guitar with a more upbeat harmonica. Turner's throbbing sax can just about be heard, but will also be excised from the later version. It's an undeniably catchy piece of urban folk music, if a little underpowered in demo form.

By contrast, '**Kiss Of The Velvet Whip**' (aka '**Sweet Mistress Of Pain**') fizzes with energy and mischief, swinging wildly between sunny Californian psychedelia, gnarly Velvet Underground-esque freak-out and Pink Floyd at their gloomiest. The rise and fall of the main riff is like the arching back of the song's sado-masochistic protagonist, flexing in pleasure and pain, the "oohs" and "aahs" of the guitar and sax mimicking their cries. It's a long way from the sonic and lyrical territory they'll come to inhabit, but Brock delivers lines such as "*Feel the pain burning, reaching up your spine / How your body shudders, higher as you climb*" with real gusto. The 'Venus In Furs'-esque subject matter is tackled head-on without a hint of prurience, demonstrating a subversive, even transgressive, edge to the band right from the start. And how many other British groups were referencing VU in 1969?

The final track is a robust cover of Pink Floyd's '**Cymbaline**', a brooding acoustic ballad from the recently released *More* soundtrack. It's an interesting choice – perhaps they don't consider their other material strong enough, or maybe they're pragmatically aligning themselves with one of the underground's most popular bands. Brock's vocal delivery lacks the subtle intonation of Dave Gilmour, and the instrumentation as a whole is rough around the edges. But it plugs them into a seam of moody English mysticism that they'll subsequently mine on their debut album.

▾          ▾          ▾

Events move quickly once the demo is complete. Doug Smith approaches **Andrew Lauder,** UK manager of Liberty Records, who agrees in principle to release a single by the band, which with a little subsequent persuasion is upgraded to an album.[7] Having shed the 'Zoo' part of their name on the advice of John Peel ("too Haight-Ashbury"), Hawkwind enter the 1970s on a high, both figuratively and literally...

<><><><><><><><><><><><><><><><><><><><><><><><><><><><><><><><><><><><><><><><><><><><><>

a    'The Hawk: Sailing In The Face Of The Wind' – Mark Plummer, *Melody Maker*, 5/9/70

1    "Myth" is an apposite word, as various parties maintain that the nascent Hawkwind played other gigs before All Saints Hall. Mick Slattery recalls an earlier appearance at Chiswick Town Hall, and the annals of Eel Pie Island Hotel had them playing there on 26 July 1969. However, Slattery describes the Chiswick show as "just a jam with various people getting up and playing, more like a party really," and the Eel Pie Island gig was also a private party. Slattery notes, "All Saints Hall was the first gig we did with the full line-up... We didn't have any numbers together at that time, so we just jammed on the riff from 'Eight Miles High'." (ref: Hawkwind and Related Album History Facebook group, 12 November 2019) Slattery also claims to have got permission on the day to play All Saints Hall, while Dave Brock maintains that the band had been invited to appear in advance by Skin Alley, one of the other bands on the bill (ref: "I Have A Perverse Mind, Don't I?" – Malcolm Dome, *Record Collector*, February 2020).

2    Or John Coltrane's 'India' depending on who you speak to, the track that inspired Roger McGuinn to write 'Eight Miles High'. They weren't the only local band jamming on 'India' at the time – for instance, Mighty Baby had been playing a version of it since their previous incarnation as The Action.

3    Guitarist Mick Slattery refers to this jam as 'Sunshine Special' before leaving the stage, the name possibly inspired by the potent strain of LSD known as Orange Sunshine popular in San Francisco at the time.

4    DikMik: "I had an audio generator, which is a radio-testing kit, [and] an oscillator, which is an octave splitter. I fed that through a Watkins Copicat echo unit, then a fuzz pedal, a wah-wah pedal and a microphone, and just experimented." (From interview with author.) The exact

9

provenance of DikMik's original kit is lost to posterity, though Nik Turner claims that it was provided by people involved with the Covent Garden-based Arts Lab (afterwards the Institute for Research in Art and Technology), who also made various pedals and effects for Turner.

5    While modern club goers are familiar with the muscle-loosening properties of sub-sonic frequencies, this would have been a relatively unusual experience in the late 60s/early 70s. Two early press features from the following year – 'Journey Into Space', Jonathon Green, *Friends*, 13/11/70, and 'When It Comes To Mind-Blowing, Hawkwind Are Really Into It' – Jerry Gilbert, *Sounds*, 17/09/70 – reference gigs where members of the audience are physically sick as a result of Hawkwind's electronic bombardment.

6    Dorian Hawkmoon is one of the recurring heroes of Moorcock's 'Eternal Champion' series of books, where the central character is fated to maintain the balance between order and chaos across intersecting worlds and ages. Other incarnations include Elric of Melniboné, Jerry Cornelius, Erekosë and Corum.

7    Signing Hawkwind was another prescient move on Lauder's behalf. Having previously brought Creedence Clearwater Revival to the British public's attention, Lauder will also introduce Krautrock to the UK by releasing records by Can, Amon Düül II and Neu! Dave Brock will write the sleeve notes for the UK/UA release of Neu!'s 1972 debut album.

# The Death And Resurrection Of British Psychedelia

## Reigniting The Flames Of The Experimental 60s

When Hawkwind first stumbled onto the underground scene, psychedelia was effectively dead in Britain. In just a few years, it had changed both the sound and look of a generation, but now it was something of an embarrassment. Its influence would echo for years throughout popular culture, but by 1969, there were few serious musicians who still actively subscribed to the idea of being in a psychedelic band.

Yet from the start, Hawkwind's music was undeniably psychedelic. But this was a new type of psychedelia, one where sonic exploration was just as likely to turn into sonic attack, with third eyes forcibly opened via a combination of propulsive raw power and mind-melting electronics. Hawkwind rekindled the ashes of 60s psychedelia and turned them into a raging chemical conflagration. Where once there had been Summer Of Love-inspired hippies preaching good vibes to all men, now there was a ragged group of freaks and renegades hurtling headlong into the void.

## Psychedelic Pioneers

In its strictest sense, 'psychedelic' refers to the altering of normal perceptions via the ingestion of psychotropic drugs such as LSD.[1] But psychedelia quickly became part of a much bigger shift in attitudes across the arts and society at large. Old certainties were questioned, traditional boundaries started to break down, new forms of expression emerged.

Listening to and playing music under the influence of drugs suggested a myriad of new sonic possibilities. Attempting to replicate the narcotic-enhanced music in their heads, bands used reverb, phasing and flanging effects to create a heavier, more distorted sound. Non-western scales and tunings were introduced, along with instruments such as sitars, tablas, harpsichords and early electronic keyboards.

In 1965, The Beatles pioneered the psychedelic sound with the sitar-driven ballad 'Norwegian Wood', then followed this up with the hypnotic drone of 'Tomorrow Never Knows'. But it was 1967's double A-side single 'Penny Lane' and 'Strawberry Fields Forever', a visionary mix of pastoral, orchestral and avant garde influences, which would define the sound of UK psychedelia.

Perhaps the most significant group to emerge from the British psychedelic scene – certainly as far as Hawkwind were concerned – was Pink Floyd. While extended jams and freak-outs were a commonplace feature of concerts by US West Coast luminaries such as the Grateful Dead and Quicksilver Messenger Service, Pink Floyd eschewed the blues scales these bands used and performed experimental improvisations based on sound manipulation. Songs such as 'Interstellar Overdrive' might stretch out towards the half hour mark not through protracted soloing, but via waves of abstract noise and sonic texture, Syd Barrett rolling ball bearings along his fretboard or Rick Wright mimicking a spacecraft's distress signal on his Farfisa.

Outlandishly outré, even unlistenable, just a few years previous, this was now the happening soundtrack to a London-based underground scene. At clubs such as UFO on Tottenham Court Road and Middle Earth in Covent Garden, LSD was readily available and the music was complemented by the phantasmagorical illuminations of coloured slides and oil wheels. Rather than alienate audiences with their exploratory, sometimes structureless songs, Pink Floyd performances became part of a synesthetic whole, a genuine psychedelic experience.

## Psychedelia In Retreat

The arrival of psychedelia led to a critical re-evaluation of pop music as something more than just ephemeral entertainment for working class teenagers. Lennon published poetry, McCartney name-dropped Stockhausen, and the cultural establishment took note. The Who's Pete Townsend talked about smashing up guitars in terms of "auto-destructive art", while classical music critic Hans Keller wondered why Pink Floyd needed to play so damn loud.[a] An intellectual subculture developed around rock music as it became the soundtrack to an entire lifestyle, with fans studying song lyrics and record sleeves for deeper meanings.

Psychedelia was an even bigger deal in America, a rallying point for an emerging counterculture fiercely opposed to the aggressive conformity of the straight world and the country's increasingly bloody conflict in Vietnam. From Haight-Ashbury to Greenwich Village, psychedelia became the radical soundtrack to the protest movement, an expression of political dissent rather than mere teenage rebellion.

Yet by the late 60s, psychedelia had become a victim of its own success, with a flood of second-rate imitators – and much of popular culture itself – having co-opted its paisley and Day-Glo aesthetic while ignoring its musical and social call-to-arms. Bands began to turn their backs on sonic adventurism and mind expansion, and started instead to make music that was less self-consciously trippy. In America, country rock became popular and the singer-songwriter scene developed, while Britain was the unlikely epicentre of a blues rock boom and also saw the staging of a folk revival.

1969 was a watershed year for the counterculture. The Woodstock festival in August may have represented the zenith of the "peace, love and music" credo, but the utopian dreams of the 60s were being savagely undercut by dark, violent forces: police brutality in response to escalating protests over the Vietnam War and civil rights; the Manson Family murders; Altamont.

1969 also saw a clutch of key debut albums from the likes of Led Zeppelin, King Crimson and The Stooges that would point the way forward for 'serious' music in the next decade: chest-beating stadium rock; brainy faux-classicism; proto-noise thuggery on the margins. While some of psychedelia's early pioneers delivered albums that acted as capstones on their original trajectories – Pink Floyd's *Ummagumma*, the Grateful Dead's *Live/Dead* – other players sought to refine and control psychedelia's whimsical excesses. The establishment in the UK of 'progressive rock' as the music that mattered for the next half-decade or so was the final nail in first-wave psychedelia's coffin.

Yet Hawkwind followed their own path, mavericks from the start. Rather than presiding over its death, they imbibed and distilled ideas and influences from the previous few years to create a new type of psychedelia, one more fitting for the spirit of the age.

## The Acid Gospel Reborn

So what did Hawkwind take from the first age of psychedelia and what did they leave behind?

An obvious point of continuity was making music intended to encourage an altered state of perception.[2] Smoking, speeding and tripping would actually become more prevalent among audiences in the 70s as recreational drugs became more widely available. But if many of the bands themselves had recanted the Acid Gospel, the members of Hawkwind were still committed users of psychedelics (and would remain so until the mid-70s), something which was clearly reflected in their dense, saturated music.

But the psychedelic visions that Hawkwind channelled predated the UFO club. This was music that reached back into a pre-history of ritual and ceremony, where naturally occurring hallucinogens such as psilocybin and peyote were routinely used as a gateway to other planes of consciousness. Hawkwind's attitude to LSD may have been less Aquarian Age holy sacrament and more basic way of life, but their ability to take the listener on a shamanic journey through an intense, sometimes frightening sonic realm became for many fans the equivalent of a religious experience.

Hawkwind's presentation of themselves as a live, multimedia spectacle was also core to the band's re-ignition of the psychedelic flame. Integral to their gig-as-a-trip philosophy was the use of lighting and slides to create an immersive environment for the music, the blobby colour wheels of the early psychedelic clubs transformed into a complex arrangement of moving images. Instead of spots to pick out the singer or the guitarist when they took a solo, Hawkwind used strobes and projections to deliberately obscure themselves and de-centralise their role as performers.

Psychedelia had fallen out of favour in Britain because of mannered, stereotypical elements such nursery-rhyme vocals, swirling middle eights, and a general air of genial bemusement. Hawkwind kept the trippiness, but ditched the whimsicality, favouring a musical approach built around riff, rhythm and freeform improvisation. But they quickly moved beyond the blues ragas of the West Coast jam bands and entered a unique zone where relentless forward motion combined with instrumentation that was amorphous rather than individualistic, a sonic dissolution of the ego more convincing than the long-winded solos of Jerry Garcia or John Cipollina.

The music press, who for the most part were baffled by Hawkwind's popularity, argued that the band's sound and style of playing was merely the result of its members' lack of musical proficiency. But what most critics missed was that this was how Hawkwind consciously chose to express themselves. At a time when virtuosity was a prerequisite for any rock band hoping to be taken seriously, Hawkwind's refusal to play the game was a bold stance to take, and one which would have a profound influence on a generation of bands to follow.

Adding fuel to the critics' fire, Hawkwind also featured avowed non-musicians in their ranks – but DikMik and Del Dettmar's contribution to the band's sound was another vital element in their unique take on psychedelia. While earlier bands had introduced new colours into their music via effects pedals and non-rock instrumentation, Hawkwind incorporated raw electronic frequencies – not so much imitating the effects of drugs as directly tapping into the brain's alpha and theta waves.

Hawkwind's embrace of technology, even at this relatively primitive level, was in contrast to the first wave of psychedelic bands, where the use of instruments such as the sitar and harpsichord suggested a flirtation with the mystic East or retreat into an imagined past, psychedelia as a return to a prelapsarian Eden. Instead, Hawkwind used technology to create futuristic soundscapes that reflected the space age their fans were actually living through.

## Not All Trips Are Good Trips

Hawkwind redefined psychedelia by accepting noise and chaos as an aesthetic in itself. Improved amplification and speakers in the late 60s had allowed bands to play louder, but a prolonged aural assault was unusual – technique and virtuosity demanded light and shade. Hawkwind didn't employ squealing feedback or strutting power chords, but they understood the psychedelic properties of sustained, metronomic noise, making music designed to engulf the listener's conscious mind and short-circuit cognitive processes rather than take them on a clearly signposted trip.

Crucially, they understood that not all trips are good trips. Taking LSD can produce a feeling of oneness with the world and inspire wonder at the intricacy of creation – but it can also lead to a derangement of the senses and the terror of self-annihilation. Hawkwind were certainly capable of evoking feelings of stoned, cosmic bliss, but their vision of psychedelia was far from benign. As Lemmy memorably put it, "We were a black fucking nightmare. A post-apocalypse horror soundtrack."[b]

Hawkwind took LSD's evocation of 'the void' literally, and used space as a guiding metaphor – yet instead of gazing in tripped out wonder at the stars, Hawkwind would blow the human mind by channelling the dark, unfathomable vastness of the universe. Like first-wave psychedelia, their music was a soundtrack to disruption – but it wasn't about burning call-up papers or fighting the police. Instead, this was existential protest music, rock untethered from its earthly orbit and blasted into the eternal night.

◇◇◇◇◇◇◇◇◇◇◇◇◇◇◇◇◇◇◇◇◇◇◇◇◇◇◇◇◇◇◇◇◇◇◇◇◇◇◇◇◇◇◇◇◇◇◇◇◇◇◇◇◇◇◇◇◇◇◇◇◇◇◇◇◇◇◇◇◇◇◇◇◇◇◇◇◇◇

a     *The Look of the Week*, BBC2, 14/5/67

b     'Any Way The Wind Blows' – Toby Manning, *Record Collector*, May 2002

1     Writer Rob Chapman describes the gradual spread of LSD into society as "the greatest pharmaceutical field experiment in the history of Western civilisation" (p33, *Psychedelia And Other Colours*, Rob Chapman, 2015).

2     As Spacemen 3 would later put it, Hawkwind embraced the maxim "taking drugs to make music to take drugs to" with some gusto.

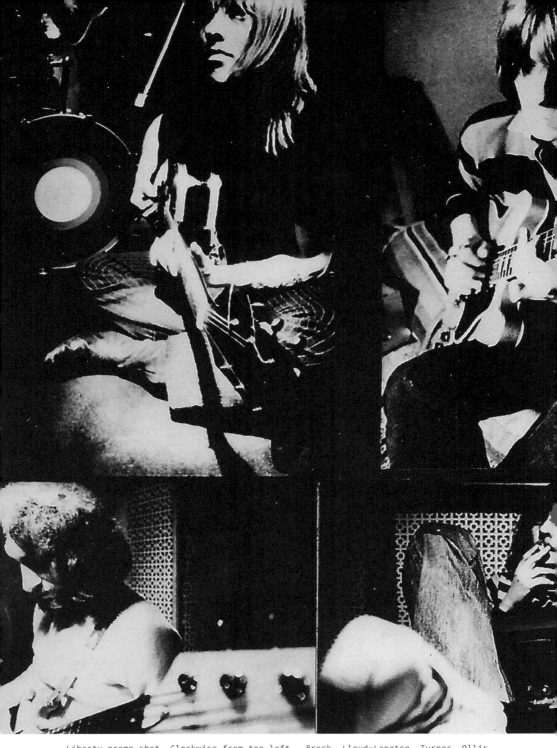

Liberty promo shot. Clockwise from top left - Brock, Lloyd-Langton, Turner, Ollis, DikMik, Harrison (source: Doug Smith archive)

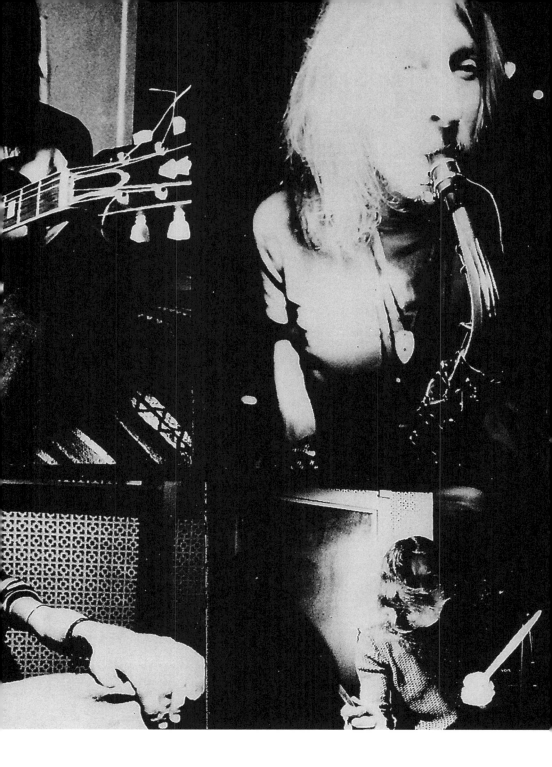

# Hundreds Of People Like You And Me

January–August 1970

*THURSDAY: Hawkwind set up inside. Generator failure. Total blackness in dome. Fans stop running... dome starts collapsing. Total silence. Broken by Terry on drums (how did he see them?). Applause. Whistles. Cheers. Freaky! Power finally goes back on. Hawkwind & Fairies play to capacity crowd. Everyone tripped out & blotto!!*
Mick Farren, `International Times`[a]

Almost exactly a year on from their first gig, another major element in Hawkwind's creation mythology happens at the 1970 Isle Of Wight Festival. A key event in the development of a nationwide underground scene, over half a million fans descend on the festival site, but only 50,000 of them are paying customers. The official stage is in a fenced-off, ticketed area – everybody else watches from the hill overlooking the site. The acrid scent of confrontation is in the air, as militant factions argue that the festival should be free for all.

An alternative festival springs up outside the fence, based around Canvas City, an inflatable dome and stage. In the company of the Pink Fairies,[1] Hawkwind spend five days performing seemingly non-stop, a precursor to every benefit gig they'll play over the next few years, enhancing their reputation as agents of chaos, the anti-establishment resistance, the ultimate People's Band...

But it's often more musical endurance test than free gig. Many participants have consumed fruit juice spiked with LSD, and even for the psychedelic veterans, it sometimes proves too much. As Dave Brock recalls, "We were playing a heavy riff for about four hours with strobe lighting going on and off, and it freaked me out so badly I just had to get away. I gave my guitar to the nearest person, something I would never do normally, and just walked up to the top of the hill, but I still couldn't get rid of this thing in my head".[b]

With Brock and Turner gone AWOL,[2] drummer Ollis, bassist **Thomas Crimble** and guitarist **Huw Lloyd-Langton** jam out extended, echo-drenched mantras, with occasional help from a troupe of Brazilian percussionists.[3] On the final day, the fences come down and Hawkwind play inside the official enclosure, part of the liberating army sticking it to The Man.

▾       ▾       ▾

On 28 January, Hawkwind officially sign to Liberty Records[4] – and almost immediately, Mick Slattery leaves the band to travel to Morocco. **Dick Taylor**, ex-Pretty Things guitarist and the man earmarked to produce their debut album, stands in for a few gigs before Brock recruits Lloyd-Langton as Slattery's replacement.

Taylor is a canny choice for producer. The Pretty Things' long hair, raucous performances and tough take on R&B had quickly earnt them a reputation as one of Britain's most 'dangerous' pop acts, yet by 1968's ground-breaking concept album *S.F. Sorrow*, they were mixing metallic riffing with psychedelic sound design and visionary lyrics. Taylor is as comfortable with Hawkwind's abstract noise as he is with their more conventional folk blues.[5]

Work begins on the album in March at Trident Studios. 'Hurry On Sundown' and 'Mirror Of Illusion' are recorded in conventional style, but it's quickly obvious this won't work for the rest of the set, which revolves around long-form improvisation anchored by a few recurring chord sequences. Instead, the band do various takes of their set live in the studio, with the best performances recorded and edited into 'songs'. The fact that each of the resulting tracks has a dynamic identity of its own is a testament to Taylor's ears, the mic-ing skills of session engineer Barry Ainsworth, and of course to Hawkwind themselves.[6]

Meanwhile, they continue to grow as an exciting and unusual live band, regularly playing the Implosion club night at the Roundhouse, now the epicentre of London's musical underground. On 9-15 March, it hosts the Atomic Sunrise festival, one of the first indoor events of its kind, with Hawkwind billed alongside scene luminaries Arthur Brown, Third Ear Band and Quintessence, plus David Bowie and the up-and-coming Genesis.[7]

On 29 March, they play their first show abroad at Le Festival Musique Evolution near Paris, alongside Pink Floyd, Ginger Baker's Airforce, Kevin Ayers and the Edgar Broughton Band. And on 28 June, they perform for the first time together with the Pink Fairies on the back of a flatbed truck outside the Bath Festival of Blues and Progressive Music, a glimpse of things to come.[8]

On 31 July, '**Hurry On Sundown**'/'**Mirror Of Illusion**' is released as a single, followed by their debut album *Hawkwind* on 14 August.[9]

〰〰〰〰〰〰〰〰〰〰〰〰〰〰〰〰〰〰〰〰〰〰〰〰〰〰〰〰〰〰〰〰〰〰〰〰〰〰〰〰〰

a    *International Times* 87, 10-24/9/70

b    'When It Comes To Mind-Blowing, Hawkwind Are Really Into It' - Jerry Gilbert, *Sounds*, 17/09/70

1    Hawkwind and the Pink Fairies would play together as one band on many occasions. Fellow denizens of Ladbroke Grove, the Fairies were The Deviants minus Mick Farren – ejected from the band during a disastrous US tour in 1969 – plus John 'Twink' Alder, formerly of Tomorrow and The Pretty Things. Farren, writer and professional agitator, was a constant presence in the UK underground scene, and one of the Isle of Wight militants. His path will cross Hawkwind's many times during the 70s.

2    Nik Turner wandered around the festival, his silver make-up attracting interest from both press photographers and Jimi Hendrix, who dedicated a song to "the cat with the silver face". Pictures of him appeared in *Vogue, Paris Match* and *The Daily Telegraph* magazine, which ran a seven-page feature – 'Was This The End Of Rocktopia?' (Anthony Haden-Guest, 30 October 1970) – that signalled changing perceptions of the counterculture: "Has the concept of the great 'peace and love' meeting grown too big to support itself, turning, instead, into a mammoth marketing event?"

3    The percussionists were at the festival with exiled Tropicália stars Gilberto Gil and Caetano Veloso, who Nik Turner played with on the main stage: "I was astonished to discover how big these guys were. They seemed so humble, so generous, so eager to jam with anyone." 'Gilberto Gil and Caetano Veloso in London' – John Lewis, *The Guardian*, 15/7/10

4    The original contract was for "six single 45rpm sides" ie three 7" singles. Doug Smith: "The band had to record at least four sides during each of the following four option periods, after the first year. This quickly just morphed into albums!" (interview with the author).

5    Pretty Things drummer Viv Prince occasionally depped for Terry Ollis, as did the Pink Fairies' Twink, who played drums on *S.F. Sorrow*. Dick Taylor: "At the time, everyone was getting very musical and precious… but this was like seeing a psych version of The Pretty Things. There was a really good atmosphere and no one was knowing quite what they were doing – but who cared, because it sounded good" (from 'Hurry On Hawkwind', Ian Abrahams, *Interstellar Overdrive, the Shindig Guide to Spacerock*, 2014).

6    Dick Taylor: "What was quite amazing was that each piece had such an individual character. I don't know quite how they achieved that to be really honest; when I heard them I thought, 'How do they do all this?'… But the essential thing was that each song had its structure… even when they went out into quite strange places, it was always quite ordered chaos" (Ian Abrahams, 2014, same source).

7    Hawkwind played on 13 March. Atomic Sunrise was professionally filmed, with footage taken of two songs from each act – in Hawkwind's case, 'Hurry On Sundown' and 'The Reason Is?'/ 'Be Yourself'. The raw footage has been in the possession of graphic designer Adrian Everett for the past thirty years, during which time (on and off) he has been assembling the performances and trying to interest various parties in producing a proper film of the event. At the time of writing, Everett was still hopeful of such a film emerging in the not too distant future.

8    An alternative festival – headlined by the Pink Fairies, to take place outside the official Bath Festival venue – was scotched by traffic delays, and no one was sure where it was being staged. "Because of this, most of the groups who had agreed to play didn't even know where the Fairies were, and by the time we left on Sunday afternoon, Hawkwind were the only other group to have appeared" (*IT*, 3-16/7/70).

9    Bought by United Artists, Liberty was still trading as a separate label. While *Hawkwind* is released on Liberty, all subsequent records made under the contract signed with Andrew Lauder are released on UA.

# The Hawk: sailing in the face of the wind

HAWKWIND are the progressive band, who, they say, are too progressive for British progressive clubs, and receive few bookings because of that fact.

" We don't do too much work. Most of Britain's progressive clubs won't have us, because they say we are too progressive for them," said Dave Brock, singer and guitarist with the electronic group.

" But work is picking up now," added Nick Turner, " mainly because of the LP. I think we have six bookings next month."

Hawkwind, a truly progressive group, don't just rely on noise and sex to create excitement. The strangely named Dikmik plays electronic noises on an audio generator which is an important part of the overall sound.

" Dikmik originally joined as our roadie, but when we found he was interested in making noises on electric things, we asked him to join.

" It was the same with Nick. He came to town to join us as our roadie, and when we found he played alto, we asked him to join as well," said Dave.

Nick added : " When they asked me to join as a musician, I said yes. Then I realised I hadn't played the alto for about five years, so I had to brush up on my technique pretty quickly."

The group — Nick, alto; Dave, vocals and guitar; Huw Langton, lead guitar; Dikmik, electronic noises; Terry Ollis, drums; and Thomas Crosbie, bass (he replaced John Harrison who played bass on the album) — were planning to do a free concert on the Isle of Wight, when I met them

last week. " We did a free concert at Bath with the Pink Fairies and we are going to do the same at the I.o.W." said Dave Brock.

" We did a free thing the other week at the Scrubs and really enjoyed it. When a concert is for free you get good vibrations because no-one has paid to see you. You are on the same level as the audience, the only difference being the fact that you are playing the guitar and not them," said Dave.

" When we played at Bath we organised a collection. The things we received were incredible. Money, acid and loads of other things," added Nick.

The subject changed to money and groups, and how it changed them, and the unfortunate fact that because Hawkwind have no money, at least half of them are sleeping rough at any one time. " A lot of bands as they become successful and earn a lot of bread seem to put

themselves above the audience. When you get successful, bread does seem to change a lot of people. A lot of bands get their bread then forget what they were before.

" They tend to turn their backs on the people they mixed with before," said Huw, sitting reading a Batman comic.

" Yeah, but when you get a lot of bread, you get a lot of hangers on," challenged Nick.

" But you have to sort them out from your real

due for release in March then put back, " and put back again, when the factory went on holiday for a week," was cut live in the studio.

" We tried double tracking, and laying down separate parts, but it was so sterile that we ended up just playing it live. Doing two or three takes of each number and picking the best, after a little polish was added here and there," said Nick.

" The studio was sterile and inhuman," added Huw.

Hawkwind are now using lights and strobes to turn their audiences on. " We want to use a complete environmental thing, where all the

much longer when we did them in the studio. Dave writes the idea for the song, then we improvise round that idea, including the words which Dave writes roughly beforehand. The trouble in the cuts were about 15 or 20 minutes each, then they cut them down to seven and things like that," added Nick.

things.

" At the moment we are rehearsing with the strobe turned on us, and it really does get you high," said Nick.

" And Dikmik is working on a thing where sheets of reflecting plastic are put in front of the speakers, and they move round with the sound waves, bending and reflected light," said Dave. " We want to get a new directions. But one of our troubles is money," said Dave. " We want to get Moog to ......

'Hawkwind...don't just rely on noise and sex to create excitement'
*Melody Maker*, 5 September 1970
(source: Jim Skinner collection)

Early all-nighter, Woolwich Poly, 30 January 1970

# FRIARS
### New Friarage, Walton Street
### AYLESBURY

## MONDAY, FEBRUARY 23rd

# HAWKWIND

Hawkwind play electronic interstellar frequencies.
This is a Special Concert.

## POETS : LEGENDARY OPTIC NERVE LIGHT SHOW
## ANDY DUNKLEY :: EVERYONE IS A BUS

'Interstellar Frequencies' – first appearance at Aylesbury Friars,
23 February 1970

# *Hawkwind*

Released 14 August 1970

| | |
|---|---|
| *Label:* | Liberty / United Artists (USA - 1971) |
| *Track listing:* | Hurry On Sundown / The Reason Is? / Be Yourself / Paranoia - part 1 / Paranoia - part 2 / Seeing It As You Really Are / Mirror Of Illusion (All songs composed by Dave Brock arranged by Hawkwind) |
| *Line-up:* | Dave Brock / Nik Turner (credited as Nick Turner) / Huw Lloyd-Langton (credited as Huw Lloyd) / DikMik / John A. Harrison / Terry Ollis |
| *Recorded at:* | Trident Studios |
| *Produced by:* | Dick Taylor & Hawkwind |

As an opening gambit, '**Hurry On Sundown**'[1] lacks the interstellar throb of their later work, but demonstrates from the off that Hawkwind can do songcraft as well as psychic derailment. It might be atypical of the 'classic' Hawkwind sound, but Brock's busking folk/blues style echoes across their first few albums. Hawkwind are an urban band, and 'Hurry On Sundown' is music from the kerbside – it may sound upbeat, but it's smog-choked around the edges.

A fingerpicked 12-string mimics the twinkling harmonics of a sitar, a melancholy signifier of the Summer Of Love. There's a cluster of down strokes, and then the main riff arrives with an all-join-in-together brio. Terry Ollis's drums clip-clop along and John Harrison's bassline ambles rather than walks, but Brock's voice and harmonica is strong and clear, accustomed as he is to cutting through background traffic. There's also some nice, though uncredited, guitar work from Dick Taylor.

Yet if 'Hurry On Sundown' harks back to the protest songs of the 1960s, there's an ambivalence here too. The title suggests an impatience for the day to be over, to "*see what tomorrow brings*". But, "*Well, it may bring war / Any old thing*", is more fatalistic shrug than brave new world. "*Look into your mind's eye / See what you can see*" suggests it's up to the individual to find their own way in life, while "*There's hundreds of people like you and me*" strikes a more communal note. It may not be widespread, but a viable counterculture has come into existence – and Hawkwind intend to reach out to its members. An antipathy to the straight world, coupled with calls for hippie self-reliance, would feature strongly in their lyrics during the first half of the 70s.

'**The Reason Is**?' plunges the street-corner busker into chilly, nebulous gloom. The dark ambient interludes the band improvise in their live sets are an essential counterpoint to their heavy-duty space rock, and this is an early recorded example of their gift for creating uncanny atmospheres, more folk ritual than space ritual, a slow processional through moonlit woods.

First there's a rumbling sibilance of percussion and a scraping of strings, then a voice high in the trees, a ghostly spirit calling on the listener to walk further into the forest. An ascending passage of minor key guitar seems to offer reassurance, but the cymbals shimmer with anxiety. An insistent bass is a brooding presence behind you, and now that voice wails piteously in your ear. Not for the last time on this album, it feels like we've entered the territory of supernatural horror.

'**Be Yourself**' is a rude awakening, announcing itself with a staccato three-chord riff that's so basic it feels slightly unhinged. This impression is reinforced when bass and sax join in on the riff, now slurring and dragging its feet. Brock barks out the title as a robotic command – once again, he wants us to look inside and not just conform to society's roles. "*I can see others like me*" – but he's still ultimately dissatisfied: "*I can't find peace of mind*". A volley of drums takes us into archetypal Hawkwind territory, a free-flowing improvisation driven by a strong melodic bassline and choppy guitar, while Turner blows along like a lone piper in an eastern bazaar.

Yet this is still a prototype of their classic sound, more psychedelic jam than nuclear-powered space rock, as is evident when Lloyd-Langton takes a long solo. His playing is fluid in the wailing blues not-quite-metal style that many guitarists favour at this time – yet his very proficiency seems at odds with the underlying groove, as it muscles everything else out of the way. Central to Hawkwind's sound-to-come will be the stripping away of such 'technical' elements.

This song also sees the first real appearance of DikMik's audio generator. Primitive and relatively limited as his set-up is, it gives the music a futuristic sheen, from the electronic howlaround of wind to the metallic laser fire cutting through the instrumental freak-out section. These wild and unruly frequencies – this belief in the liberating qualities of abstract noise – will become a defining part of Hawkwind's sonic identity.

'Paranoia' is the word that defines the 1970s, a nagging accumulation of dreads and fears – of nuclear war, the population bomb, rising pollution, the energy crisis. For Hawkwind and their milieu, this feeling of mental siege mixes uncomfortably with the residual love and peace vibes of the previous decade. They also have to contend with the day-to-day suspicions of the straight world, hassle from The Man being an ever present threat.

The thin sliver of '**Paranoia – part 1**' which ends side one is like the edited highlights of a horror movie trailer, the spectral unease of 'The Reason Is?' ratcheted up to nerve-jangling suspense: a creeping death bassline with sax and guitar in lockstep suggests something truly unpleasant is about to happen. A little too garish even for Hammer, it might have been ripped from one of the violent 'giallo' thrillers produced by the Italian film industry in the 60s and 70s.

'**Paranoia – part 2**' opens with a murmur of querulous bass notes recalling Pink Floyd's 'Careful With That Axe, Eugene', but the vibes here are even darker. It's a rising assault on the senses, again with a strong ritualistic aspect – and these droning voices chanting "*higher, higher*" aren't about to transport you to some benign astral plane. An insistent, migraine-inducing riff leads back into the lurching, we're-coming-to-get-you bassline of 'Part 1', this time possessed by the unquiet spirits of the audio generator, an approaching steam train morphing into an exploding meteor. The tempo increases and there's more laser blasts before it peaks, slows and grinds to a halt. It may seem brutish and crass to music fans of a nervous disposition, but 'Paranoia' is an effective distillation of its title.

'**Seeing It As You Really Are**''s title returns to the theme of being true to yourself – the world is full of illusions and it's up to the individual to see through them. It also extends the sense of eerie desolation underpinning this album. The mechanical breathing and echoing whispers could be the sounds of deep space slumber – suspended animation is a recurring motif in Hawkwind songs. But this is more like a disorientating voyage into inner space, a blown mind trapped in the claustrophobic corridors of the brain.

A two-note bass pulse emerges and a witches' chorus of androgynous voices wails along,[2] building towards a stoned, ecstatic singularity. Remember that 1970 is the year of Led Zeppelin's 'Whole Lotta Love',[3] Deep Purple's 'Hard Lovin' Man', and Free's 'All Right Now', songs where the male ache of the blues has morphed into lascivious hard rock. Yet as Plant, Gillan and Rodgers howl and ululate their mystic macho virility, Hawkwind are sighing and shouting out in surrender to the *Om* of universal consciousness. Rock culture may be giving in to its lusty id, but here's an outpost of the underground still intent on dissolving its ego.

Lloyd-Langton's spirited solo moves the track into more routine territory – but the banshee shriek and spectral choir of the audio generator are calling time on such rock & roll conventions. The galloping midpoint is pretty thrilling, even if the clompy interlude that follows is more tea break than dynamic breakdown. In the final stretch, Turner's sax scrambles free – we hear him playing through a wah-wah pedal for the first time, producing the distinctive bubbling, babbling tone so characteristic of the early Hawkwind sound. It's a decent enough freak-out, with most of the key elements already present – they're just not in alignment yet.

'**Mirror Of Illusion**' ends the album as it began, with another of Brock's busking numbers. A discordant opening riff resolves into cantering bass and rhythm, and a voice that's reassuringly earthy after our trip. Brock's still dissatisfied and alienated, though: "*In the cold grey-mask of morning I cry out / But no-one feels the sound that I shout.*" Rejecting the chemical wisdom of the 'tune in, turn on, drop out' generation, he sings of "*a dream world that you've found will one day drag you down,*" before pointing the finger at the counterculture's holy sacrament: "*You think you've found perception doors / They open to a lie*".[4] This is an intriguing stance from a band notorious for its ingestion of LSD. Brock seems to say that anybody seeking instant, acid-fuelled enlightenment is in for a nasty surprise – whatever your drug, the world is a harsh and difficult place. And the sooner you realise it the better.[5]

Yet the song itself is upbeat and melodically compelling, with a more evolved arrangement than 'Hurry On Sundown' and a proper verse/bridge/chorus construction. Lloyd-Langton's bluesy solos have a nice Keith Richards feel, and the audio generator mews sweetly in the background. Another nice touch is the way the bass mirrors the lyric melody. John Harrison may not have Lemmy's bone-crunching heft, but he's the first of many surprisingly tuneful bassists who'll supply the ear-worming undercarriage to the crunching guitar and controlled electronic chaos that make up much of Hawkwind's early output.

Fading into the distance, 'Mirror Of Illusion' returns to its initial discordancy, until a last electronic chirrup signals closedown. They don't achieve escape velocity on their debut recording, but in an underground scene accustomed to experimentation and spontaneity, it's still a bold assertion of Hawkwind's essential otherness.

◇◇◇◇◇◇◇◇◇◇◇◇◇◇◇◇◇◇◇◇◇◇◇◇◇◇◇◇◇◇◇◇◇◇◇◇◇◇◇◇◇◇◇◇◇◇◇◇◇◇◇◇◇◇◇◇◇◇◇◇◇◇◇◇◇◇◇◇◇◇◇◇◇◇◇◇◇◇

1   The origins of this song are likely in 'Hurry Sundown', a gospel blues released in 1944 by Richard Huey & His Sundown Singers, which includes the refrain "See what tomorrow brings".

2   These voices presumably belong to Brock, Turner and DikMik.

3   While 'Whole Lotta Love' charted around the world in 1970, it wasn't released as a single in Britain. Nevertheless, it became a staple of rock radio and clubs for years to come, and was adapted as the *Top Of The Pops* theme 1970-1977.

4   A reference to Aldous Huxley's *The Doors Of Perception*, a key text for advocates of psychotropic drugs and a popular countercultural tract.

5   These sentiments aren't new to Brock. 'Mirror Of Illusion' shares its lyric with 'Illusions', a dour but affecting piece of acid folk recorded by Dave Brock & Friends for the 29 January 1969 edition of John Peel's *Night Ride* show.

# Hundreds Of People Like You And Me

August–December 1970

Nik Turner and Thomas Crimble
(Doug Smith archive)

*Hawkwind* comes in an eye-gougingly psychedelic gatefold sleeve, its purple, orange and green palette enough to make even the most ardent trippers feel queasy, while inside is a colourised shot of the band playing in front of a speaker stack Stonehenge. So far, so hippie, and there's a definite West Coast 60s vibe to Arthur Rhodes' artwork: alligator men are born from conical piles of leaves on the cover, while a reptilian truck writhes around the edge of an idyllic bayou scene on the flipside. It's an intriguingly surreal piece of work, but how well it reflects the record's penumbral, uncanny mood is debatable.[1]

The sleeve notes are just as anachronistic, each member expressing in a couple of sentences where they're coming from. Brock is focused and pragmatic ("I don't really do much except play music"). Turner is free-spirited ("I just dig freaking about on saxophones"). DikMik is upfront and unapologetic ("I've got practically no musical knowledge, but I figure if you let it become your whole trip... you can do anything you like"). Only Harrison directly professes an interest in "electronic music" – ironically enough, as by the time of Hawkwind's release, he's been replaced by Thomas Crimble.[2]

They end with what amounts to an early mission statement, laying out their ambitions for the future: "This is the beginning. By now we will be past this album. We started out trying to freak people (trippers), now we are trying to levitate their minds, in a nice way, without acid, with ultimately a complete audio-visual thing. Using a complex of electronics, lights and environmental experiences."

There had been worries about capturing the Hawkwind sound in the studio, with Lloyd-Langton complaining that Trident was "sterile and inhuman".[a] According to *Friends*, the band are unhappy with the way the improvised tracks were edited, and with Taylor's sense of how they should sound.[b] But overall, the members are generally pleased with the album.[3]

It fails to chart, but receives positive reviews.[4] What's interesting is that, despite DikMik's input being relatively low in the mix, the write-ups all focus on Hawkwind as makers of 'electronic music'. *Melody Maker* applauds them for using sonic effects "discriminatingly, and only when they are needed to convey a feeling... It's tremendous."[c] *Disc And Music Echo* are quick to identify them with Pink Floyd,[d] while *Music Now* is impressed by the way the album sprawls, unconstrained for the most part by traditional song structures.[e]

The band is already being promoted as a 'space rock' act, despite no overt references to the cosmos on this first album. The press ad superimposes the group shot from the inner gatefold on the curved surface of a dark planet, the Earth rising behind it, while the text simply states: "Space Rock.... a new album". Another early poster features a bizarre hawk/man/skeleton bestriding the moon and holding a flaming sword aloft, the slogan proclaiming "Hawkwind does live!"[5] It all points to a band ready to fill the vacuum left by the increasingly earthbound Pink Floyd.

▾       ▾       ▾

On 18 August, Hawkwind record their first radio session for John Peel's *Top Gear* at the BBC's Maida Vale Studios.

'**Hurry On Sundown**' is once again the friendly, getting-to-know-you song, its languid intro backed by electronic bird calls. Crimble subtly embellishes the bass line, while Lloyd-Langton's wandering blues vamps work well against a staccato version of the riff. DikMik and Turner combine like angry ghosts haunting one another before the song slows to a halt. It's certainly a more fully realised group effort than the album version.

'**Seeing It As You Really Are**' is much darker, a past-life therapy session gone wrong. Close mic'ed breathing and cymbal clicks create an unsettling vibe, the slowly chanted "*You – Go – You – Know*" turning to jagged screams of "*No!!*" as Lloyd-Langton lets rip with a strident solo, his playing less tentative than on the album.[6]

'**Some Of That Stuff**' is something else. It starts as a bluesy jazz band stomp, with whooping and whistling aplenty, before Brock as a drug-addled hepcat entreats his "big fat mama" to "try some of this stuff" – sure enough, "she opened her mouth and I popped one in". But soon we're in more familiar territory: a moody riff, DikMik and Turner wailing away, and a first-take solo from Lloyd-Langton that might lack technique, but fizzes with energy. A brief return to the jazz pastiche, then mercifully it ends. Brock is evidently finding his jocular busker persona hard to leave behind.[7]

▾       ▾       ▾

Between the session's recording and its broadcast on 19 September, there's the Isle of Wight, and a descent into lysergic madness. Assailed by acid-induced demonic visions, Lloyd-Langton drops to his knees onstage and prays for salvation. Turner tells him to do it at every gig ("It looked really cool"),[£] but the young guitarist's torment is real, and he leaves the band soon after.

Hawkwind elect not to replace him, a momentous decision for their sound and direction. With no traditional soloist in their ranks, they're forced to find other ways to embellish their extended improvisations.

Rather than levitating minds "in a nice way", they begin experimenting with sonic attack: "There was this gig at Nottingham and no-one listened to the first set, they were all too busy getting pissed in the bar. When it came around to the second set and we played 'Paranoia', the electronics were too much for them".[9] Brock expands on the idea: "You can force people to go into trances and tell them what to do; it's mass hypnotism and you're really setting yourself up as God".[h]

The Isle Of Wight and their appearance at the Pilton Pop, Folk & Blues Festival in September[8] enhance their underground credibility, but it's the free gigs they play around their Ladbroke Grove base that really cement their status as a community project. The first of these takes place as part of the 1970 Notting Hill Carnival on a stage in front of Wormwood Scrubs. Despite rain and intimidation by local skinheads, the gig – afterwards known as 'Wormstock' – is deemed a success.[i] They also start playing gigs under the concrete arches of the Westway.[9]

Naturally sympathetic to alternative causes and willing to play for free, Hawkwind are a popular choice for the organisers of benefit gigs. In their first extended press feature, Jonathon Green in *Friends* opines that, "Hawkwind sometimes sound, in their ideas, like some hip anachronism. Love, peace and flowers are all well and good, but isn't it a bit late for that?" Yet the band are in a fighting if somewhat paranoid mood: "In the next couple of years, something is going to happen, good or bad: young people everywhere know this... At the moment, things are moving towards a complete invasion of privacy, everyone's surveyed, assessed and annihilated... The system still preserves itself and destroys those who question it".[j]

▾     ▾     ▾

On 5 November, Hawkwind record in front of a live audience at London's Paris Theatre for John Peel's *Sunday Concert*, which is broadcast ten days later.

Crimble extracts as much dread as possible from the bass riff to '**Paranoia**' as Ollis rumbles threateningly underneath: Turner's sax is like an alarm trying to wake us from what sounds like a nightmarish, deconstructed take on contemporary Krautrock.

Crimble's muscular bass is again prominent in the positively malevolent '**Seeing It As You Really Are**'. There's a controlled barrage of laser fire from DikMik and the amorphous vocalisations still disturb – but there's a sense of expectation being created that, in the absence of Lloyd-Langton's guitar, the band don't seem entirely sure how to fulfil. There is, however, a brief appearance of Brock's distinctive damped strumming style, and the song is brought to an explosive, well-executed end.

Peel introduces the band, and says they want to buy a synthesiser: "I can't help but feel that they'll use it more effectively than some of the people who already have them." Their next song is **Untitled**, something he approves of, because the show is all about the ability to "stretch out".

What follows is 15 minutes of uncompromisingly propulsive and astonishingly intense out-rock, perhaps inspired by those long-form Canvas City jams. Crimble lays down a driving, looping bassline that Ollis matches with a pounding *motorik* beat. Turner's sax burbles at the fringes and Brock chops at his guitar, but it's the dense, hypnotic rhythm track that holds the attention – it's completely unlike anything else that's happening in the British music scene at the time. Bass and drums thud in manic unison, overwhelming in the best possible way, while electronic artillery shells whistle overhead. Retrospectively named '**I Do It**' (then '**We Do It**') from the song's only distinguishable words, it's a major leap forward, and a definitive, early peak in Hawkwind's trance-cendent sound.[10]

▾          ▾          ▾

In just 18 months, Hawkwind have gone from a Putney rehearsal basement to spearheading the post-60s countercultural scene and the development of electronic music. "Most of Britain's progressive clubs won't have us, because they say we are too progressive for them," claims Brock,[k] but they're a busy and popular live attraction around the country, ambassadors of the underground to wannabe heads everywhere.[11]

In December, *Disc And Music Echo* describes them as "the freakiest and most electrifying band doing the rounds at the moment",[l] and they end the year playing the 'Christmas Spaced Party' benefit for the underground press at the Roundhouse, alongside the Pink Fairies. Less festively, and much to his surprise, Thomas Crimble then finds himself sacked.

## 'You can force people to go into a trance'

**HAWKWIND MAY not be the world's most affluent group, or the world's most successful group, but they are certainly one of the most mind-blowing.**

Their single release in no way reflects the kind of sounds they are into, and the album only serves to scratch the surface. The fact is that their engineer, Dikmik, uses apparatus which emits strange electronic force waves.

And recently the band noticed that the waves being produced by their audio generator was having a profound effect on audiences, not to mention themselves.

Dikmik has fitted a ring modulator to his audio generator, which produces arcs of sound in three different frequencies. But Dikmik can change the pitch of these drones and the top register sound gradually spirals higher and higher until it reaches a piercing, screeching pitch.

Says the group's guitarist Dave Brock: "The sounds send out a force field and things really came to a head at the Isle of Wight.

"We were playing a heavy riff for about four hours with strobe lighting going on and off, and it freaked me out so badly I just had to get away. I gave my guitar to the nearest person, something I would never do normally, and just walked up to the top of the hill, but I still couldn't get rid of this thing in my head."

Dave Brock realises the potential danger and is endeavouring to learn more about forces so that he can be sure of the effects Hawkwind's excursions into the unknown will have.

He described recent scenes at Norwich and Nottingham where people were being physically sick, tearing their hair out, or just totally transfixed by the sound.

● *DAVE BROCK: 'We're like a magnet.'*

# WHEN IT COMES TO MIND-BLOWING, HAWKWIND ARE REALLY INTO IT

'You can force people to go into a trance.' *Sounds*, 17 October 1970 (source: Paul Windle collection)

〰〰〰〰〰〰〰〰〰〰〰〰〰〰〰〰〰〰〰〰〰〰〰〰〰〰〰〰〰〰〰〰〰〰〰〰〰〰〰〰〰〰〰〰〰

a     'The Hawk: Sailing In The Face Of The Wind' – Mark Plummer, *Melody Maker*, 5/9/70

b     'Journey Into Space' – Jonathon Green, *Frendz*, 13/11/70

c     Mark Plummer, *Melody Maker*, 29/8/70

d     *Disc And Music Echo*, 8/70

e     'It's All Part Of The Trip' – *Music Now*, 27/6/70

f     p75, *Spirit Of Hawkwind*, Nik Turner & Dave Thompson

g     Jonathon Green, same source. Unattributed, probably Brock

h     'When It Comes To Mind Blowing, Hawkwind Are Really Into It' – Jerry Gilbert, *Sounds*, 17/09/70

i     'Oh! What A Scene', *The Kensington Post*, 4/9/70

j     Jonathon Green, same source. Hawkwind quotes unattributed, likely Brock or Turner

k     'The Hawk: Sailing In The Face Of The Wind' – Mark Plummer, *Melody Maker*, 5/9/70

l     "'Free' Hawkwind slam expensive bands like Free!' – Caroline Boucher, *Disc and Music Echo*, 12/70

1     Arthur Rhodes believes that alternative cover illustrations were under consideration. One may be the image of a bird-man warrior on horseback riding through the clouds that features on the 1971 debut album by Welsh hard rockers Budgie. Originally commissioned by Hawkwind, but then rejected, artist David Sparling merely replaced the rider's hawk head with that of a budgie (ref: 'Heavier Than A Cast Iron' – Michael Heatley, *Record Collector*, June 2015). Ironically, Budgie used another illustration originally intended for Hawkwind on the cover of their 1981 *Nightflight* album, after artist Derek Riggs became worried that Hawkwind wouldn't pay for his work. Huw Lloyd-Langton was briefly a member of Budgie in 1978.

2     The exact manner of some departures from the band remains both mysterious and contentious to this day. Crimble had been bass player in Skin Alley, another Clearwater group.

3     Perhaps surprisingly, Brock, Turner and drummer-to-be Simon King have all named the debut album as their favourite.

4     As Hawkwind built a live reputation outside London, reviews appeared in local papers as well as the specialist music press. The *Leamington Spa Morning News*: "Like the Floyd, Hawkwind feature electronics – constructively, not just as a gimmick… But they are not just a copy. Their music is unique, in my experience at least" ('More Winners For Liberty', 20/9/70). *The Barnsley Chronicle*: "a slightly Floydish feel about it, but the group have sufficient individuality to make them a potent force in the music business… I liked it immensely" ('Pick Of The Records', 19/9/70).

5 "Hawkwind does live!" is an adaptation of the "Hawkwind Lives!" stickers found throughout the London Underground around this time. The hawk-skeleton poster is by Alan Tanner, a Margate friend of Turner's, who produced artwork for Clearwater and also designed the cover of the Groundhogs' *Thank Christ For The Bomb*. "In my original drawing, various 'body parts' of a hawk and a human skeleton were hurtling off in all directions through space… But the band said they wanted all the parts put together again… It's nearly 50 years since I drew this, but I still think my 'exploding' version was better!" ('Alan Tanner's 'Music Is The Revolution'' – *Govanhill Voice*, 1/8/16).

6 During the 12 December repeat broadcast of this session, Peel characteristically punctures the atmospheric opening of 'Seeing It As You Really Are', interrupting himself mid-preamble to exclaim, "What's this extraordinary hissing?? Oh, never mind: Hawkwind… Oh I see, that's what the hissing was." A final interjection to someone in the studio ("Another marshmallow?") suggests he's forgotten to turn his mic off.

7 This is the only recording of this song. It's referred to as 'Came Home' on most bootlegs and semi-official releases.

8 Organised by Michael Eavis, the Pilton Festival is the precursor to the first Glastonbury Free Festival held the following year.

9 Pink Fairies-in-waiting The Deviants had already staged similar gigs under the Westway, as had various local reggae sound systems. Despite complaints, the council eventually recognised their community value and installed a dedicated power point.

10 The only recording of this song, it first appeared in 1983 on *The Text Of Festival*, a semi-official collection of radio sessions and live tracks, and in edited form on *Hawkwind, Friends And Relations – Twice Upon A Time*. It's unclear why a studio recording wasn't attempted for *In Search Of Space* – perhaps the band felt it was too much like 'You Shouldn't Do That'.

11 Spreading the word of the underground, Hawkwind often distributed *Friends* magazine at gigs outside London. This sometimes led to conflict with local authorities. At a court hearing in Durham following a Winterland Ballroom gig on 8 August, it's claimed that the group, "appeared naked; drugs, contraceptives and magazines were handed to the audience and 'free love' was encouraged from the stage" ('Court Cleared At Hippy Flower Power Trial', *Northern Echo*, 17/12/70). In January 1971, *Sounds* reported that the band were forbidden from handing out *Friends* at Malvern Winter Gardens: "Somehow copies were obtained by some of the kids… A fracas ensued in which Hawkwind were forcibly ejected and told not to return. The band have now been blacked by the area's theatres and dance halls, who will refuse to deal with any package on which Hawkwind are playing" (From 'Thou Shalt Not Hear, Thou Shalt Not Read', *Sounds*, 28/1/71).

# The Origins Of Space Rock

## Parallels And Precursors To The Hawkwind Sound

No one else sounds quite like Hawkwind, and they're often described as the progenitors of the 'space rock' genre. But many of the components they used to build their style of propulsive, deep space psychedelia had already been road-tested by a variety of bands and artists before them, whether it be via free-form experimentation, electronic manipulation or the raw power of noise…

### Darlings Of The Underground

The band whose influence is perhaps most apparent in Hawkwind's early sound is **Pink Floyd**. While capable of writing brilliant, off-kilter pop songs, what really interested them was expanding the dimensions of sound in London's oil-lit psychedelic clubs via ambience, atonality and abstract vocalisation. How much could a track like 'Interstellar Overdrive' be bent and elongated in real time? This was improvisation as a free-form energy, an action painting in sound – and of course, the press were already calling their music 'space rock'.

Important Floydian touchstones for Hawkwind's own journey into the void include the metronomic chug and eerie discordance of 'Astronomy Domine', the shamanic repetition of 'Set The Controls For The Heart Of The Sun', and the cosmic battle and celestial voices of 'A Saucerful Of Secrets'. Even the melancholic pastoral folk of 'Cymbaline' would help to shape the nascent Hawkwind.[1]

Like Floyd, the playful and inventive **Soft Machine** were also darlings of the psychedelic underground, though leant more towards jazz and the avant garde. Yet they too could channel the trance-inducing power of the locked groove, with live versions of 'We Did It Again' using its hypnotic two chord riff as a platform for extended improvisation, sometimes stretching to 40 minutes in length. Subsequently exiled to France, Soft Machine co-founder Daevid Allen formed **Gong**, a surreal troupe of hippie rock pranksters, spiritually if not musically aligned to Hawkwind.[2]

## America Turns On

The San Francisco psychedelic scene also provided inspiration for Hawkwind's improvisational spirit. The entire raison d'être of bands such as the **Grateful Dead** and **Quicksilver Messenger Service** was to jam their songs into the unknown each night, and Hawkwind clearly embraced this ethos of music being about the trip rather than the destination. And of course, their first public performance at the All Saints Hall in August 1969 was a free-form exposition around **The Byrds'** 'Eight Miles High'.

But there are two American bands in particular outside of the West Coast who anticipate the proto-electronic riff rock of the Hawkwind sound.

New York's **The Velvet Underground** specialised in a similar minimal/maximal repetition, and performed at Andy Warhol's Exploding Plastic Inevitable shows, where strobes, slides and film projections were used to create an immersive, sometimes disorientating atmosphere, much as Hawkwind would develop during the 70s. Brock and Robert Calvert were both serious fans – drop the needle at 9.45 into the epic murk of *White Light/White Heat*'s 'Sister Ray' and there's the pounding drums, grinding guitar and spacey keys that would define Hawkwind's sound circa *Doremi Fasol Latido*.[3]

The other band is Texas psychonauts **The 13th Floor Elevators**, whose sound mixed twangy, adrenalized surf rock with raw garage punk via a prodigious consumption of hallucinogenics. The insistent, bass-heavy rhythm of tracks such as 'Roller Coaster' and 'Reverberation' suggests a parallel, but what makes them particularly reminiscent of early Hawkwind is the chirruping of Tommy Hall's amplified electric jug, which uncannily resembles DikMik's ring modulator on tracks such as the driving, feverish 'Slip Inside This House'.

## Psychedelic Electronics

A number of bands in the late 60s experimented with combining psychedelia and electronics.

The New York duo **Silver Apples** – singer and electronics player Simeon Coxe and drummer Danny Taylor – used a rig of oscillators and controllers (dubbed 'The Thing') to produce undulating bass melodies and primitive arpeggios, overlaid with Coxe's tremulous voice and Taylor's cyclical drumming. Tracks such as 'Oscillations' and 'Velvet Cave' are like off-kilter hymns sang to some alien god, while the tougher atonal grooves of 'You And I' and 'A Pox On You' could be Hawkwind's funky second cousins.

*Cauldron*, the sole album from San Francisco's **Fifty Foot Hose**, is a fascinating mix of sad-eyed melodic psychedelia and electronic tonalities. The album's opening track 'And After' anticipates the droning build towards lift-off that would become a staple of Hawkwind albums and shows, while the title track is a strange, spoken word incantation across a chaotic noisescape of electronics and tape loops. 'Red The Sign Post' is the stand-out of the more conventional songs, a fuzzed-up slice of anti-war doom rock, churning guitars versus howling sine waves.[4]

**The United States Of America** were the brainchild of ex-Fluxus member Joseph Byrd, who sought to combine pop music and electronics with radical socialist politics. Their self-titled album is a cleverly conceived and executed collection of songs that move between dream-like psychedelia, Beach Boys-esque pseudo-baroque and up tempo rockers, swirling oscillations constantly pushing through the mix.

**White Noise**, a London-based trio of experimental musicians, included Delia Derbyshire and Brian Hodgson from the **BBC Radiophonic Workshop**. Using the tape manipulation techniques learnt in their day job, plus the legendary EMS Synthi VCS3, their debut *An Electric Storm* shifts bewilderingly between novelty pop and avant garde nightmare – DikMik was a fan. Even in the heart of the swinging 60s, the seeds of a dark electronic cacophony were being sown...[5]

## Cosmic Soundtracks

While unrecognised at the time, the Workshop's Derbyshire had also been responsible for realising the 60s' most recognisable piece of electronic music, the eerie/terrifying theme to the children's science fiction series *Doctor Who*. Its pulsating rhythm and shrieking, ghostly melody would fill the bad dreams (and possibly bad trips) of generations of young people.

The future members of Hawkwind would already have encountered similar electronic tonalities in the SF movies of their youth such as *The Day The Earth Stood Still* (1951) and *Forbidden Planet* (1956). The former featured the high-pitched wailing of a Theremin as part of Bernard Hermann's orchestral score, while the latter boasted a purely electronic soundtrack created by husband and wife Louis and Bebe Barron using a ring modulator, which still sounds utterly alien today.

Pre-dating Hermann's use of the Theremin, Miklos Rozsa had already used it on the main theme to Alfred Hitchcock's *Spellbound* (1945), while Les Baxter would feature it on the easy listening exotica of *Music Out Of The Moon* (1947). Tom Dissevelt and Dick Raaymakers (aka Kid Baltan) produced a series of incredibly prescient abstract electronic pop records in the late 50s such as *Song Of The Second Moon*, while Jean-Jacques Perrey pioneered the use of early electronic keyboard the Ondioline, releasing records such as *Musique Electronique Du Cosmos* (1962).

The first all-electronic album to really capture the mainstream's attention was *Switched-On Bach* (1968) by **Walter** (now **Wendy**) **Carlos**, which featured interpretations of various Bach standards using an early Moog synthesizer. Other similarly themed Moog albums of space-age lounge music would follow,[6] but Carlos herself was keen to avoid accusations of making novelty records, and would go on to produce the sinister electro-classical score for *A Clockwork Orange*.

While early modular synthesizers were too complex and unreliable for most musicians, the Mellotron – a tape-based proto-sampler featuring banks of pre-recorded string, wind and choral sounds – gained favour. Early adopters included The Beatles and The Rolling Stones, but **The Moody Blues** – a favourite of Brock's – were the first band to make it the core of their sound.[7] Though indelibly associated with progressive rock acts such as Genesis and King Crimson, the Mellotron's otherworldly sound also became central to Hawkwind's music with the arrival of Simon House.

## Raw Power

Of course, Hawkwind's music wasn't just about incorporating electronic sounds – it was also about unleashing the anarchic spirit of noise and spontaneity into the calcifying rock format.

When Jimi Hendrix channelled feedback to suggest both agony and ecstasy, he did so with the skill of a virtuoso. In contrast, **MC5** and **The Stooges** favoured a punkish simplicity and sense of nihilistic abandon. On MC5's interpretation of Sun Ra's 'Starship', the detonations of the opening riff and cries of "*Leaving the solar system!*" trail off into a rhythmless plateau of guitar sustain. The grinding, mechanical riff of The Stooges' 'I Wanna Be Your Dog' conveys a visceral belligerence, its block chords like a bludgeon to the senses.[8]

It wasn't just Detroit experimenting with sonic violence. In Stockholm, **Pärson Sound** were blasting a way towards transcendence, their music based around pounding riffs, driving rhythms, exploratory sax and an experimental aesthetic – archival recordings of the band sound strikingly similar to Hawkwind in full flight a few years later.[9]

But perhaps the band that Hawkwind most resembled in their earliest incarnation was **Amon Düül II**. Emerging from the radical commune scene in

60s Munich, they brought together many of the same elements as Hawkwind's sound: rhythm-heavy jams; wailing chants; minor key guitar arpeggios; spacey drones. Their 1969 debut *Phallus Dei* and 1970 follow-up *Yeti* even feature *In Search Of Space* bass player Dave Anderson.

Another significant German release from 1969 is **Can**'s *Monster Movie*, which opens with the propulsive, invocatory thrust of 'Father Cannot Yell', and features a rougher, harder version of the mesmerising polyrhythmic sound the band would develop. Anticipating Hawkwind's deep space mantras, the original Music Factory credits also read like something Robert Calvert might have dreamed up: Malcolm Mooney is "linguistic space communicator"; Michael Karoli is "sonar & radared guitar pilot"; Jaki Liebezeit is "propulsion engineer".[10]

(For relevant bands from the Ladbroke Grove scene see p.71, 'The Making Of A People's Band')

## Influences And Favourites

Finally, we shouldn't forget Hawkwind's own formative influences and favourite bands.

Brock had busked his way round Europe and Britain, and played in bands for almost a decade before forming Hawkwind. With a bare-boned rhythmic thump at the heart of his playing, he's repeatedly cited folk-blues guitarist **Big Bill Broonzy** as an influence on his style.[11] Another early passion was trad jazz, the insistent beat and improvisational imperative of bands led by **Chris Barber** or **George Lewis** also finding their way into the Hawkwind sound. **Jimi Hendrix**'s cosmic *sturm und drang* and sci-fi-inflected philosophy made an impression, as did Jim Morrison's concept of shamanic theatre with **The Doors**. And crucial to ultimately breaking the band out of the underground, Brock enjoyed the solid, melodic songwriting of the aforementioned Moody Blues and the **Steve Miller Band**.

Nik Turner, DikMik and Lemmy also admired Hendrix, but despite the bassist's appearance as the ultimate rocker, his go-to band remained **The Beatles** – hence his sometimes McCartney-esque playing, perhaps. Simon King was also a big Beatles fan, and an admirer of **David Bowie** and **The Who**, while Del Dettmar was a secret jazzer, naming **Charles Mingus** and **Thelonious Monk** as favourites.[a]

Less surprisingly, Turner is a life-long jazz lover, favouring sax players like **Charlie Parker**, **John Coltrane** and **Roland Kirk**, as well as trumpet magus **Miles Davis**. Also important to his discursive, abstract playing is the free jazz philosophy

– in particular, the musicians he encountered at Berlin's Blue Note club in the late 60s helped him realise that 'feel' was more important than technical proficiency.[12]

◇◇◇◇◇◇◇◇◇◇◇◇◇◇◇◇◇◇◇◇◇◇◇◇◇◇◇◇◇◇◇◇◇◇◇◇◇◇◇◇◇◇◇◇◇◇◇◇◇◇◇◇◇◇◇◇◇◇◇◇◇◇◇◇◇◇◇◇◇◇

a      'The Hawkwind File' – *Melody Maker*, 11/11/72

1      Mick Farren makes clear the connection with Hawkwind's aesthetic, including "the horror and sadness of the tiny human juxtapositioned against the infinite universe… [Pink Floyd] seemed so Oxbridge cold in their merciless cosmos: the Steven Hawkings of rock & roll" (p91, *Give The Anarchist A Cigarette*, Mick Farren, 2001).

2      Gong exist in a parallel dimension to Hawkwind, with a significant cross-over of fans and personnel – Tim Blake, Gong's synth player from 1972-75, would eventually join Hawkwind at the end of the decade.

3      In 'The Hawkwind File' (*Melody Maker*, 11/11/72), Brock lists VU as an influence, while Calvert cites both *The Velvet Underground & Nico* and *White Light/White Heat* as his most influential LPs and Lou Reed as his favourite singer. The lyrics to 1969 demo track 'Kiss Of The Velvet Whip' clearly owe something to 'Venus In Furs', and Hawkwind would cover 'I'm Waiting For The Man' in 1977. See also 'Down On Her Knees', a demo from 1975 featured on the eighth *Weird Tape*, which is practically a VU homage – its title is taken from the lyrics to 'There She Goes Again'.

4      Brock: "I think it was in 1966 [sic] that I saw [Silver Apples], they had banks of oscillators and the other band Fifty Foot Hose were using audio generators with weird guitar sounds" ('Dr Rock Goes Intergalactic: An Interview With Hawkwind's Dave Brock' – *The Quietus*, 6/1/11).

5      Other artists experimenting with electronics in the late 60s include singer-songwriter Buffy Sainte-Marie (*Illuminations*, 1969) and the jazz duo of Paul Bley and Annette Peacock (*Revenge*, by the Bley-Peacock Synthesizer Show, recorded live in 1969, released 1971).

6      Another popular synthesizer break-out album was *Moog: The Electric Eclectics of Dick Hyman* (1969), with a mock-up on the cover of the Apollo 11 moon landing, plus various Pop Art Hymans. Taken from this album, 'The Minotaur' (a Top 40 hit in the US) is one of the first singles to feature a drum machine. The space theme was infectious: *Switched-On Bach II*, Carlos's 1973 follow-up, had the German composer on its cover floating in space attached to a Moog.

7      Tracks such as 'Higher And Higher' and 'Gypsy', from the space-themed Moody Blues album *To Our Children's Children's Children* (1969), overlap with the Hawkwind universe musically and thematically.

8     *Funhouse*, the second Stooges album, fleshes out their wired, chaotic sound with sax – tracks such as '1970' can arguably be heard as an American garage punk take on classic Hawkwind.

9     These recordings from 1967-68 are available on *Pärson Sound* (Subliminal Sounds, 2001). The band then became International Harvester (whose 1968 album *Sov Gott Rose-Marie* is also quite Hawkwind-like on such tracks as 'There Is No Other Place' and 'I Mourn You'), then Harvester, then Träd, Gräs Och Stenar, a legendary group in the Scandinavian underground. Their ethos – playing far and wide throughout the region, involving the audience as much as possible – has much in common with the Hawkwind approach.

10    *Monster Movie* was released in the UK in 1970 by United Artists. The Music Factory edition features a plug for *Canaxis 5* by Technical Space Composer's Crew (T.S.C.C.), "The space story of the CANAXIS 5 sounds expedition to the star ZUR," an album of experimental short-wave radio recordings by Can bassist Holger Czukay.

11    Dave Brock: "When you listen to guys like Lightning Hopkins, Sonny Terry, and Big Bill Broonzy, who I based myself on, they're using their thumb to play the rhythm on the bass strings. You listen to what they're doing, it's very rhythmic, and that's my influence" ('Returning Volumes Of Sound' – Joe Banks, *Shindig*, February 2018).

12    Nik Turner: "They were banging away on a piano with hammers, feeding back on a double bass with a microphone on it, very experimental, and they said, 'You don't need to be technical to express yourself,' and I thought, 'Oh, great!' Free jazz in a rock band – that was what Hawkwind were to me eventually" ('The Prog Interview – Nik Turner' – Joe Banks, *Prog*, January 2018).

UA promo shot 1971. L-R - Anderson, DikMik, Ollis, Turner, and Brock, who holds a
copy of *Friends* (10 July 1970) with Enoch Powell on the cover
(source: Doug Smith archive)

# Charged With Cosmic Energy

January–October 1971

Hawkwind still regard themselves as an open collective with a shared musical vision, and 1971 sees a number of key collaborators drawn into their orbit. Under the influence of these new members, their performances become increasingly intense and ritualistic, immersive multimedia experiences far removed from the workaday shows of rival bands. This is the year when the Hawkship achieves escape velocity and starts accelerating into the void.

▾　　▾　　▾

First and foremost among these collaborators is **Robert Calvert**, the man who provides a thematic framework for the band throughout the 70s. Another of Turner's Margate friends, Calvert is a classic small-town autodidact, a creatively unfulfilled manic depressive who binges on culture and longs to escape the confines of his young family. He writes poetry, sings in local bands, and dreams of becoming a fighter pilot, though a defective ear rules him out of the RAF. With Turner's help, he moves to London and countercultural Ladbroke Grove.

*Friends* magazine publishes his poetry and short stories. He checks out Turner's new band, intrigued by his friend's description of them playing 'space rock',[1] and it's not long before he's performing onstage with Hawkwind – on 26 May, he introduces their set at the Seven Sisters Club in north London with a reading of his poem 'Co-Pilots Of Spaceship Earth'. Its words act as a manifesto for the band's increasingly millenarian musical vision: the old order teeters on the brink of destruction and only the void offers salvation.

Calvert performs sporadically with Hawkwind throughout the year, his space-age oratory injecting an air of menacing theatricality, and becomes an official member in October. But he's already been conceptualising away like mad on their behalf, the most obvious fruits being *The Hawkwind Log* booklet that comes with their second album.

Another key collaborator is Colin Fulcher aka **Barney Bubbles**. A colleague of Calvert's at *Friends*, Bubbles will create a complete visual identity for Hawkwind via sleeve artwork, poster design and decorated stage gear. As Calvert incorporates the band into his own heroic and fantastical version of the universe, Bubbles brings this quasi-mystical science fictional worldview to life.

Both share an enthusiasm for arcane knowledge, and Bubbles incorporates images from cosmology and eastern spirituality into his work – but unlike other underground artists, he also has a background in commercial design and understands what engages an audience. This combination of interests and skills will see his association with Hawkwind take the art of the album sleeve to a new level.[2]

▾    ▾    ▾

As these conceptual and visual elements coalesce around a half-apocalyptic, half-ecstatic vision of man's destiny among the stars, the music changes to match. Improvisation is still at its heart, but the songs are now less nebulous and more propulsive. Pushing relentlessly into deep space, Hawkwind divest themselves of Floydian influences and become more closely aligned with the German avant rock of Can and Amon Düül II.[3] Indeed, their new bassist is **Dave Anderson**, formerly of the latter group.[4]

There's no better illustration of this tightening up and focusing of Hawkwind's sound than their next *Top Gear* session for John Peel. Recorded at the Playhouse Theatre on 19 April (broadcast 24 April), the three songs they showcase prove the band has learnt to channel its live energy into exciting new shapes.

'**Master Of The Universe**'[5] is assured and powerful, the ominous drone straining for release before the stuttering riff kicks in, a punchier intro than the more deliberate take on their forthcoming album. Turner's vocal is icily aloof, an alien sliver of otherness, but this is a bona fide Rock Song, the naked re-statement of the riff packed with dynamic tension. Aqueous sax is underpinned by industrial-strength drumming, before Turner delivers a passage of stream-of-unconsciousness spoken word not found on other versions – "*Mind controls freak me out!*" is one of its few discernible lines.

'**You Know You're Only Dreaming**' is swathed in choppy wah-wah. Anderson's bass is loud and groovy while Brock's vocal is decidedly ragged – no angelic backing voices here, just the devil's choir of the audio generator.[6] It mellows to make way for Turner's flute, and as the bass becomes *bolero*-esque, there's an uncanny flash-forward to the instrumental section of 1975's 'Assault And Battery'. Unlike the later recording, the verse is repeated, followed by an outro featuring an organ pitch-shifted towards infinity.[7]

The brutal one chord chug of 'You Shouldn't Do That' is less trance-inducing here, more last-train-out-of-hell psychosis. Over a barked, claustrophobic chant, Turner sounds like a man undergoing an extreme sleep deprivation experiment before being obliterated by an eruption of molten guitar. For all its skilful arrangement, the album version will never reach this level of feral intensity, Anderson's discordant ascending bass line screaming out 'Can'.

In May, there's a week of acid-induced torpor at George Martin's AIR Studios, before the band moves to Olympic Studios to record their second album, the process overseen by experienced in-house engineer George Chkiantz.[8] On 19 May, they decamp to the BBC's Maida Vale Studios and record a session for *Sounds Of The Seventies*, which is broadcast a week later (and presented by Stuart Henry) and features versions of the three songs aired previously.[9]

▾　　　▾　　　▾

It's tempting to credit the sonic violence of their sound to the internal turmoil that Hawkwind experience during this period. As Brock notes, "The sound waves we're sending out is really affecting (our) equilibrium. We saw our ex-guitarist Mick Slattery the other day, and he could see that we'd all gone a bit mad."[a] DikMik temporarily leaves after the *Sounds Of The Seventies* session, badly shaken by a head-on collision while riding in the band's equipment truck, although this transition is relatively smooth: roadie and soundman **Del Dettmar** takes over the electronic arsenal – soon expanded to include a VCS3 – and though unskilled as a musician, introduces a more melodic approach to the frequency wrangling.

More collaborators take up their positions. Dancer **Stacia Blake** is perhaps the person who will make the single greatest impression on-stage over the next few years. Invited to join the party after performing with the band at a gig in Redruth, Cornwall, she becomes a vital part of Hawkwind's audio-visual experience, a human lightning rod interpreting the music in movement or improvising routines with the increasingly theatrical Turner.

Also starting to appear with the band in 1971 is **Andy Dunkley**. One of the underground's top DJs, with regular nights at both the Roundhouse and Friars Club, Aylesbury, Dunkley works with Hawkwind first as crowd warm-up, then as master of ceremonies. His choice of music – from Neil Young and the Grateful Dead to Van Der Graaf Generator and Terry Riley – plays a significant role in bringing the sounds of the underground to the provinces.[10]

Another key figure who starts to perform with the band is writer **Michael Moorcock**. Living in Ladbroke Grove, and having encountered Robert Calvert via *Friends* (now re-branded *Frendz*), it's not long before he's seeing and meeting the band. Memorably describing them as "barbarians with electronics", Hawkwind are more than happy to accept his offer of doing some readings with them at gigs under the Westway.[11]

Moorcock's passion for some years has been *New Worlds* magazine.[12] Since becoming editor in 1964, he has transformed it from a staid and parochial SF journal into the leading platform for New Wave science fiction, which rejects the traditional 'hard' sci-fi of the 40s and 50s to engage instead with present-day concerns and anxieties: inner rather than outer space. Brock and Turner are fans of his Eternal Champion fantasies, but it's this New Wave sensibility that Moorcock brings to the first 'song' he writes and performs with them, the cynical, satirical 'Sonic Attack'.

These comings and goings of personnel are perhaps proof of the band's essential fluidity within its ever-expanding conceptual universe. For example, in June they play the first Glastonbury Free Festival minus an unwell Brock. Thomas Crimble – a prime mover behind the festival – is surprised to be asked to temporarily rejoin the band that recently kicked him out. But despite the set having significantly changed since his sacking, the Hawkwind template is strong enough for both he and the band to play on regardless.[13]

▾        ▾        ▾

When DikMik rejoins in August, there's no question of Dettmar stepping aside, with Hawkwind's growing armoury of keyboards and electronic devices now looked after by two players. In contrast to the pseudo-classical maestros of the emerging British progressive scene, both regard their instruments as noise-making, atmosphere-creating technology rather than colourful relatives of the piano, aligning them more with the textual experimentation of Tangerine Dream or Kraftwerk.

However, DikMik's return – plus the arrival in the band's inner circle of his amphetamine-loving drug buddy **Ian 'Lemmy' Kilmister** – exacerbates a growing split in the ranks, and Anderson becomes yet another Hawkwind bassist to leave only months after joining.

Lemmy had played guitar in Blackpool beat group The Rockin' Vickers before moving to London in the late 60s, where he had roadied for The Nice and Jimi Hendrix, and played with Sam Gopal and Opal Butterfly. A forceful personality with a none-more-rock biker image (despite neither owning nor riding a motorbike), he's a talismanic but divisive figure who brings a bellicose edge to Hawkwind's music. As a professional player, he's also used to getting paid, which moves them further towards becoming a 'serious band' rather than just a community project.

Despite having never played bass before, Lemmy does his first show with Hawkwind at a free open-air concert in Powis Square on 1 September. It's not long before he's the band's latest official member.[14]

*In Search Of Space* is released on 8 October, as the band traverse the UK on an extended tour.

◇◇◇◇◇◇◇◇◇◇◇◇◇◇◇◇◇◇◇◇◇◇◇◇◇◇◇◇◇◇◇◇◇◇◇◇◇◇◇◇◇◇◇◇◇◇◇◇◇◇◇◇◇◇◇◇◇◇◇◇◇◇◇◇◇◇◇◇◇◇◇◇

a     'When It Comes To Mind Blowing, Hawkwind Are Really Into It' – Jerry Gilbert, *Sounds*, 17/09/70

1     Calvert later admitted he simply hadn't heard the term 'space rock' before: "But it seemed like the magic key to a movement that was afoot. It was like Ezra Pound and the Imagists discussing the new movement in poetry. And to me it sounded like something brand new – which it was" (ref: audio recording, interview by Tim Gadd, 1982).

2     Doug Smith: "Hawkwind would not have sounded the same with anybody else's designs" p40, *Reasons To Be Cheerful*, Paul Gorman (2008).

3     In an October 71 *Melody Maker* article that will be used as the sleeve notes for the UK release of Can's *Tago Mago*, Duncan Fallowell says, "the only outfit in England with anything in common with them is Hawkwind." Hawkwind subsequently attend Can's first UK gig in April 1972 (ref: p57, Nick Kent, *Apathy For The Devil*). German rock magazine *Sounds* votes *Hawkwind* best new album by a new group, and Hawkwind no.2 best new group of the year (*IT* 96, 28 Jan-10 Feb 1971) – in June, they play a series of dates in West Germany where the audiences are bigger than many British gigs.

4     Dave Anderson's exact time of arrival has been a source of debate, but he confirmed to the author that he joined "straight after the [1970] Christmas show, so about 4 or 5 months earlier than [some] reports."

5     Confusingly, John Peel calls this track 'Inwards Out'. Hawkwind's 70s BBC sessions are a tangle: historically, 'Inwards Out' has commonly been assumed to be the track known as 'We Do It'. However, recordings came to light during the writing of this book that proved 'We Do It' is

in fact the 'Untitled' track from the November 1970 *Sunday Concert* session (see p33), and that 'Inwards Out' was the original title of 'Master Of The Universe' (or at least that's what Peel had written down).

6    The song is subtitled 'Visions of Beyond Recall' on the inside cover of *ISOS*, and while that phrase is sung here, it isn't on the album version.

7    There's no organ on a Hawkwind album until Simon House's arrival on *HOTMG*. Perhaps there was one at the Playhouse Theatre.

8    Often credited as the inventor of flanging (as heard on the Small Faces' 'Itchycoo Park'), Chkiantz liberally applies this psychedelic effect to the instrumental section of 'Master Of The Universe'. Parts of that track may remain from the pre-Chkiantz sessions, as the inside cover of *ISOS* notes that 'Master Of The Universe' was "first recorded at Air Studios".

9    The May 1971 *Sounds Of The 70s* session is another source of confusion. It has previously been assumed that the tracks recorded for the April *Top Gear* session were from the *SOT70s* session, but this is incorrect (see note 5 above). Given that it features the same songs, it's tempting to assume that the May 'session' is just a repeat of April's, but the BBC archives show there were separate recording sessions in April and May at different locations (Playhouse Theatre and Maida Vale Studios) – and Dave Anderson also recalls doing two BBC sessions with the band. BBC sessions expert Ken Garner has suggested that the May session might have just added overdubs to the April tracks – but would Hawkwind have done this? Exactly what was recorded and broadcast by the BBC in May 1971 remains a mystery.

10   Dunkley would even occasionally 'play in' records during Hawkwind's set. Doug Smith to the author (2018): "On a few occasions when the synth had problems, Andy and Del used a couple of Stockhausen albums and created some wonderful noises." When Dunkley died in April 2011, journalist Kris Needs wrote a tribute on the Friars Aylesbury website: "The tireless trio of John Peel, Jeff Dexter and Andy Dunkley were London's scene-stoking DJ giants." All three played a significant role in the Hawkwind story.

11   Michael Moorcock: "I liked Hawkwind because they weren't anti-technology, they celebrated it... When I first saw them they seemed like barbarians who'd got hold of a load of electrical gear; instead of being self-conscious and pseudo-intellectual, they were actually *of* the electronic age. They weren't impressed by their own gear." ('The Hawklords Riddle' – Mike Davies, *Melody Maker*, 13/11/78). Moorcock had himself been involved in staging gigs under the Westway with *Frendz* editor John Trux.

12   Although in 1971, he had just stepped back from full-time editorship.

13   Crimble says that it took him all of three minutes to learn 'Master Of The Universe' (ref: p67, *The Saga Of Hawkwind*, Carol Clerk, 2004). Still, the template had its limits. Nick Kent, an early supporter in the press, recalls a show at the Starlight Club in Crawley (3 August 1971) where

just three members turned up. "The audience that night was treated to Hawkwind's very own stripped-down version of 'Jazz Odyssey'. I'd love to have been a fly on the wall backstage when they tried to get their fee from the promoter afterwards." (p55, *Apathy For The Devil*, Nick Kent).

14     Interviewed for the 2007 documentary *Hawkwind: Do Not Panic*, Lemmy remembers first seeing the band at the Roundhouse: "They were terrifying. I thought, I've got to join these guys, cos I can't watch 'em!" His sobriquet has various origin stories. Perennially skint, legend says he was often heard to say "Lemme a fiver 'til Friday!" A more fittingly SF origin is Lemmy Caution, the hard-boiled detective in Jean-Luc Godard's *Alphaville* (1965). However Keith Emerson, who knew Lemmy when he was the road manager for The Nice, maintained that Kilmister was a big fan of the BBC sci-fi radio drama *Journey Into Space* (1953-58) and it came from radio operator Lemuel "Lemmy" Barnet.

Robert Calvert and Dave Brock share a joke
(source: Doug Smith archive)

Terry Ollis
(source: Pedro Bellavista collection)

# *In Search Of Space*

Released 8 October 1971

| | |
|---|---|
| *Label:* | United Artists |
| *Track listing:* | You Shouldn't Do That (Brock/Turner) / You Know You're Only Dreaming (Brock) / Master Of The Universe (Turner/Brock) / We Took The Wrong Step Years Ago (Brock) / Adjust Me (Hawkwind) / Children Of The Sun (Anderson/Turner) |
| *Line-up:* | Dave Brock / Nik Turner / DikMik / Del Dettmar / Dave Anderson / Terry Ollis |
| *Recorded at:* | Olympic and AIR Studios |
| *Produced by:* | Olympic and AIR Studios |

What a difference a year makes. While *Hawkwind* eased unwary listeners in with a folk/blues singalong, *In Search of Space* makes good on the promise of its cryptic title, whether you're strapped in for the journey or not.

'**You Shouldn't Do That**' starts with the sounds of a ramshackle but powerful craft rising up from the primordial soup to take its maiden flight. This sonic approximation of lifting off and accelerating into a space/time wormhole is a Hawkwind trope that we'll hear again and again – but it never gets old.

Then there it is: Brock's chugging guitar – not even a riff at this point, just sheer propulsion, ratcheting up anticipation. This mantric, robotic pulse will become the core of Hawkwind's sound, its metronomic simplicity setting them apart from just about every other UK band. Dave Anderson's bass teases us with little melodic vamps… and then WHAM! The band hit the boosters and we're pushed back into our seats by a savage hyperspatial ur-riff, high-pitched electronic whistles like faster-than-light particles striking the ship's hull, meandering sax like the laughter of alien gods…

Let's just pause and revel for a moment in the astonishing sound that Hawkwind are making here. It's trance-like, but also smacks of pure adrenaline – and this lays bare the duality at the heart of their appeal. It's a powerful soundtrack for getting out of your head, but something deeper is going on here too, as if we're eavesdropping on a shamanic ceremony, the repetition of simple rhythmic elements acting as a gateway from profane to sacred space. There's plenty of worship happening elsewhere in the British music scene – of virtuosity, or the latest teenybopper idol – but little true invocation of rock's primal, transgressive spirit.

Now the riff stands to attention, as guitar, bass and sax play in clipped unison over a series of drum rolls from Ollis.[1] It's an anchor point before everybody hurtles off into the sonic ether again – but it also shows how carefully the track is arranged to sustain engagement over its 16 minutes. It's no free-form jam: there's a dynamic ebb and flow, the players alive as a team to what's going on around them. It never flags or gets dull. With Lloyd-Langton gone, Turner's sax is next in line as lead, but he tends towards the discursive and the decorative, rarely asserting dominance within the sound. Similarly, while the VCS3 and audio generator are deployed with increasing precision, their role is purely textural – no chance of any Keith Emerson-style rococo solos here.

The singing has also evolved, with the ritualistic chanting of 'Paranoia' and 'Seeing It As You Really Are' fine-tuned into percussive mouth music. Over a rumble of bass, a sibilant approximation of *"Shouldn't do that"* hisses like a hi-hat, until Turner begins a heavy-lidded litany of woe – and a higher, more aggressive chant of *"Shouldn't!"* kicks in. The three vocal lines weave together woozily, our attention dragged around the stereo field.

If Brock sounded like a clear-eyed but embittered sage on *Hawkwind*, Turner is here the epitome of the put-upon hippie, all child-like hurt in the face of The Man. The drawled words are hard to pick out, but lines like *"They put you down and cut your hair / They're saying you're no good, they just don't care"* surely resonate with the intended audience. As with many songs to come, the theme of escape from a repressive, paranoid reality is implicit throughout. The repetition of *"You're trying to fly / You're getting nowhere"* suggests a cycle of failures to launch, but there's hope too as the words morph into *"You're getting aware"*: recognise the inherent restrictions of the straight world and you might start to break free from it.

This is the first of Hawkwind's quintessential space rock tracks – and it more or less defines the sound the band pioneers from now on, one based around relentless forward motion. It's in marked contrast to the tangled arrangements of the progressive groups and the verse/chorus/middle eight platitudes of just about every other contemporary rock band. Hawkwind embrace light and shade, but avoid the hand-holding peaks and troughs of traditional songcraft, refusing to signpost the listener's emotional response. Instead, they want to transform perceptions via this hypnotic, linear rush, where the exact result of the trip depends on the individual as much as the music.

'You Know You're Only Dreaming' signals the return of Brock the cosmic troubadour, a change of pace after that prolonged flaming of the engines. Over an already familiar descending chord sequence, the snarling squelch of his guitar counterpointed by a cooing angelic choir,[2] he's here to tell us once again that the world is not a happy, benign place – instead it's full of *"screaming souls in the night"*. It's not the easiest lyric to decipher, the title refrain suggesting some meditation on the illusory nature of reality. Or it could just be about drugs. Either way, there's a sense of uneasy fatalism among the seductive sounds.

The vocal ends and a bass-led switch-up leads into looser, even jazzier territory, with Turner on flute and Brock tentatively extemporising on guitar. With a narrower range of expression, Brock is a less fluid player than Lloyd-Langton, but perhaps a more thoughtful one. The sound provides room for less 'technical' types of improvisation, which certainly benefits Turner, whose flute runs through delay and reverb to create the gauzy impression of seagulls in fog. The track builds towards trance-out, and again it's Anderson's bass leading the charge, with Brock working the same few notes in quick succession. Even at their trippiest, this combination of insistent rhythm and underlying conflict defines Hawkwind's music, visions of a golden age subverted by real-world uncertainty.

'Master Of The Universe' also starts with a rising drone, heralding something from afar.[3] It's almost cinematic, the mysterious stranger riding into town as Hawkwind's (arguably) most recognisable riff starts to play, a metallic chug with a double punctuation at the end, loaded with portent. First bass, then drums and finally the filthy belch of a second guitar lock together as one, an entrance so perfectly judged that it never fails to raise the hairs on the back of the neck.

No wonder then that Turner's lyric is so gloriously over the top, an ego trip of galactic proportions, but also the first song where their interest in science fiction is signalled. His earlier somnambulant drawl is gone: every word here is arrogantly enunciated for maximum effect. The cosmos is a place of judgement and reckoning, and Turner's pay-off lines – *"Has the world gone mad or is it me?"* and *"If you call this living I must be blind*" – suggest an impatient deity wondering if free will was such a good idea after all.

As a song, it's a brilliant exercise in letting space into the music – different combinations of instruments drop in and out, allowing the riff to shine. The rest of the band even display restraint when Turner plays an extended passage of duck-quacking sax, concentrating on maintaining a clear through-line, with some heavy flanging courtesy of producer Chkiantz. At 4.50, everyone pauses for breath, and then – perhaps the best moment in the song – the bass re-enters alone, refreshing the riff with the springy lope of a predator moving in for the kill.

This song will become a mainstay of their 70s live set, no gig complete until it's been performed. So it's perhaps surprising that they didn't emulate its particular dynamic more in future recordings.

But now we're back at the fag end of 60s utopianism. The anti-nuclear, pro-ecology credo is slowly filtering into the mainstream, but the folk-rock hardline want us to get back to the land, to re-engage with more traditional ways of life. '**We Took The Wrong Step Years Ago**', another of Brock's 12-string polemics, fits right in with this trend, especially with the more pessimistic, finger-wagging aspect of it.

After confident picking, and lonesome bird calls from the audio generator, a rustic Brock – like Roy Harper with a head cold – laments how the modern world has turned its back on Mother Nature. It's unclear when this wrong step occurred – Post-Eden? Industrial Revolution? Hiroshima? – but you can picture the bedraggled heads and freaks at Brock's feet, nodding glumly in agreement as he sings, "*Look around and see the warnings close at hand / Already weeds are writing their scriptures in the sand.*"

Just as it starts to feel rather morose, a vigorous middle eight revives our spirits. The crowd is on its feet, pitchforks and mandolins in hand, ready to march on the cities and reclaim the pavements for pasture. Ollis and Turner join in enthusiastically, then it's back to the verse for one last ticking off. A lovely finger-picked coda will end up being recycled – in a more cosmic context – for 'Space Is Deep' on the next album.

The mournful, lost-in-space start of '**Adjust Me**' will also sound familiar from later recordings such as 'Seven By Seven' and 'Welcome To The Future', Brock gently strumming in a minor key as the audio generator wails in sympathy. Then a downward-spiralling riff over a spoken word section pitch-shifted from low to high, like a robot having a nervous breakdown. Hard to distinguish, the words are some of the most interesting here: "*World full of men, who all are blind*

*/ Who walk and talk and say as one / 'Androids are we', heir to no son."* Then a final plea: *"Adjust me!"*

But now the song halts and fails to re-ignite, some aimless jamming suggesting more of a filler track in contrast to the careful structuring earlier on.[4] At one point, they seem to be reverting to some psychedelic trace memory – trying but failing to recall the riff from 'Paint It Black', or possibly 'Eight Miles High' again – but the craft is stuck in low orbit. If it picks up momentum towards the end, it's only because we're being sucked down towards the planet below…

And we're back on Earth with a perky acoustic intro to welcome the starfarers home. Except something's wrong, the finger-picking soon turning into a sombre agrarian death march. '**Children Of The Sun**' is a song suffering from severe cognitive dissonance. The lyrics celebrate flower children basking in the glory of a new day: *"The golden age of the future comes… Where freedom reigns on minds of peace."* But Turner delivers them in a bombed-out drawl, while the primitive backing trudges on remorselessly. *"We are the children of the sun / And this is our inheritance"* becomes a dismal wail of resignation, less hippies enjoying an endless summer, more survivors in a post-apocalyptic landscape hacking away at the barren ground.

Turner gets his flute out to cheer up these dishevelled remnants, but the trippiness has turned listless, like a medicated Jethro Tull. It's a strangely downbeat end to an album that starts in such an energising, transcendence-or-bust way, but Hawkwind's next three LPs conclude on a similarly pessimistic note. Dance free while you can, because the brain police are not far behind…

---

1    The rampaging judder of Anderson's bass before and after this section reminds me of John Entwistle charging into the start of The Who's 'My Generation', another song about The Man pushing young people around.

2    Brock's love of The Steve Miller Band perhaps gets the better of him here, as there's an uncanny resemblance to 'Jackson Kent Blues' (from 1970's *Number 5*). An earlier version of 'You Know You're Only Dreaming' (recorded during the sessions for *Hawkwind*) has quite a different arrangement – it's available on the archival collection *Parallel Universe* (2011).

3    Nik Turner: "The siren sound at the start of 'Master Of The Universe' is actually me" ('The Prog Interview – Nik Turner' – Joe Banks, *Prog*, January 2018).

4    'Adjust Me' is the only 70s composition credited to 'Hawkwind'. 'Honky Dory' (the B-side to 'Kerb Crawler') is credited to the band, but with each member individually named.

# Charged With Cosmic Energy

October–December 1971

Band in a van: Anderson, Turner, Brock, Ollis, DikMik
(source: Michael Scott collection)

Resplendent in its Barney Bubbles packaging – enough on its own to keep a listener entertained through repeated spins – *In Search Of Space*[1] spends 19 weeks on the UK album charts, peaking at number 18.[2] On the front, a stylised technicolour hawk is surrounded by a circle of stars – in its centre, a rainbow-haired space maiden tilts her chin defiantly at the void. It could be the crest of some psychedelised galactic empire, or a particularly cosmic motorcycle club. Flip it over and there's a quotation from the retitled 'Technicians Of Spaceship Earth' above a glorious colour shot of a naked Stacia in mid-gyration, the blurring of the image suggesting the reality-melting immersion of a Hawkwind live show.

But the fun is only beginning, because the front cover is interlocked down the middle via die-cut serrated edges and opens out to reveal portraits of the band: Turner, Ollis and Dettmar project friendly vibes; Brock glances moodily to the side; Anderson's just woken up from a bad dream; an elongated DikMik is apparently decomposing.[3]

There's another surprise inside, a 24-page booklet entitled *The Hawkwind Log*, an assemblage of pictures, illustrations and text drawing on astrology, mysticism, sci-fi pulps and comic strips. The photographs of Stonehenge and Glastonbury Tor are entirely in keeping with the countercultural memes of the day, and there's a fragmented, hallucinatory drift to the words and layout. The introduction states that the "spacecraft Hawkwind was found by Captain RN Calvert of the Société Astronomae", which makes clear Calvert's plans to flesh out the Hawkwind concept as he sees fit.[4] (For more about *The Hawkwind Log*, see p.273 of 'Cosmic Dada Nihilismus!')

When fully folded out, the inner cover features another blocky, stylised hawk in flight, lyrics, and some striking black and white photographs taken during one of the Westway gigs, which tellingly feature more of the crowd than the band. It's a vision of a peculiarly urban idyll: heads sit on the bare earth floor and watch politely; local kids look on bemused; the police keep a beady watch.

*Melody Maker*'s Richard Williams identifies *ISOS*'s parallels with German avant rock – "In the rush to applaud the Amon Düüls and Cans from across the water, we've all tended to forget the prophets in our own backyard" – even as he decides the album is "imaginative" though "not unduly so".[a] Noting the improved arrangements and structure, *Beat Instrumental* concludes it's "more thoughtful than the first album and musically a lot more complex".[b]

But following the album's belated US release in March 1972,[5] it's the American media who really go to town in terms of critical analysis. In *Rolling Stone*, Lester Bangs riffs excitedly on the idea of space rock and describes *ISOS* as "music for the astral apocalypse" and "psychedelic from the cover to the fadeout of the last groove."[c] Jeff Walker in *Phonograph Record* is even more enthusiastic: "The music itself is an adventure in sound, full of raw excitement, suspense and rich climaxes."[d] For Steve Ditlea of *Circus*, "Hawkwind extends the limits of what were once familiar musical frontiers",[e] while *Billboard* reckons that, "Listening to this LP is virtually a 'trip' in itself."[f]

It's left to *Creem*'s Greg Shaw to irreverently compare 'Master Of The Universe' to the "swirling electronic gibberish sound effects of every 1957 science fiction flick", and poke fun at 'We Took The Wrong Step Years Ago', imagining future listeners thinking "if only those stupid hippies… hadn't loaded the ancient teachings down with all this moralistic self-righteousness".[g6]

▾    ▾    ▾

Recurrent in many of these reviews are mostly favourable comparisons with Pink Floyd. But a subtle yet distinct division is beginning to occur within the British rock music audience. The emerging progressive scene – of which Floyd are reluctant members – feels increasingly aimed at an intellectually aspirational audience, college-based and/or middle class, rather than the trad rock & roll crowd. Hawkwind on the other hand appeal across a surprisingly broad spectrum, from countercultural freaks to Tolkien obsessives, working class Hells Angels[7] to aristocratic hippies. There's something peculiarly levelling about them and their boundary-dissolving live experience.

In interviews to promote *ISOS*, Brock observes that, despite a lack of support from the mainstream music press, "We're a people's band… and now we're packing places everywhere,"[h] but admits, "We still seem to freak people out. They come up to us after gigs and say our music terrified them."[i]

Del Dettmar paints a more communal picture: "We use [the audiences] to give us the power to play. It's like the way that one guy can get into what the band are playing and his excitement just spreads to the people around him. We pick it up, build it up and pass it back to the audience… a spiral of musical energy that just builds up and up."[j]

The notion of the 'star trip' and technical proficiency also comes up. Brock: "A lot of musicians get into ego scenes and lose contact with the audience… I don't necessarily think you have to be a fantastic musician to experiment. Rather than have a guitarist out front playing flashy bits, the guitar and bass [can] provide the basic pattern which allows the electronics to become the lead instrument."[k]

Reviewing a gig at Birmingham's Kinetic Playground on 3 December, Jim Simpson of *Melody Maker*[l] paints the most eloquent portrait yet of the group in action: "Hawkwind's entire act takes place in a gloomy, doomy, space-age atmosphere – shadow figures of the band lit up by flashing footlights – luminous cymbals, decorated drums and speaker cabinets – and a disturbingly hypnotic strobe directed at the audience. The music is heavily electronic, repetitive and compelling…"

Simpson mentions two other significant things: drummer Terry Ollis is absent (deputised in this instance by the Pink Fairies' Twink), and the airing of a new song called 'Silver Machine'…

〈〈〈〈〈〈〈〈〈〈〈〈〈〈〈〈〈〈〈〈〈〈〈〈〈〈〈〈〈〈〈〈〈〈〈〈〈〈〈〈〈〈〈〈〈〈〈〈〈〈〈〈〈〈〈〈〈

a      Richard Williams, *Melody Maker*, 23/10/1971

b      *Beat Instrumental*, December 1971

c      Lester Bangs, *Rolling* Stone, 6/22/72

d      Jeff Walker, *Phonograph Record*, 5/72

e      Steve Ditlea, *Circus*, 7/72

f      *Billboard* 1972

g      Greg Shaw, *Creem*, June 1972

h      'Hawkwind: The Spaced Out People's Band' – Richard Williams, *Melody Maker*, 27/11/71

i      'Hawkwind More Serious Now' – James Johnson, *NME*, 27/11/71

j      'Del On The Beat' – *Beat Instrumental*, December 1971

k      James Johnson, same source

l      Jim Simpson, *Melody Maker*, 12/71


1      For reasons best known to Bubbles, the front cover title – by which the album is sometimes referred – reads *Xin* (or *X In*) *Search Of Space*, inviting allusions to Brit sci-fi films such as *The Quatermass Xperiment* and *X The Unknown*. But spine, label and inside cover all clearly refer to it as plain *In Search Of Space.*

2      A reflection of their status at the time as the country's most popular underground band, no other Hawkwind album stays in the charts this long (next longest being *Warrior*, at just eight weeks). When it sells 100,000 units, *ISOS* becomes their one BPI-certified gold disc.

3      Anderson is in fact the dead man walking, while DikMik's design-crashing inclusion was a result of his return when the artwork was mostly finished. Note also the hawk pendant at Turner's neck and the hawk tattoo on Brock's forearm.

4      Later in the year, Calvert is keen to expand on this concept, "crackling with excitement" at his plans for a space opera involving dancers, mime, lights, poetry, and one continuous piece of music: "[W]e can hit people with the use of words, sound and light, and we can hypnotise an audience into exploring their own space. Space is the last unexplored terrain, it's all that's left, it's where man's future is" ('Hawkwind – Still The Naughty Boys Of Pop', Caroline Boucher, *Disc And Music Echo*, 30/10/71).

5      As *ISOS* is released in the UK, *Hawkwind* is released in the US. "They're not just experimenting, they obviously know that they're doing," writes John Morthland. "Plus there isn't a hint of pretension here, as is often the case with Pink Floyd, the only other group I can think of, off hand, still doing anything like this. *Hawkwind* reminds me of Steve Miller's 'Song For Our Ancestors'" (*Creem*, 1/11/71).

6    Ironically, Shaw would go on to work for United Artists in America and become involved with the promotion of Hawkwind's albums there.

7    A close association with Britain's Hells Angels did much to burnish Hawkwind's outlaw image. However, *Hells Angels* – a BBC documentary from 1973 – highlights how mundane most members' lives were. For example, we see 'Mad John' unpacking a suitcase after being forced to move out of the family home – it includes a copy of *The Hawkwind Log*, and underneath, a vicious-looking hatchet: "The bits and pieces that really matter to him," deadpans the commentary.

# Nik Turner

Saxophone, flute and vocals
1969–October 1976 (and 1982–84)
*Hawkwind* to *Astounding Sounds, Amazing Music*

Nik Turner
(source: Doug Smith archive)

What were the early 'Group X' rehearsals like?

Just jamming on a chord, not tunes particularly. [Dave Brock and Mick Slattery] were playing the blues and managing to accommodate what I was doing, which was free-form. John Harrison the bass player used to play with Joe Loss, so he had a big band background. He wasn't that much of a jammer, but when you threw him in at the deep end, he was good! That was how it developed, John playing bass, Dave and Mick on guitar, and me playing weird noises!

We were rehearsing at the Royal College of Art. Dave had a friend there, and Mick says, "Oh, there's this gig going down in Notting Hill Gate, do you think we should go and play there?" and we all said, "Yeah!" All totally stoned and ready to rock. So we climbed in my van with what little equipment we had, got to the gig, spoke to one of the organisers at Clearwater, I think it was Doug Smith, and he said, "Yeah, OK, ten minutes."

What were those early gigs like?

I had all these friends who were LSD dealers, they had their own factory, and they'd come to the gigs and give me bottles of all this liquid LSD. I thought, 'Good god, what am I supposed to do with these?' So I thought, 'Oh I'll take it to the gigs and give it away to the fans!' I think it really compounded the band's popularity, because people still come up to me and say, "Wow, that gig you did in 1971 changed my life!" And I say, "You sure it wasn't the LSD??"

It had a resounding effect. We were doing gigs in the provinces, in the middle of nowhere, giving away all this LSD, and I think it really did change people's lives.

You were heralds of the underground culture…

I think so. We took back issues of *Friends* and gave them away, spreading the word of the underground. Mick Farren, Hoppy [John Hopkins], Barney Bubbles, Mike Moorcock: we were taking this information and knowledge to people who never imagined this was going on. We were the bearers of new news.

Were any other bands doing similar things?

I don't think anybody else gave away free drugs and newspapers! Edgar Broughton and other London bands were playing out there, but their agencies got them really straight gigs. We were more subversive and underground.

How did your 'free jazz in a rock band' idea influence the other members?

They thought I was completely mad, but they liked it. As I was playing an E flat instrument, they tuned their guitars down to E flat for me. I could play on my instrument in C, so I could play anything. It all seemed to gel together into this bizarre noise, this self-expressionist, wacky sound. It was so new, nobody else was doing anything like it.

Guys from the Arts Lab in London came to gigs and made me pedals and boxes and ring modulators to distort the sound I was playing. I had a microphone on my sax and put it through all these boxes, and played this distorted, convoluted music! And DikMik was very influential when he got involved, as well. I think he was the sound of Hawkwind.

How important were drugs to this creative experience?
I think I took LSD every day for about two years. I took it all the time, I think we all did to some degree in the early days. It was just what we did. It wasn't "Let's take a trip and write a song," because I was already tripping. I was driving my van around doing removal jobs under the influence of LSD. As long as I had somebody with me who knew where we were going, I was quite happy to drive all day, all over London! It was just a way of life. I was able to function normally without any misgivings.

Hawkwind quickly become a big underground band...
We were unique, it wasn't as if we were competing with Free or Quintessence. We were an entity in our own right and I think people saw us as that, as something completely different. We had this image of doing benefits, helping people and being around socially. I did all the benefits. People would come up to me when I was out of my head on LSD, and say, "Oh I'm organising this benefit, do you think you could come and play?" and I'd say, "Yeah, why not?"

From the start, Hawkwind has a strong anti-establishment ethos...
Not only did we align ourselves with [groups such as the Angry Brigade], they aligned themselves with us. And we did benefits for them. I wasn't totally into the Angry Brigade, I wasn't into letting off bombs, but for me it was about freedom of expression.

We released 'Urban Guerilla' [in 1973], but the BBC wouldn't play it and the record company withdrew it, rather embarrassed about it. I had the bomb squad round my house, tearing up floorboards, looking for bombs. In hindsight, releasing a song like that was a fucking stupid thing to do! You're just asking for trouble. I'm amazed that the record company put it out at all. [But] there was publicity to be gained from all the negative aspects of these things, and we were advertising the virtues of anarchy! We were getting it without trying really.

Anti-authoritarianism runs through the music as well...
[We had] this thing about this terrible, dystopian future going to happen. Other bands weren't doing things like that. The Edgar Broughton Band had 'Out Demons Out', but it's hard to think of any bands that were actively political. Mick Farren's Deviants, I suppose – but we were out there doing it, getting publicity for it, and seen to be the ones.

You wrote lyrics for 'Seeing It As You Really Are', but they're not recorded…

I used to do them live. "*Our saucers have landed, we've come to take your mind away / You know what we are after, we've come back for our property / You know exactly who we are, you knew us ten million years ago / When time was light… We're going to take it now!*" Then it builds up with this climactic screaming: "*Now, now, now!!*"

I'd put the microphone under the cymbal, and Terry would hit it, getting a cymbal splash, a hissing noise, and I'd move it from the centre to the edge to get this phasing effect. While that was going on, I was doing the lyric.

The Isle Of Wight festival in 1970 is a turning point…

As soon as we arrived, it was "Do you want this orange juice?" "Yeah, thanks." I drank down a pint. "Oh, that was California Sunshine." "Oh great, you got any more?" I was bombed out on LSD and dressed up in weird clothing – a pair of trousers made of purple leather with silver stars and moons all over them, and a fringe jacket. And I painted myself silver all over! I'd hang out in the press enclosure too, and as soon as they saw me, all the cameras turned my way!

Around *In Search Of Space*, you begin to take on more of the role of front man…

I wasn't singing until I wrote 'Master Of The Universe', and sang it on the album. I wrote the lyrics and said, "Who's going to sing them?" They said, "You are!" "Me? I don't sing!" "You do now!" So that was my first foray into vocalising. I thought, "I can actually sing!"

It was an emotional thing for me, you know, "*I am the centre of the universe… Has the world gone mad or is it me?*" A sort of self-assessment, an observation of myself.

You have a very particular style. Sometimes it sounds as if Calvert was influenced by it…

A lot of the time I can't distinguish between him and me. Listening to *Space Ritual*, I think, 'Is that me or Calvert?' A lot of the time he couldn't do gigs because he was having a nervous breakdown, so I ended up doing the stuff he would have done. I wasn't impersonating him, I was singing naturally. [But] I never thought about the influence he had on me, or I had on him.

# The Making Of A People's Band

## A Brief Trip Through The British Counterculture, Arriving At Ladbroke Grove

**HAWKWIND: the spaced-out people's band**

WHEN Hawkwind were last interviewed in these pages, some 14 months ago, they expressed pleasure and surprise that, during the following month, they were scheduled to play no less than six gigs. "We're picking up," reed - player Nick Turner told our correspondent, in optimistic tones.

His feelings were fully justified. For some months now, Hawkwind have been very busy indeed, playing to packed clubs everywhere and receiving ovation after ovation. Their new album, "In Search Of Space," zipped into the chart days after it was released, reflecting the strength of their grassroots support.

But you haven't read much about them in newspapers like this one. Why? I don't know . . . some bands achieve fame through publicity, while

HAWK-WIND: appeal to dope freaks and acid heads

'You haven't read much about them in newspapers like this one.'
*Melody Maker*, 27 November 1971
(source: Jim Skinnner collection)

Hawkwind's initial reputation was built on their status as a community project. They were tirelessly active at a grassroots level, appearing at numerous benefit gigs or playing for free on the fringes of festivals or on common ground in Ladbroke Grove. They made themselves available and the counterculture loved them for it.

By embodying the spirit of the alternative society, Hawkwind became the new figureheads of the underground. They played for their audience rather than for critical approval, taking their show around the country and creating a focus point for heads, freaks and disaffected youth everywhere. They were avatars of a lifestyle and attitude that was suspicious of deference and conformity, but open to new ways of being yourself. Hawkwind were the band that turned the 1970s into the true "days of the underground".

## The Coming Of The Counterculture

Britain has a rich alternative heritage of visionaries and mavericks who re-conceptualised the world, often in opposition to the laws and morals of mainstream society. William Blake railed against the religiosity of the Church and called for sexual freedom. William Morris propagated a utopian socialism and helped found the Arts and Crafts movement. Bertrand Russell challenged our sensory perceptions and led public opposition to both nuclear weapons and the Vietnam War. R.D. Laing saw mental illness as a response to the pressures of modern society itself. Each inspired pockets of resistance to the conformity of everyday life – and called for change.

The countercultural scene that developed in Britain in the 1960s lacked the intellectual rigour of previous revolutions in thought, but it was exceptional in one sense – it was the first popular 'political' movement driven by young people. Rock & roll might have scandalised their parents by telling teenagers to cut loose and have fun – but psychedelia and LSD heralded a new way of seeing and being, a challenge to the post-war status quo. Preaching a fuzzy doctrine of personal liberation, mind expansion and free love, the counterculture mounted – via actions and events – a soft attack on the institutions and assumptions of the straight world.

A key event in the development of the counterculture was the International Poetry Incarnation, held on 11 June 1965 at the Albert Hall. Initially conceived as a platform for beat poet Allen Ginsberg, it rapidly ballooned into a full-scale convention and attracted a near-capacity audience of 7,000 people, with many attendees expressing astonishment that such a like-minded crowd existed.

There were other signs of a counterculture coming into being. Notting Hill's London Free School was founded in March 1966 by Rhaune Laslett and John "Hoppy" Hopkins (a key figure in all this). At first a centre for alternative adult education, it became a space where activists could scheme and bands could rehearse, and the focus for benefit gigs, including several by Pink Floyd at the All Saints Church Hall. There were also happening shops like Granny Takes A Trip and Indica Books, with Hopkins and Barry Miles founding *International Times* (*IT*), the first of the British underground newspapers, in the basement of the latter.

And at the end of 1966, perhaps most significant of all, Hopkins and Joe Boyd opened UFO at the Blarney Club in Tottenham Court Road, introducing the full-on psychedelic experience of music, lights and acid to a British audience for the first time. By 1967, the counterculture had its own soundtrack, with the Summer Of Love seeing the release of *Sgt Pepper's Lonely Hearts Club Band*, *The Piper At The Gates Of Dawn*, and *Are You Experienced?*.

But as the underground began to go overground, there was an inevitable backlash, with the commercialisation of the scene denounced by the more hard-bitten idealists. Hopkins was jailed for possession of cannabis, and peace and love suddenly seemed in short supply. In March 1968, an anti-war demo outside the US embassy in Grosvenor Square descended into a pitched battle between police on horseback and protestors. The authorities were fighting back.

By the end of the 60s, the original scene was faltering. UFO and Middle Earth had long since closed, while the underground press was now facing the realities of keeping a business afloat. Co-optation by opportunistic parties – from unscrupulous music promoters to new age religious cults – was everywhere. It's perhaps why the popular narrative insists that the counterculture died with the decade.

## The Underground Spreads

Yet while some of the idealism was stripped out, the underground spirit was still very much in evidence at the dawn of the 70s, with music its primary vehicle. Eager to cater to an expanding audience, record companies set up specialist 'progressive' labels. Across the country, arts labs and club nights sprang up, with the college gig circuit better connected to switched-on tastes than the cabaret-style tours bands had suffered previously. And London's happenings had moved to bigger venues (such as Implosion at the Roundhouse) to accommodate the growing crowd of heads looking to turn on in a safe space.

The growth of the rock festival also had a major impact on the spread of countercultural values around Britain. Tens of thousands could now congregate outside of London, and experience an alternative way of life to the drab, post-war existence that much of the country was still living through.

It didn't matter that, rather than hitting the hippie trail to India, the crowds then returned to their day jobs, colleges or schools. It didn't matter if they only enjoyed the freedoms of this lifestyle for the weekend. It didn't matter because the broader message of the counterculture – of questioning both authority and reality – had been assimilated at an intrinsic level by a new generation. And this was where the underground now resided.

For all the focus on 'big figures' in a social movement, actual change – in outlook, attitudes and values – comes from the grassroots. As it was, the audiences continued to turn up and turn on, the underground continued to spread – and Hawkwind became a rallying point for the alternative society throughout the 1970s.

## The Alternative Society

A key focus for the underground in London was Ladbroke Grove. Encompassing most of Notting Hill, including Portobello Road and its famous market, and bounded to the north by the raised concrete ribbon of the A40 known as the Westway, the whole area was pivotal to post-war culture.

Today gentrified beyond recognition, Ladbroke Grove was for much of the 20th century seen as little better than a slum. When the 'Windrush' generation began arriving in the late 40s from the Caribbean, it was one of the few areas that their less-than-welcoming hosts allowed them to settle in. This led to a blossoming there of semi-illicit 'blues parties', where black youth danced to ska and bluebeat (and later reggae) and smoked weed. In 1958, the first 'race riots' took place in Ladbroke Grove, as Teddy Boy gangs launched attacks on West Indian homes. The police were accused of failing to prevent these attacks, and a state of antipathy developed.

As one of London's cheapest places to live throughout the 60s and beyond, it became a hotbed of youthful creativity, as students sought affordable accommodation just a short walk from the West End's schools of art, design and theatre. Unsurprisingly, musicians were also drawn to its cheap housing and air of bohemian lawlessness. One such was Mick Farren, proto-punk provocateur and a man who could be relied on to cause chaos wherever he went. In 1967, his band **The Deviants** released *Ptooff!*, an album of raw, Troggs-meets-Zappa R&B, and the first significant signal from this new west London scene. Taking on more psychedelic and blues rock influences, and recruiting future Hawkwind player Paul Rudolph, the band jettisoned Farren and re-formed as the **Pink Fairies** in 1970.[1]

Moving to Ladbroke Grove from Warwick, The **Edgar Broughton Band** captured the heavier atmosphere of the times better than the hippie whimsy of yore. 'Death Of An Electric Citizen' and 'Evil' from their debut album *Wasa Wasa* (1969) showcased a gnarled, often sinister take on blues rock, while 'Out Demons Out' (originally a sorcerous anti-war chant written by The Fugs to levitate the Pentagon) became the unofficial anthem of the underground, a catch-all anti-establishment rant for audiences to shout along with.

And then there was **High Tide**, whose debut album *Sea Shanties* (1969), despite its deceptively jaunty title, was a study in crunching, post-Hendrix psych/prog. Featuring the swooping, distorted violin of future Hawkwind member Simon House, it's an often overlooked but essential staging point in the development of heavy music.[2]

For a snapshot of the area and its attitudes, there's a fascinating BBC documentary entitled *New Horizons – The Alternative Society* (first broadcast in 1971) which petitions the views of various community members. Charismatic *OZ* editor Richard Neville talks about the new libertarian attitudes towards sex and drugs and decries the drudgery of traditional working life. Ian King of BIT (a 24/7 information and advisory service founded by John Hopkins) talks about love and compassion being "eroded and destroyed by materialism". Caroline Coon of drugs campaign group Release proposes an engagement with straight society about a "more spiritual way of existing". Among the long-haired young people sewing and knitting in the Friends bazaar, there's a blink-and-you'll-miss-it appearance from Nik Turner. And Barney Bubbles is seen attending to the layout of the magazine.[3]

## The People's Outsiders

This was Hawkwind's milieu in their formative years. Brock busked on Portobello Road and worked semi-professionally as an electrician. Turner was a delivery driver for The Family Dog head shop. Moorcock sold books on the local market and helped stage gigs under the Westway. And as a contributor to *Friends/Frendz*, Calvert was a regular presence in shops and cafes.[4] Essentially, Hawkwind lived and worked alongside the people who would become their hardcore audience.

Yet the term 'people's band' was more often than not used as a back-handed compliment by music journalists, denoting groups whose records sold well regardless of what the press wrote (or didn't write) about them. It also implied that, despite being popular with their audience, a band was artistically inferior if they failed to win critical approval. To be a people's band was to exist outside of the 'official' 70s rock mainstream.[5]

This suited Hawkwind just fine, because they were determined wherever possible to operate apart from the traditional music business – for them, the record industry remained a cog in the establishment machine, however much it tried to re-brand itself as 'underground-friendly'. Also, Brock and Turner were in their late twenties when Hawkwind began, an age when most musicians who hadn't already made it were generally looking to rejoin straight society. This perseverance – combined with their independent, entrepreneurial outlook – strongly coloured the way they regarded and interacted with the business.

So despite its negative connotations, Hawkwind were happy to be known as a people's band, because it was how they saw themselves. None of them were exceptional musicians, so they didn't have the sense of entitlement that 'talent' sometimes produces. None of them really looked like rock-stars-in-waiting. And avoidance of the "star trip" was paramount – they were more likely to invite an audience member to do an interpretive dance than hog the limelight themselves.[6] The strobes and slides of their live experience was another way to de-focus their roles as performers. For now at least, they were the "technicians of spaceship earth" rather than its imperial commanders.

## Performing On The Frontline

And then there was their sheer visibility and willingness to travel and minister to provincial freaks. In 1970, they played over 100 gigs; in 1971, over 150, rapidly accruing a sizeable following simply by being almost permanently on the road. Their willingness to play for free – whether for deserving causes (striking firefighters and miners, CND, Release, Greenpeace, White Panthers, the underground press) or as a gesture of community good will – was also a huge factor in their early success and ongoing mythology.

Particularly notable were the gigs they staged under the Westway. The photographs inside *ISOS* show the band surrounded by a protective henge of amps, the flyover's concrete supports forming a bleak modernist backdrop. The broken ground and huddled crowd add to the sense of some post-apocalyptic ritual taking place – but in bringing music to the people like this, Hawkwind reclaimed an ugly urban space and imbued it with good vibes, if only for a couple of hours every Saturday.

This philosophy of just turning up and doing it was epitomised early on in their history by their appearance at the 1970 Isle Of Wight festival. Performing free for hours, Hawkwind became a symbol of the underground spirit, an expression of freak defiance in the face of the encroaching corporatisation of the music industry.

In its own way, playing for free was a political act, and Hawkwind were the most prominent band to do this regularly. But inevitably, it also brought them into routine conflict with the authorities, suffering numerous drugs raids long after most fellow travellers had made themselves less conspicuous. This sense of trying to escape the clutches of conformity in the face of persecution would become the over-riding thematic driver of Hawkwind's early music and shows. They were the people's band reporting back from the frontline as the fragile underground battled the harsh, increasingly turbulent reality of the straight world.[7]

▾　　▾　　▾

Already a melting pot of culture before they arrived, Hawkwind did more than any other band to imbue Ladbroke Grove with a vibe of anarchic possibility, where music could be made and shows put on beyond the confines of what was allowed or acceptable. This sense of empowerment and breaking down of barriers would spread far beyond West London, and by the mid-70s , begin to fan the first flames of punk.

◇◇◇◇◇◇◇◇◇◇◇◇◇◇◇◇◇◇◇◇◇◇◇◇◇◇◇◇◇◇◇◇◇◇◇◇◇◇◇◇◇◇◇◇◇◇◇◇◇◇◇◇◇◇◇◇◇◇◇◇◇◇◇◇◇◇◇◇

1    Initially distributed via the underground press, *Ptooff!* was funded by Nigel Samuel, the young heir to a property fortune (and an investor in *IT*). There's an argument for The Deviants being another influence on Hawkwind's sound, certainly their attitude. On 'Somewhere To Go' from 1968's *Disposable*, Farren's delivery is near-robotic as he fantasises about escaping mainstream society, while Sid Bishop's guitar solo is strangely Brock-like. And then there's the downright eerie 'Last Man' from the same album, with Farren as a deranged sole survivor of the apocalypse.

2    High Tide were also the band headlining the All Saints Hall the night that Group X gatecrashed their gig.

3    Norwegian state TV (NRK) had already cast a perplexed eye over the Ladbroke Grove scene in a 1968 report which featured Dave Brock busking on Portobello Road

4    Nick Kent describes how *Frendz* became the band's centre of operations before local shows. They'd gather in the office in the afternoon, "and the room would duly become transformed into an ongoing scene from a *Cheech And Chong* movie" (p54, Kent, *Apathy For The Devil*, 2010).

5    The Aylesbury Friars newsletter of 22 April 1972 makes a more positive use of the term: "Someone recently told me that in their opinion Hawkwind were the only real band we've got, because unlike other rock bands, they were strictly a 'people's band', as opposed to being a 'musician's band'. Bands like TYA [Ten Years After] or ELP etc are the mountains whilst Hawkwind is more like the air itself. Either way, Hawkwind are a very important band now."

6    Dettmar: "One night at a Roundhouse gig, there was some guy dancing on the stage and we found that we were gradually able to 'play' him. The rest of the audience became caught up in the same thing and they were able to 'play' us" ('Del On The Beat' – *Beat Instrumental*, December 1971).

7    Brock: "Every time we arrived back in the early hours in our van, we'd be stopped by the police in Notting Hill and searched. In those days, anyone with long hair was a drug addict" ('Returning Volumes Of Sound' – Joe Banks, *Shindig!*, February 2018). According to Pete Frame's 1979 Hawkwind family tree (available with *PXR5*), Doug Smith claimed the band were "subjected to police investigation 68 times in the first few years: roadblocks were commonplace, searches were expected."

# HAWKWIND

## DAGENHAM - JAN. 22

### An Apology

IMAGINE . . .

*You are a band, rushing about the country trying to do benefits and helping people and in between, fitting in the gigs to make ends meet — and your van breaks down in the middle of nowhere.*

*We can imagine how it felt for you when we didn't turn up at Dagenham. Can you imagine how we feel? Signed: HAWKWIND.*

Hawkwind will be appearing at Dagenham Roundhouse on Saturday, March 25th. All those present last Saturday will be admitted free with the tickets they were given.

*We'd like to see you if you'd like to see us*

'Can you imagine how we feel?'
(source: Wolfie Smith collection)

Advert for The Wild One featuring Nik Turner
(source: Wolfie Smith collection)

At Rockfield to record *Doremi Fasol Latido*... L-R – DikMik, Dettmar, King, Brock, Turner, Lemmy
(source: Michael Scott collection)

# The Other Side Of The Sky

January–November 1972

It's early evening on Thursday 13 July, 1972, and something strange and rather wonderful is about to happen. We're midway through *Top Of The Pops* and dance troupe Pan's People have just finished their interpretation of The Stylistics' 'Betcha By Golly Wow'. Eccentric DJ Jimmy Savile makes a noise like a rutting seal,[1] then introduces the next band. They're not in the studio, but have been filmed playing live for the purpose of promoting their latest single.[2] Cut to a darkened hall, and for the next few minutes, the freaks are let loose in the nation's living rooms. For many young viewers, music will never be the same again.

Over the coming weeks, repeat showings of this extraordinary footage will propel 'Silver Machine' into the top three. Its opening shot is of a crowd already in the grip of what looks like religious ecstasy, hands aloft flicking peace signs in the air, the provincial underground in all its scuzzy glory. As the radiophonic oscillations of the intro give way to the thunderous whoosh of the riff, the camera focuses on the striking figure of Stacia, her short black dress embroidered with stars, her face painted silver and white. She gets up from her knees, stands to attention and salutes. Acting out a sequence of moves at stage front, she's rapt in her own secret ceremony, implacable and mesmerising.[3] The flouncing of Pan's People seems a long way off now.

The camera alights on **Simon King**, the drummer's pale, almost emaciated body buzzing with kinetic energy, and then Lemmy steps up to the mic, the very essence of grimy biker chic. With his shaggy hair and leather trousers, Nik Turner is the coolest looking member of the band, furiously shaking his flute above his head like a space-age sceptre. DikMik is the more animated of the electronics crew, stooped over his table like a carnival showman; Del Dettmar is seated, heavily bearded, more serious. Dave Brock is barely glimpsed, content to shun the spotlight.

Shot and edited in an impressionistic style, the camera roves between the band, lights and crowd to convey the immersive nature of the Hawkwind live experience. Cutting back to the gaudy *Top Of The Pops* studio and a mimed performance by Johnny Nash of 'I Can See Clearly Now' is like emerging from a temporary wormhole in the artificial fabric of everyday reality. 'Silver Machine' offers a disruptive vision, a bold assertion of a music scene and lifestyle that rejects straight society's conventions. It's a clarion call to nascent heads and freaks everywhere.[4]

▾     ▾     ▾

The unlikely success of 'Silver Machine' will change everything for Hawkwind, but it's business as usual at the start of the year, with another band member given their marching orders. Ongoing substance abuse has left Terry Ollis increasingly unable to keep time properly – his replacement is Simon King, formerly of Opal Butterfly and a friend of Lemmy's.[5] With his hard-hitting but unflashy style, King is the perfect fit for the band's increasingly muscular space rock – for many, his addition completes the 'classic' line-up, its core relatively stable for the next three years.

An early gig for the new line-up is the Greasy Truckers benefit show on 13 February at the Roundhouse.[6] It's a major turning point in the band's fortunes, though initial auspices aren't great: the band prepare for the occasion by getting completely off their heads, with Lemmy and DikMik's preferred cocktail – speed, downers, acid – proving to be particularly debilitating. The event is sold-out, but when a power cut requires everybody to leave the building, hundreds more join the original audience on return. Hawkwind's electronics devices are affected, and they re-start with mumbled apologies – but deliver a surprisingly cogent set. The show is recorded, with edited highlights appearing on the *Greasy Truckers Party* album – released on 28 April in a limited edition of 20,000, it quickly sells out.[7]

Hawkwind occupy side four of the album. '**Master Of The Universe**' rides in on a volley of electronic whistles, King immediately making his presence felt. Here is the pounding engine of Hawkwind at its most densely metronomic, riff and drums in almost robotic unison. There's evidence of their chemically-altered state – Turner's vocals are wavery, and either Lemmy changes too early or Brock comes in late after the first verse – but the tension-ratcheting breakdowns are as effective as ever. Turner sounds like he's drowning in mountainous waves of cosmic sludge, but there's real excitement whenever the drums burst explosively back in to pick up the beat.

'**Born To Go**' is less focused than future versions, but still the epitome of Hawkwind in full flight, a nihilistic battering ram *"breaking out of the shell"* and smashing through the celestial ceiling. It's their first recording with Calvert on vocals, a snarling space rat compared to the more controlled voice he later adopts. Brock, DikMik and Dettmar create sheets of near-white noise, but as the song locks into a single-minded chug, it's Lemmy who takes the lead, weaving in and out of the groove before it collapses in a fusillade of electronics and acid rock meandering.

But these aren't the most important recordings made at this event. New song 'Silver Machine' is a powerful slab of interstellar boogie which always gets a good reaction. There's a clanging of strings and cymbals before the riff kicks in, and Calvert seems to forget both his words and where the microphone is. Turner joins in, but sounds jostled, as though in the midst of a stage invasion. They pretty much miss the chorus altogether, which nevertheless drags on aimlessly. And yet despite its shambolic nature, there's still something about that riff…

The song halts abruptly, and the band segues into a recitation of 'Welcome To The Future' over minimal backing, illustrating how they can move from stoned boogie to icy morbidity in the space of a moment, good vibes tempered with a cold blast of reality. This builds to an ascending elevator of noise, the Hawkship escaping the dying earth, to which *"you are welcome."*[8]

▾      ▾      ▾

The papers can't argue with the sold-out shows, but seem nonplussed by Hawkwind's appeal. Even the band are sometimes at a loss: "In the beginning," says Turner, "I never thought our music would appeal to anybody, simply because we've never pandered to public taste, never compromised… By a happy accident, people seem to be digging it." Brock suggests it's because they genuinely value their audience: "If you go round dance halls in the country and see the miserable conditions people are in, you feel you should give them as much in a live show as you possibly can. Most groups don't."[a]

Some journalists do however offer a more serious analysis of the group's music, and how it reflects the conditions that Brock alludes to. *Melody Maker*'s Andrew Means speculates on the band's role as explorers of both outer and inner space during a time of apocalyptic foreboding: "While this new age of mechanical space travel suggests unlimited horizons, the situation upon Earth promises the opposite… The fact that doomsday is all too viable sets the background for the group's activities."[b]

▾      ▾      ▾

On 9 June, an overdubbed and remixed version of 'Silver Machine' from the Greasy Truckers concert is released as the band's second single, the post-production cladding its fuselage in steel and mounting a new engine on each wing – and expunging Calvert's vocal. It opens now with a squelchy, radiophonic call-sign which, even as its grimy Chuck Berry riff fades up,[9] sets the song apart from the lumpen boogie being played by countless other bands. But the real difference comes from Lemmy's imperious revoicing and the cosmic biker vibe he brings to the song. He bellows the opening "*I!*" like a man asserting his will to power while sat astride a gleaming missile heading straight for the sun – as the casing gets hotter and hotter, he struggles manfully to hit the high notes, "*still feeling meeeeeeeann!*".[10]

Brock beefs up the chorus with extra guitar and a faltering but determined solo, and adds screechy, golem-like backing vocals which suggest "*the other side of the sky*" might be a good place to lose your mind. But it's Lemmy who gives the song its irresistible charm, inspiring teenyboppers and Hells Angels alike to shout along with its chorus.

Flip the single and you hear a very different Hawkwind.[11] '**Seven By Seven**' starts with a lilting, melancholic chord sequence, before lurching into a serious downer rock riff, Brock uncomfortably at the top of his vocal range: "*Lost am I in this world of timelessness and woe!*" Adding to the gloom, there's a spoken word section full of metaphysical mumbo jumbo delivered by a stoned and rather camp Calvert.[12] It's audaciously contrived, but as the electronics whistle away, and Lemmy vamps like mad, it's pulled off through sheer strength of conviction.

'Silver Machine' becomes a bona fide phenomenon. Initial sales are a testament to Hawkwind's position as the "country's number one alternative band"[c] – but when the single starts getting plays from Radio 1's Tony Blackburn and Jimmy Young, it enters the chart on 1 July. Two weeks later, it's on *Top Of The Pops*.[13] The following week, *NME* gives them their first music press front cover, Nik Turner playing his flute under the headline "Hawkwind Lift Off".[14]

'Silver Machine' features four times on *Top Of The Pops*, peaks for two weeks at number three (19-26 August) and remains on the chart for a total of 15 weeks. It eventually sells over 500,000 copies in the UK alone, and becomes a worldwide hit, charting in France, West Germany, Portugal, Spain, Sweden, Rhodesia, Japan and Australia – it even gets to number one in Switzerland. By any estimation, it's one of the songs of the year.

▾       ▾       ▾

More in demand now than ever, with major venues beckoning, Hawkwind struggle to reconcile commercial success with maintaining credibility as a community band. At Finsbury Park Rainbow on 13 August, hundreds of fans without tickets storm the doors to get in for free.[15] The benefit gigs are also taking their toll. Brock: "People are beginning to take it for granted that they can get us, so that sometimes we're advertised as playing somewhere and people turn up and pay to get in only to find that they've been ripped off."[d] Turner demurs: "What's left of the underground is worth preserving: I'd like to do more free gigs".[e]

The success of 'Silver Machine' blindsides the music press even further, and an acerbic edge creeps into their coverage. *Melody Maker* publishes an article entitled 'Hawkwind – The Joke Band That Made It', while *NME*'s Nick Kent writes 'How Will Success Affect The Freaks?'.[16]

Yet Hawkwind claim to have planned it all along. Brock says "It didn't surprise us, man. We knew it was going to be a hit",[f] while Turner is positively Machiavellian: "We've become involved in the singles market by choice because we want to get a few things moving... We calculated that a good single would put us in a strong bargaining position because as a rule [UA] don't give us a great deal of support".[g] Calvert later claims to be unsurprised for more innocent reasons: "I was so naive in those days that I couldn't see any way that if you made a single it wasn't a hit. I assumed if you got into the process of making singles than you're in the business of making hit singles and that was it".[h]

▾ ▾ ▾

On 2 August, the BBC invite them to record a session for the more mainstream *Johnnie Walker* show. They take the opportunity to try out '**Brainstorm**', one of the newer songs in their set. Relatively truncated, this early take features none of the frantic chanting of later versions, but the grungy simplicity of its ramalama riff is effective from the outset. Turner sounds less stoned than usual, and the combination of wailing electronics and King's pounding drums indicates a band reaching peak power. Brock's buzzsaw guitar and Turner's wah-wah sax radiate garage-punk attitude, while Lemmy makes some adventurous runs amid the cosmic debris.

They're also obliged to do a version of '**Silver Machine**', the riff starker and Lemmy's vocal sounding a little less Wagnerian. Inevitably less powerful than the skilfully bolstered single, it's possible they're already getting a little tired of it –

# Win 200 Bangla Desh tickets

## NEW MUSICAL EXPRESS

**JULY 22**    U.S./Canada 50c    6p

### THE DAVID BOWIE
#### INTERVIEW

## REX, STEWART
### NEW ALBUMS REVIEWED

# HAWKWIND LIFT OFF

NICK TURNER (HAWKWIND)

## Six-hour Rainbow marathon, British tour

HAWKWIND — who take a major leap towards popular acceptance with the entry of their "Silver Machine" in the singles chart this week — are to put on a 6-hour "party" at the London Rainbow in August.

For so long dismissed as a lower division British band despite their potential as crowd pullers, Hawkwind are also currently being lined up for their first major U.K. tour.

The Rainbow gig, on August 13 starting at 4 p.m., will be Hawkwind's own promotion.

Other bands they've chosen to join the marathon "party" are Man, Keith Christmas, Magic Muscle and "The first ever London appearance" of Bristol all-girl group Beryl Billabong and the Sheilas.

The British tour will take place late autumn, with the band playing major venues — four a week — over a two-month period.

From the U.K. tour, Hawkwind depart for their first tour of America.

The band's "Silver Machine" single is at No. 19 in its first week in the NME Chart.

## HAWKWIND'S NICK TURNER INTERVIEWED ON PAGE 6

First *NME* front cover, 22 July 1972
(source: Wolfie Smith collection)

Spain

Angola

Israel

Portugal

West Germany

Yugoslavia

A selection of 'Silver Machine' picture sleeves (source: Johan Edlundh collection)

while it's fun to play, it's not representative of their main vibe. At least you can hear Turner's flute on this version. When the session is broadcast on 14 August, the DJ seems faintly ambivalent: "the interesting and unusual sounds of Hawkwind." [17]

▾     ▾     ▾

Following a short European tour and a big show at the Oval Cricket Ground supporting Frank Zappa,[18] the band travel to Rockfield Studios on 17 September to record their third album. Situated in the South Wales countryside, Rockfield is a relatively basic residential facility, but has the advantage of being as far away as possible from the distractions of Ladbroke Grove and their new found fame.

As Brock explains: "We just let the tapes run and play like we do when we're playing live; do a three-hour track and then cut it up into pieces, use one piece as a complete section, and join it up to another piece with a synthesiser link or something... We've got enough down for two albums in fact, because it's so nice down here".[i] And this time, Brock and Dettmar are producing.[19]

On 23 September, Hawkwind play the Windsor Arts Festival, and are billed as the main attraction above fellow stars of the underground including Pink Fairies, Arthur Brown and MC5.[20] And on 28 September, Hawkwind return to London's Paris Theatre for what will be their final session for the BBC during the 70s. A live in-concert broadcast, it shows how ambitious the band have become in turning their gigs into rock theatre, and the direction they're going in.

The only 'official' recording of her voice, Stacia recites the pre-show '**Countdown**' in an adenoidal tone of detached amusement, or perhaps embarrassment: "Mothership control in readiness. Sonic Assassins cleared for space flight." DJ Andy Dunkley is more game: "Audience receptor units activated – now!" Cue a big cheer from the crowd. This is the type of thing that gets Hawkwind written off as a 'joke band' by serious music critics, but the audience clearly love it.

"All units functioning, movement commencing, we have lift-off, we have music, we have Hawkwind!" concludes Dunkley as the stinging circular riff of '**Born To Go**' takes over. Brock's guitar is more metallic than ever, King's drums are huge, and the electronics crew seem to have invested in a Theremin. Brock and Turner's combined vocals are a declaration of intent, sturdy pioneers at the galactic frontier, not yet succumbed to deep-space cabin fever. Brock also sounds increasingly confident as a soloist, charting the peaks and troughs of the hyperspatial byways while Turner's sax gibbers away like rats mutated by the ship's reactor.

'The Black Corridor' emerges from rattling strings, electronic rumblings, cosmic atmospherics – Turner's spoken word delivery is even bleaker than the absent Calvert's. '**Seven By Seven**', with lovely flute and synth over its introduction, has one of their most intense and unremitting riffs (such that Brock barely attempts the vocal). '**Brainstorm**' begins in the middle of the chanting. It feels like we're eavesdropping on an interstellar-sized bad trip, until Lemmy and King find the main riff and batter their way back to sanity. '**Master Of The Universe**' has a fantastic crunch to its opening riff, but Brock's guitar loses power, Lemmy playing louder to compensate. It's a brutal bludgeon compared to the studio original, with some crazed knob-twiddling towards the end.

'**Paranoia**' is the one track surviving in their set from *Hawkwind* – but as the slow bass riff takes over and Brock and Lemmy have fun chanting "*fly, high, die*", it's as malign as ever. '**Earth Calling**' is an ambient interlude, and '**Silver Machine**' is inevitable, even a little incongruous after what's gone before. But the chorus is still great: the office party at the end of the universe, everyone joining in before the brain police arrive. Finally, the lovely opening chords of '**Welcome To The Future**' leave you entirely unprepared for the sudden and impressive explosion of noise that brings proceedings to an abrupt halt.

It's hard not to smile as Dunkley signs off: "BBC is the Earth-based unit of Galactic Audio Services. All Terran listeners will now be returned to Earth-based channels. As Hawkwind flies on, this is Andy Dunkley wishing you good evening and open space."

▾     ▾     ▾

This is just a taster. 'Silver Machine' has supplied the financial leverage to create their most ambitious and extensive tour yet. Ever since Calvert climbed onboard, he's been telling anyone who'll listen about the immersive multimedia presentation that will become the 'Space Ritual': "The basic idea of the opera – for want of a better word – is that a team of starfarers are in a state of suspended animation, and the opera is a presentation of the dreams that they're having in deep space. It's a mythological approach to what's happening today… the mythology of the space age, in the way that rocket ships and interplanetary travel are a parallel with the heroic voyages of man in earlier times".[j] He wants the idea to be taken seriously: "Our show will include electronic music, strobe lights, dancers, mime and space hero costumes. The only danger is that it collapses into carnival; for this reason, it is necessary to always maintain a certain distance".[k]

The band too are enthusiastic, seeing it as a natural extension of what they've been doing, playing continuous live sets that ebb and flow rather than break for applause. Various ideas are mooted for the staging, including touring the show like a circus in an inflatable plastic tent. More outlandishly, it's suggested Del Dettmar be seated on a revolving tower above the heads of the audience. Brock is typically concerned with practicalities: "It's coming along slowly, but there's so much work, really a lot, and you just don't realise how much there is until you start. Our normal number of people on the road is 16, but with this we'll need 24, and they've all got to be paid. When I see it all written down, I tend to freak out, because apart from all that we've got to get it all together musically too".[l]

The expanded road crew that Brock refers to includes a new lightshow team. **Mike Hart** and **Alan Day** of Proteus Lights – who have been working on and off with Hawkwind for the past two years – are joined by **Jonathan Smeeton**, a veteran of Middle Earth and the Roundhouse, who's recently been doing tour lighting for Frank Zappa. Smeeton sees Hawkwind as the perfect musical counterpoint to his increasingly ambitious lighting effects, using multiple slide projectors to create crude but effective five-cell animated loops. Coming together as **Liquid Len and the Lensmen**,[21] Smeeton, Hart and Day develop a ground-breaking spectacle that becomes another defining aspect of the Hawkwind experience.

A Space Ritual 'manual' is sent out to the press, which *Melody Maker* treats with unusual seriousness: "Cultural change is an essential part of Hawkwind's image. Cultural, never the obsolescence of politics".[m] And then a quote from the manual itself: "The basic principle for the starship and the space ritual is based on the Pythagorean concept of sound. Briefly, this conceived the Universe to be an immense monochord, with its single string stretched between absolute spirit and at its lowest end absolute matter. Along this string were positioned the planets of our solar system. Each of these spheres as it rushed through space was believed to sound a certain tone caused by its continuous displacement of the ether. These intervals and harmonies are called 'The Sound Of The Spheres.' The interval between earth and the fixed stars being the most perfect harmonic interval."

This is actually Bubbles rather than Calvert, keen to make mystical cosmology central to the realisation of the show. He adds: "I've designed new speakers in chromium boxes which gives us a metallic appearance more in keeping with the group's image, and we've painted various areas in opposition to the Pythagorean musical scale. All the speakers and boxes in that area will be painted those colours and the musicnauts Del, Dik, Simon, Lemmy and Dave will stand in positions relative to their signs".[n]

▼ ▼ ▼

The band return to Rockfield to complete *Doremi Fasol Latido*, a punningly titled reference to the Pythagorean scale and a "preview" of the tour. After four months, 7 October marks the last week that 'Silver Machine' is on the charts. The following week, BBC Radio 1 broadcasts the Paris Theatre recording in its *In Concert* slot.

Another short hop to Europe, and then the Space Ritual tour officially begins at the King's Lynn Corn Exchange on 8 November. Throughout the tour, every audience member receives a free programme containing lyrics and Calvert's tongue-in-cheek "extract from the Saga of Doremi Fasol Latido". On the first night, the band's 2,500 watt speaker stacks blow the venue's PA. The following evening only a few of the customised stacks are in use for the press performance at Dunstable's Queensway Hall. Regardless, crowd and journalists all seem gratifyingly overwhelmed.[22]

*Record Mirror* describes the gig as, "Nothing short of sensational",[o] a thought echoed by Martin Marriott at *Disc*: "2,000 people were up on their feet, arms over heads, clapping."[p] *NME*'s John Pidgeon is similarly fascinated with the audience's reaction: "Whenever the stage gave off electronic pulsations, the crowd became uneasy, restless, perturbed; when the characteristic heavy metal riffs started up the sense of relief was made physically manifest."[q]

Martin Hayman at *Sounds* gives the best description of the event, and how it defines the provincial underground: "The bass pulses through the hall, itself like a massive space capsule, the dull insistent hypnotic boom of a nuclear reactor. Spidery figures wield guitars and crash drums in the flickering half-light at the end of the hall, packed with a dense mass of people, a sort of freaks' convention. A mass in another sense too, come to celebrate not only Hawkwind's accession to the ranks of bands whose gigs have 'All Tickets Sold' on the door, but of those who share Hawkwind's populist philosophy."[r]

Pidgeon describes, "A montage of meteorological, astronomical, sonic and electronic images flashed in front onto the three dancers. The familiar, almost stolid figure of Stacia has been joined by John May (who looks like someone who crashed the stage and didn't get bounced) and (Miss) Renée, whose white-wrapped shape appeared to fragment under the UV's and strobes.[23] The effect on the band, obscured between this sandwich of light, was to eliminate individuality in the same way as their music does."[s]

▼　　▼　　▼

On 24 November, and with advance sales of 80,000,[24] *Doremi Fasol Latido* hits the shops.

a　'The Truth About Hawkwind' – James Johnson, *NME*, 05/02/72

b　'Hawkwind: A Space Odyssey' – Andrew Means, *Melody Maker*, 29/04/1972

c　'The Alternative Band' – James Johnson, *NME*, 22/07/72

d　'Hawkwind – A Fantasy Of Sound And Colour' – Peter Erskine, *Disc*, 15 July 1972

e　'Hawkwind: Some Facts From The Freedom Freaks' – Keith Altham, *NME*, 30/9/72

f　'In Search Of Hawkwind' – Steve Peacock, *Sounds*, 23/9/72

g　James Johnson, same source

h　Audio recording, interview by Tim Gadd, 1982

i　Steve Peacock, same source

j　'Hawkwind: The Spaced Out People's Band' – Richard Williams, *Melody Maker*, 27/11/71

k　'Il Falco Spaziale' ('The Space Hawk') – Alberto Gioannini, *Ciao 2001*, 21/5/72

l　Steve Peacock, same source

m　'Hawkwind: Watch This Space' – Andrew Means, *Melody Maker*, 28/10/72

n　'Hawkwind Musicnauts' – Keith Altham, *Music Scene*, 1/12/72

o　*Record Mirror*, November 1972

p　Martin Marriott, *Disc*, November 1972

q　John Pidgeon, *NME*, 18/11/72

r　'All Aboard Hawkwind's Space Ritual' – Martin Hayman, *Sounds*, 18/11/72

s　John Pidgeon, same source

1　There can be no greater illustration of the darkness at the heart of the British establishment in the 70s than a dangerous sexual predator like Jimmy Savile hiding in plain sight on primetime TV.

2　Something of a holy relic for fans given the dearth of 70s live footage of Hawkwind, this film was shot at the Queensway Hall in Dunstable (7 July). Brock: "They only had one camera so we had to do it twice. If you look at the footage you can see that we're wearing different stuff in every shot!" ('The Making Of Hawkwind's Silver Machine'", Paul Moody, *Uncut*, September 2007).

3　Stacia would later refer to this sequence of movements as her "robot routine."

4    The charts were awash with unthreatening MOR in 1972. This edition of *Top Of The Pops*
     included The Partridge Family's 'Breaking Up Is Hard To Do', The New Seekers' 'Circles' and
     Donny Osmond's 'Puppy Love', the current number one. Less saccharine, the show also featured
     The Who's 'Join Together' and Alice Cooper's 'School's Out', one of the songs that would stop
     'Silver Machine' from reaching the top spot. David Bowie's eye-popping *TOTP* performance of
     'Starman' had occurred the previous week – the fact that 'Starman' and 'Silver Machine' were in
     the hit parade at the same time is a pleasing coincidence. 'Silver Machine' spent 15 weeks on
     the charts and peaked at number three. 'Starman' charted for 11 weeks and peaked at number
     10. Space-themed hit singles were definitely a thing in 1972: Elton John reached number two
     in the charts in June with 'Rocket Man' and The Kinks got to number 16 in the same month
     with 'Supersonic Rocket Ship'.

5    Prior to Ollis's departure, a show was attempted with both drummers. Brock: "There was a gig
     where both Terry Ollis and Simon King played, and some guy in the front freaked out and
     had to be strapped into a stretcher and taken away. Terry was slowing down while Simon was
     speeding up, and the band was playing weird electronic music – it must have been terrifying!
     That was the last gig that Terry did with us..." ('Returning Volumes Of Sound' – Joe Banks,
     *Shindig!*, February 2018).

6    The Greasy Truckers were a Ladbroke Grove-based community organisation led by
     *Frendz* editor John Trux. Trux can be seen standing next to Barney Bubbles on the inside
     cover of *ISOS*.

7    Also featuring Man, Brinsley Schwarz and Magic Michael, *Greasy Truckers Party* was a prized
     fan possession and collector's item until its expanded re-release in 2007.

8    Both the unedited version of 'Silver Machine' and 'WTTF' appeared on the *Glastonbury Fayre*
     triple album released in June. The previous year's Glastonbury Festival had been organised by
     an idealistic coterie of upper-class hippies – including Arabella Churchill, granddaughter of
     Winston – and had run up significant debts. *Glastonbury Fayre* was conceived as a way of paying
     these debts off, though with a complex fold-out sleeve designed by Barney Bubbles, a limited
     pressing of 5,000 copies and a retail price of just £3.99, it's debatable how much they recouped.
     Other acts who donated tracks include David Bowie, the Pink Fairies, the Edgar Broughton
     Band, Gong and the Grateful Dead.

9    Simon King: "[Greasy Truckers] was about my third gig, and I didn't know what I was doing.
     I hadn't done any rehearsals and I thought that 'Silver Machine' *was* a Chuck Berry number –
     really" ('No Change in the Wind' – Geoff Barton, *Sounds*, 1/75).

10   Calvert's words for 'Silver Machine' were actually inspired by the essay *How To Construct A Time
     Machine* by French symbolist writer Alfred Jarry. Calvert interpreted it as a guide to building
     a bicycle, and wrote a mock-heroic space-age tribute to his own two-wheeled (silver) machine.

As the cover of the single's sleeve is apparently composed of bicycle gear cogs, its designer – long assumed to be Bubbles – seems to be in on the joke. It was actually created by Tony Vesely: "It was the innards of an old clock that was lying around. Used simply because it was 'machine'-like. Pennie [Smith] photographed it and 'posterised' it (making the image contrasty and easy to separate into two or three colours). The monkey was inserted as a sort of background "Deus ex machina" reference. I also worked in a very rough head of Christ in the centre, there if you want to see it sort of thing" (Interview with the author, 2018). Vesely worked alongside Bubbles and Smith at *Frendz*. Alfred Jarry also wrote the play *Ubu Roi*, from where US garage-punk experimentalists and Hawkwind fans Pere Ubu took their name.

11    The post-production of 'Silver Machine' took place at Morgan Studios in north London, but 'Seven By Seven' was Hawkwind's first recording at Rockfield Studios in mid-April. Doug Smith remembers Calvert listening to a live radio broadcast of the latest lunar mission while recording his vocal: "Underneath his headphones was a small earpiece connected to a transistor radio in his pocket… I seem to remember that in the middle of a take he cried out, 'They've landed!'" (Interview with the author, 2019).

12    The section may be inspired by the seven planes and subplanes of existence in occult cosmology, or by the Seven Rays of various esoteric philosophies, or merely an abstract verbal riff on the number seven. Song and lyrics are attributed solely to Brock, but the spoken section sounds like Calvert's work.

13    The press finds the idea of Hawkwind on *Top of the Pops* hard to process. *IT*'s enthusiastic review of 'Silver Machine', written just before this happens, concludes: "A crazed record for all you nutters to buy, I mean wouldn't you really dig to see these boys on *Top Of The Pops*? (God what a horrid thought!!!)" (27/7/72). *NME*'s Steve Peacock, after the fact: "So how did you feel when that friendly bunch of freaks, the ones you always liked to go and see when you got really out of it, are at number two in the singles chart? 'Was I tripping or did I really see Hawkwind on *Top Of The Pops*?' someone wrote to us, and a lot of people were similarly astonished" ('In Search Of Hawkwind', Steve Peacock, *NME*, 23/9/72).

14    Further front covers this year include Turner & Lemmy on *Disc* in September, and Lemmy sharing an *NME* cover with Alice Cooper (14/10/72). *Sounds* includes a full colour poster of the band inside the paper on 2/10/72.

15    Turner's habit of compiling gigantic guest lists can't have helped: "I was always hanging out on Portobello Road, and fans would ask me to be on the guest list. We did a gig at the Rainbow Theatre, an indoor festival where we gave away free food and had all these guests, and the promoter said, 'Look, you've got 400 guests! I can't let them in,' and I said, 'If you don't, I can't go onstage!'" (Interview with the author, 2017).

16    Andrew Means, *Melody Maker*, 12/08/72 and Nick Kent, *NME*, 12/08/72. Ironically, both writers were early champions of the band. The Means article is actually very positive, while a month earlier, Kent had compared Hawkwind favourably to Pink Floyd and Amon Düül, and half-jokingly described them as "the cosmic Prophets of the Unalterable Apocalypse" ('Gone With The Wind', *Frendz*, 14/07/72).

17    This comment is heard on the archival album *At The BBC-1972* (EMI - 2010) – but confusingly, it's made by veteran DJ Brian Matthew, not Johnnie Walker. The source of this recording is evidently a BBC transcription disc of the *Top Of The Pops* export show, which was sent to radio stations around the world and presented by Matthew.

18    Supposedly added to the line-up after poor ticket sales, Hawkwind in fact play *after* Zappa, in an evening slot, so that their lightshow can be properly appreciated: "Then the lights darkened, the boggies leapt to their feet as they heard Del and Dikmik's oscillators speeding up, and we all faced our private crises on Spaceship Earth" (*IT* 139 – Oct 72).

19    Of this surfeit material: 'Take What You Can', recorded during the *Doremi* sessions, was released on the 2011 archival collection *Parallel Universe*. Whether studio versions of other contemporary tracks such as 'Born To Go' were attempted remains unknown. Calvert wasn't at Rockfield, and makes no musical contribution to the album.

20    Nick Kent gives a fairly dismal account of this event, but ends positively: "And then there was a flash in the sky and a hand reached out and switched on the luminous sign amid the heavens which read 'Hawkwind'. And it was good." (NB MC5 failed to show) (Nick Kent, *NME*, 30/9/72).

21    A reference to E.E. 'Doc' Smith's *Lensman* stories, a cornerstone of 'Golden Age' space opera.

22    During the writing of this book, I've been sent memories of Hawkwind concerts by many fans, particularly of the Space Ritual tour. This, from Grahame Lake, is typical: "I was fortunate to see the Space Ritual at Middlesbrough Town Hall. This certainly wasn't a bunch of acid head hippies playing drippy post '68 rock. It was an aural and visual assault that left you blown away. The vacant looks on everyone's face as they left highlighted how exhausting and brutal these concerts were" (ref: 'A Case For Sonic Attack' – Joe Banks, *The Quietus*, 29/08/13).

23    *Sounds'* Martin Hayman was particularly taken with Renée, an American dancer who had previously worked with Quicksilver Messenger Service and Jefferson Airplane, describing her as, "blonde and sylph-like, a space fairy, frozen at perhaps ten frames a second, (she) does a futuristic parody of the can-can across the line of the strobe" ('All Aboard Hawkwind's Space Ritual' – Martin Hayman, *Sounds*, 18/11/72). May, one of the writers at *Frendz*, would be replaced after the first few dates by dancer and mime artist Tony Crerar.

24    According to Nick Kent ('Cosmic Calypso And Sonic Surprise', *NME*, 11/11/72). The album's release was put back two weeks from the 10th – so much for the Space Ritual 'preview' idea.

Topping the bill at the Windsor Arts Festival
(source: Paul Windle collection)

| Doors open | 3.30 p.m. |
| Keith Christmas | 4.00–4.30 |
| Man | 4.45–6.15 |
| Beryl Billabong | 6.45–7.00 |
| Magic Muscle | 7.10–8.00 |
| Hawkwind | 8.30–10.00 |

Natural Theatre Company will perform on the stage during one of the 30 minute changeover periods, and possible in the aisles/audience at another period.

THIS BOOK COMES FREE FROM NASTY TALES—DESIGNED BY EDWARD BARKER & MICK FARREN

From the *Nasty Tales* programme handed out at the Rainbow show,
13 August 1972

Lemmy
(source: Michael Scott collection)

# THE TRUTH ABOUT HAWKWIND

*revealed to JAMES JOHNSON*

**HAWKWIND (From left): Bob Calvert, Dikmik, and Dave Brock.**

**LIKE THEM or not, you must admit that Hawkwind are honest. Guitarist Dave Brock is not loath to admit that most of the band's musicians are at best mediocre, while Nick Turner (sax) never ceases to be amazed by their success.**

Partly, it's all due to the band beginnings. When they first came together Hawkwind was just a means of having a good time — "a pleasurable side-line," as Brock puts it. Only when people actually seemed to like their music did they begin to take it seriously. And even now the main motive of the band is to provide fun both for the audience and themselves.

theatrical event, with dancers, mime and a new way of using light techniques which will cover the whole audience. Hopefully we want to get together the best-ever light show ever put on the road. And it won't just be complementing the music but actually part of it. The guy operating the lights will be playing them, if you like, just as the others play their instruments.

"I really don't think groups give enough to their audiences," said Brock. "They don't seem to have much contact. If you go round dance halls in the country and see the miserable conditions people are in, you feel you should give them as much in a live show as you possibly can. Most groups don't do it. They go through the same routine so much that they might as well be working in a factory."

Hawkwind, of course, have always had special connections with what's lovely called the alternative society. Again it stems partly from the beginnings of the group — as Brock explains: "When the group formed we were

all hustlers and dealers on the scene, and now we still see the same people and go to the same places."

But do the group see themselves as any different from others?

Bob Calvert replied: "I suppose if the underground has any meaning at all we're part of it, simply because we don't see ourselves as part of the music industry or aligned to the profit motive which is what that industry is about.

"All generations have had some sort of revolutionary feeling in them but this is the first that isn't based on any political ideals or programmes. Consequently it's the job of the musician to put these feelings into music that people can recognise.

"Gigs seem to get into a very ritualistic, tribal thing where people come to lose their personal identity and expand their consciousness collectively."

Probably the greatest link the band have with the underground is through playing numerous benefit gigs for various organisations. Trouble is, though, as the group become more successful more requests for them to play benefits pour in. Obviously this presents problems.

"Quite honestly the benefit scene has got completely out of hand," said Brock. "Because so many bands don't do them, people rely heavily on those that do. Then when you can't manage all of them people say you've sold out.

"Also there are a lot of rip-offs at benefits when you just can't tell where the money has really gone. It's a pity because there are so many people who are really into nice things but can't get the bread to do it that we feel we should try and help as best we can."

'We don't see ourselves as part of the music industry or aligned to the profit motive...' - *NME*, 5 February 1972
(source: Paul Windle collection)

Nik Turner
(source: Doug Smith archive)

Del Dettmar and Simon King at the Bickershaw Festival, 5-7 May 1972. The festival
programme claimed that Salvador Dali was a Hawkwind fan.
(source: Doug Smith archive)

# *Doremi Fasol Latido*

Released 24 November 1972

| | |
|---|---|
| *Label:* | United Artists |
| *Track listing:* | Brainstorm (Turner) / Space Is Deep (Brock) / One Change (Dettmar) / Lord Of Light (Brock) / Down Through The Night (Brock) / Time We Left This World Today (Brock) / The Watcher  (Kilmister) |
| *Line-up:* | Dave Brock / Nik Turner / DikMik / Del Dettmar / Lemmy / Simon King |
| *Recorded at:* | Rockfield Studios |
| *Produced by:* | Hawkwind (Dave & Del) |

If you wanted to capture the essence of Hawkwind in all their gonzoid space rocking glory, the first thirty seconds of '**Brainstorm**' is a good place to start. It crashes straight into a body-pummelling, pulse-quickening ur-riff – a thrashed 'A' chord with three exclamation marks – which channels both the unstoppable momentum and crushing inertia of interstellar travel. After *ISOS*'s relatively airy sound, this is a dense, muggy blast of exhaust fumes and amphetamine acceleration. It forces the listener's head against the metal door to the engine room, where Moorcock's barbarian spacemen can be heard partying while there's still fuel to burn.

More prosaically, it sounds like the band have been playing for 24 chemically enhanced hours, and someone's finally thought to hit the record button. The block riffing and wayward electronics we know, but the rhythm section has gone up a gear: Lemmy's rumbling, growling bass hammer plus Simon King's brutal, relentless drum propulsion. If Krautrock's *motorik* beat is a cruise-controlled drive down the Autobahn,[1] Hawkwind's 'King Beat' is a lairy foot-to-the-floor dash along an ill-lit B-road. What King lacks in technical finesse he makes up for in sheer physical power.

This heads-down sonic attack is new. The sound may be like black treacle oozing from the speakers, but the attitude is pure punk, down to Turner's lisping, snotty vocal, craving escape from an oppressive world: "*I can't get no peace 'til I get into motion / Sign my release from this planet's erosion.*" It's not stoic non-compliance, either – it bursts with passion and anger: "*You gotta help me or there'll be an explosion!*" There's a brilliant call and response bridge – the fear of turning 'android' highlighted again – with Lemmy's gruff shouts of "*Body of mine!*" counterpointing Turner's angsty pouting, and the chorus is their punchiest yet. Compare the background ritualistic yodelling and Turner's hyper-ventilating orgasm with the grunts and screams of a Plant or Gillan: this isn't climax as an expression of macho sexual conquest, but of union with the cosmos.

"*I'm floating away*", trills Turner, his escape to the stars clearly more drug-assisted than rocket-powered. But Brock kicks into warp drive anyway, a militantly minimalist wah-wah solo splurging over the instrumental section, its few notes both regimented but thrillingly amorphous. Meanwhile the FX on the sax are like the gibberings of crazed cosmic beings glimpsed in the rear-view mirror.

It builds to another invocatory space chant, Lemmy and Brock panting, "*This is a…!*", Turner answering, "*Brainstorm…*" in a state of stoned languor. Hawkwind surrender to the flow of their own music, the insistent rhythm a gateway to an altered state of consciousness. But if the earlier incantations and mantras tended towards the shamanic, here there's a palpable edge of frenzy. After 11 minutes of almost non-stop skin pounding, King finally downs sticks, and 'Brainstorm' lumbers off into the distance…

Whether it's the reverb on Brock's shimmering 12-string or the throaty authority of his voice, '**Space Is Deep**' feels like a hymn to the Summer Of Love on Altair IV. The electronics chirrup and purr along in sympathy as he challenges our arrogance – "*Why does Man try to act so tall?*" – while urging us onward: "*Into the void we have to travel.*" Just as the contemporary folk rock movement is busy reviving the mystical traditions of Albion, Brock gazes with wonder at the infinite reaches of the universe and invests it with a similar numinous significance: "*Beyond the realms of ancient light.*"

As we're contemplating our destiny among the stars, the Hawkship's engines start to buzz. The rhythm kicks in, and a spiralling heraldic fanfare – Turner or Dettmar or possibly both – announces the grand entrance of the back cover's Bedouin space pirate, Lemmy's bass his euphoric imperial bearer. It's one of the most joyfully uplifting passages in Hawkwind's music, and as the parade passes by and winds down, we're left with a surprising feeling of peace. So much of the band's output until now has been about stimulating the backbrain, but 'Space Is Deep' mines the emotions and goes for the heart.

'**One Change**', a short piece of treated piano from Dettmar, fits in nicely with this mood, its vaguely oriental melody moving gracefully across the keyboard. It's an indication of an expanding tonal palette that will see the band increasingly reference both the progressive and *kosmische* scenes.[2]

'**Lord Of Light**' takes us back into familiar territory. Through scraped strings and phased cymbals comes a damped, expectant chug – and then King comes in and it's off, despite an awkward entry from Lemmy.[3] One of their most expansive and tuneful tracks live, this studio version is more of a prototype, Brock's vocal in particular feeling strained and breathless. 'Lord Of Light' is the first of many Hawkwind songs to take its title from a novel,[4] although its lyrical allusions to ley lines and standing stones don't reflect the book's contents.

There's a terrific bass-led change-up into the song's instrumental section, Lemmy's trademark muscular-but-melodic playing providing structure and driving the arrangement forward. But the core elements – Brock's phased guitar, Turner's meandering sax – don't quite hang together. Brock has fondly reminisced that all of Hawkwind's early albums were mixed on acid – either the desk crew were hearing something very different here, or were just freaked out by Brock's mind-blown repetition: "*Flying is trying is dying…*"[5] By the final verse, everybody's so ripped that the tape sounds like it's about to disintegrate – it's a relief when they make it to the end.

'**Down Through The Night**' has another insistent 12-string intro, which resolves into a gloomy minor chord riff buoyed by a wonderfully fluid bassline. Brock's vocals are heavily reverbed and panned, while Turner's flute tiptoes round the edge of the mix as though afraid to wake us from our contemplation of the universe. Lyrically at least, *Doremi* is Hawkwind's most mystical album – the mind must be freed in preparation for our appointment with the stars. 'Down Through The Night' is like an astral traveller's last transmission, and leaves you both beguiled and disquietened.

But then it's back to stark reality and '**Time We Left This World Today**', the ominous sound of an iron giant approaching, bearing down on the listener, until everything locks together and the head-stomping begins. Under a monolithic call-and-response riff, King's drumming threatens to turn funky at any moment. It's a song full of paranoid forebodings – "*They watch you as you walk the street /*

*Cast sly glances at who you meet*" – and an urgent entreaty to get on the Hawkship right now. Like a preacher, Brock rasps out the first part of each line for his flock to complete – though it's clear not everybody's singing from the same hymn sheet.

Testifying done, the band begin breaking the riff down, digging in for the long haul. You can practically hear the drugs kick in as the music turns discordant and disorientating, Lemmy's bass a nightmarish squall, Brock's churning wah-wah backing a stoned chant of "*Today!*" As Lemmy mutates the riff, inspiring Brock to some fine soloing, you sense the 'telepathy' that exists between the two players. Turner twitters peripherally, perhaps eyeing this new partnership with surprise and suspicion.

Hawkwind's willingness to let the music splurge messily outside the lines – to overwhelm a song's structure without destroying it – is what sets them apart from the rest of the British rock scene, and this is a prime example. It's not just psychedelic excess – instead, they seem to be accessing some seam of transcendent primitivism, performing spontaneous alchemy rather than the same old tricks. In a scene dominated by music that values technical flash over visceral noise, Hawkwind are travelling in the opposite direction by unlearning the rules of traditional blues-based rock.

If 'Time We Left…' is a manifesto for the immediate evacuation of all heads from the planet, then the morbid, eviscerated blues of '**The Watcher**' details the fate of everyone left behind. It's a lyrical sequel to 'Master Of The Universe', a demi-god sorely disappointed by their creation. Over plucked guitar and a swarm-like drone, Lemmy delivers his judgement in a mocking, small hours voice: "*There's no room for you out here / This is the end now…*"[6] Cue the sound of lasers turning the earth to ashes.

It's another downbeat conclusion, but its sentiments are entirely in keeping with the apocalyptic pall that's fallen across the world in the early 70s. Hawkwind's next major project and album will further embrace this growing sense of impending doom while plotting an escape route to the stars.

<hr />

1    Klaus Dinger of Neu! preferred to call it 'Apache Beat'.

2    Though arguably what 'One Change' most resembles, and in fact anticipates, is something from Brian Eno's *Another Green World* (1975).

3    This stumble at the start of 'Lord Of Light' may be the mistake that Lemmy variously says was left in either 'Brainstorm' or 'Space Is Deep'.

4    In this case, a Hugo award-winning novel by science fiction author Roger Zelazny published at the height of the countercultural 60s, which voguishly borrows various Hindu myths and reimagines them on an alien world. While Brock's lyrics don't directly reference the book, they perhaps touch on similar themes of reincarnation: "Perhaps the dying has begun... Here our lifetime has begun."

5    An expression soon to be immortalised on the cover of *Space Ritual*.

6    'The Watcher' recalls a song Lemmy had earlier written and sung with Sam Gopal, 'You're Alone Now'.

# The Other Side Of The Sky

November–December 1972

L-R Dave – Brock, Simon King – unused photos from Space Ritual programme
(source: Michael Scott collection)

Peaking at number 14, four places higher than its predecessor, *Doremi* is for many fans the epitome of Hawkwind as purveyors of anarchic, drug-fuelled space rock. And while not the elaborately packaged explosion of cosmic colour that was *ISOS*, it does feature another sumptuous Barney Bubbles design. Reflecting a toughening up of the music, the sleeve is printed in black and metallic silver, the front cover dominated by a gleaming heraldic shield – or perhaps the radiator grille of some intergalactic warship. It also features Hawkwind's most durable logo, letters sloping to suggest acceleration.

On the back, chromium-plated nymphs throw their arms wide to the cosmos, conductors of mystical energy, as a Bedouin space pirate leers threateningly. The

Calvert-penned commentary on 'The Saga Of Doremi Fasol Latido' describes the album as "a collection of ritualistic space chants, battle hymns and stellar songs of praise as used by the family clan of Hawkwind on their epic journey to the fabled land of Thorasin".[1] No gatefold this time,[2] but the inner sleeve depicts armour-clad warriors on horseback, with flying saucers skimming overhead. And there's a poster: the band members' faces arranged in a six-pointed star around a central image of grinning red-eyed skulls, bearing the palindromic legend 'Star Rats'.[3]

All the major papers are primed to review *Doremi*, and most notices are positive, even as the writers struggle with the sheer otherness of Hawkwind's music. *Melody Maker*'s Andrew Means calls it, "The spaced-out slipstream, the rushing, gurgling torrent of weightless sound…"[a][4] Martin Hayman in *Sounds* says, "The bass and drums batter on with unflagging pace, synthesizers twirl and whistle around the thunderous block riffs whose endless repetition generates that numbed hypnosis".[b] For *NME*'s Nick Kent, it's "the strongest high energy cosmic hubcap this side of the Metal Zone".[c]

▾　　▾　　▾

The Space Ritual tour continues until the end of the year, playing to packed houses at 2,000+ capacity venues. The shows at Liverpool Stadium and Brixton Sundown on 22 and 30 December respectively are recorded for future release.[5]

And when the credits roll on the *Top Of The Pops* festive special on Christmas Day, the crowd bop along to 'Silver Machine', a song that's secured a special place in the nation's affections.[6]

<hr />

a　'Hawkwind: A Group In Search Of Melody' – Andrew Means, *Melody Maker*, 16/12/72

b　'Hawkwind: A Few Surprises' – Martin Hayman, *Sounds*, 16/12/72

c　'Hawkwind: A Good One' – Nick Kent, *NME*, 9/12/72

1　A jokey reference to Thorazine, an anti-psychotic drug that Calvert was probably familiar with.

2　Although Nick Kent says this was briefly mooted ('Cosmic Calypso And Sonic Surprise', *NME* –11/11/72).

3   Bubbles' primary inspirations here are Marvel's Jack Kirby, Michael Moorcock illustrator James Cawthorn, and Philippe Druillet, creator of *Lone Sloane*, a French comic-book space opera that Bubbles was particularly keen on.

4   Andrew Means championed the group at *Melody Maker*, but the editor who headlined his piece 'Hawkwind: A Group In Search Of Melody' was clearly less of a fan. See also the Means-written 'Hawkwind – The Joke Band That Made It'.

5   The poster for the Brixton and Edmonton Sundown shows advised that, "Trip circuit will function only when head is turned to high." The show at Sunderland's Locarno on 23 December was also recorded, but not used.

6   'Silver Machine' was voted British single of the year in the *NME*'s 1972 readers' poll. Another indication of 'Silver Machine''s status as a song of the year was its re-recording for easy listening consumption by various pop orchestras. There were swinging, horn-led instrumental versions by James Last (from *Non Stop Dancing 1973*) and Hugo Strasser (from *Tanzhits 3*), plus a vocal version on Music for Pleasure's *Hot Hits XIII* compilation.

# DikMik

Electronics and Vocals
1969–August 1973
*Hawkwind* to *Space Ritual*

DikMik (source: Michael Scott collection)

How did you become involved with Hawkwind?
I knew Mick Slattery and Brock from when we were teenagers around Richmond.
And I knew Nik and Bob from down around Broadstairs and Margate a lot later
on. And we all sort of met up again on Portobello Road.

How did you start to play electronics?
I got all this electronics stuff laid on me when we were rehearsing early on, when
we were Group X, and I thought, 'Hmmm, I can do something with this.' I was
laying stuff on top of what they were playing, not music as such, but moody stuff,
sound effects.

Did you have a technical background at all or a previous interest in electronics?

No, nothing, I'm not even a musician! I wanted to study the piano, but I never got around to it.

Did you have an interest in electronic music?

The German bands. And the album by White Noise, that impressed me.

How about people like Stockhausen or Morton Subotnick?

I tried to get into Stockhausen and stuff like that, but I couldn't get my head round it!

Early reports suggest the audio generator had 'profound effects' on the audience…

A lot of people said it was, well, "mind-blowing" I suppose is the term they used. But that was the intention! I understood how ultra-sonics affect the brain and sub-sonics affect the body. Especially when people were drunk down the front of the stage, the sub-sonics could make them physically sick if you wanted to. Which I think I achieved a couple of times on purpose!

How important were the drugs to the creative process?

It was just what everybody was doing then. We liked to think that it helped with the process. [And] personally I think it did, but it's up to the individual.

You hear music in a different way on LSD…

Some of the live gigs were pretty weird in that respect. The noises going on weren't just affecting the audience but the people on stage as well!

The first album is very atmospheric in places – lots of strange wordless vocals as well as your electronics. Are you one of the voices?

A little, but it was mainly Brock and Nik, and then Bob when he came along. I fed my microphone through my boxes, so it didn't come out like a voice as such, more a chanting noise in the background or over the top. The sole purpose was to add atmospherics.

**Did you ever discuss with Del Dettmar how the sounds would work together?**

No, it was more do what you wanted. There was no competition between us, and no organised parts. Sometimes one of us would stop and let the other carry on, and vice versa. It was all very loose.

**When did you first encounter Robert Calvert?**

In Broadstairs, on a bus. I thought, "This is a strange one!" I used to go round his house and he'd be up all night telling crazy stories, reciting poetry off the top of his head. I'd be speeding and he'd just be doing his thing. I thought he was brilliant, I spent a lot of time round his place just listening to him. Then he'd go on a manic turn, because he was suffering even then, not that we knew it at the time. It was 1966-67 when I first met him and Nik, who had a stall on the front of Margate selling soppy hats and sticks of rock to the tourists.

**And you start hanging out with Lemmy...**

When we were off the road, I was knocking about with various dodgy characters. That's how I met Lemmy, at Earl's Court doing speed deals.

**How did he actually join?**

We'd gone through so many bass players, and Lemmy was desperate to get into a band again. So I said to the others, "Look, do we want a good bass player or don't we? 'Cos I've got somebody." Lemmy had never played bass in his life, but that was beside the point. He was a really good rhythm guitarist, we'd sit up all night playing when we were in the squats. So he did an audition and it kicked off from there. There was a bit of aggravation – they didn't want another speed freak in the band – but we overcame that.

**By the time *In Search Of Space* is released, Hawkwind are pretty much the biggest band in the underground. How do you account for this?**

The originality of the music. And doing free gigs for various organisations obviously helped...

Were you a science fiction fan?

I had been as a teenager. But then I was backtracking to people like Kerouac, the beat side of things. William Burroughs, what a crazy fucker he was! [I liked] that side of science fiction, if you want to call it that.

Are you doing the high vocal at the end of 'Silver Machine'?

No, that's Brock. Funnily enough, I was discussing this with mates recently. I thought it was either me or Nik, but it turns out it was Brock.

What was your reaction to success of 'Silver Machine'?

It was weird, because after recording it, we all thought it was going to do well. We didn't know how well, but we knew it would do some business. And we were right!

Were you aware how big it became – that it was a hit around the world?

In Germany in particular, they were into us as much as the British fans, more or less from the beginning. Some of the gigs we did in Germany in 1971 were pretty big. You could get 10,000 people in the *sporthalles* – whereas over here we'd still be doing pubs and clubs. Maybe colleges and universities.

Were you ever on the same bill as any of the German bands?

Yes, Can, Amon Düül, Neu!, Tangerine Dream. There was some sort of affinity. I liked Can a lot, they were a good band.

Did you regard Hawkwind as a UK equivalent?

I think it was recognised more back then than it is now.

Why did you leave?

I'd just had enough, there were other things I wanted to do. I was never a dedicated musician unfortunately. To me the whole thing was like a little adventure for four years, one of many, many adventures throughout my life. People say, "Didn't you miss it or have any regrets?" But no, not really. It was all good fun at the time and that was it.

What's your abiding memory?

What can I say that can be published?? It was just a great fucking crazy time. It was of its time, all that acid craziness, the whole psychedelic experience. It'll never be repeated.

Your use of electronics was pioneering, particularly in relation to drone and ambient and industrial music. Do you ever reflect on what you achieved with Hawkwind?

Yes, I do. I'm reminded of it all the time by different people. If it wasn't for you, you wouldn't have this, that and the other. Which is nice in a way.

Silver Surfers, live 73. L-R - Turner, King, Lemmy, Brock
(source: Michael Scott collection)

# We Were Born To Blow The Human Mind

## January–May 1973

In February, the Space Ritual tour restarts. One of the less conventional venues is Wandsworth Prison. Doug Smith has somehow persuaded the Home Office that a one and a half-hour blast of anti-establishment cosmic noise is exactly what its inmates need as part of their rehabilitation. "There wasn't much resemblance to Cash at San Quentin," reports *Melody Maker*,[a] but Stacia's arrival on stage cheers everyone up, while new song 'Psychedelic Warlords' has the apposite opening line: "*Sick of politicians, harassment and laws.*"

A no less radical gig takes place the following month when Hawkwind become one of the few major rock bands in the early 70s to play Belfast, a city that has become a byword for sectarian violence. Scenes of street battles between protesters and soldiers are a depressingly regular feature of TV news – while it's not exactly Vietnam, there are plenty of allusions to the British Army as an occupying force in Northern Island.

*NME*'s James Johnson goes with them, describing the blasted bars and houses as a "war zone". Yet Hawkwind have spread the spirit of the underground to every corner of the land. Their name emblazoned on the backs of denim jackets, they play to a large crowd: "Few in Belfast had ever experienced anything quite like this before, as the slides and colours drifted behind the band, the heavy-metal insidious sound grew and grew and the Hawkwind space machine went into orbit... As a spectacle, as an entertainment, [it] is unsurpassed in British rock and can be utterly involving".[b]

▾        ▾        ▾

After a short tour of Ireland, the band find time for some extra-curricular musical activity. Despite erratic onstage appearances and routine hospitalisation for manic depression, Robert Calvert has managed to charm Andrew Lauder at UA into funding a solo project, *Captain Lockheed And The Starfighters*. Obsessed with military aviation from an early age, Calvert is fixated on the Luftwaffe's ill-fated roll-out of the Lockheed F-104G Starfighter, a tragi-comic story that resulted in the deaths of over 100 pilots.[1] At the end of March, Calvert, Paul Rudolph (lately of the Pink Fairies) and Hawkwind (minus Brock and DikMik) record a teaser single in Olympic Studios, entitled '**Ejection**'.[2]

Where 'Silver Machine' was a chugging battlecruiser, 'Ejection' is a crazed death-or-glory attack ship on fire, a driving, pumping surge of adrenaline-spiked garage rock worthy of the Stooges or MC5. Turner's sax dampens the punky aggression and Dettmar's trilling is a little random, but the rush of the chorus is irresistible and Rudolph's guitar solo stings. Calvert is more English raconteur than Motor City rabble-rouser, but his effete delivery contrasts nicely with the primal noise around him. His lyrics are amusingly anti-heroic too: "*When a ship meets with destruction, the captain stays to drown / But no tin contraption is going to drag me down.*"

If 'Ejection' is three minutes of high energy kamikaze skronk, the B-side's '**Catch A Falling Starfighter**' is completely different. Backed by the dull thump of a funeral drum and sounds of air crashes, it's a blackly comic lament sung by a chorus of dead pilots. Calvert also plays the Gremlin, a snide pricker of hubris interrupting their afterlife fugue. Classic British irreverence in the face of death, it could have been a *Monty Python* sketch.

▾　　▾　　▾

As one of the bands of the moment, Hawkwind merit a *Melody Maker* 'Band Breakdown' article in April: a short interview with each band member (including Stacia and Smeeton) plus an overview of their equipment. Frustation runs throughout the piece, painting a picture of a band under pressure. Turner says, "I'd like to do benefits… but I'm thwarted in this to a large extent because of the business aspects of being involved in such a large organisation as we are now." Dettmar complains, "There are [those] in this band who give you a musical slap across the face and it puts you off trying anything new… Producing space effects is like going to work in a factory. You know – produce space effects for two years." Brock worries, "I can't get anything together at the moment. I've run out of ideas." He's also critical of 'Silver Machine': "Very boring number that is. I really hate playing it. There's no way you can do it different, it's a restricted number."

Not everybody's downcast though, with "the legendary Bob Calvert, writer and conceptual thinker" keen on imposing his own vision on the band: "I think really that discipline is needed to keep all this conglomeration of sounds together. If you're producing experimental electronic music… it does help if the sounds are related to a concept of some kind. Otherwise it's just noise".[c]

Luckily, there's no immediate requirement for Hawkwind to produce new material, as the shows recorded at the end of last year have been mixed and overdubbed, and prepared for release as a double live album. Such records are a staple of the early 70s rock scene, but Hawkwind's will be unlike any other band's attempt to reproduce their live show on vinyl.

A one-sided single of '**Sonic Attack**' is sent out to press and radio in a plain cloth bag, its title stamped on the front in red military-style stencil. Predominantly a spoken word piece, it's a curious way to promote the album, yet definitively signals that Hawkwind are no longer about "levitating minds in a nice way", but the threat of "imminent sonic destruction".

*Space Ritual*[3] is released on 11 May.

◇◇◇◇◇◇◇◇◇◇◇◇◇◇◇◇◇◇◇◇◇◇◇◇◇◇◇◇◇◇◇◇◇◇◇◇◇◇◇◇◇◇◇◇◇◇◇◇◇◇◇◇◇◇◇◇◇◇◇◇◇◇◇◇◇◇◇◇◇◇◇

a    'Hawkwind In Jail', writer unknown, *Melody Maker*, 17/2/73

b    'The Sonic Warlords in Belfast' – James Johnson, *NME*, 24/3/73

c    'Hawkwind – Band Breakdown' – Andrew Means, *Melody Maker*, 7/4/73

1    A fair-weather jet fighter converted into a ground-attack, reconnaissance and interceptor aircraft, the defective F-104G was over-burdened by technology and flown by under-trained pilots who found it difficult to control. Known as the 'Widowmaker', the Starfighter caused a major scandal, with West Germany's Minister of Defence Franz Josef Strauss accused of receiving $10 million from American aerospace giant Lockheed to secure the contract.

2    According to *Parallel Universe*, the tape box for this single version of 'Ejection' actually names Hawkwind as the recording artist.

3    The label gives the full title as *The Space Ritual Alive In Liverpool And London*.

Dave Brock (Source: DikMik archive)

DikMik (Source: DikMik archive)

Nik Turner (source: Doug Smith archive)

Lemmy (Source: DikMik archive)

(DikMik archive courtesy of Mica Davies/Pedro Bellavista)

Performing the Space Ritual, Brixton Sundown, 30 December 1972
Line-up: Calvert, Brock, Turner, Stacia, Dettmar, DikMik, Lemmy, King, plus Miss Renée & Tony Crerar
(photos by Laurie Lewis)

‘The results were positive: Permanent Brain Damage’
Advert in *Rolling Stone* ahead of the first US tour

# Space Ritual

Released 11 May 1973

*Label:* United Artists

*Track listing:* Earth Calling (Calvert) / Born to Go (Calvert/
Brock) / Down Through the Night (Brock) / The
Awakening (Calvert) / Lord of Light (Brock) / The
Black Corridor (Moorcock) / Space Is Deep (Brock)
/ Electronic No. 1 (DikMik/Dettmar) / Orgone
Accumulator (Calvert/ Brock) / Upside Down
(Brock) / 10 Seconds of Forever (Calvert) /
Brainstorm (Turner) / 7 By 7 (Brock) / Sonic
Attack (Moorcock) / Time We Left This World
Today (Brock) / Master of the Universe (Turner/
Brock) / Welcome to the Future (Calvert)

*Line-up:* Dave Brock / Nik Turner / Robert Calvert / DikMik
/ Del Dettmar / Lemmy / Simon King

*Recorded live at:* Liverpool Stadium (22 December 1972) and Brixton
Sundown (30 December 1972) using the Pye
Mobile Studio

*Produced by:* Hawkwind

Here it comes, slowly looming into view from the cosmic depths… 'Earth Calling'
teases the audience with the first two notes of Richard Strauss's 'Thus Spake
Zarathustra'[1] as a disembodied voice from home tries to raise the crew. But nobody's
listening, and it's drowned out by the rattles, scrapes and shrieks that echo along the
ship's empty corridors. Within these first few seconds, it's clear that Hawkwind's
transmutation from psychedelic hopefuls to sci-fi rock overlords is complete. The
space race in the real world may be running out of money and losing the public's
attention, but Hawkwind are about to embark on their greatest voyage yet.

From the moment its brutal, cyclical riff pummels the air, '**Born To Go**' is an utterly thrilling exercise in velocity and propulsion. King is an unstoppable human piston, the craft's restless pounding heart, while Brock and Lemmy are locked together in frantic, murky unison. There's a switch to a straighter riff and beat, then Turner raggedly proclaims their manifesto for survival: "*We were born to go / We're never turning back / We were born to go / And leave a burning track.*" As he sings, "*We're hatching our dreams into reality,*" his body seems subjected to tremendous forces, the last word painfully elongated as though he's straining to remain conscious. This is no sightseeing trip among the stars, but space travel as gritted-teeth ordeal.

This super dense layering of sound is like nothing else committed to vinyl. DikMik and Dettmar generate a violent white noise canvas for the vocals and riffs, while Turner's disembodied flute swirls around like debris from a meteor strike. We're surfing a spectrum of shifting frequencies, from pitch black to sudden bursts of magnesium brightness, barbaric electronics fused with the raw power of rock at its most monolithic.

Brock launches himself at his pedals, scouring the sky with wah-wah – while most players use this effect as a bit of exotic colour, Brock stomps the hell out of it and turns his guitar into a futuristic weapon, pushing at the boundary between cosmic noise and proto-punk. There's also a great example of his 'robot skiffle' style, the fast strumming of muted strings giving a crunchingly percussive sound. Counterpointing Brock's six-string fireworks, Lemmy alternates between chord shapes and melodic note clusters. The driving, primal energy of his playing is often commented on, but there's nothing Neanderthal about it – instead, it's fluid and nimble, even jazzy in places.

These elements combine with an uncanny logic, the musicnauts continually re-marshalling their efforts to mould the main riff into different shapes. But it's the immersive intensity of the experience that grabs hold and refuses to let go. Just as Turner plays as though he's forever trying to find his way back to the control room, you may feel dizzy – perhaps even the need to vomit – but compelled onwards nonetheless.

Just as well then that the ship finally decelerates and we get the chance to steady ourselves. This album is made up of clever transitions, and the segue into '**Down Through The Night**' is particularly graceful, the teasing guitar and wandering bass still magically entwined. The verse is more driving than *Doremi*, Brock singing from the middle distance as flute and electronics wrap around him. The song pushes into the upper atmosphere and expands to nearly twice the length of the studio original, but there's a yearning melancholia here – the type you might experience if you were light years away from Earth, with no hope of ever seeing your home or family again…

Right on cue, here's 'The Awakening'… The thing I found most reality-warping about *Space Ritual* when I first heard it – more so even than the black hit of space oozing from the speakers – were these strange poems read by what sounded like a half-man, half-machine oracle. I had literally never heard anything like them before – they were fantastical, but excitingly serious.

Despite shaping the band's sci-fi aesthetic for some time, this is Robert Calvert's first appearance on a Hawkwind album, and it's quite an entry. Against plaintive warbles and cries from the electronic chorus line, he contemplates the cryogenically frozen members of his crew, his voice a chilly combination of precision and dispassion. While not really a concept album, a theme does run throughout it – of men struggling to survive in a hostile environment, haunted by the world they've left behind. It's also full of ear-catching rhymes and imagery: "*The nagging choirs of memory / The tubes and wires worming from their flesh to machinery / I would have to cut.*"

Calvert and his poems are a coolly intellectual presence at the heart of the chaos engine. They challenge the listener with their sheer audacity, and they certainly confounded some of the band's audience – there's the occasional heckle during his readings. But to skip them is to miss out on a vital element of the *Space Ritual* experience, this delicious layer of brooding android hauteur.

The electronics work themselves into a howling frenzy before being quelled by the opening riff to 'Lord Of Light'. Where the *Doremi* version had a stuttering, drug-soaked uncertainty, the song here soars with confidence. With bass and guitar locked in place against shivering peals of VCS3, Brock's strident vocal gives the words added space and emphasis. The switch-up from the verse is magnificent, a showcase for some of Turner's most cogent and melodic sax playing to date, vamping lazily over thumping bass with carefree, child-like wonder. With its tightly structured arrangement, this is easily one of Hawkwind's most euphoric songs –

Which is just as well, because a freezing sonic mist descends as soon as it ends. A lonely distress signal bleeps in the gloom as Calvert steps forward, the ship's captain going out of his mind as he confronts the vastness of space. 'The Black Corridor' takes its name and words from a Michael Moorcock novel which explores the sense of abjection and existential crisis that space travel might give rise to. It's a keystone work for Hawkwind, and Calvert plays the lead role perfectly – his reading of the book's opening passage is clinical and detached, yet suggests a barely suppressed mania about to spill over into full-blown psychosis: "*Space cannot be measured / It cannot be angered / It cannot be placated / It cannot be summed up / Space is there.*"

'**Space Is Deep**' is the song originally inspired by *The Black Corridor*, its gloriously drowsy opening like the gentle lapping of waves on an alien shore, perhaps the new Eden at journey's end. This elegiac side to the band's music is like a reminder of the beautiful future that briefly seemed possible, before being snuffed out by the harsh reality of the 1970s. Hawkwind might have no truck with Earth being rescued by golden people in the sky, but they still harbour the dream of a better type of society. There's a gathering buzz of excitement after the verses, then King kicks in and carries us high above the clouds for some free-form improv. The song ends with more soft magic as it morphs into the ecstatic croon of an unlisted '**You Know You're Only Dreaming**'.

There's a strange atonal clattering that recalls the Krell from *Forbidden Planet*. The archly-titled '**Electronic No.1**' is a showcase for the sonic technicians at the side of the stage, but it's still a long way from Rick Wakeman. Brock conjures spindly runs over a bubbling undercurrent as crazed geometric waveforms cut at the air. It occurs that this angular machine-chatter sounds like nothing so much as TV's *The Clangers* enraged by all the man-made space junk that keeps crashing into their little planet.

By contrast, '**Orgone Accumulator**' is a head-nodding, hip-swivelling, foot-stomping slab of space-age biker boogie that channels the carnal power of rock & roll like no Hawkwind track before it.[2] But just as 'Silver Machine' sneakily eulogised a bicycle, here we get a tongue-in-cheek tribute to Wilhelm Reich's crypto-scientific energy device.[3] Calvert runs with the concept like a wired cross between renegade scientist and snake oil salesman: "*Energy simulators just turn your eyeballs into craters / But an orgone accumulator is a superman creator!*" You can tell he loves the sound of those words in his mouth, his nasal monotone a perfect counterfoil to the music's murky groove.

Lemmy wrests control of the wheel once again, his high bass lines cutting through the sonic smog. Over a series of audio generator 'claps', his finest moment comes at the 7.00 mark, with a breakdown that's positively funky. Any number of contemporary bands were churning out similarly extended blues rock jams as an excuse for grandstanding solos, but Hawkwind prefer to dig into the rhythmic loam of the song and revel in its gritty metronomic power. If 'Born To Go' is all brutal interstellar thrust, this evokes the simple joys of freewheeling through the galaxy.

But now we hit a particularly jolting patch of turbulence. Over Brock's most jarringly clipped riff yet, '**Upside Down**' is a strange and disorientating song, with a nightmarish middle eight that sounds like the ship's been invaded by a gaggle of unquiet spirits. There's a flanging effect on Brock's bemused voice, as if space is warping his reasoning: "*I stand upside down / Can't get a thing together and I don't know why...*"⁴ It may of course just be the drugs.

There's a gentle gurgling and swooshing in the background as Calvert begins to recite '**10 Seconds Of Forever**'. He seems more agitated than before, and slowly his voice becomes vulnerable. Most of *Space Ritual* is fabulist rock theatre, but an edge of real emotion creeps into this poem, the most indebted to science fiction's New Wave. (For more analysis of the SF content of Calvert's poetry, see 'New Worlds And Dangerous Visions', p.322.)

Calvert's final, resigned delivery of "Never..." is mimicked by the mocking voice of Lemmy, and then the exuberant, headlong dash of '**Brainstorm**' kicks in: woozy and desaturated on *Doremi*, this is the full fat, technicolour version. Hawkwind are essentially an acid and pot band, but this buzzing, amphetamine-wired ramalama strongly suggests the influence of a different drug. Think of all the nascent punks in the audience when they first heard this.

This is Hawkwind ram-raiding the gates of perception, the paranoia police in hot pursuit. Verse and chorus are shouted out, and the teasing build to the main riff is bigger than ever. Brock unleashes his caustic wah-wah again, even recycling parts from 'Born To Go', but who cares – by this point in the proceedings, it's as much about bloody-minded stamina as it is sonic boundary pushing, and you're either digging in for the duration or lying semi-conscious on the floor. The chant in the middle is particularly frenetic, the same chord thrashed over and over again, King hammering away throughout.

'**7 By 7**' (as it's titled on *Space Ritual*) fades up from silence into a mysterious realm of weeping electronics. Brock moves between two jazzy chords and Lemmy paddles softly underneath, caught between reflection and melancholy. Then we plunge into its chin-strokingly heavy riff, full of portents and omens. Brock's delivery is less hysterical than on the studio version, but the terror of the soul being cast adrift is starker than ever, a dark mirror to the psychedelic experience.

An ominous rattling, a siren call, and then Calvert recites Hawkwind's most iconic piece of performance art. '**Sonic Attack**' has become short-hand for the brain-blasting, gut-punching shock and awe of Hawkwind in full flight – but the track itself is all creeping dread and terror. It's a blackly comic extrapolation of the paternal authority found in British public information films distorted by the chilly logic of the Cold War, from the absurd – "*It is imperative to bring all bodies to orgasm simultaneously*" – to the bleakly Darwinian – "*Survival means every man for himself.*"

Calvert is born to play this role, his voice full of malicious contempt for the people he's ostensibly warning. Lemmy is similarly wonderful as the gloating strong arm in the background reiterating the rules, a finger-wagging hunchback to Calvert's box-ticking sociopath. The integration between the sound design and words is superb, the mechanical shudders of the audio generator underlining the inhumanity of the instructions, with Turner's flute providing impish emphasis. Its ending – Calvert urging "*Do not panic! / Think only of yourself!*" over a throbbing, marching beat – is Hawkwind at their most frightening.

The mighty riff of '**Time We Left This World Today**' crashes straight in, packing even more muscle than the *Doremi* version. Brock has whipped the choir into compliance this time too, his barked exhortations met with present and correct responses – less a prophet addressing his ragged disciples, more a sergeant major drilling his troops. The riff burrows in deep, with King's drumming solid but loose. The peel-off from the verses is also much more controlled – it's no longer a rambling druganaut of a song but a well-oiled excavator digging at the earth's roots, making space for Turner to play his approximation of free jazz without fear of being crushed in an avalanche of noise. Then it fades, to make way for something even bigger…[5]

While the version of '**Master Of The Universe**' on *ISOS* was an exercise in hold-and-release dynamics, this is just monstrous. The light-sucking density of the opening riff and the cosmic hurricane of electronics raging around it is the sound of the Hawkship tearing a hole in the fabric of space-time. The primal energy and relentless propulsion of the main riff as it kicks in are literally mind-blowing: all higher brain functions shut down, overwhelmed by its raw power. A unique seam of avant-futurist rock is opened up here which eradicates any vestige of the blues in the white heat of technology.

Turner's vocal is more arrogant than ever, while the skull-rattling velocity of the rhythm section is tremendous. We're hurtling through the far reaches of the universe – or perhaps crashing down to Earth as the ship comes apart. Brock's playing is arc-light intense, while Turner blows harder and harder to be heard above the maelstrom. The guitar sound in the final breakdown is so gritty it could grind bones to dust. Nothing in the contemporary rock canon comes close to the pummelling, brain-frying black-out of this track.

There's a pitiful wailing of electronics, an acknowledgement that the end is nigh. And here's Calvert, Hawkwind's resident prophet of doom, to ram the message home. '**Welcome To The Future**' is a condensed hit of eco-horror – "*Welcome to the oceans in a labelled can / Welcome to the dehydrated land*" – that sounds increasingly prescient. Being Hawkwind, we get apocalypse instead of a happy ending as this exhilarating, exhausting journey draws to a close.

After an enormous, final flaring of the engines, the first stunned cheers of the crowd build to a crescendo of applause and stamping feet.[6]

◇◇◇◇◇◇◇◇◇◇◇◇◇◇◇◇◇◇◇◇◇◇◇◇◇◇◇◇◇◇◇◇◇◇◇◇◇◇◇◇◇◇◇◇◇◇◇◇◇◇◇◇◇◇◇◇◇◇◇◇◇◇◇◇◇◇◇◇◇◇◇

1       Most familiar from the opening titles of *2001: A Space Odyssey*.

2       Ironically for a biker anthem, 'Orgone Accumulator' bears more than a passing resemblance to Mod favourite 'Green Onions' by Booker T. & The MGs.

3       In June 1975, William Burroughs interviewed Led Zeppelin's Jimmy Page for *Crawdaddy*: "Before getting down to business, Burroughs proudly showed Page his orgone accumulator, which looked like a big plywood crate. Sitting in this box, Burroughs explained, concentrated certain energies in a productive and healthful manner according to theories developed by the psychiatrist Wilhelm Reich. Jimmy Page declined Burroughs's offer to give the orgone box a try." Reich believed that orgone energy was a mysterious life force which suffused the universe. His ideas were taken up by the beat generation in the 50s, Burroughs in particular. Common currency in the 60s, they were ripe for parody by the 70s. But only Calvert could celebrate what was essentially a large wooden box in terms of "dig my hog!"

4       There are several vocal overdubs on *Space Ritual*. The one on 'Upside Down' is particularly significant given the song was played as an instrumental at the Brixton Sundown show.

5       At 13 minutes in length, 'Time We Left' was brutally edited down. The full length version also incorporated the main riff to 'Paranoia'.

6       It's worth searching online for bootleg recordings of the Brixton Space Ritual show to hear just how ecstatic the audience response is. There's a palpable sense of having experienced something remarkable.

# We Were Born To Blow The Human Mind

May–December 1973

'Some say that Hawkwind are screwballs. Others say that
Hawkwind are the band of the future' *Bravo*, 1973
(source: Wolfie Smith collection)

*Space Ritual* is Hawkwind's highest UK chart placing, peaking at number nine. Released in the US later in the year, it reaches 179, their first album to enter the US *Billboard* 200.

Etched in retina-sizzling technicolour, the cover leaps out at you like some quasi-mystical alien artefact: a stylised Stacia as a cosmic messiah flanked by gape-mouthed starcats.[1] The sleeve folds out into six 12 inch panels, one half adorned with blurred but evocative colour pictures of the band in mid-flight onstage, the other with the 'Master of the Universe' depicted as a steely-eyed Incan or Aztec god, a pictogram resembling a Mensa puzzle (Viking? scarab? control panel?), and a colourful brainwaves-and-bullets design with what looks remarkably like a modern graffiti tag.

On the monochrome reverse is an Edwardian nude, a mottled planet that on closer inspection turns out to be a breast, and an image of the Starchild inspired by *2001: A Space Odyssey*. As an addendum to *The Hawkwind Log*, there are further writings on the meaning of existence, from the cosmological insignificance of Earth to the wonders of DNA, with references to Atlantis, the Great Pyramid and ancient messenger of the gods the Thunder Bird. There are unattributed quotes from various sources, including: *The Epic Of Gilgamesh* ("He said to me, 'Look down at the land'"); William Blake's *Auguries Of Innocence* ("To see a world in a grain of sand"); Alexander Scriabin's *The Poem Of Ecstasy* ("The universe resounds with the joyful cry I am"); Alfred North Whitehead's *Science And The Modern World* ("It is the business of the future to be dangerous").[2]

The records themselves come in orange-and-yellow sleeves with a tessellating pyramidal flower design that, like the front cover, is more Art Deco than psychedelic. Art direction is by UA's in-house sleeve designer Pierre Tubbs; modest and ever-more anonymous, Barney Bubbles is credited with 'packaging'.[3] More unusually, Calvert's credit is "Poet and swazzle". A swazzle is a small metal device placed in the mouth to produce the harsh, high-pitched voice of Mr Punch. So perhaps Calvert is responsible for some of the 'electronic' effects in the show.

Reviews are mixed, and certainly less enthusiastic than for the shows themselves. At *NME*, Nick Kent considers the songs from *Doremi* "rejuvenated by the complete improvement in texture". He praises the presence of Calvert and sees the band as an antidote to Pink Floyd's "superficial cosmic wallpaper". Don't pay for that horrible Yes triple, he writes: save instead for this, *Raw Power* and *Blue Öyster Cult* – "after *Space Ritual*, everything else is just horse tranquilliser".[a4]

*Sounds* is less impressed, describing it as *Star Trek* without Mr Spock: jargon, atmosphere, technology, "but not really things that I can feel a part of".[b] *Melody Maker* notes, "It takes time to adjust to this monstrous four-sided, 88 minute long sound journey," concluding it's mainly for the fans.[c5] As Hawkwind enter the rock mainstream, their reviews aren't just doled out to the faithful, and many writers continue to find their appeal elusive.

▾      ▾      ▾

On 27 May, Hawkwind play Wembley Empire Pool – with a capacity of 10,000, it's the biggest and most prestigious indoor show that Hawkwind will headline in the UK. But as their pulling power grows, so does their talent for self-sabotage. The papers report internal upheavals, and a UA spokesperson admits they're "having their problems." Brock is "getting uptight and refusing to play with the band," with plans afoot to replace him.[d] But by the time of the show, Brock is firmly back at the helm.[e6]

After sets from support acts including the Quiverland Brothers (Quiver and The Sutherland Brothers combined), Danny And The Racing Cars (the Pink Fairies) and Magic Michael, Hawkwind take to the stage as heroes of the underground – yet when Turner tries to stir the countercultural spirit ("We'd like to dedicate this to the righteous people"), he's undercut by Lemmy ("Nice to be back at Wimbledon Stadium again") and Brock ("We'll have a general jam tonight").

One member of the band has different ideas though. Instead of powering into 'Born To Go', the audience are treated to the spectacle of Calvert tearing into the Günter Grass poem '**In The Egg**'. It's a passionate performance, Calvert possessed by a desire to communicate, even if the poem's meaning – replete with revolutionary sound and fury, and flashes of New Wave SF surrealism – is opaque to all but him. He particularly relishes the lines, "*Our prophets inside the egg for a middling salary argue about the period of incubation. They posit a day called X*". Over a minimal backing not unlike 'The Black Corridor', Calvert builds to a climax, yelling, "*What then my brethren inside the egg*?!"[7]

It's about now that he starts to swing the sword he's brought on stage, and Lemmy finds himself under attack.[8] The way that Calvert allows himself be taken over by the role playing out in his head makes him a forceful and magnetic presence, but also a potential danger to anybody sharing the same stage. It's a symptom of his yo-yoing mental health, the hypomania that he openly talks about in interviews. But for all his stays in sanatoria or hospital – sometimes voluntarily, sometimes not – he's wary of any treatment that might rob him of what he considers to be the wellspring of his creativity.

Judging by his performance at Wembley, he's approaching the upper limits of a manic phase. His next reading is an extract from the book *Steps* by Jerzy Kosiński,[9] subsequently referred to as '**Wage War**'. It's an incredibly violent piece of writing which imagines the destruction of society and the killing of the rich: "*Their last screams would suffocate in their ornate curtains… Their dead bodies pinned down by broken statues…*" Calvert spits the words out with rapid-fire fury, an existential terrorist glorying in this visceral imagery, utterly committed to its murderous vision. We're suddenly a long way from allegorical tales of starfarers escaping Earth, and right at the dark heart of the 1970s. As if to confirm this trenchant stance, the band launch into a new song entitled '**Urban Guerilla**'.

Hawkwind are no longer just a "general jam" band, but a well-drilled musical unit whipped into shape by months of non-stop touring. For *Melody Maker*, they're "far more recognisable as a rock band. There's a singer behaving like Jagger, shaking the mike stand about, a guitarist getting worked up as he solos… more than once the Stooges came to mind".[f] Yet still, how many other groups are declaiming nihilistic poetry in front of thousands of people?

▾　　▾　　▾

Fired up by Wembley, the band immediately go into Olympic Studios to record their new single. 'Urban Guerilla' is an English garage-punk take on the Creedence Clearwater Revival sound, a compact slice of blood-pumping, knuckle-cracking rock, that on the face of it, seems to be a worthy successor to 'Silver Machine'. But where Lemmy's bellow invited the listener to sing along, Calvert's speed-freak delivery is like being beaten over the head with a rolled-up copy of *The Anarchist Cookbook*.[10] And more problematic for a song hoping to get national radio play, it appears to offer unequivocal support for armed resistance against mainstream society. Calvert describes it to *NME* as a "definitive statement"[g] – and "*I'm an urban guerilla / I make bombs in my cellar*" is a provocative opening couplet, to say the least.

However, Calvert may be many things, but homicidal ideologue isn't one of them. The song is a satirical character study with a mocking undertow to the chorus – "*So let's not talk of love and flowers / And things that don't explode*" – which rejects hippie-dippy utopianism, but implies that blowing things up isn't much of a solution either. As Calvert writes in *Music Scene*: "The words of the song… are not meant to be taken too literally. There is quite a bit of irony behind them. It certainly isn't advocating violence in the streets".[h] And yet, he inhabits the first-person with absolute conviction. It's what makes him such a compelling performer, but will keep causing problems for himself and the band.[11]

'**Brainbox Pollution**', the single's B-side, barrels in on another Chuck Berry riff – perhaps Brock is hankering after a simple life of knocking out good-time pub boogie given what's in his head: "*Screaming sounds are buzzing through my brain / Am I mad or am I sane?*" There's an ongoing rock & roll revival in full swing, with 50s acts like Berry, Little Richard and Jerry Lee Lewis suddenly finding themselves in demand again. It's seen as a back-to-basics reaction against progressive rock and sappy MOR, and part of its audience – bikers, old rockers, counterculture elders – overlaps with Hawkwind's constituency. If nothing else, 'Brainbox Pollution' suggests a bridge away from the murk of *Doremi*, and when the song moves into more recognisably space rock territory, there's some great upbeat jamming around its ascending riff.[12]

Yet Brock remains downcast by the realities of financing the band. "Hawkwind are broke," he tells *Melody Maker*.[i] "We own our equipment, but we've no money to pursue our direction in music... We've been forced to bring out another single, because we need the bread to advance. It's not from choice – I mean, who wants to be a pop star?"

Nevertheless, he displays a militant edge in line with the single's subject matter: "We can see the world and the way it's being run and we're trying to awaken people to the fact that it's wrong... Hawkwind is city music and it's trying to relate to what's happening. Too many laws against this and that." But the article ends on a positive note: "For four months now the group has been on a downer – thankfully we're just getting over it. We don't know where we're going, but something will come along. Musically we're improving all the time."

▾    ▾    ▾

'Urban Guerilla' comes out on 3 August,[13] promoted in a double-header advert with Calvert's 'Ejection', which is credited to Captain Lockheed And The Starfighters.[14]

'Ejection' gets a glowing, if possibly facetious, write-up in *Melody Maker*: "There's not been a hit like this since 'Satisfaction' by the Stones".[j] Interviewed in the same paper a few weeks later, Calvert also assumes it will be a hit ("over 10,000 sold in its first week"). Alas, it doesn't bother the charts, but it gives Calvert a good excuse to talk up both the *Captain Lockheed* concept as a stage production and himself as a poet, playwright and general raconteur: "I want it to be a theatrical event in the true sense. Like those in the Elizabethan era. Not like one of Alice Cooper's egotistical displays, which in spite of what people say, is nothing to do with theatrics... Being a hypo-manic and consequently having mental disturbances means that I need to be settled in one place at a time and by staging the play, I'll be able to do just that".[k15]

'Urban Guerilla' reaches number 39,[16] but climbs no higher. Co-opting the radical chic of the Baader-Meinhof gang might have made for an edgy but effective marketing angle,[17] but the troubles in Northern Ireland have intensified, with fatalities on both sides. In August, the IRA commences a mainland bombing campaign that targets Harrods, Conservative Party Central Office, the Stock Exchange and the Bank Of England. UA and the band elect to withdraw the single. A statement explains: "Although the record was selling very well, we didn't want to feel that any sales might be gained by association with recent events".[L18]

▾　　▾　　▾

The fall-out from this episode is more attention than ever from customs officials and the drug squad. Hawkwind and their crew have become expert in ensuring that members and vehicles are clean at the relevant times, and no major busts ensue, although Nik Turner's flat is turned over by MI5.[19] But it's the monotony of touring that's really getting to them.[20] DikMik in particular is tired of life on the road. He packs up his audio generator for the last time and leaves the band for good.

The band are trying to move away from the Space Ritual-based set. On 25 August, Calvert and Moorcock perform on stage together at the Windsor Free Festival, one of the few times this happens. The show is framed by spoken word pieces drawing on Moorcock's Eternal Champion books, locating the band and their music in a more earthbound, heroic fantasy mould.[21] It's one of the last shows that Calvert will play with Hawkwind for the next two years, as he concentrates instead on *Captain Lockheed* and other writing projects.

More gigs take place in Scandinavia and Switzerland. At the Olympia in Paris, the British press are flown over in chartered prop planes and Turner partly recites 'Sonic Attack' in French ("*pas de panique*"), but reviews are mixed. *Melody Maker* reports audience high spirits,[22] while *Sounds* complains that nothing much else happens.ᵐ

On 23 November, their first American tour begins at the Tower Theatre in Philadelphia.[23]

▾　　▾　　▾

Hawkwind and their management have been touting these US shows for some time, with *Melody Maker* swallowing the line that "Hawkwind are headlining the 5-date tour – uniquely, for a British band on their first visit to the States."ⁿ *NME* isn't far behind, noting that, "Their Chicago date has already sold out before any advertising appeared in the US trade papers. Promoter Howard Stein is quoted in *Billboard* as saying, 'I have never seen such enthusiasm since the early days of Hendrix and Joplin.'"⁰

The tour itself, which actually extends to 10 dates, gets off to a shaky start, with various technical problems on stage in Philadelphia. Jeff Ward cheerleads on their behalf for *Melody Maker*, though implies it's the staging of the event that has the most impact.[24] However, it's the following night's gig at the New York Academy Of Music that garners the most attention, though mostly for the after-show party at the Hayden Planetarium, which attracts over 1,000 guests, including Stevie Wonder and Alice Cooper. Unused to such star treatment, Hawkwind retire early from the party.

*NME* describes scenes of "gentle chaos" at the sold-out Chicago Auditorium Theatre show, the band setting up their own equipment when the roadies fail to show.ᴾ Reviewer James Johnson is less convinced than the audience: "Their two-hour cosmic tour de force on stage does have a shattering effect, even if it's hard to tell sometimes whether it's for good or bad." For Johnson, Hawkwind are indicative of the gulf that often exists between critics and public, noting that the US press have given the tour "horrendously bad reviews".[25] But the shows are all well attended, and for the band it's an exciting and successful adventure.

▾      ▾      ▾

The US gigs lay the Space Ritual set officially to rest. The band determine to move away from the overtly cosmic and embark instead in a new direction, even if no-one's entirely sure what that might be. It's apt then that their next British tour – which begins on December 10 at Manchester Trade Hall, just days after returning from America – is called 'The Ridiculous Roadshow'.[26]

◇◇◇◇◇◇◇◇◇◇◇◇◇◇◇◇◇◇◇◇◇◇◇◇◇◇◇◇◇◇◇◇◇◇◇◇◇◇◇◇◇◇◇◇◇◇◇◇◇◇◇◇◇◇◇◇◇◇◇◇◇◇◇◇◇

a       'Live Goods from the Sonic Assassins' – Nick Kent, *NME*, 19/5/73

b       'Star Trek Revisited' – *Sounds*, 19/5/73

c       'Hawkwind In Earth Orbit' – *Melody Maker*, 19/5/73

d       'Upheaval In Hawkwind' – *NME*, 12/05/73

e       'Hawkwind: Problems Resolved' – *Melody Maker*, 19/05/73

f       'Hawkwind: We Have Lift-Off!' – Michael Oldfield, *Melody Maker*, 2/6/73 g     *NME*, 5/73

h    'The Days Of Future. Now' – Robert Calvert, *Music Scene*, September 1973

i     'Hawkwind... Heroes Of The Cosmos, Flat Broke On Earth' – Michael Benton, *Melody Maker*, 30/6/73

j     Chris Welch, *Melody Maker*, 14/7/73

k    'Take Me To The Pilot' – Michael Benton, *Melody Maker*, 4/8/73

l     'Hawkwind Withdraw "Guerrilla"' – *NME*, 01/09/73

m    'Hawkwind's Rocket Goes Astray' – Pete Erskine, *Sounds*, 24/11/73

n    'Hawkwind's Silly Show' – *Melody Maker*, 17/11/73

o    'Hawkwind: Four London Dates In Six-Week Tour' – *NME*, 10/11/73

p    'The Ridiculous Roadshow' – James Johnson, *NME*, 26/1/74

1    The style of illustration suggests the work of Art Nouveau painter Alphonse Mucha. The cats' elongated heads resemble his *L'Emeraude* (ref: Hawkwind artist John Coulthart's *Feuilleton* blog).

2    The Russian composer Scriabin was fascinated by chromatic music and its colour associations. The Whitehead quote will become the title of a 1993 Hawkwind album. Given the nature of these quotes, it's likely Barney Bubbles was involved in their selection.

3    An alternative design by David Hardy for the *Space Ritual* sleeve is reproduced in *The Spirit Of Hawkwind* (Nik Turner & Dave Thompson, 2015). Renowned for both his astronomical and sci-fi art, Hardy's illustration depicts the band playing on a barren, crater-pitted planet, as Calvert descends from the sky on a silver disc.

4    Kent refers to *Yessongs*, the triple live album released a week after *Space Ritual*.

5    The advert for *Space Ritual* describes it as "88 minutes of brain damage". While this rather undersells Calvert's contributions in particular, the reference to 'brain damage' could be a sly poke at Pink Floyd, as a song of that name appears on *The Dark Side Of The Moon*, released two months previously.

6    Lemmy had missed the start of a short German tour owing to "illness" (failing to catch a plane, he was briefly sacked by an exasperated Brock). DikMik and Calvert had returned after brief sabbaticals.

7    As with other Grass poems, 'In The Egg' combines the absurd with the everyday. It may have been an inspiration for Calvert's 'Born To Go': "*breaking out of the shell*" and "*hatching our dreams.*" Calvert also wrote an unpublished experimental novel entitled *A Day Called X*.

8    Lemmy: "[Calvert] came on stage wearing a witch's hat and a long black cape, carrying a sword and a trumpet. Then halfway through the second song, he attacked me with the sword! I was yelling, 'Fuck off!' and batting him about the head with my bass... It was the biggest gig we ever played in our lives, and he was attacking me with a fucking sword – what's wrong with this picture, you know?" (p.77, *White Line Fever*, Lemmy with Janiss Garza, 2002).

9    Novelist and 'literary celebrity' Jerzy Kosiński's *The Painted Bird* (1965) was a semi-autobiographical account of a young boy's experiences in WW2, some of it allegedly plagiarised. *Steps* (1968) is a series of surreal, Kafka-esque vignettes. *Being There* (1970) inspired the acclaimed 1979 film starring Peter Sellers.

10   Written by teenager William Powell to protest America's involvement in Vietnam, *The Anarchist Cookbook* contained instructions for the manufacture of both explosives and LSD. First published in 1971, it became a key underground text, popular with wannabe revolutionaries everywhere.

11   A promo film for 'Urban Guerilla' exists, made with footage taken from an unidentified 'live' performance. This was an exciting find when it was discovered during the last major reissue programme of the UA period, and was included with the 'Collector's Edition' of *Space Ritual* (2007). Given Stacia's nudity in the film, it seems unlikely that it was intended for public broadcast, but Doug Smith speculates that it was made by UA to promote the band internally to the label's US HQ ahead of Hawkwind's first American tour. It's previously been suggested that the footage comes from the Wembley Empire Pool show, but Smith believes it was a staged performance filmed at a Wardour Street studio owned by the production company 24 Frames. During the writing of this book, I tracked down 23 minutes of further footage from the same performance, in the possession of the original film maker Cynthia Beatt. It is currently unknown which other songs were performed, although the footage was accompanied by tape recordings from *Space Ritual* (sides 1 & 2, 'Orgone Accumulator', 'Master Of The Universe' and 'Welcome To The Future'). The film was being restored at the time of publication.

12   Also recorded, but unused, is 'It's So Easy'. A live version appears on the B-side of 1974's 'The Psychedelic Warlords'.

13   In June, German fans had already been treated to a new single, an edited version of *Doremi*'s 'Lord Of Light' (misspelt 'Lihgt' on the picture sleeve) with an edit of 'Born To Go' from the *Greasy Truckers Party* on the B-side. Why the more recent (and superior) *Space Ritual* versions weren't used instead is a mystery.

14   The advert promoting both appeared in the 28 July edition of *NME*, and the most likely release date for 'Ejection' is 13 July. 'Urban Guerilla' is promoted with the image of a fantastical warrior known as 'Fanon Dragon Commando', taken from a series of Philippe Druillet-indebted posters produced by Barney Bubbles to coincide with the Space Ritual tour. The Calvert single features a robotic skeleton ejecting into space drawn by Rodney Matthews, who will become one of science fantasy's most popular illustrators, providing covers for some of Moorcock's Eternal Champion novels. Matthews was unhappy with how the 'Ejection' sleeve had been colourised (ref: *In Search Of Forever*, Rodney Matthews, 1985). 'Ejection' comes in a picture sleeve, 'Urban Guerilla' (in Britain at least) in just a plain bag.

15     Interviewer Michael Benton notes that Calvert looks "incredibly un-Hawkwindish in suit, short hair, rolled umbrella and staying at the Dorchester Hotel."

16     No thanks to John Peel. Reviewing 'Urban Guerilla' for his singles column in *Sounds*, their one-time supporter is unenthusiastic, mysteriously describing the lyrics as "fairly unremarkable", and concluding, "I prefer the idea of Hawkwind to the actuality – so far." ('Singles Reviews By John Peel' – *Sounds*, 23/7/73). Yet later in the year, reviewing Can's 'Moonshake' single, he'll describe its "urgent, thrusting rhythm" as what "some of you may think of… as 'the Hawkwind beat'."

17     Ulrike Meinhof's 1971 manifesto, *The Urban Guerrilla Concept*, helped popularise the term, and Andreas Baader was well aware of the Gang's pop-cultural appeal, hiring a designer to create the Red Army Faction logo of a machine gun against a red star. By the time of 'Urban Guerilla''s release, Baader and Meinhof were in solitary confinement in Stuttgart's Stammheim Prison. However, a second, far deadlier campaign of RAF violence would begin in 1975.

18     Speaking later, Brock was unimpressed: "It was stupid to withdraw it. [UA] were paranoid they'd get bombed. I thought that record was what everything was about in the 70s" ('Any Way The Wind Blows' – Toby Manning, *Record Collector*, May 2002). However, for Doug Smith and other band members, its withdrawal was as much to do with the single's poor performance.

19     Turner will later claim they're searching for explosives, but they're actually on the trail of a visiting US Hells Angel in connection with the death of an FBI officer.

20     "Hawkwind get so bored they have competitions to see who can wind the van windows up and down the fastest, or at least, that's what Lemmy says" ('Blowin' In The Wind' – Peter Erskine, *Disc*, 14/07/73).

21     Revised versions of both pieces will appear as 'Standing At The Edge' and 'Warriors' on 1975's *Warrior On The Edge Of Time*.

22     "One moment there were rows of swaying heads in the seats, the next the seats were being jumped on wildly, with an abandon rarely seen on the English side of the Channel" (Jeff Ward, *Melody Maker*, 17/11/73).

23     'Victim Of Sonic Attack!' screams the headline of the poster promoting this first US tour, featuring an open-mouthed rock fan with cracked glasses and the text: "We flew little Johnny Kaye all the way from Los Angeles to London so he could witness a Hawkwind Space Ritual performance first-hand. The results were positive: Permanent Brain Damage."

24     "The crowd got the works: strobes spinning blue squad car light, layer upon layer of film, and when a neon strip burst into life across the stage, it brought the house down. A guy in the row behind yelped 'Jeeesus Ch-rist!'" ('Spaced Out USA!' Jeff Ward, *Melody Maker*, 1/12/73).

25     For example *The New York Times*: "[A]ll the effects… could not disguise the fact that it was the same old mid-60s rock – heavy on the serious, decked out in science fiction, and promoted with much sound and fury attempting to signify something" ('Britain's Hawkwind Gives Earthy Rock The Cosmic Touch' – Ian Dove, *The New York Times*, 27/11/73).

26  Thanks to industrial action and restrictions on resources, several of the ideas mooted for this tour were abandoned. "10,000 tin cans containing dried peas and Frisbees were to have been given away during the course of the shows – but all tin cans being manufactured are being retained for foodstuffs due to steel production shortages, and Frisbee production too is down as all plastics are petroleum by-products" ('Shortages – Hawkwind Hit' – *Sounds*, 12/73). Magill, one of the tour supports, featured Huw Lloyd-Langton (ref: 'Hawkwind's Silly Show' – *Melody Maker*, 17/11/73). Fans who recall seeing the guitarist play with Hawkwind after 1970, but before his 1979 return, may be thinking of this tour.

Urban Guerilla.

I'm an urban guerilla,
I'm a po-tential killer.
I keep guns in my cellar,
I'm a derelict dweller,

I'm a two-tone panther
~~I'm a side-long glancer~~
I'm a revolution romancer
I'm a side-long glancer
and a street-fighting dancer

So let's not talk of love & flowers
and things that don't explode
You've used up all your magic powers
It's time to do it in the road.

I'm a longhair political bandit,
and you just don't understand it,
I'm an anarchist defector
I'm ~~a hand-grenade collector~~

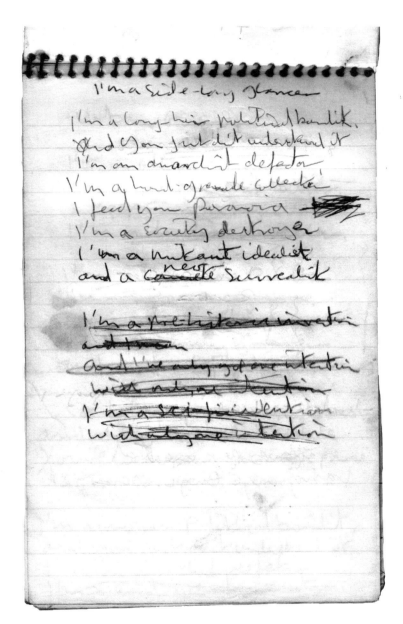

I'm a side-long glance

I'm a long-hair political bandit,
And you just don't understand it
I'm an anarchist defector
I'm a hand-grenade collector
I feed you paranoia
I'm a society destroyer
I'm a mutant idealist
and a ~~complete~~ neo Surrealist

I'm a ~~prehistoric invention~~
~~and then~~
~~And I've only just been~~
~~with only one intention~~
I'm a sci-fi invention
with only one intention

An early draft of 'Urban Guerilla'
(source: Robert Calvert archive)

# Michael Moorcock

Vocals, lyrics and inspiration
1971–1986
*Warrior On The Edge Of Time*

Michael Moorcock (& Nik Turner)
(source: Michael Scott collection)

**How would you sum up the Ladbroke Grove scene in the late 60s/early 70s?**
A brief golden age. It was inspiring in general to be part of it. I knew it couldn't last, but was determined to enjoy it.

You called Hawkwind "astronauts who'd been on their ship for a thousand years and gone insane." How did they compare with other bands at the time?

They had a barmy, visionary innocence. Absolutely nothing pretentious about them. They seemed chaotic, a bit unsure of themselves, but I knew nothing like them. All the other 'psychedelic' bands seemed pretentious and pale in comparison.

The perfect band for the entropic universe you were writing about?

Certainly in their early days. Later they lost some of that quality – but by way of balance their musical skills increased, and their technical understanding.

Did you sometimes feel like you'd conjured them into existence?

I have to say yes.

Attitudinally if nothing else, were they the SF New Wave's house band?

It depends. Very few *New Worlds* regulars, staff, writers or illustrators liked them. I was very surprised how little most of my peers were interested. Mike Harrison was, more than most.

What do you think they took from the acid experience, in terms of music and outlook?

Dave could get pretty mystical over a mushroom, but essentially he took the band in a more urban direction. Which was why so many lyrics had a grittiness the punks liked. Two band members were speed freaks taking acid for the trip, and not a sense of personal enlightenment. We were sometimes irritated by Nik's 'hippieness'!

What was the inspiration behind 'Sonic Attack'?

World War 2 and Cold War public service broadcasts, my ongoing narrative of the future.

What were your impressions of Calvert as you got to know him better?

He was genuinely bipolar and received bad advice from his friends against staying on medication and so on. He could also be very self-indulgent. He had problems working, mostly anxiety-based. He was a brilliant rock and roll performer and given more solid self-confidence might in my view have been Bowie's equal. A great waste.

Was he specifically influenced by any of the New Wave SF writers?
He read very little at length. He was attracted to New Wave SF writers –
Zelazny, Ballard, me – and borrowed a lot of the imagery. Like Bowie, he was
primarily a synthesist.

Did he work with an overall aesthetic in mind?
I don't think he had. It depended more on what fantasy he was playing out. Much
of it involved a *Biggles/Battler Britton* kind of image derived, ironically, from the
comics I wrote for Fleetway! He also had fantasies of being an upper class squire,
a Hammett-style private eye, and so on.

*Warrior On The Edge Of Time* is loosely based around your Eternal
Champion books. What was your brief?
None, really. Dave and Nik both asked me for material. I drew on my Eternal
Champion ideas. Of course the title was one of mine.

How would you assess your performance on the album?
Hasty. I was in a hurry to see a movie, so I dropped in at Olympic [Studios], did
all the numbers too quickly and rushed off. I should have spent more time on them.

What was the overall concept behind *The New Worlds Fair*?
A funfair as a kind of modern *Vanity Fair/Pilgrim's Progress*. A symbol of the
unexamined life, if you like.

Why was it a one-off?
I fell out with UA. I could have used some more studio help. Looking back I now
realise we had a failure of understanding.

About what you were trying to achieve and what they thought they
were getting?
Partly. I think they wanted something more spacey, like the single, 'Starcruiser'.
And originally, that was what I wanted to do, just to work on that. But they offered
me a three-album contract on the basis of the demo, and they didn't really know
how to handle it. They tried to put me out as a space-rock singer. It was sort of
dumb, and I felt let down.

What sets the 70s apart from the 60s – or is it reductive to want to package decades neatly?

It is a bit reductive. My own view is that 'the sixties' lasted as long as a relatively progressive government was in power, and ended around 1980 with the last Stiff tour. I think we need a different term for that period of relative optimism! The dystopian element in Hawkwind was the 'warning' sort, which is hopeful of change!

Did Britain feel like a country on the brink then? Or is this too apocalyptic an interpretation?

It's a Thatcher-ish myth, I think. There have always been people who see the apocalypse everywhere, so of course there were just as many "if this goes on" warnings. I think some were well-based, and therefore all the more in need of urgent attention.

What impact do you think that New Wave SF had on the wider culture?

A lot of current media people seem to have been inspired by us. A lot of journalists read us then, and filtered what we were doing out to their readers. I think we pointed the way for a number of new techniques in the arts, and our attitudes were taken up by 'mainstream' authors more than by SF people, perhaps. We wanted to develop a new kind of fiction by using SF techniques – and when you look at modern literary fiction, I think you see this everywhere. While amongst younger people, pop SF is the boss form. I think we had quite a strong impact on the wider culture.

Mainstream SF on film and TV seemed particularly apocalyptic and dystopian in the 70s…

SF was seen predominantly as a 'warning' genre. I think it took *Star Wars* in 1977 to bring the fun to it. Most of our models were 'warning' ideas – *Nineteen Eighty-Four* for example.

Before the 70s, the SF mainstream seemed more about "our destiny among the stars". Why did it become so 'warning'-based?

I think this was more the media's obsessions. We really were embracing the future, from computers to crashed cars! Offering an alternative to all those knocking knees! The media reflected middle-class after-dinner concerns. It was absolutely banal. We shared some of those concerns, but also saw how computers weren't going to do a HAL on us, but could be used as extensions of our creativity.

Why do you think the public fell out of love so quickly with the Apollo missions, but became fascinated with UFOs, extra-terrestrial life, Erich von Däniken and so on?
People prefer myths to facts. I certainly do.

Why do you think that is?
Ask your nearest existentialist! People are sustained by myth. Without myth, there is only the fact of death. It's the language and imagery of survival.

Does Hawkwind's development of their own mythology explain their success and longevity?
Absolutely! [It was] why I wasn't bored by them!

How do you think Hawkwind and the rise of punk were connected?
Closely. We were essentially an urban band with urban lyrics and so were the punks. We all had that in common. That's why the Pistols, Siouxsie and others so liked Hawkwind. I was made very welcome at punk gigs. Siouxsie liked Lemmy mostly, but was enthusiastic when she heard I'd worked with Hawkwind. I liked her a lot. Classy lady.

Do you think that Hawkwind in the 70s captured the "spirit of the age" - and if so, what was it?
Technology, space, a sense of the future, all these ideas were impinging far more on us than ever before. Many were scared by novelty. We embraced it. That was the spirit of the age.

# Radical Escapism In The Age Of Paranoia

## How Hawkwind Channelled The Apocalyptic Mindset Of 1970s Britain

by Andrew Means

HAWKWIND: Top (from left), Del, Simon, Lemmy, Nick Turner. Below: Bob Calvert, Dik Mik, Dave Block.

'They regard Hawkwind as primarily a mobile communications system'
*Melody Maker*, 29 April 1972
(source: Jim Skinner collection)

If the 1960s in Britain was a time of increasing prosperity and optimism, the 1970s was one of confusion and crisis, the decade that gave us the "Three Day Week", the "State Of Emergency" and the "Winter Of Discontent". The post-war dream of social and economic re-development had collided head-on with political inertia and industrial unrest, with the country now constantly on the brink of chaos.

Threats to humanity's very survival loomed on all sides: the oil crisis, international terrorism, pollution, the population bomb, and the ever-present prospect of nuclear war. It felt like the world was spinning out of control, with fear and conspiracy dominating popular culture. After the Age of Aquarius had come the Age of Paranoia…

Hawkwind were a band made for these times. While most artists peddled rock & roll banalities or were too wrapped up in their own self-importance, Hawkwind connected with the world at ground level. The dark, dangerous noise they made reflected the turbulence of the age back at their audience, 'sonic attack' as a form of self-defence against a messed up straight world. Anti-establishment to the core, Hawkwind delivered a unique brand of 'radical escapism' to society's disillusioned and disenfranchised.

## Idealism Into Radicalism

In 1964, Labour Prime Minister Harold Wilson had promised that our future would be forged in the "white heat of technology". Instead, infrastructure and institutions remained doggedly stuck in the past. Despite the "Swinging London" propaganda, growth and GDP were in decline and unemployment was creeping up. In 1950, the UK had controlled nearly 25% of world manufacturing trade; by 1970, its market share was barely 10%. When Conservative leader Edward Heath became Prime Minister in June that year, he promised to bring technocratic rigour to the business of government – but inflation was spiralling out of control and the unions were spoiling for a fight.

The 1960s had seen the emergence of new ways of thinking, with the psychedelic explosion only one part of a cultural revolution that sought to do away with the conformity and dogmas of the old world. But the 60s also saw a dramatic upswing in both military and civil violence, with hatred and anger as much in evidence as love and understanding.

The Vietnam War epitomised this new world disorder. In 1970, America began bombing Cambodia, and killing protestors at home, with four students shot dead that May at Kent State University, Ohio. The brutal response to anti-war demonstrations turned countercultural idealism into radicalism – chanting "love and peace" and placing flowers in the barrels of rifles wasn't going to be enough to stop centuries of state-sponsored carnage. The uprising of Parisian students and workers in May 1968 had already established a new template for militant underground resistance, which argued that nothing short of revolution was required to change things.

A wave of terrorist organisations began to wage war against the state: the Weather Underground in the US; the Red Brigade in Italy; the Red Army Faction in West Germany; the Angry Brigade in Britain.[1] Their objectives were often ill-defined, but all were committed to a violent disruption of the establishment status quo via headline-grabbing bombings, kidnappings, and even murder. But the most havoc was wrought by those with specific political demands, such as the resurgent IRA and the Palestinian Black September. It was as though the idea of dialogue and negotiation as a way towards social harmony had completely broken down, replaced instead by the blunt diplomacy of direct action and the gun.[2]

For many on the home front, the moral consensus had collapsed. Self-appointed guardians of propriety such as Mary Whitehouse regarded the counterculture's 'permissive society' as a cancer that was destroying traditional values and the British way of life from within: sex and violence were now mainstays of TV, film and theatre, while rock and pop promoted free love and drug-taking...

In truth, mainstream society was as conservative and reactionary as ever. Yet new rights and equalities were being battled for by the radical fringe. Much of what was first mooted during the 60s started to happen in the 70s – Germaine Greer's *The Female Eunuch* and the feminist *Spare Rib* magazine were published, and the UK Gay Liberation Front (GLF) was formed. The 1970 Miss World show at the Albert Hall was stormed by Women's Lib activists armed with bags of flour, while GLF members dressed as nuns disrupted a 1971 Festival Of Light meeting by releasing mice into the event hall.[3]

Even as the average family sat through yet another power cut, eating meat paste sandwiches by candlelight and trying not to think about the rats swarming over the uncollected rubbish outside, modern Britain was coming into being.

## A Retreat From Reality

As often as not, when we think about the 60s, we're actually envisioning the early 70s: men in all walks of life now wear their hair long; furnishings and fashions feature bold new colours and patterns; young people are more sexually aware and active; recreational drug use is relatively widespread, with cannabis and even LSD readily available in most towns. The once outré images and ideas of the Summer Of Love are now mainstream, co-opted and mass-produced. Historians refer to this effect as the "long 60s".

Hawkwind themselves are a product of the long 60s. The social, cultural and musical roots that define them were planted in the 60s. They see the use of drugs as basic to their lifestyle and essential to the composition and performance of their music. They embody the "let's do the show right here" spirit of the underground. Yet what's different about them is the way they not only reflect the turbulence and paranoia of the early 70s, but also create an entire mythology that offers a way out of these times, a new brand of radical escapism.

Of course, escapism had always been a major part of popular music's appeal. In the early days of rock & roll in particular, it channelled dreams of fast cars and the perfect wave, surrendering to the latest dance craze or being consumed by the ecstasies (and miseries) of romance.

But this changed in the 60s. For artists such as Bob Dylan, songs were no longer just mundane fantasies or idle distractions. Instead, they became a way of interrogating the world and smuggling ideas into listeners' heads. Pop and rock changed from being a purely escapist medium and became something altogether more meaningful in peoples' lives, the driving force behind an emerging underground consciousness.

The 1960s was the great era of the protest song: Dylan's 'A Hard Rain's A-Gonna Fall', Barry McGuire's 'Eve Of Destruction', Donovan's 'Universal Soldier', John Lennon's 'Give Peace A Chance'. The Beatles and The Rolling Stones alternately critiqued and celebrated countercultural radicalism ('Revolution' versus 'Street Fighting Man'). Jefferson Airplane advocated drugs while disavowing legal pharmaceuticals ('White Rabbit'). Jimi Hendrix eviscerated 'The Star-Spangled Banner' at Woodstock, a tortured indictment of the horrors of Vietnam.

Yet by the turn of the 70s, things were changing again. Singer-songwriters preferred to catalogue the inner life of their soul rather than engage with issues. A more aggressive form of blues rock reflected the heaviness of the times, but was lyrically retrograde, rock & roll clichés about wicked women and sexual omnipotence allied to blitzkrieg guitar heroics. Progressive rock gestured towards the apocalyptic, but mainly traded in lyrical opacity and pseudo-intellectual posturing. And the charts were filled with feelgood MOR and sentimental novelty songs – 1970's UK number ones included Mungo Jerry's 'In The Summertime', Lee Marvin's 'Wanderin' Star', and the England Football Squad's 'Back Home'.

On the one hand, an arms race between self-indulgence and navel-gazing; on the other, saccharine pap designed for an unending procession of light entertainment shows. The twin spectres of economic meltdown and global annihilation haunted the collective unconscious, but popular music was looking the other way. If you wanted music that acknowledged what was happening beyond the studio doors, you had to venture into the underground...

## Hawkwind: Space Rock In Opposition

In terms of dogma or ideology, Hawkwind never claimed to be political. Yet Hawkwind clearly *were* political through their proactive opposition to the mainstream.

Their commitment to playing innumerable benefit concerts made them standard bearers for the alternative society. And who else was releasing singles like 'Urban Guerilla' and 'The Psychedelic Warlords (Disappear In Smoke)' – sample lyrics: "I'm society's destructor, I'm a petrol bomb constructor" and "Sick of politicians, harassment and laws"? They refused to pander to traditional songwriting narratives of finding solace in love or boasting about sexual prowess. And at a time when instrumental mastery was viewed as a prerequisite for success, their lack of interest in virtuosity, and the inclusion of 'non-musicians' in the band, was deeply provocative to the status quo.[4]

Yet the truly oppositional statement is the music itself: unruly and hypnotic, it was unlike anything else being made in Britain at that time, a point which can't be emphasised enough. Hawkwind create a unique strain of existential protest music that eschews direct engagement with 'issues', but channels the queasy atmosphere of paranoia and anxiety that looms like a black cloud over the 70s.

More than any other band, attendance at a Hawkwind gig is synonymous with "getting out of it" and "taking a trip". But it's a journey that feeds on the darkness outside the concert hall rather than the Aquarian impulses of just a few years previous. Hawkwind's shows are fired by an apocalyptic urgency that reflects both a disgust at the state of the world and a determination to leave it behind as soon as possible. Their songs criticise the oppressive nature of society, while embracing space as a site of new possibilities. The 'radical escapism' they offer is revelation plus liberation: not just fleeing from the world, but envisaging a new reality as well.[5]

The fact that Hawkwind use the imagery of science fiction and space travel to express their disillusionment with the straight world shouldn't detract from their message. As the Moorcock-helmed *New Worlds* was demonstrating, SF was ideally placed in the early 70s to interrogate the new existential and psychological challenges facing the human race. Hawkwind are one of the very few artists of the time who understand how SF can be used as a way to dramatise and critique what's happening in modern society.

## Galactic Psychodramas

Hawkwind develop this notion of radical escapism, increasingly expressed in science fictional terms, over the course of their first four albums. *Hawkwind* still trades in 60s platitudes, urging us to "*be yourself*" while fatalistically accepting that the new day "*may bring war*". But the music itself conveys the message, nagging motifs that worm into the sub-conscious like phantoms lurking behind the façade of polite society, 'Paranoia' in particular.

*In Search Of Space* ups the ante, the shuddering, pulsating groove of a craft achieving escape velocity, its very title a call for physical and psychic freedom from enclosure. 'You Shouldn't Do That' is explicitly anti-authoritarian while 'We Took The Wrong Step Years Ago' anticipates our impending doom. And the 'Master Of The Universe' makes clear his disappointment with us: "*If you call this living, I must be blind.*" This first excursion into science fiction proper comes with packaging that's a *tour de force* of cosmic mysticism and New Wave SF-derived philosophy.

By *Doremi*, Hawkwind have become the definitive SF rock band, with a dense deep-space sound and songs that directly address "*this planet's erosion*" ('Brainstorm') and the Orwellian "*brain police*" ('Time We Left This World Today'). It's time to free yourself from your earthly bonds before 'The Watcher' issues his stark decree: "*This is the end now.*"

And then *Space Ritual* turns radical escapism into galactic psychodrama, with Hawkwind as renegade colonisers, hurtling headlong into the eternal night on a one-way mission to oblivion. The crazed evangelism of 'Born To Go' blasts a "*new clear way through space*", but by 'The Black Corridor', we're staring into the void, and the void is staring back...[6]

## The Revolution Personified

With Britain itself staring into the void, riven by strikes and power cuts, and seemingly on the point of some catastrophic collapse, Hawkwind travelled ceaselessly around the country to bring their show to the huddled masses. A liberation mythology quickly built up around Hawkwind, nurtured by both the band and its audience. For many fans, they were the literal harbingers of a new way of life, "*a way out of the maze that held the human race.*"

As Andrew Means reported in *Melody Maker* in August 1972, "There's a Hawkwind cult now that's almost as vital to their gigs as the music... Hordes of dedicated teenagers regard them as the revolution personified, and with 'Silver Machine' slicing through the chart, some of them must be ticking off the days to the take-over with increasing impatience."[a]

◇◇◇◇◇◇◇◇◇◇◇◇◇◇◇◇◇◇◇◇◇◇◇◇◇◇◇◇◇◇◇◇◇◇◇◇◇◇◇◇◇◇◇◇◇◇◇◇◇◇◇◇◇◇◇◇◇◇◇◇◇◇◇◇◇◇◇◇◇◇◇◇◇◇◇◇

a       'Hawkwind – The Joke Band That Made It' – Andrew Means, *Melody Maker*, 12/08/72

1       The Angry Brigade were active in the UK from 1970-72, with a total of 25 bombings attributed to the group, none of which caused any serious injury. Contrast this with the series of kidnappings and murders carried out by the Red Brigade and Baader-Meinhof gang.

2       Robert Calvert would become obsessed with terrorist groups. From the ironic salute of 'Urban Guerilla' to references to Black September in 'Hassan I Sahba', events would come to a head in October 1977 when Calvert became convinced that a gig in Paris was being attended by representatives of all the major terrorist organisations.

3       The Nationwide Festival Of Light was a short-lived evangelical Christian movement that railed against sex and violence in the media and arts.

4       Am I the only person who reads the word 'awkward' as 'Hawkwind' when they see it in text? To paraphrase Groucho Marx, they wouldn't be a member of any club that would have them.

5       J.R.R. Tolkien was one of the first to articulate this notion. In his 1939 essay 'On Fairy-Stories', he talks about "profound 'escapisms'" that distinguish between "the escape of the prisoner" and "the flight of the deserter" – and requests critics not to confuse them.

6       It's interesting to note that all of Hawkwind's main writers make the theme of escape central to their songs in 1972 – Nik Turner with 'Brainstorm' ("I've got to get out of this void"), Robert Calvert with 'Born To Go' ("We're breaking out of the shell") and Dave Brock with 'Time We Left This World Today' – while Lemmy gets the last laugh as 'The Watcher', sealing the fate of those left behind.

Stacia, Turner & Lemmy — from *NME* photo shoot for 23 November 1974 issue
(photo by Pennie Smith)

# World Turned Upside Down Now

January–September 1974

Maintaining their reputation as one of the UK's hardest-gigging bands, Hawkwind resume the Ridiculous Roadshow tour on New Year's Day at Blackburn's King George Hall, and tour solidly until mid-February. Keen to defuse the hype grown up round them, the mood is one of consolidation.

Speaking to *Record Mirror* in January, Simon King says, "We still get people who come because we made the top 20, but we're winning back the hardcore, the faithful from the underground days." For Hawkwind, it's still more important to be credible than successful, though King also wants to dispel any notion of them being too obscure: "Some might talk of the space image as a serious trip, but we're really a fun band. We enjoy playing more than anything else".[a]

With Calvert busy recording *Captain Lockheed*, the shows miss his unpredictable intellectual edge. Turner performs the spoken-word material, but his habit of taking to the stage wearing a green frog costume tends to undercut any attempt at gravity.

The Edmonton Sundown gigs on 25-26 January are recorded with a view to them forming the basis of another live album, but the performances aren't deemed strong enough. However, one of the Edmonton shows is notable for the first appearance with the band of ex-High Tide violinist **Simon House**, mooted as a replacement for Del Dettmar, who's announced he's leaving soon.[1]

▾    ▾    ▾

In March, Hawkwind are back in America. This time the tour runs to 22 dates, including shows in Canada. Hawkwind may lack the inclination to become arena rock stars, but memories of the Beatles-led British Invasion are still potent in the 70s and given the potential money and kudos at stake, 'breaking America' is a general industry obsession.[2] Despite being told by UA to "Stay at home until you get some new product",[b] Doug Smith works with US management team Steve Leber and David Krebs (Aerosmith, Ted Nugent, the New York Dolls) to build on last year's attendances, promoting the tour as "The '1999' Party".

The press remain baffled by the amount of tickets Hawkwind continue to sell, especially in the US.[3] But is it so surprising? Hawkwind put on a proper multimedia show with projections, lights and dancers at a time when 10-minute drum solos are most bands' idea of a good time. And their intense riffadelica is a genuine alternative to the schmaltzy pop, ersatz country rock and southern boogie that dominates the American music scene. Hawkwind's anti-establishment ethos appeals both to the Haight-Ashbury old guard and a new generation of fans, all disillusioned with the state of the nation.

In March 1974, the news everywhere is bad. After ripping the country apart, America is still coming to terms with 'defeat' in the Vietnam War. The Watergate scandal is in full swing, severely undermining faith in US politics. And the domestic headlines play out against a backdrop of industrial decline, rising unemployment, inner city turmoil and general lawlessness – New York City has become a byword for spiralling crime and police corruption, while Chicago, where the band play again on 21 March, will see its murder epidemic peak in 1974 with 970 deaths.[c4]

Yet US rock audiences are still very much invested in the countercultural ideals of smoking dope and sticking it to The Man. And with former musical icons either disbanded (Jefferson Airplane) or mellowed out (the Grateful Dead), the way is clear for a band with suitably radical credentials to fill the vacuum that exists. Hawkwind fit the bill nicely and do themselves no harm playing a benefit gig at Berkeley on 10 March for acid evangelist Timothy Leary, recently extradited from Afghanistan and now in solitary confinement in Folsom Prison.[5]

The novelty of playing America for the first time may have worn off, but the shows are still well-attended, with audiences much bigger than back in Britain. New songs are honed while 'The Watcher' is fleshed-out into a full band version. Turner performs the Moorcock-penned '**Standing At The Edge**' and '**Veterans Of A Thousand Psychic Wars**' with aplomb – with its sneering nihilistic cry of "*Death to all things living / Only death will cleanse the world*", the latter is a bracing corrective to the West Coast diktat of love, peace and understanding.[6]

Mick Farren analyses the make-up of the Chicago audience for *NME*: "Hawkwind are attracting a capacity crowd. And the crowd are young. There's a lot of blue jeans and combat coats, not an eight-inch platform or a speck of glitter to be seen… One section seems to think that the 'Wind are some weird kind of Sha Na Na flower power revival parody band. Others put them in a Blue Öyster Cult/Black Sabbath bag. And others mutter about Sun Ra and John Cage." The crowd loves it as the band take their "hypnotic, early Velvet Underground pulse to almost psychotic extremes".[d]

At *Melody Maker*, Geoff Brown is less convinced, describing the spoken word pieces as "laughably banal" and "recited like speeding Daleks". But he also makes a Velvet Underground connection, declaring that, "Brock and Lemmy have that [same] frantic simplicity, that basic earthy drone and tumble".[e] Brown also notes the tense, sometimes violent atmosphere at US shows – at the St Louis Henry Kiel Auditorium on 16 March, an over-excited fan clambers on-stage and tries to strangle Stacia.

Upon their return to Britain in mid-April, House – who has been shadowing Dettmar during the US tour – becomes an official member.[7] In May, work begins at Olympic Studios on the next album.

▾      ▾      ▾

For fans thirsting after new Hawkwind product, 10 May sees the release of Robert Calvert's *Captain Lockheed And The Starfighters*, which combines spoken-word skits with songs that range from gonzoid garage rock to primitive electro-punk. The skits are performed by Calvert, Vivian Stanshall and Traffic's Jim Capaldi, while Paul Rudolph is musical director. Roy Thomas Baker produces,[8] and the album also features Arthur Brown and Brian Eno. All of Hawkwind play on it, and with a number of its songs entering their live repertoire over the years, many fans regard *Captain Lockheed* as a Hawkwind album by proxy.[9] But for all the similarities, there are differences too.

'**The Aerospaceage Inferno**' taxies into view on the back of a throbbing, rubbery bassline before guitar and drums burst into the insistent rhythm and riff combination that Hawkwind fans know and love,[10] although Rudolph's guitar is pitched higher than Brock's favoured tone. Calvert's voice is sneering and aloof, his idealised fighter pilot staring death in the eye and declaring, "*What a good way to go!*" One couplet sums up the cynicism of the German military's attitude, while also referencing Pink Floyd and Hawkwind: "*Set the controls for the heart of the earth / The silver machine is worth more than you're worth.*"

'**The Widow Maker**' is less controlled nosedive, more hellish biker stomp, Lemmy's swampy bass dominating the sound, Turner's sax occasionally breaking through the sonic fug. Relishing his fatalistic tough-guy role, Calvert spits the line: "*Do you wanna try a good way to die?*" Brock's solo is barely audible, but there's some 'Orgone Accumulator'-style swagger towards the end.

Pick of the aerospace rock tracks is '**The Right Stuff**', a song inspired by the combination of steely-eyed heroism and flying skills necessary to become an ace

Alex Cooley
presents
Midnight
at the
FOX THEATRE
HAWKWIND
WITH FRIENDS MAN
PRESENT
1999 PARTY
LIQUID LEN & THE LENSMEN
ANDY DUNKLEY
Friday. March 29
at Midnight
$5.00   6.00
advance   day of show

Cowtown Productions
Presents
HAWKWIND

with guest
RUSH

Friday          Memorial Hall
Oct.18          K.C., Ks.
8pm             Tickets
                $5 Adv.
                6 Door

TICKETS AVAILABLE AT: CAPERS CORNERS, RECORD BAR (Metcalf South), RECORD BAR (Independence, Center),
BUDGET TAPES, BARRY'S RECORD RACK, MEMORIAL HALL.
SEND MONEY ORDERS TO: COWTOWN PRODUCTIONS, P.O. BOX 10314, KANSAS CITY, MISSOURI 64111

SUPERB
MARCH 10, 8:00
HAWKWIND
&
M A N
- - - - - - - -
BENEFIT FOR
DR. TIMOTHY LEARY
ZELLERBACH
AUDITORIUM
U. C. BERKELEY
TICKETS $3, $4, $5

a.s.u.c. box office

On tour in the USA

pilot. [11] The riff is like a train hammering over tracks at high speed, while Calvert's vocals do the manic robot: "*My reflexes and reactions are as fast as a machiiiiine!*" The Starfighter's barrel-roll acceleration is mimicked with reverb and the tinkling echo of a piano, as Rudolph's needling guitar and Turner's honking sax add to the mounting disorientation.

There's a new version of '**Ejection**', with a chunkier, fuller sound and slapback echo on Calvert's voice, though it feels a little sluggish compared to the original's garage punk. But like all the tracks above, it shares a single-minded verse/chorus momentum – once the main riff is established, there's practically no deviation from it. In contrast, the great majority of Hawkwind's tracks have some form of middle eight or dynamic shift in them, Brock being at heart still a fairly traditional songwriter.

Yet Calvert doesn't intend to just copy the Hawkwind sound. One of the album's most striking tracks is '**The Song Of The Gremlin (Part One)**', featuring Arthur Brown as full-on pantomime villain. Over silent movie-style piano, Brown breathlessly incants, "*I focused the magnifying glass that brought the downfall of Icarus.*" As his voice reaches operatic fever pitch, the song pauses and a jabbing synth line takes over, joined by what sounds like an early electronic snare drum, a slice of robotic punk-funk years ahead of its time. Keyboards are attributed to Adrian Wagner, but the treatments applied to voice and drums are Eno's, running them through his VCS3 and other contraptions. Brown's Gremlin – a mischievous elemental being responsible for mechanical failures on aircraft – is magnificently deranged, screaming and scatting against Rudolph's wailing guitar. [12]

**Part Two** of the song is even more over the top, Brown violently declaiming his lines against a discordant crashing and Turner's atonal sax, before the song finally resolves into a mournful epic rock groove that fades out all too soon.

Different again, '**Hero With A Wing**' is a parodic Nordic folk hymn with a dismal atmosphere that looks ahead to the series of musical pastiches that will constitute Calvert's next album. The title comes from a 1905 etching by Paul Klee which depicts a classical figure with a feathered wing replacing one of his arms. [13] Calvert's lyrics are blackly poetic: "*But still I was a hero, with one wing more than most / Almost half an angel, a whirling holy ghost.*"

'**I Resign**' is a short barbershop acapella and '**Catch A Falling Starfighter**' is the same version as appears on the B-side of the 'Ejection' single. The booklet stapled into the gatefold sleeve also contains the words to 'The Widow's Song', but it doesn't make the tracklist, presumably because Nico – who Calvert had talked about working with – isn't available.[14]

Alongside the songs, Calvert and the voice actors clearly enjoy bringing the comedy skits to life, with the Goons, Monty Python, Pete & Dud, and *The Navy Lark* as touchstones. In 1974, the British perception of Germany is still shaped almost entirely by memories of World War Two (with the 1966 World Cup thrown in for good measure). The television schedules are full of triumphalist films like *The Dambusters* and *The Great Escape*, and Freddie Starr playing Hitler as a madcap grotesque, while re-enacting WW2 via Action Man dolls, Airfix models and *Victor* comic is a popular pastime for boys.

Defence Minister Franz Josef Strauss is portrayed as a despotic blowhard with a thick Teutonic accent, still smarting at defeat by the British, who orders the Starfighters to restore national pride and honour.[15] However, all the other 'German' characters are played as officer-class Englishmen with stiff upper lips, hinting that perhaps there's not such a difference between the Luftwaffe and the RAF after all. Meanwhile, the Americans selling the planes to Strauss are all smooth-talking con artists – "*G for Germany!*"[16] – hoovering up the post-war spoils and treating the arms trade as a Wild West sideshow.

It's not hard to imagine some of these skits being quoted in college bars around the country, along with the 'Dead Parrot' sketch: "They don't always crash, you know" – "*It would be an honour to crash in such a plane!*"[17] For all its playing to the crowd, Captain Lockheed is often genuinely funny and clearly the product of a literary mind rather than a rock star dilettante.

It fails to chart, but will go on to become a cult classic. In *Sounds*, Martin Hayman notes Calvert's obsession with a "particular brand of kamikaze heroism," where the "quest for individual glory, fame in perpetuity assured at the moment of oblivion, intersects with childhood absorption with the technical and atheistic attractions of autonomous jet-powered flight".[f] In *NME*, a sniffy Mick Farren is more dismissive: it's an "adequate Hawkwind spin-off", but to achieve real art, Calvert has to go beyond "Freudian psycho-jokes about the airplane as a phallic symbol, and a certain nostalgia for *The Wizard* and *Hotspur*".[g]

Meanwhile, Calvert has announced a series of *Captain Lockheed* stage shows and is discussing his next project, a reinterpretation of Hamlet set in Prohibition-era Chicago entitled *The Rise And Fall Of Luigi Brilliantino*.[18] However, nothing comes of either. Due to start on 19 May at the Kings Road Theatre in Chelsea, the *Lockheed* shows are nixed by Python Productions, Calvert's new management

– yes, that *Python* – for logistical reasons, though it's just as likely that Calvert has had another meltdown. As a spokesman tells *NME*, "he is not keen on the idea of touring. In fact, he is seriously considering giving up his musical career altogether, to concentrate on being a poet".[h]

▾     ▾     ▾

Ironically, Calvert takes part in several recording sessions during the year, including a bizarre cricket-themed novelty single to cash in on a possible visit by the much-feted West Indies team. Calvert and the First Eleven includes Rudolph, Turner, King and former T. Rex percussionist Steve Took. '**Crikit Lovely Reggea**' [sic] is a fairly broad pastiche, while the mooted B-side, '**Howzat**', is a catchy if flimsy pop song. An acetate is made, but UA aren't keen to release it, particularly when the West Indies tour is cancelled. However, this single will have a second life later in the decade.

Also in the First Eleven is Adrian Wagner, who releases *Distances Between Us* in 1974, an ambitious electronic album with Calvert's vocals on two tracks. '**Messengers Of Morpheus**' is essentially a poem read against a discordant, Ligeti-esque backing – but perhaps more interesting for Hawkwind fans is '**Steppenwolf**'. A track of the same name, with very similar lyric and melody, will feature on *Astounding Sounds, Amazing Music* two years later. But the music here, a proto-industrial rumble of minimal synth rock, is quite different.[19]

Finally, Calvert also features on *Down To Earth* by Nektar, a German-based British space-prog group who enjoy more success in continental Europe and America than in their homeland.[20] Still very much in *Lockheed* mode, he provides spoken links in the persona of a crazed Teutonic ringmaster.

▾     ▾     ▾

In June, with the recording of their new album mostly complete, Hawkwind travel once again to Europe for shows in West Germany and the Netherlands. *NME* runs a long feature based round the Concertgebouw show in Amsterdam – only a third full, blamed on poor promotion. There's a torturously protracted interview with Turner, the tone is patronising throughout, and the piece is headlined 'Dorkwind In Dutchland'.[j]

Here, writ large, is the ever increasing "credibility gap" that exists between Hawkwind and the industry, which Martin Hayman explores in *Sounds*: "Punters who congratulate themselves on their good taste groan when they are mentioned. Music journalists devise a thousand and one excuses, each more ingenious than the last, to avoid going to their gigs… Record companies throw up their hands in horror at the idea of trying to market a cult." He notes they remain a legitimately underground band, but maintaining autonomy creates business problems – the money they have to borrow to make albums, to attract American promoters, to stay on the touring treadmill. This trade-off between industry expectations and countercultural credibility will dog them throughout the 70s – as Turner laments, even the word 'hippie' is "now used as a term of abuse".[j]

There are personnel changes too. Prior to their trip to Europe, Simon King fractures his ribs playing football and is replaced by **Alan Powell**, formerly with Vinegar Joe. When King rejoins the band, they retain Powell and adopt a double drummer line-up – the beginning of what Lemmy will later witheringly refer to as "the Drum Empire". The June dates also mark the end of Del Dettmar's time with the band – having already retreated behind the sound desk to give Simon House more room on stage, he leaves to start a new life in Canada.

▾     ▾     ▾

On 2 August, an edit of 'The Psychedelic Warlords (Disappear In Smoke)' is released as a single.[21] A sinister synth drone heralds an urgently chopped out riff that's downright funky – it's quite a departure in sound from their previous singles.[22] The song slinks forcibly along under an aggressive vocal from Brock, and its angry chorus of "*That ain't no joke / You can disappear in smoke*" taps into the pall of fear that's descended on the country following the IRA's attack on the Houses Of Parliament in June. For those who think Hawkwind are relics of a bygone age, the title is an open goal, although *NME*'s review is jokily positive.[k] *Sounds* is blunter: "If you're into quasi-political, cosmic doom rock then this is your river of blood. Otherwise, skip it".[l] It doesn't chart.

Maybe they didn't put the right song on the A-side. Recorded at the Edmonton Sundown and later overdubbed at Olympic, flipside 'It's So Easy' is a more melodic take on the space rock template and another subtle departure. The angelic choral introduction resembles Popol Vuh's soundtrack for Werner Herzog's *Aguirre, The Wrath Of God*, while Brock's tentative guitar is like a searchlight in fog. His vocal is open, expansive, even hopeful: "*Revolution's coming / The chaos will soon end.*" And the chorus is a three-part cosmic football chant that begs to be bellowed along to.

Edited into shape, 'It's So Easy' could have caught the ear of radio programmers and fans alike, but it isn't even deemed strong enough for the upcoming album. It's one of the band's more mystifying decisions.

▾    ▾    ▾

In August, the band do their first UK concerts since the Ridiculous Roadshow, all festival appearances. The most memorable is at Harlow Park, where Turner runs onto a rain-soaked stage in his green frog suit, skids and slides off the edge. Michael Moorcock is also present – *NME* calls him a "lunk of a fella wearing a smock and a hat decorated with all manner of things including a feather"[m] – but keeps his footing.

On 6 September, the punningly-titled *Hall Of The Mountain Grill*[23] is released.

◇◇◇◇◇◇◇◇◇◇◇◇◇◇◇◇◇◇◇◇◇◇◇◇◇◇◇◇◇◇◇◇◇◇◇◇◇◇◇◇◇◇◇◇◇◇◇◇◇◇◇◇◇◇◇◇◇◇◇◇◇◇◇◇◇◇◇◇◇

a    'Hawkwind – In Search Of New Space' – Tony Jasper, *Record Mirror*, 05/01/74

b    'America Sees The Light' – Geoff Brown, *Melody Maker*, 23/3/74

c    '1974 Was A Deadly Year In Chicago' – Stephan Benzkofer, *Chicago Tribune*, 8/7/12

d    'Trippin' USA' – Mick Farren, *NME*, 6/4/74

e    'America Sees The Light' – Geoff Brown, same source

f    'Calvert: Hero With A Wing' – Martin Hayman, *Sounds*, 27/04/74

g    'Starfighter Crashes; Public Demand Enquiry' – Mick Farren, *NME*, 25/5/74

h    'Calvert Cancels 'Lockheed' Dates' – *NME*, 4/05/74

i    'Dorkwind In Dutchland' – Chris Salewicz, *NME*, 6/7/74

j    'Hawkwind: Winning Or Waning?' – Martin Hayman, *Sounds*, 6/7/74

k    *NME*, 3/8/74

l    *Sounds*, 3/8/74

m    'An English Comedy Of Manners' – Steve Clarke, *NME*, 17/8/74

1    Bizarrely enough, classical music critic and composer Michael Nyman (who will go on to write the scores for films including *The Draughtsman's Contract* and *The Piano*) was briefly mooted as Dettmar's replacement. Ads for the Edmonton shows state, "These concerts are dedicated to Timothy Leary – a jailed philosopher." They also announce a competition: "A prize of a weekend on the road with Hawkwind with all expenses paid… will be awarded to the best masks worn by a male and a female to the concerts." A mask template based on Barney Bubbles' two-headed

hawk design, to be cut out and decorated, was printed as a press ad.

2    For example, Led Zeppelin played more than 100 US shows in 1969, and did nine tours there 1968-1971. Jethro Tull and Foghat, the latter little regarded in their home market, also became big live attractions in the US, with huge record sales.

3    Even Doug Smith seems perplexed: "They made more bread off live appearances last year than any other group in Britain and they're still just a bunch of freaks" ('The World Ends In Half An Hour' – Charles Shaar Murray, *NME*, 4/5/74).

4    Another top story during the band's second tour of America was the kidnapping of newspaper heiress Patty Hearst by revolutionary militants the Symbionese Liberation Army. America was further scandalised in April when Hearst, apparently brainwashed to the SLA's cause, helped to hold up a bank in San Francisco.

5    There's a telephone hook-up with Leary during the concert, although it occurs during support band Man's set, and is largely incomprehensible. By 1974, Leary was increasingly drawn to matters cosmic: *Starseed* (1973) is a paranoid screed full of extra-terrestrial salvation and impending doom on earth; *Terra II: A Way Out* (1974) includes a proposal for the colonisation of space. Turner visited him in jail, and learnt of an escape plan that involved Hawkwind being suspended from a helicopter and performing above the prison as a diversion (ref: p150-51, *Spirit Of Hawkwind*, Nik Turner & Dave Thompson, 2015).

6    These tracks appear on a recording of the Chicago Auditorium show released in 1997 as *The '1999' Party*. The March 23 Detroit Palace show was also recorded, but remains unused. 'Veterans…' was renamed 'Soldiers At The Edge Of Time' and recorded for *Warrior*, but was left off the finished album, only becoming available in 2013 on the Atomhenge re-issue.

7    House was Hawkwind's first 'proper' trained musician, though no less committed to sonic attack: "I used to have these speakers I called the illuminators. One on each side of the stage, huge things with a big horn. In conjunction with the VCS3, I could stun a badger at 20 paces" (ref: *Hawkwind: Do Not Panic* documentary, 2007).

8    Around the same time, Roy Thomas Baker was masterminding the sound of the first two Queen albums – if *Captain Lockheed* occasionally feels a little flat ('The Aerospaceage Inferno' being a prime example), there are instances of sonic invention that suggest he wasn't completely asleep on the job.

9    Hawkwind credits in full: Calvert/vocals, Brock/lead guitar on 'The Widow Maker' (though it sounds like he's elsewhere too, 'The Right Stuff' for instance), Lemmy/bass & rhythm guitar, Turner/sax, Dettmar/synth, King/drums. Eno is credited as Brian Peter George St John La Baptiste De La Salle, his full name less Eno. Like Calvert, Stanshall was a talented artist beset by demons whose coping mechanism was to play an eccentric English gentleman. A key contributor to the Dada cabaret of The Bonzo Dog Doo Dah Band, Stanshall had also created a series of

comic radio sketches based on *Journey Into Space*, aired on BBC Radio 1 in August 1971 while he depped for John Peel. These too featured Jim Capaldi, plus Keith Moon as "likeable cheeky cockney Lemmy". Moon was booked for a *Lockheed* session, but failed to turn up.

10 Which Lemmy will later lift for the start of 'Motorhead'.

11 For all Calvert's desire to explore the Starfighter tragedy, he's also indulging his childhood fantasies. An expression describing the bravery and machismo of a certain breed of test pilots, "the right stuff" is later associated with the early US space programme (specifically the Mercury Seven astronauts) via Tom Wolfe's 1979 book of the same name, and its 1983 film adaptation.

12 Best known for his 1968 hit 'Fire', Arthur Brown was a pioneer of theatrical cosmic/prog rock. The three albums he made with his band Kingdom Come, particularly the debut *Galactic Zoo Dossier*, are not far outside the Hawkwind universe, and Brock and Turner were both fans. Brown sang on Hawkwind's *Take Me To Your Leader* (2005) and continues to guest with them live. Wagner (who died in 2018) was one of Britain's few solo electronic musicians at the time – and the great-great grandson of the German composer. He went on to design, manufacture and market the Wasp, the world's first portable digital synthesiser.

13 In Klee's own words: "[A] tragicomic hero, perhaps an antique Don Quixote… In contrast to divine beings, this man has been born with only one angel's wing, and makes incessant attempts to fly. In the process he breaks arm and leg, but nevertheless perseveres under the banner of his idea." It's not hard to see what Calvert saw in this picture.

14 'The Widow's Song' was eventually recorded as 'The Widow Song' in 1984 with Calvert's third wife Jill Riches on vocals, and released on *Hawkwind: Friends And Relations Vol III* (1985). A simple waltz-time ballad played on electric harpsichord, it's surprisingly affecting.

15 While overstated for comic effect, this is not inaccurate. The unwillingness of figures such as Strauss to fully confront Nazi atrocities, and accept the establishment's culpability in the rise of Hitler, was a key factor in the post-war birth of both the Baader-Meinhof gang and the early Krautrock bands.

16 Calvert as Strauss approvingly notes that the 'G' in F-104G could also stand for "Gott strafe England", a German saying dating back to WW1 that translates as "May God punish England". It's also where 'strafing' comes from to describe a method of German air attack in WW2.

17 'Ground Control To Pilot' is another example of Calvert sending himself up – the list of drugs, including Largactil, Valium and Haloperidol, are all anti-psychotic medications.

18 Calvert had previous 'theatrical' form – upon first moving to London, he formed (or possibly joined) a Camden-based street theatre group called "Street Dada Nihilismus", though their main recorded action was spraying red paint at unfortunate passersby.

19 The CD reissue of *Distances Between Us* includes 'Stranger In A Strange Land' (after the Robert Heinlein novel), an unreleased track featuring another Calvert vocal/lyric, though possibly recorded later.

20    *Down To Earth* went gold in America, making it the most successful record Calvert appears on.

21    In July, a single featuring edited versions of 'You'd Better Believe It' and 'Paradox' (from Edmonton Sundown) had been released in France and West Germany. 'Paradox' is significantly remixed from the album version to highlight vocals and Mellotron.

22    This is an edit of the song that appears on *HOTMG*, with extra sax and guitar overdubbed in the middle section. The words to 'Psychedelic Warlords' originally appeared in the Space Ritual tour programme, but the opening couplet – "*We're the psychedelic warlords / Playing spaced out rock and roll*" – is omitted in the recorded version, presumably considered too gauche.

23    A conflation of Grieg's 'In The Hall Of The Mountain King' and The Mountain Grill café in Ladbroke Grove, a popular Hawkwind hang-out. It's a metaphor for the band itself at this point, fantastical music meets greasy spoon, Mellotron and chips.

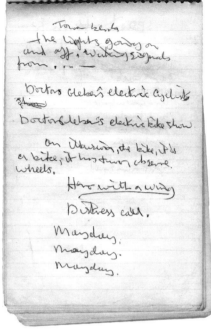

'Hero With A Wing' –
Robert Calvert doodle
(source: Robert Calvert archive)

Mayday
(source: Robert Calvert archive)

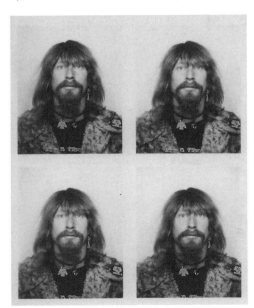

Nik Turner's passport photo
(source: Doug Smith archive)

# POP SHOP

**STACIA . . . she delights in being outrageous**

## By MICHAEL CABLE

HER name hasn't always been Stacia.

It used to be something quite ordinary, though she won't say what.

Then one day, while hitch-hiking, she was given a lift by gypsies.

They studied her birth date numbers and decided that she ought to be called Stacia.

She thought it was kinda groovy. So Stacia she's been ever since.

If you think all that is pretty unlikely, you ain't heard nothing yet.

Stacia is the lady who, at 17, anticipated the streakers by several years, when she jumped on stage in front of top rock group, Hawkwind, and danced stark naked.

As Stacia is 6ft tall and boasts a 43-28-39 figure, this caused an outsize sensation.

### Plans

Hawkwind invited her to do it on a regular basis.

That was four years ago, and she has been with them ever since. But not still stripping.

Plans are afoot to turn her into a star in her own right. She is likely to release her first single, New York City Retch, later this year.

"That's right. Retch not wretch," says Stacia, who seems to delight in being out-rageous. She arrived at The Sun office wearing only a black leotard and fishnet tights, which caused a near riot as she strolled along Fleet Street.

She explains: "People stare at me anyway, because I'm 6ft tall and I've got a big bust. So I feel, what the hell

"In fact, I'm basically rather shy.

"And I get very angry when people accuse me of being a groupie.

"If anyone says it to my face, I'll punch them on the nose. At first,

## How shy Stacia took off for fame!

when I stripped off, people accepted it as an art form.

"But then a lot of people just came along to gape and giggle."

And the act was upsetting her Mum.

"She loves Hawkwind," Stacia says. "She's been to several of their gigs.

"Although she is happy for me to dance with them, she didn't like me being naked in front of all those people."

So now Stacia keeps her clothes on, which is a big relief for mum.

## NEW SINGLES

### THE ANGEL
### FLY HIGH

NEW group Angel are, on the face of it, a textbook example of what is known as hype. A prettily-packed, cleverly-marketed pop product. But one thing may cause the cynics to think twice before dismissing the group as just that.

'She is likely to release her first single, New York City Retch, later this year.'
Stacia in *The Sun*, 7 June 1974
(source: Doug Smith archive)

# *Hall Of The Mountain Grill*

Released 4 September 1974

*Label:*  United Artists

*Track listing:*  The Psychedelic Warlords (Disappear In Smoke)
(Brock) / Wind Of Change (Brock) / D-Rider
(Turner) / Web Weaver (Brock) / You'd Better
Believe It (Brock) / Hall Of The Mountain Grill
(House) / Lost Johnny (Kilmister/Farren) /
Goat Willow (Dettmar) / Paradox (Brock)

*Line-up:*  Dave Brock / Nik Turner / Del Dettmar / Simon
House / Lemmy / Simon King

*Recorded at:*  Olympic Studios and Edmonton Sundown (live
tracks, recorded 26 January 1974)

*Produced by:*  Hawkwind & Doug Bennett (& Roy Thomas Baker –
'YBBI' only)

Almost two years since the last studio album, and the buzzing klaxon-call that opens 'The Psychedelic Warlords (Disappear In Smoke)' is like a wiping clean of the slate. Except who still calls their music 'psychedelic' in 1974?[1] Maybe Hawkwind see themselves as standard bearers for the boundary-pushing experimentation that defined psychedelia at its best, unbowed warriors proudly declaring that the underground is still alive and kicking. Maybe they just think it sounds cool.

It doesn't so much charge the barricades as stealthily slink under the wire. Brock chops out a flurry of funky, tape-delayed chords, as a smoother sustained guitar eases against it like a cat arching its back. Lemmy slides in and King lays down a hypnotic mid-tempo beat, before Simon House's Mellotron creeps up on the song, an almost subliminal orchestral colouring. The sound is crisper and more direct – we're no longer hurtling at full pelt into the void, but cruising on high altitude thermals.

But there's still an undercurrent of unrest, an edge, and as the sound surges and swells, Brock delivers an unambiguously angry lyric: "*Sick of politicians, harassment and laws / All we do is get screwed up by other people's flaws.*" Always implicitly anti-authoritarian, always critical of straight society, this nevertheless feels newly militant. That opening couplet – plus a later reference to "*concrete jungles*" – feels like it's tapping directly into the political turbulence around them, and the tub-thumping chorus only reinforces this impression.

The instrumental section showcases the lush textures and deft musicality that House has brought to their sound, his Mellotron weaving airily against Lemmy's flanged, distorted bass, which seems to be belching in disgust. With its otherworldly arsenal of choirs and flutes, the Mellotron is a totem of the progressive rock scene – are Hawkwind now competing with Genesis and Yes? Even Turner's soloing recalls the type of sax breaks heard on recent Pink Floyd and King Crimson records.

Yet Hawkwind continue to shun prog's knotty time signatures and multi-part arrangements. They still prefer to dig into the rhythm, such that the skittering wah-wah, spare bass and phased cymbals of the extended outro could almost be a lost piece of classic rare groove – in fact, it bears more than a passing resemblance to Isaac Hayes' iconic *Shaft* soundtrack. It ends with the dull boom of an explosion, the concrete jungle being blown to pieces perhaps.

And then comes the wind to clear the dust away, nature's renewal after man's destruction. '**Wind Of Change**'[2] builds slowly and gracefully, first with organ, then Mellotron, then the wordless, cosmic voices of Hawkwind's proletarian choir. Lemmy's pendulum-like bass provides the anchor for House's violin to weave elegantly around. If its quasi-classical melody also hints at prog, it possesses a wide-eyed quality that stops it from becoming too lofty – though the spectre of Pink Floyd haunts the song, with nods to both 'A Saucerful Of Secrets' and 'Echoes'. After a dramatic climax, the lonely organ line remains, lowering us gently back to the ground.

'**D-Rider**' feels both expansive and intimate, the clipped reverb of guitar and twittering of synthetic birds suggesting a wide open space, even as the sound itself feels womb-like. The bass skips carefree, and Turner's innocent vocal matches his words: "*We're children playing in the sun / A sense of freedom on the run / We never knew what time it was / We just knew how sublime it was.*" There's an emotional clarity here that's unusual for Hawkwind, the song pregnant with yearning for a childhood that's irretrievably lost.

The chorus is like one long flashback, a vast memory palace filled with phasing celestial voices. Dramatic stabbed chords punctuate the second verse, but we keep returning to the amorphous kindergarten *kosmische* at its heart, Turner's oboe like an infant's melodica. It's a song that seems to slip in and out of focus, resisting interpretation as it floats off into the sky, lifted heavenwards by an army of birds. With wordless, devotional voices – human and Mellotronic – combining into abstract harmonies, it could almost be a precursor to 10cc's ethereal pop classic 'I'm Not In Love'.

Brock pulls out his trusty acoustic for '**Web Weaver**' and basically delivers a faster take on 'You Know You're Only Dreaming'. But in the background, a squall of electric guitar churns away uneasily, and his words are full of icy fatalism: "*A chord was struck that chilled the nerve... The voices pleading went unheard.*" But its brisk pace overcomes any morbidity, and when the band break into an uncomplicated canter, House's piano vamping pushes it towards the West Coast. It's as close as Hawkwind ever get to the rootsy country rock of Ladbroke Grove contemporaries Cochise and Quiver, and highlights by its absence their music's usual undertow of agitation and anxiety.

'**You'd Better Believe It**' is the first of the album's two 'live' tracks. There's another Martian call to prayer from Dettmar, then the familiar ascending chug in search of a groove. The King Beat kicks in and the crowd are on their feet for another upbeat number with a commanding vocal performance from Brock, while Lemmy delivers the chorus with the aggressive fervour of a radicalised starchild. After the trippiness of the verse ("*Now I'm just a cosmic man*"), such strong-arm tactics seem a bit incongruous, but the clue perhaps is in Brock's rejoinder: "*It's so easy to say*". Hippie rhetoric is all well and good, but it won't achieve anything on its own.

Sermon over, the track blossoms into a space-rock hoedown, House's bluegrass fiddle sawing in conjunction with Dettmar's radiophonic parps. This is a new colour to their sonic palette, suggesting the folk-and-countrified Grateful Dead, or images of Ken Kesey and his Merry Pranksters wending their way through the Midwest, preaching the Acid Gospel. Brock and Lemmy seem content to take a back seat, as House shifts to a more romantic style of playing, and Turner squeezes in some heraldic sax before the final verse. Yet while it ebbs and flows nicely, it misses *Space Ritual*'s zoned-out live attack.

'**Hall Of The Mountain Grill**' is Hawkwind's first title track, and pretty much a solo turn from House. It's the second of three instrumentals on the album, and if anything, even more prog-leaning than 'Wind Of Change'. It's quite different from what's gone before, but it's also rather wonderful, built around a rolling classical piano melody that pricks at the skin. The Mellotron's sweeping entrance is sublime, and pealing synth, keening violin and mysterious "*ha ha ha*" motif create a disquieting cinematic atmosphere. It's an elegant pocket symphony to moisten the eyes of even the hardiest Hells Angel, assuming they're not scratching their beard and wondering what's happened to the hog-revvin' space boogie of yore.

Well, here it is. '**Lost Johnny**' is the grungiest slab of biker rock that Hawkwind (or rather Lemmy, Dettmar and King) will ever record, an ode to excessive drug intake that sounds like a bleary-eyed comedown of gigantic proportions. The bass squelches like a warthog in a mudhole, the guitar oozes like treacle, the synth slithers like wet jelly. It's not pretty but it is very funny, with some startling imagery from Mick Farren: "*And here inside the waiting room, the radio still screams / And we're all taking Tuinal to murder our young dreams*".[3] It's like a wonky salute to the Ladbroke Grove underground: the truculent garage blues of the Pink Fairies, Edgar Broughton with a sore throat. Dank and swampy, though not without a grimy charm, it's what Hawkwind sound like when they're running on fumes.

Then just to disorientate the listener further, '**Goat Willow**' is Dettmar's last hurrah, another proto-ambient/new age miniature that could almost come from Eno's *Another Green World*. There's a strange whistling drone, a short stretch of kalimba, then a soothing if incongruous conclusion with harpsichord and flute. There's no obvious connection between its components, but it functions perfectly well, a testament to Dettmar's interest in discreet but telling musical gestures.[4]

'**Paradox**', the second track from the Edmonton Sundown, ends the album, Brock's style of stun-guitar riffing so recognisable by now that this could only be Hawkwind. His vocal is heavily reverbed and the melody is sombre, the lyrics again lamenting our inability to divine what's really important in life: "*See the signs, they're always there / But you know you never care / You're always looking for another reason.*" There's a negativity to many of the words on *HOTMG*, but the elegant Mellotron and bobbing bass keeps our spirits up here.

But then the song shifts up a gear into an angry gallop, Brock the moody seer becoming pissed off agitator, railing, "*Always, always it's the same thing / Try it, try it, you just can't win!*" But he runs out of energy, and falls back on a dismal, fatalistic chant: "*Down, down, down, down you go.*" There's a rousing guitar solo, some melodramatic Mellotron, and a lovely piano-and-bass coda – yet I always come away from this track, and the album, feeling a little deflated.

1     Though its title and lyrics predate *HOTMG*, first appearing in the 1972 Space Ritual tour hand-out.

2     A politically charged expression, "wind of change" was most famously used by Harold Macmillan in a 1960 speech addressing African independence, and has been appropriated ever since. Perhaps it's a reference here to Hawkwind's change in direction, with the introduction of more traditional keyboard arrangements on this album. The song itself was composed as a soundtrack to Jonathan Smeeton's 'Tree & City' sequence of slides, a popular feature of the 70s live shows, in which a city grows up round a tree – the city ultimately crumbles, but the tree survives .

3     Tuinal was a popular recreational sedative at the time.

4     The kalimba is also known as a thumb piano. 'Goat Willow' was originally titled 'African Wild Piano', and featured an "unnamed six note steel-and-wood African instrument" (from 'Del Quits Hawkwind', *NME*, 29/6/74). Goat (or pussy) willow is a deciduous broadleaf tree.

# World Turned Upside Down Now

September–December 1974

Live 74 - Turner, guest percussionist Al Matthews, Stacia, Powell

Hawkwind's ability to sell albums is apparently undiminished – *HOTMG* peaks at 16 in the UK charts and reaches 110 in the US *Billboard* charts, a vindication perhaps of their recent focus on the American market.[1]

If the lyrics are less cosmic, Barney Bubbles' airbrushed depiction of a crashed Hawkship in a misty lagoon is their most on-the-nose science fictional sleeve image yet. It suggests various metaphors: the band as a broken-down craft, its mission at an end; or more hopefully, landfall has been achieved on a strange new world. This latter thought is supported by David Hardy's glorious back sleeve: an alien mountain range and river bathed in the light of a thousand stars.[2] The inner sleeve is more perfunctory – a photo-strip of the band sat on a climbing frame on one side, a picture of the Mountain Grill cafe on the other, above a verse (presumably by Calvert): *"...and in the grove, by gate and hill, midst merry throng and market clatter – stood the Hall of the Mountain Grill where table strain'd 'neath loaded platter* (from the Legend of Beenzon Toste)".

However, the prevailing critical wind is definitely not in their favour. *Melody Maker's* Geoff Brown praises House, but deplores Brock's "simplistic, chunky chording" and "lumpy writing style" – he's nevertheless duty-bound to admit their popularity, and that they're essentially operating in a field of one.[a] *NME's* Charles Shaar Murray is equally dismissive, criticising the band for its "persistent habit of bashing their riffs around for several minutes on end with no appreciable textural variation," though he admits "a sneaking fondness for this album."[b]

Yet reviews such as these miss what Hawkwind are essentially about. Their psychedelic space punk of "simplistic, chunky chording" and "bashing their riffs around for several minutes on end" functions as an antidote to the enervating bombast of the trad rock dinosaurs and the pseudo-classical fripperies of the prog crowd. More tellingly, Hawkwind are a nagging reminder of a countercultural outlook that many writers are keen to move on from and/or discredit as a failed experiment. And while, for instance, the press are happy to eulogise the primitive ramalama and drug-hip lyrics of the Bowie-endorsed Velvet Underground, Hawkwind's 'low culture' sci-fi nihilism brings out the snob in them.

But there's a younger generation of fans emerging who enjoy noise and repetition, and are tired of being told what to like by the 'serious music' brigade...

▾          ▾          ▾

By the time of the album's release, the band have already embarked on their third US tour in 12 months. The mood is more upbeat, and various members express their satisfaction with *HOTMG's* sound and musical development. And the crowds are getting bigger – Doug Smith tells *Melody Maker* that ticket sales for Milwaukee's Riverside Theatre have doubled on their previous visit from 2,000 to 4,000.[3] But there's a serious stick in the works after their show at the Civic Center in Hammond – the band are surrounded by police and served by IRS officers with an $8,000 tax bill owing from their last visit. Unable to immediately pay, their equipment is impounded and the band are effectively placed under house arrest in their hotel.

They take a break while the problem is sorted out, but back in Britain the story blows up, with excitable headlines about the band being thrown in jail. In *Sounds*, Geoff Barton jokes about "hearing what seemed to be hour-by-hour bulletins about the band's welfare on some radio stations",[c] but this level of coverage – from music press to tabloids such as *The Daily Mirror* – is indicative both of Hawkwind's totemic status and their ability to sell papers. The band downplay the incident and resume the tour in October.

The UK press still doesn't understand their US appeal. Interviewing Simon House, *Melody Maker's* Allan Jones cites their "eccentricity and inspired amateurism" as surely a "peculiarly English phenomenon." House merely observes that, "We always seem to go down best in heavily industrialised areas." He suggests the Midwest is "like the north of England, it's a very oppressive heavy environment. I suppose Hawkwind are a very dramatic escape, in both visual and audio terms."[d]

Mick Farren's evocative report from the final gig of the US tour at New York's Academy of Music seems to confirm this – unlike the capacity crowds in the Midwest, it's only two thirds full. Those attending are "older, less enthusiastic and far more solemn than the frenzied kids who flock to see Hawkwind at the Chicago Auditorium or the Detroit Palace" – they're "more like a Pink Floyd audience," he concludes. But he's impressed by the band's performance, constant touring having turned them into "a tight, efficient unit", with Lemmy "commanding the front of the stage and rocking with almost demonic energy." Alan Powell brings new interest and dynamics, and the "melodic top line" of Brock and House is "far in advance of anything they have done previously."[e4]

▾     ▾     ▾

On 23 November, Hawkwind make the *NME* front cover again – or at least three of its members do. Lemmy sits astride a chopper with Stacia riding pillion,[5] while Nik Turner looks on from inside a large Cadillac. In contrast to the inset picture above them – Paul McCartney in tartan, Rod Stewart in a leotard – all three wear black leather jackets and radiate rock & roll attitude.[f]

And all just to announce their now traditional winter tour, the band slogging their way around nearly every town and city in the UK, stretching from 10 December to the end of February.

<svg>≈≈≈≈≈≈≈≈≈≈≈≈≈≈≈≈≈≈≈≈≈≈≈≈≈≈≈≈≈≈≈≈≈≈≈≈≈≈≈≈≈≈≈≈≈≈≈≈≈≈≈≈≈≈</svg>

a     Geoff Brown, *Melody Maker*, 14/9/74

b     Charles Shaar Murray, *NME*, 7/9/74

c     'Impounded' – Geoff Barton, *Sounds*, 12/10/74

d     'House Of Keyboards' – Allan Jones, *Melody Maker*, 19/10/74

e     'The Regular 'Wind Miracle' – Mick Farren, *NME*, 30/11/74

f     'Hawkwind: 19 New Dates' – *NME*, 23/11/74

1     The first Hawkwind album to be released near simultaneously in the UK and America, *HOTMG* will be their highest charting record in the US.

2     Hawkwind had originally purchased a set of 36 35mm 'AstroArt' slides from Hardy via an advert in *NME*, which they used throughout the 70s to complement Liquid Len's light show and projections. Hardy would also produce a series of revolving panoramic slides for the band.

3     "Actually we lost between 2,000 and 3,000 dollars on that tour," Smith later admits, which rather contradicts the more upbeat picture he's keen to paint. The fact that Hawkwind toured America with 21 people may have had something to do with this ('How Hawkwind Fell Foul Of The Revenue Men' – Chris Charlesworth, *Melody Maker*, 28/09/74).

4     Of course, as co-writer of a track on *HOTMG*, Farren may not be entirely dispassionate.

5     Unhappy with this cover, Brock later describes Lemmy's identification with the Hells Angels as "a complete fantasy trip, man… It's what he'd like to be, but can't" ('Hawk-Lord Of The Manor' – Allan Jones, *Melody Maker*, 22/02/75).

**MUSICAL EXPRESS**

November 23, 1974     US 50c/Canada 35c     10p

FOUR-PAGE GUITAR BOOK

**P. Floyd roll into town...**
PAGES 22/23

**Queen Jethro Essex**
PAGES 5/6     PAGE 12     PAGE 15

**NME VIRGIN CRISIS TOUR**

**Now it's Paul and the Faces**
PAGE 15

# HAWKWIND:19 NEW DATES
FULL DETAILS PAGE 2

*Hot Choppers: NME roadtests the new-model Stacia*

Incident in Ladbroke Grove. NIK TURNER (in auto), LEMMY and STACIA. Pic: PENNIE SMITH.

Hot Chopper – 'NME roadtests the new-model Stacia'
NME, 23 November 1974

# Stacia Blake

Dancer
April 1971–August 1975

Stacia Blake circa 1974

**You first met Nik Turner at the 1970 Isle Of Wight festival?**
That's right. I'd ran away from home. Most people then headed up towards London, I headed to St Ives, where the artists and writers were. A bunch of us then hitchhiked to the [Isle Of Wight] ferry and went over. We were walking around outside the barriers of course, all spaced out, and I saw Nik and a friend. Nik had his silver paint on, and I thought, "He's interesting." The performer in me saw the performer in Nik. We got talking and he told me about the band playing in this inflatable tent. I didn't actually go, but he told me all about it.

[Then when] they played in Barnstaple, I went along, I think in October 1970. And I hitched down when they played the Flamingo Ballroom in Redruth [on 15 April 1971].

**How did you come to dance with them that night?**
I just asked Nik, "Can I get up and dance?" The band made some silly remark like, "Yes, if you take your clothes off and paint your body." I don't think they expected me to do it, but I did! I thought, 'OK, don't challenge me!' Don't forget, the women's lib thing was going on at the time.

**When your dancing is written about now, it's often described as provocative.**
I'm sure it was for some people. It was probably the first time a lot of young guys saw a woman without her clothes on! I was never treated with anything but respect by the people I met. Girls were a bit wary of me, and I don't think the women libbers liked me at all. I went to a few meetings and I wasn't very popular. They were burning their bras and cutting their hair, and some were becoming very anti-men. I thought, 'That's not what the whole movement is about, it's about equality.'

**You were coming from a similar place…**
Absolutely. You know, "Here I am, this is me, I'm a woman." I'm severely dyslexic, so I've always been very shy about speaking, very afraid to voice my opinion. And no one was interested in interviewing me about what I thought, so all I had was my art form, which was my body and mind. But I get a lot of abuse now for what I did in the 70s.

**Do you have any memories of dancing that first time?**
The feeling of total freedom is the over-riding memory of that first appearance. And it was the same whenever I danced. There wasn't a difference for me being in front of the band or being on stage with the band. I always gave the same amount of energy.

**At what point did you become an official member of the band?**
Not at that point. Obviously it was something I wanted to do, so I headed to London. I didn't really think, 'I'm going to be a part of this band,' but that's where [everything] was happening. I started doing gigs here and there and getting a few quid. I think we were playing somewhere near to Putney, and I said to Lemmy, "Look, I can't do this anymore, I can't keep a place to live." He spoke to the band, and from then on I was put on a wage.

**Was there any discussion about what your role should be?**
No, I was given total freedom, which was wonderful. Until the point that costumes came into play. We were playing up in Scotland, and there was a problem in Glasgow. I couldn't go on unless I wore nipple tassels. I said, "Fuck that, I'm not a stripper," and refused. After which Doug [Smith] suggested costumes, I think with the knowledge of the band.

**How much of your movement was pre-planned?**
The majority of the time it was spontaneous. 'The Robot' came into being with 'Silver Machine', but it could crop up at any point. A robot is given a pill and it suddenly becomes fluid and free, but then towards the end, the robotics start to take over again. That was from 1972.

**Did you adopt the 'Miss Stacia' persona when you got on the stage?**
It wasn't 'put on' – that would be like acting. I allowed the music to permeate me, it went through me like a channel.

**The music was like your canvas…**
Yes, that's a good way of putting it. And I was theirs. It came from both directions.

**Was there something you were trying to convey to the audience?**
Yes, it was more than just dancing. In photos you can see that I'm reaching out to people, trying to connect with them. I was very aware of people's faces, because I was in front of the lightshow line. Further back, you couldn't see faces properly, whereas I could. It's difficult to explain, but it was much more than dancing, and I would have liked to have gone further with it.

But being a woman in the music business at the time wasn't easy, and nor was being a dancer or performance artist, or being me. When we toured America, there must have been 20 guys including roadies and the lightshow. I was one woman on her own. It wasn't an easy time.

**Were you interested in what was happening in SF at that time?**
Not as much as the others. The science fiction was in the brain I think! Maybe not as consciously as the others, they would be more intellectual than I am.

Robert Calvert was very upfront about what he was doing…
He was an incredible person, a genius. The blurgh that goes on about his so-called illness really pisses me off. It's like Spike Milligan. They were manic depressives, bi-polar, but they were way ahead of their time. If they flipped out sometimes, it was because people didn't get them. Like a pressure cooker, now and then they'd explode. People talk too much about Bob's illness, rather than his genius.

You can only be heard on one Hawkwind album, the BBC live recording, doing the introductory 'Countdown' with Andy Dunkley…
I was absolutely terrified and I think you can hear it. Starting off OK, then going too fast.

Was it ever suggested you do vocals?
No. I was visual. And why would they think of it at that time? It was a totally different era. Everything had opened up more by [1989], when they had Bridget Wishart.

I wrote songs myself and recorded them on tape, and they obviously knew about it, but I stupidly took them to America with me, and left it on the plane along with my Stetson! I still have some of the songs, which are absolutely crap. There's one I still have on a piece of Hawkwind-headed paper, which is called 'Only If You Are'. I wrote it in Los Angeles, and it's about a musician who's no longer at the top of the game. The refrain is something like, "*They only want to know you if you're a star, only if you are.*"

I did backing vocals in Germany, on an album for a guy called Jan Ten Hoopen. The producer was called Frank Dostal, from The Rattles, who were like the German Beatles. He was trying to get this certain type of flow in this one number, and the normal backing girls couldn't get it, so his wife Mary – who had been in The Liverbirds, one of Brian Epstein's bands – suggested that I do it. I actually got paid for doing it!

What are your main thoughts when you look back on this part of your life?
I loved it, and I loved each and every one of them, with all their good and bad points. It was a wonderful and exciting time. It was very difficult when I was no longer with them.

Atco promo shot. L-R - Turner, Stacia, Powell, House, King, Brock, Lemmy
(source: Michael Scott collection)

# We're Tired Of Making Love

January–May 1975

In the first week of January, Hawkwind enter Olympic studios to record two songs for their next single, 'Kings Of Speed' – a co-write with Michael Moorcock[1] – and 'Motorhead'. The Drum Empire are pleased, particularly with the first of these. Powell tells *Sounds*: "It's very powerful – it's got two drums on it and it sounds fucking great. It's like a Phil Spector thing." King more accurately says, "It's the same as 'Silver Machine'. Well, near enough, anyway".[a]

Amid a flurry of music press front covers,[2] Hawkwind get back on the road again. In February, they play four shows in London in quick succession: the East Ham Granada Cinema, twice at the Hammersmith Odeon, and of course the Roundhouse. *Melody Maker* editor Ray Coleman's Hammersmith review contains a familiar dig at the audience's "grubby Afghan jackets and carefully dirtied-down sneakers," but makes an eye-catching assertion: "Their music sounds like good, solid punk rock to me." And the headline is 'Hawkwind: Punk Masculinity'.[b]

'Punk' is a term initially popularised by US writers such as Lester Bangs to describe a stripped-down, no frills approach to rock – and it's telling that Hawkwind are now being tagged this way. Coleman describes audience and band as "creating an intensely private event", and being "members of a secret society." In other words, the UK's biggest cult band, a gathering point for those still committed to the values of the underground, but also the crucible of a new type of anti-establishment feeling, as some in the audience prepare to cut their hair and embrace anarchy.

For Brock, it's like a war. After a show at the Birmingham Odeon, *Melody Maker's* Allan Jones describes him as shell-shocked, "an exhausted counterfeit of his dramatic space warrior stage persona." Touring has become a ceaseless military campaign – he's conflicted by their level of success, but also worries that they might have peaked. Like Turner before him, he's concerned about losing contact with the community that spawned them. Unlike Pink Floyd's middle class audience, who "sit there comfortably", Brock says, "ours is a predominantly working class audience, and we want to keep tickets as cheap as we possibly can. We want to get close to the audience."[c]

It's not a complete surprise then when the final British dates are cancelled. A spokesman explains that after two UK and three US tours in 12 months, everyone is physically and mentally shattered: "Matters came to a head at London Roundhouse last Sunday when about a thousand people who had been unable to get in tried to burn down the side entrances, and the police had to be called." Even Turner accepts there is no alternative. He apologises for the cancellation, but "there was no way the band could continue without time for a rest."[d]

▾     ▾     ▾

After time out to recuperate, they return to Rockfield to record the next album. While they're away, the new single is released on 7 March.[3]

**'Kings Of Speed'**'s opening salvo of guitar and drums has a buoyant, knees-up-down-the-local feel, which is apposite – while it climbs back on board the cosmic boogie train, it also taps into the South-East's burgeoning back-to-basics pub rock scene, of which recent support act Dr. Feelgood are one of the leading lights. But in comparison with their lean and angular R&B, Hawkwind sound decidedly shaggy, not helped by the cowbell that clunks away throughout. Still, House's eastern-ish synth and hoedown fiddle add interest, and while it appears to be a none-too-subtle celebration of drug-taking, it's actually the only Hawkwind track from the 70s that explicitly references Moorcock's Jerry Cornelius novels.

**'Motorhead'** on the other hand is exactly what it appears to be, a Lemmy-penned paean to amphetamine abuse, with rumbling bass line and Brock's glammy slash-and-burn guitar. This version of the song[4] feels curiously underpowered though, Lemmy's delivery caught between good-time rock & roll and the gruffer, more aggressive style he later adopts. It sometimes sounds as if he's trying to sing too many words at once – though that's arguably in keeping with the song's subject matter. Certainly it's one of rock's more bizarrely literate drug songs: "*Fourth day, five day marathon / We're moving like a parallelogram*".[5]

'Kings Of Speed' fails to set the charts alight. Speaking in April, King seems sanguine enough – "I didn't like the number anyway" – but gives an insight into how Hawkwind are becoming increasingly alienated by the mechanics of the music business: "We had to do a single to fulfil our record contract... People kept on saying to us that it had to have this, had to have that. In the end, the band didn't want to know."

He's more satisfied with the album, despite only having three and a half days to record at Rockfield, and three days to overdub and mix at Olympic. Why the rush? "We're soon to tour America. Atlantic, our recording company over there, needed an album to coincide with our visit".[e6]

▾       ▾       ▾

At the end of April, Hawkwind fly to the US, and begin their latest tour at St Louis' Ambassador Theatre. But this time, the campaign will lead to a rupture in their ranks which significantly alters the band's direction, and creates more cracks in the line-up further down the road.

The band is also in flux business-wise. 'Kings Of Speed' is the final release under their original contract, and Doug Smith is still trying to negotiate a better deal. With a stop-gap licensing deal struck with UA to cover its pressing and distribution, *Warrior On The Edge Of Time* is released on 9 May, just nine months after its predecessor.

〰〰〰〰〰〰〰〰〰〰〰〰〰〰〰〰〰〰〰〰〰〰〰〰〰〰〰〰〰〰〰〰〰〰〰〰〰〰〰〰〰〰〰

a       'No Change In The Wind' – Geoff Barton, *Sounds*, 1/75

b       'Hawkwind: Punk Masculinity' – Ray Coleman, *Melody Maker*, 15/2/75

c       'Hawk-Lord Of The Manor' – Allan Jones, *Melody Maker*, 22/2/75

d       'Hawkwind – Eight Gigs Called Off' – *NME*, 22/02/75

e       'Not A Single-Minded Band' – Geoff Barton, *Sounds*, 10/5/75

1       A version of 'Kings Of Speed' had already been demoed by Moorcock for possible inclusion on *The New Worlds Fair* – available on Esoteric's 2008 re-issue, it's faster and punkier than the Hawkwind take, and well worth seeking out.

2       They get two front covers on 18 January – Stacia writhing on the floor for *Melody Maker*, Turner in his frog outfit for *Sounds* – with a third for *Melody Maker* on 14 February, featuring both Stacia and Turner.

3       'Kings Of Speed' is issued in different picture sleeves in the UK, France and Germany.

4    A demo of 'Motorhead' with Brock on vocals from the January 1975 Olympic sessions is fuzzier and more ramshackle, but has an energy missing from the released version. And then of course there's the versions that Lemmy will record with his next band…

5    "Parallelogram" is possibly a reference to the shape of a speed wrap.

6    A one-off deal is struck with Atco (a division of Atlantic) for *Warrior*'s release in the US.

MUSIC IS THE MESSAGE

**sounds**

JANUARY 18, 1975    10p

**GIANT BOOST
FOR ROCK TV**

SEE PAGE THREE

## MOON

in Los Angeles.
Tales of the Who,
of wild nights
and broken
windows.
All is revealed.

## DE PAUL

...de presses de
people. So we
said when we
reviewed her LP,
but she still
speaks to us.

## MOTT

An appreciation,
a thankyou, an
epitaph...our
man pays tribute
to the
Saturday gigs.

## SLADE

are back—on
film for the
first time. Our
reviewer thinks
'Flame' betters
'Stardust'.

**BIGGEST-EVER TOUR AND
ALBUM FOR 10cc — P.2**

*Is it Genesis? A
Beatle in a mask?
Bowie gone mad?
Or the new Stone?*
... *perhaps none of these. See page 4*

**HAWKWIND DATES — P.4**

Nik/Frog, *Sounds*, 18 January 1975

# Melody Maker

JANUARY 18, 1975    12p weekly    USA 60 cents

# BEDSITTER GIANTS TOUR

## McTell, O'Sullivan hit the road

R ALPH McTELL and GILBERT O'SULLIVAN — two big heroes of bedsitter land — are both hitting the road for separate tours this Spring! And, for O'Sullivan, it will be his first British tour in two years.

McTell, who this week hit the number one spot in the MM singles chart with "Streets Of London", starts his tour at the end of next month.

But before the first concert, McTell will be releasing a new album — which includes a new version of "Streets Of London". The album, "Streets", will be available on January 30 and McTell has re-recorded his famous song which first appeared — on an album — six years ago.

The tour will start at Exeter University on February 22 and the concerts will continue at Plymouth Guildhall (23), Regal, Redruth, (24), Cardiff University (25), Nottingham University (26) and the New Theatre, Oxford (28).

A full schedule for March is being finalised.

And deb-set darling GILBERT O'SULLIVAN will be touring throughout Britain in March. The concert schedule will include a date at Croydon's Fairfield Halls early in the month and, altogether, 10 dates have been planned for the tour.

O'Sullivan last toured in Britain during 1973, although he appeared at the London Palladium last year. A new O'Sullivan single, "You Are You", is released this week.

## Elton's big soccer kick

E LTON JOHN, Superstar! One week it's sell-out concerts in New York, Los Angeles or the Houston Astrodome. And the next week it's . . . cabaret in Watford!

Yes, Watford. Elton is to play one night's cabaret at Baileys Club there on February 18. The gig is a testimonial benefit for Johnny Williams, a player with the Third Division football team, Watford. Elton is a director of the club.

The show, from 8 pm to 2 am, will feature Baileys resident band, a support cabaret act and Elton, who may persuade some of his star friends to appear.

Elton has already appeared on a number of shows for the club.

H AWKWIND will be appearing in Leeds next month — despite a ban imposed on the group after their last appearance in the city.

The band visit Leeds University on February 1 as part of their mammoth British tour.

" In 1973, the six-year-old daughter of dancer, Tony Carraba, appeared on stage with the group and, apparently, a student in the audience thought we were exploiting children and reported us to the police," says Paul Fenn, Hawkwind's agent.

" So the Students' Union put a ban on the group and, originally, refused to let us play there on this tour. After a lot of negotiations, however, they have lifted the ban."

New Hawkwind concerts are Leascliff, Folkestone, on February 22, Civic Hall, Guildford (23), Worthing Assembly Hall (24), Johnson Hall, Yeovil (28), Queensway Hall, Dunstable (March 2), Aberystwyth Great Hall (7), Afan Lido Sports Centre, Port Talbot (8), Halifax Civic Theatre (10) and Preston Guildhall (11).

A new Hawkwind single, " Kings Of Speed," will be released in April.

*Melody Maker* front cover, 18 January 1975
(source: Jim Skinner collection)

# *Warrior On The Edge Of Time*

Released 9 May 1975

*Label:*          United Artists (UK & Europe) / Atco (USA)

*Track listing:*  Assault And Battery (part 1) (Brock) / The Golden
                  Void (part 2) (Brock) / The Wizard Blew His Horn
                  (Moorcock/House/Powell/King) / Opa-Loka (Powell/
                  King) / The Demented Man (Brock) / Magnu (Brock)
                  / Standing At The Edge (Moorcock/House/Powell/
                  King) / Spiral Galaxy 28948 (House) / Warriors
                  (Moorcock/House/Powell/King) / Dying Seas
                  (Turner) / Kings Of Speed (Moorcock/Brock)

*Line-up:*        Dave Brock / Nik Turner / Michael Moorcock /
                  Simon House / Lemmy / Simon King / Alan Powell

*Recorded at:*    Rockfield Studios

*Produced by:*    Hawkwind

If *HOTMG* ended with the crashed Hawkship still struggling to fire its engines, *Warrior* blazes into life, instantly seizing the listener and transporting them to a place with an awe-inspiring view. The rippling, muscular bass and bold Mellotron chords that open '**Assault And Battery**' are a bracing reassertion of the band's indomitable spirit. The sabre-sharpening kiss of the hi-hats builds anticipation, then comes the dry thump of the drums and blackened drone of the guitar, and an eldritch army surges over the horizon…

Those opening bars evoke Moorcock's realm of order and chaos just perfectly. *Warrior* may not strictly be a concept album, but in terms of atmosphere, it's the only one to match *Space Ritual*'s sense of thematic cohesion. It's also sonically one of Hawkwind's most ambitious records, thanks largely to the free rein that Simon House has to embellish the music wherever possible. And the mix is a thing of blurry wonder, like a (J.M.W.) Turner painting in sound.[1] Compared to the impressionistic bombardment of the senses that Hawkwind have created here, the likes of Genesis and Yes seem very mannered indeed.

'Assault And Battery' is one of Hawkwind's best simulations of LSD's perceptual whoosh, its elements at once indistinct and startlingly present. Yet Brock's powerful vocal cuts through, very much captain of the ship as he confidently pushes at the edge of his range.[2] Perhaps the melody follows the song's chords a little too closely, perhaps the chorus doesn't quite flow properly, but there's a joyful insouciance here that carries the day. Even so, the instrumental interplay is the main event: the swirling Mellotron brushstrokes, Turner's nimble flute, what sounds like a distorted medieval psaltery, the clattering battle drums that feature throughout. Plus that outrageous phase of the mix three minutes in, like the tantalising opening of a gateway in space-time.

What follows is one of the most breath-catching moments in the Hawkwind catalogue. As the rhythm breaks down into a crash of cymbals and the Mellotron crests dramatically, a piercing electronic cry rends the air, saturating the sound field with a ringing intensity, and seguing seamlessly into '**The Golden Void**'. The pace slows to that of a majestic processional, Turner serenading the party with elegiac sax. Brock delivers one of his most defiantly affecting vocals, despairing: "*Is there something wrong with me? / I cannot hear, I cannot see.*" It's a simple line with a terrible directness, Lear on the brink of madness, cast out onto the blasted heath…

The rhythm section strikes up an intense, *bolero*-style tattoo as Brock calls down apocalyptic taunts: "*So you think the time has passed / The life you lead will always last.*" What's striking about this passage – and about much of their 70s output – is the sheer commitment to the music they're making. Taken in isolation, Brock's repeated, forlorn refrain ("*On the edge of time*") could feel over-egged, ridiculous even, but music and vocal combine to banish any such thoughts.[3] Sweeping into the final section, House coaxes sounds from his keyboards that belie the claim synths don't have soul, before a glorious Turner sax solo takes us into the fade over a blazing Mellotronic sunset.

'**The Wizard Blew His Horn**' is the first of *Warrior*'s spoken word pieces, a cold blast of dank air inspired by Moorcock's Eternal Champion novels. Lacking Calvert's power and precision, Moorcock's delivery swings between fey menace and camp hysteria – but these pieces for me are an essential part of the *Warrior* experience, retaining the uncanny charge they had when I first heard them as a pre-teen.

There's more to them than just the words. The atmospheric, discordant backing on 'Wizard' sounds like a Hammond organ being dredged up from a "*lake of tears*" as watchers on the shore flail at cymbals suspended from skeletal trees – avant-garde even by Hawkwind standards. And I still experience a frisson at "*The eagle laughed! / And the world grew black*!!" It takes me back to that feeling of nervous uncertainty: why would this man, this adult, lay himself so bare?

A surge and a whoosh, and we're free of the dead forest, soaring above the surf of an endless sea. '**Opa-Loka**' left me similarly confused as a child, because it didn't seem to be a proper song at all. Instead, it's the pulse of something alive, pure kinetic energy as art. With a minimal, metronomic bassline dominating the mix, it's also the most obvious intersection between Hawkwind's King Beat and Krautrock's *motorik*, both drummers playing as one for added oomph.[4]

For an apparently simple song, there's plenty of peripheral detail peeping out from behind its relentless propulsive backbone. Brock's wah-wah is a stone skipping through waves, Mellotron and flute drift and trill dreamily, there's even some Dettmar-esque squiggles. The effect is utterly hypnotic, and could go on for days.

But now there's the cry of gulls around a white clifftop building. Figures wander absently in its grounds – one of them is Brock, and he's got his busker's guitar with him. Despite its stark title, '**The Demented Man**'[5] is one of his loveliest acoustic-based songs, with a warm woodiness to its finger-picking and weathered resignation in his voice. Little scorchmarks of feedback burn into the song as the Mellotron looms like a faery carousel. It's a sympathetic and affecting portrayal of someone losing touch with sanity and the life they've known – perhaps a parent slipping into senility, or one of the underground's many acid casualties, a cosmic traveller who pushed out too far: "*Smiling faces watching me / Helping hands just wait and see, which way I'll go…*"

Night now, as wind and rain lash at the castle gates, and lightning startles the huddled guests in the banqueting hall. '**Magnu**' starts in classic Hammer horror style, Brock's stun-guitar riff scything through the sound effects, ready to slay the monster. The drums kick in, and the riff gains a purposeful spring in its step, the mystical fatalism and bombed-out paranoia of earlier albums left behind. Brock's in commanding voice again, a *Terminator*-style knight possessed by the spirit of the Eternal Champion, come in from the dark to kick some arse: "*Sunbeams are my shafts to kill / All men who dare imagine ill*".[6]

But it's the interplay between violin and sax that best conjures into life Moorcock's multiverse of fabulous beasts and magical weapons. There's a wonderful spiralling motif after the vocal bridge – and then House leaves Turner in the dust with a Stéphane Grappelli-type gypsy pirouette. It's impossible to catalogue all the sonic detail in this track: broad brushstrokes have given way to dense cross-hatching and embellishment, driven by House's wild flights of musicality.

As the battle rages, squalling guitar against banshee violin, it's like being trapped in a fever dream. An insidious whisper drills into the skull: "*Until we're diminished by the reign of night*". Brock's voice becomes ever more distorted and machine-like, as though the armour is absorbing the man.

If 'Wizard' made me uneasy as a child, '**Standing At The Edge**' completely terrified me, its bleak, pulsating chill evoking a purgatorial netherzone of lost souls condemned to live forever. Turner hams it up even more than Moorcock, but his petulant affront and self-pity is perfect. The tolling of a bell, the desolate cawing of crows: "*We're tired of making love.*" This is the final nail in the coffin of the hippie dream, calling time on the long 60s as the cold grip of the 70s takes hold. Trapped in a world of political stagnation and industrial crisis, it could be the next generation chanting "*Where is our joy? / Where is our hope? / Where is our fire?*" It's practically a rallying cry for punk.

House takes centre stage again on '**Spiral Galaxy 28948**',[7] the growling synth peals and lumbering bass like the approach of something large, Lovecraftian, and many-tentacled. Then the track bursts into life, switching up into jazzy 6/8 time – while Brock's swinging guitar and Powell's rolling drums hold it together, House has the time of his life with his armoury of keys. It's such a joyous sound: he's one of the great players of the 70s, and just as greatly under-acknowledged. Turner makes a telling contribution on flute, but what's fascinating is the way 'Spiral Galaxy' never resolves into a core melody, as though we're gazing at different facets of the same complex jewel.

'**Warriors**' is the final spoken word piece.[8] The Drum Empire provide the main backing, clattering and crashing behind Moorcock's Dalek-ised voice. The words are sly and self-aware – an excitable litany of ways to smite enemies simply concludes: "*They make us less than happy…*" It ends with House running amok through the BBC Radiophonic Workshop.

If the *Warrior* 'concept' seems to have run its course, think of the two remaining tracks as diverting postscripts. '**Dying Seas**' has a querulous bassline that's unsure whether to get funky or not – after a strong initial showing, Lemmy feels distinctly less present on this album. There's something slippery and ungraspable here, its aqueous sound and strange, mannered vocal like the plotting of servants under the stairs, the mangled syntax of the lyric reinforcing this impression: "*Past rotting hulks of culture drifting / Lost souls ghostly trawl nets* *lifting.*" House's impish violin is the highlight, and it churlishly fades out just as Turner's sax gets into its stride.

Released two months before as a standalone single, '**Kings Of Speed**' really does feel tacked on. Biker rock boogie *in extremis*, it's the first of several similar-sounding singles over the rest of the 70s, perhaps a bid to grab a piece of Status Quo's chart action. But incongruous as it is musically, there is a lyrical link to the core theme: Moorcock references "*Mr C*" – which is to say Jerry Cornelius, one of his many Eternal Champions, and a poster-boy for the SF New Wave. With prominent cowbell and bluegrass fiddle, it's good shambling fun – and also makes *Warrior* the first Hawkwind album since their debut that doesn't end on a colossal downer.

◇◇◇◇◇◇◇◇◇◇◇◇◇◇◇◇◇◇◇◇◇◇◇◇◇◇◇◇◇◇◇◇◇◇◇◇◇◇◇◇◇◇◇◇◇◇◇◇◇◇◇◇◇◇◇◇◇◇◇◇◇◇

1   Not everybody agrees with this assessment. Speaking to the author, Alan Powell called the recording and mix "Awful! How can anyone actually listen to that?" Steven Wilson's remix of the album (on the 2013 Atomhenge reissue) is cleaner, yet removing the muck and murk also robs it of its strange shape-shifting magic.

2   The opening verse ("*Lives of great men*") is a straight lift from 'A Psalm Of Life' by Henry Wadsworth Longfellow, best known for his epic poems 'Paul Revere's Ride' and 'The Song of Hiawatha'.

3   Brock's no-nonsense, no-messing persona is what makes his vocal delivery on this and other fantastical songs so convincing.

4   Bass on 'Opa-Loka' is played by Brock rather than Lemmy, who had fallen asleep/passed out at the time of recording.

5   While it's listed as 'The Demented Man' on the inner sleeve, the label calls it 'The Demented King', which harks back to the Lear-like mental desolation of 'The Golden Void'.

6   These words are adapted from Percy Shelley's 'Hymn Of Apollo', while the song's opening verse is a direct lift from the Slavic fairy tale 'The History of Prince Slugobyl; Or, The Invisible Knight', as written by Alexander Chodsko and translated by Emily J. Harding.

7   28948 is nearly, but not quite, House's date of birth. He was actually born on 29 August 1948 – which means that the High Tide gig at All Saints Hall gatecrashed by Group X was also House's 21st birthday.

8   Parts of it are adapted directly from Moorcock's 1970 novel *The Eternal Champion*.

# We're Tired Of Making Love

May–December 1975

Hawkwind in the studio, possibly Olympic, 1975. L-R - Powell, Brock, King, House
(source: Doug Smith archive)

Peaking at number 13 in the UK charts, *Warrior* is the highest placed of Hawkwind's studio albums, and the last to feature on the US *Billboard* chart, at 150. Not only does it confirm Hawkwind's ongoing popularity, it also consolidates and reinforces their position as musical flagbearers of a thriving science fantasy subculture.

Ever since J.R.R. Tolkien's *Lord Of The Rings* became required reading for heads everywhere, the counterculture has been drawn to both the imagery and philosophy of fantasy literature[1] – its portrayal of alternative societies locked in battle with the forces of darkness chimes with a new generation banging its head against the strictures of the straight world. The likes of Led Zeppelin may have amped up Tolkien's romantic, 'mystic macho' vibe, but Hawkwind are drawn to Moorcock's more nuanced treatment of order and chaos.[2]

The sleeve is another fantastical construction, a gatefold with two further curved fold-down die-cut panels inside. On the front, a knight in silhouette is poised on the right of two opposing, not-quite-symmetrical cliffs, contemplating the abyss below. The sky is a sickly yellow and black, with a pair of pink suns under heavy clouds. From a distance, the composition resembles a malevolent, elongated skull.[3] But reverse the sleeve, and it opens up into an impressive Shield of Chaos.

Concept and art direction are credited to Comte Pierre D'Auvergne and Eddie Brash, aka UA's in-house designer Pierre Tubbs and Barney Bubbles, whose wood-cut style illustrations on the inner sleeve transform the Hawkship into a swan-necked longboat. It's a striking, if slightly garish, package, with Nik Turner in particular having envisaged a more allusive sleeve than the final, decidedly on-the-nose product.[4]

Predictably, certain critics can't wait to put the boot in. *Melody Maker*'s Allan Jones, a man seemingly condemned to write about a group he has little time for, criticises its "sweeping synthesiser passages contrasting ethereal space with the violence of monotonous bass and rhythm guitar", inadvertently nailing Hawkwind's appeal. He makes concessions about the album being their most professional yet with improved musicianship, but the main thrust of Jones' antipathy is that he simply doesn't like the *idea* of Hawkwind – they're not what he thinks a rock band should be.[a] Critics have never really 'got' the band – but the tone is now changing, from bemusement to something approaching anger.[5]

The partisan Geoff Barton at *Sounds* is more positive – but even he feels the need to defend "their extra-terrestrial meanderings, their out-of-date hippy ideals". House is singled out for praise and the expanded sonic palette is "mature and varied". Yet Barton concludes, "Even the band's publicist admits that you can't really expect too many people to enjoy the band's albums."[b] Presumably said publicist was given their marching orders soon after.

▾　　▾　　▾

May also sees the release of *The New Worlds Fair*, Michael Moorcock's concept album with his once fictional, now real band The Deep Fix,[6] which features singer-guitarists Steve Gilmore and Graham Charnock. Before becoming a writer, Moorcock had been a Woodie Guthrie-style folk-blues singer/guitarist on Soho's coffee bar circuit in the late 50s, so the idea of him doing a record isn't completely fanciful. And with various Hawkwind members involved, it's no doubt viewed as a reasonable investment by UA.[7]

With a rough concept of a dystopian funfair haunted by teenage delinquents, this is a much more traditional rock & roll affair than Hawkwind, and some of its stylistic quirks – such as Moorcock's hectoring, operatic singing voice – take a little getting used to. Songwriting is shared equally between Moorcock, Gilmore ("a lean eager-looking youth with fair hair and elastoplast reinforced glasses,"[c]) and Charnock (who had written for *New Worlds*, and would subsequently help to edit the magazine).

Of the Moorcock compositions, **'Fair Dealer'** and **'Sixteen Year Old Doom'** are the highlights, the former a West Coast-style ballad with nice wandering bass and folky violin from Simon House, the latter a slightly camp piece of glam boogie. Charnock's contributions include the Lou Reed-ish **'You're A Hero'** and the slow-burning anthem **'In The Name Of Rock & Roll'**. But Gilmore's songs are the most accomplished, from the Stooges-lite garage pop of **'Octopus'** to the gothic melodrama of **'Ferris Wheel'**, featuring House on mournful Mellotron, and his old High Tide bandmate Pete Pavli on cello. Also notable is the Stonesy country rock of **'Song For Marlene'**, a co-write between Gilmore and the soon-to-be-acclaimed Sam Shepard (playwright, actor, and one-time drummer with The Holy Modal Rounders).

It comes in a colourful Bubbles sleeve – a homage to EC Comics' *Tales From The Crypt* on the front, a post-apocalyptic fairground on the back – but the fact remains that, despite having the right space rock connections, much of *The New Worlds Fair* is exactly the type of *Old Grey Whistle Test*-style music that Hawkwind continue to be an antidote to. The press dismiss it and it becomes a collectable curio, leaving Moorcock entirely disillusioned: "I've worked with book publishers, magazines, film companies and record companies. Record companies are unquestionably the worst".[d8]

▾　　▾　　▾

While UK fans mull over these releases, a drama is unfolding overseas. On 11 May, crossing from the US into Canada, the band are stopped and searched. As a long-haired rock band with a reputation for narcotic indulgence, this is an entirely common occurrence and they're used to ensuring that all vehicles and personnel are drug-free. But this time, their luck runs out: Lemmy is found in possession of two grams of white powder. Believing it's cocaine, the border police arrest him and cart him off to jail. The rest of the band make it into Canada and apply for

Lemmy's bail. But they have a gig in Toronto scheduled the next day, and Dave Brock instructs Doug Smith back in London to put **Paul Rudolph** on the first plane over.

The charges against Lemmy are dropped when the powder proves to be speed rather than coke, and he arrives in time to play the show. But at a band meeting afterwards, Lemmy is sacked. His arrest is the final straw, grievances having built against him due to his constant lateness and continued enthusiasm for amphetamines. "They must have wanted me out," Lemmy surmises glumly. He claims that Turner declared he'd leave if Lemmy returned, though Brock does ask him back – but by then, Rudolph has taken his place, and Lemmy has decided to form his own band instead.[e9]

Lemmy's departure is arguably the most significant personnel change to occur within the band so far. A firm favourite with both fans and media, and a defining presence during Hawkwind's rapid ascent from the underground, his playing has had a profound effect on the group's sound, injecting both rhythmic drive and unexpected melody. If not the heart and soul of Hawkwind, he's certainly been their guts, the low-end throb that Brock has relied upon to provide a flexible backbone during passages of improvisation. And for many, he's forever the guy who sang 'Silver Machine' and encapsulates the band's anarchic outlaw spirit.

But there's little time to worry about the ramifications of this change. As soon as they're back from America, they're off on their most extensive European tour yet, as part of a package with Gong, Man and Henry Cow, which takes up all of June. It culminates in a chaotic gig in Paris at La Gare de la Bastille attended by over 8,000 people – a tear gas canister explodes during Man's set which leads to a near-riot inside the venue and a brutal crack-down by the French security force.

▾    ▾    ▾

On 25 July, Hawkwind begin 'The Mind Journey', a series of UK dates leading up to a headline slot at the Reading Festival on 22 August, which turns out to be another watershed event for the band – it's not only the last time Stacia performs with them, but features a guest appearance from Robert Calvert, who quickly makes his presence felt as an augur of things to come.[10]

The following day, they get back in touch with their countercultural roots at a disused airfield outside Swindon for the Watchfield Free Festival, a Government-endorsed replacement for the Windsor Free Festival, after the previous year's event

Dave Brock

Nik Turner

Polaroids taken during 'The 1999 Party' US tour, March 1974
(source: Doug Smith archive)

Lemmy

Simon King

Del Dettmar

Andy Dunkley

Dettmar, Dunkley and Steve (sound engineer)

Dettmar and Steve

Bob Batty (backline and crew chief) and Alex 'Higgy' Higgins (road manager) - note the Starfighter and Princess Anne wedding t-shirts

Barbara Scott, United Artists US press officer - these t-shirts could be bought from Hawkwind's merchandise stand

Turner

Lemmy

Brock and Lemmy, somewhere in Kansas - Brock's horse was called Dynamite...

Lensman John Lee, Simon House, King and Jonathan Smeeton at Disneyland LA

Postcards home - Brock, Turner and Smeeton

had descended into a pitched battle between police and attendees. Despite poor organisation, inclement weather, and lacking King and House, Hawkwind deliver a set that recalls the looser improvisations of their earlier days. Their dense, trance-like repetition might perplex the press, but their set delivers music of consolation and defiance for the beleaguered festival audience.[11]

▾      ▾      ▾

In September, Robert Calvert releases his second solo record, *Lucky Leif And The Longships* – notable for being Brian Eno's first production job. Where *Lockheed*'s comedy came mainly from the skits, *Leif*'s comes from the music itself, which pastiches various genres. It's loosely based on the Icelandic saga of explorer Leif Erikson, who reputedly discovered America nearly 500 years before Columbus, naming it Vinland. Calvert imagines what might have happened if America had been colonised by Vikings instead of the Pilgrim Fathers.

With its leaden riff and brooding mid-tempo rhythm, '**Ship Of Fools**'[12] is more Black Sabbath than Hawkwind. Violent whooshes of synth mimic the wind and sea lashing Leif's vessel, the harsh North Atlantic an analogue for the unknown depths of space. There's a rousing, harmony-laden chorus (including Eno's distinctive voice, though he's unlisted as a performer), a piercing bluesy solo from Paul Rudolph and at the song's conclusion, Simon House's stately violin.

'**The Lay Of The Surfers**' is a brilliantly executed and very funny homage to the Californian sunshine pop of The Beach Boys, its perfect refrain "*I guess you could call us bar-bar-ians! Ba-ba-ba bar-bar-ians…*" '**Voyaging To Vinland**' begins as a parody of folk-rockers Steeleye Span (Eno again in the harmonies), but turns into a credible fusion of plainsong and urgent, shuffling beats – there's even some Robert Fripp-esque guitar in there.

'**Brave New World**' channels the mellow, West Coast vibes of Crosby, Stills & Nash; '**Magical Potion**' is twitchy Buddy Holly-style rock & roll; '**Moonshine In The Mountains**' is a jokey hillbilly hoedown. They're well-played and passably amusing, but they lack any satirical bite. '**Storm Chant Of The Skraelings**'[13] is more interesting, with vocal incantations over what sounds like an electric digeridoo, before a crushed, barely in tune guitar ramps up the feeling of ritual dislocation. Along with the tape collage '**Phase Locked Loop**', it's one of the few times where Eno's interest in voice and sound manipulation is evident.

'**Volstead O Vodeo Do**' is a jazzy, dubbed-up skank featuring Nik Turner on sax and a questionable white reggae vocal from Calvert, its title referring to the 1919 Volstead Act (which led to Prohibition in America). With references to Al Capone and "Chicago pianos",[14] it's the most obvious leftover from the "Jacobean gangster musical" that Calvert had mooted as his next work after *Lockheed*. The album ends in fine style, however, with '**Ragna Rock**',[15] an ascending horn-driven intro leading into the type of nervy funk rock that Eno will go on to explore both solo and with Talking Heads.

*Leif* is less well-received than *Lockheed*, the variation in musical styles being the chief criticism – Calvert tells *NME* this is missing the point, loftily citing playwright Peter Barnes' "magpie" approach to theatre as an influence. But he concedes the experiment may not have been entirely successful, before tetchily adding, "I'm not the Dick Emery of pop." But a deeper issue is that Calvert simply doesn't feel as manically present here as he did on *Lockheed*. Given their reputation as rock mavericks, it's ironic that Calvert and Eno seem to have had a civilising effect on each other, two intellectuals at play rather than a creative clash of egos.

But even as he claims a desire to pursue non-musical projects, it's his on/off involvement with Hawkwind that excites him the most. "I hated the weak impact of straight poetry, and realised that the only way to get through to people is through music… What I liked about Hawkwind is that they were experimenters you could understand."[f] It's no surprise then when he rejoins the band in time for their December tour of the UK.

▾     ▾     ▾

However, another member of the Hawkcrew has already departed. Dismayed by the removal of Lemmy, Doug Smith decides he's had enough of trying to sort out Hawkwind's internal wrangles and business affairs when they reject a further deal he's negotiated with United Artists.[16] He'll be back – but for many fans, this marks the point where the 'classic era' ends.

a     'Warriors Lose Kosmic Klash' – Allan Jones, *Melody Maker*, 10/5/75

b     Geoff Barton, *Sounds*, 5/75

c&d   'Deep Fix In A Deep Fix' – unknown writer, *NME*, 5/75 e   'The Trials Of Lemmy' – Tony Tyler, *NME*, 28/6/75

f   'Some Thoughts On The Underground From Hendon Cemetery' – Vivien Goldman, *NME*, 20/9/75

1   The Middle Earth club is an obvious example.

2   Moorcock has often criticised Tolkien's simplistic moral universe, most notably in a 1978 essay entitled 'Epic Pooh'.

3   Or ovaries and vagina, or cock and balls, depending on your perspective.

4   No Vikings and longboats are mentioned on *Warrior* – and none play a role in Moorcock's Eternal Champion series – so it's tempting to speculate these illustrations were originally mooted for Calvert's *Lucky Leif*. Press adverts for *Warrior* feature two ornately armoured warriors standing sentry-like, a modern cityscape behind them. The style is Jack Kirby-esque, so it's likely by Barney Bubbles. Was this the more allusive image that Turner preferred?

5   While often unvoiced, both class and age are factors in Hawkwind's critical reception. Already in their mid-thirties in 1975, Brock and Turner are literally "old hippies" – younger journalists wonder how they can still function, let alone produce top 20 LPs.

6   'The Deep Fix' was a Burroughs-esque experimental short story by Moorcock before becoming a band in *The Final Programme*, the first Jerry Cornelius novel.

7   The most prominent Hawkwind members on the album are House, King and Powell. Brock and Turner also make appearances, as does future Pink Floyd sideman Snowy White. Moorcock and The Deep Fix recorded a single – 'Dodgem Dude'/'Starcruiser' – ahead of the album, but it was rejected by UA. Moorcock subsequently liberated the tapes of this lost single from Doug Smith's office, and released it in 1980 on the Flicknife label.

8   Moorcock himself wasn't keen on how the album turned out. The rejected 'Dodgem Dude'/'Starcruiser' single has a noticeably tougher, less conservative sound, as does the unused demo of 'Kings Of Speed'. Speaking at the time, Moorcock admitted, "I think that perhaps we made too determined an effort not to include any heavy stuff. As a result the album is perhaps lacking a little in funk" ('Hawklord In A Deep Fix' – Steve Lake, *Melody Maker*, 10/5/75). More recently, he added, "There were problems with the production… There's scarcely a track I'm happy with" ('Michael Moorcock Interview' – Klemen Breznikar, *It's Psychedelic Baby*, April 2015).

9   The name Bastard having been nixed, Lemmy settles on Motörhead. On 20 July, a hastily assembled line-up – Kilmister plus ex-Pink Fairies guitarist Larry Wallis and drummer Lucas Fox – makes its debut at the Roundhouse, supporting Greenslade of all bands. Geoff Barton notes the "Adolf Hitler shouts and jack boot stomps" of the intro tape, and calls the set a "rather untogether blitzkrieg" (Geoff Barton, *Sounds*, 26/7/75).

10     Calvert was probably in high spirits, having recently won Capital Radio's 1975 Poetry Award for his poem 'Circle Line'.

11     Apparently still doing penance for crimes committed in a previous life, Allan Jones attends Watchfield: "Perversely, [Hawkwind] played a commendable set, obviously dispensing with their usual lighting effects, with Brock proving that he can get as psychedelic as any West Coast guitarist when he has the space. It was hopeless, though, to form any critical opinion. They played, and they revived the crowd who, by this time, seemed close to extinction" (Allan Jones, *Melody Maker*, 6/9/75). Part of this set subsequently appeared on one of Brock's semi-official early 80s *Weird Tapes* compilations, and more recently on the 2013 reissue of *Warrior*.

12     The expression 'ship of fools' originally comes from Plato's *Republic*, being an allegory for any political system or significant undertaking that is not managed by experts.

13     Skraelings was the Norse name for Native Americans.

14     A nickname for the Mafia-favoured Thompson sub-machine gun.

15     A deliberate misspelling of 'Ragnarök', the so-called 'Twilight of the Gods' of Norse end times.

16     Inevitably, the band considered Smith's departure their own decision, since they no longer wanted to work with UA. As King told *Sounds* the following year: "The management thing was tedious – there were no legal hassles, it just took a long time" ('Have The Hawks Become Doves... Or Just A Vision Of The Future That Went Wrong?' – Geoff Barton, *Sounds*, 20/3/76). For his own part, Smith concentrated on managing Motörhead instead.

# Doug Smith

Manager
1971–75 & 1978–80

Doug Smith, with Gilly (secretary) and Simon King
(source: Doug Smith archive)

**Were you aware of 'Group X' before that first appearance at the All Saints Hall in 1969?**
Oh no, they were a bunch of guys who drew up in a van. A couple of rehearsals and that was it! At the time, they didn't even have a drum kit. To be honest, they were a bunch of people who all enjoyed a similar drug. They walked in as we were setting up in the late afternoon and said, "Give us a go, mister!"

**What were your initial impressions?**
Hypnotic, repetitive, marijuana and acid played out in music. They didn't stop me in my tracks. But [John] Peel said to me, "I liked that, you should get involved."

They quickly built a profile…

They recorded 'Hurry On Sundown' in March 1970. By the time it was released in August, they'd done 40-50 gigs: Woolwich Poly, Tottenham Court Road Blarney Club, Wardour Street Temple, All Saints Hall obviously, places that were quite important. We also did Paris, a great festival but complete chaos, and they hung around places like Middle Earth, putting themselves about. The Isle Of Wight festival brought them to [wide] attention. *The Sunday Telegraph* did a big thing, and the band was featured in that, with a picture of Nik. And it all kicked off from there.

Did you have a business plan?

We thought we did! We learnt we didn't. It was basically hustling. We were very chaotic, totally into the whole band thing, and all part of the Notting Hill, *Frendz*, *IT* magazine scene. As success happened, you knew which way you were going to take it, and we eventually became more efficient.

Barney [Bubbles] and I planned far in advance. We realised if we kept the branding and image going all the time, you would benefit from it. Much as every bust was a pain in the arse, the publicity from it was milked. And if there was a story that was a bit of a myth, you wouldn't stop it. For example, everybody thought that Lemmy was the [band] leader, or heavily associated with the Hells Angels. Let the myth do the work.

'Silver Machine' was a major turning point…

I knew it was going to be a hit one night at a club in Wallington.[1] [It] just tore the place to pieces. They performed it at Greasy Truckers a couple of weeks later, and we took the backing track to Morgan Studios to see if we could do something with it. I was ostensibly producing it, though later on Dave decided he was "Dr Technical".

The 1973 Wembley Pool concert is Hawkwind's biggest headlining show in the UK...

There's a picture of me sitting behind these big Wenn speakers that we'd hired from Pink Floyd. We'd invited the head of United Artists in America to see us, and there's just this look on his face of, "Fucking hell, I can't believe I'm sitting here!" We'd been dubbed the poor man's rock & roll band, and it just proved a point, that's what I liked about it.

You then started to focus on the US market...

Greg Lewerke [international A&R for UA in America] fell in love with the band, and Barbara Scott the press officer got the same vibe, so off we went. However, prior to the tour, Miles Copeland – dangerous man! – said to Barbara, "I don't know how the hell they're going to get into America, they've had so many drug busts." So I got this panicked call from her, "Oh my God, we've booked this tour, done all the advertising, why didn't you think about this?" All this verbal down the phone. I just said, "We are coming," and slammed the phone down! Then I get a call from the Chicago promoter, pleading with me, "You've got to come, we've sold out." The Chicago Auditorium, 6,000 people.

How did US audiences react?

Oh, phenomenally. It was a complete surprise. None of the other gigs sold out, but the others all did 60-70%, LA nearer 90%. When we arrived in San Francisco, we were met by a convoy of cars and vans, Hawkwind posters all over, flags flying, and they drove us into the city, about 20-30 vehicles.

Was Lemmy's sacking in 1975 a mistake?

A terrible mistake. Not because he was the greatest player, but he was one of the major focal points on stage, and in the media. The media loved him. Dave was a little bit in the background, slightly coy. Getting rid of key actors is often the death of a band. I was staggered when it happened. The fact that he wasn't even busted and had made the gig should have counted for something, even if he'd been stupid to have something in his pocket. But Dave had called me up in the middle of the night. Nobody said anything to him, they let him do the gig. Then afterward they told him he was fired.

[Getting rid of] Stacia was also a bad move. She wasn't sacked, but they decided she was an expense they couldn't afford any more. I was saddened and surprised.

Why did you part company with them the first time?

I'd struck a deal with UA, because audience attendance was slacking off, and I thought, "We've got to come up with something that's a little bit more than a run-of-the-mill live show, we have to think of something new." I got them a year off, fully financed, roadies paid for, band paid for, they didn't have to work. They could do the odd live show or festival if they wanted to. A whole year, to develop a new stage show, new lighting plan. They had a meeting, and Simon House got on the phone and said, "We've decided we don't want to do that. Dave said we're a gigging band, and we should just carry on gigging." And I said, "Well, I can't help you then."

Why did the band leave UA?

We'd instigated an audit and discovered that there was an unaccounted amount of money. It was an accounting error. A simple mistake, a zero in the wrong column, but quite a lot of money. Alex their accountant and James their lawyer continued to pursue the situation after I'd left. They tried through [head of UA UK] Martin Davis to get it paid. They threatened to leave, and then they did.

You bump into them again on the flight to the US at the start of their ill-fated 1978 tour…

I saw them at the Bottom Line, and I just knew it was over. It's a really tiny room, a typical American bar-type place, all tables and chairs and jugs of beer. They were on a small stage, and there must have been a lot of anger – Calvert had a sword, sweeping it around in great swishes, and he must have missed Dave closely on four occasions! Simon [King] spent the next day hanging out with me and he wasn't very happy. They just knew they shouldn't be playing on this level. They were doing clubs.

Sure enough, by the middle of [the Charisma era], they'd broken up. Dave asked me down to Devon for a chat, and I agreed with Dave and Robert to see if we could put it all back together again. The motivation of the Hawklords was to break it back open again, and to a certain extent we did. They went back to being Hawkwind and started doing decent business again, though not like the early days of UA.

‹‹‹‹‹‹‹‹‹‹‹‹‹‹‹‹‹‹‹‹‹‹‹‹‹‹‹‹‹‹‹‹‹‹‹‹‹‹‹‹‹‹‹‹‹‹‹‹‹‹‹‹‹‹‹‹‹‹‹‹‹‹‹‹‹

1      Wallington Public Hall, 30 December 1971

# Existing In A Genre Of One

## Hawkwind In Context Of The Pre-Punk British Rock Scene

Hawkwind emerged from a brief golden period at the end of the 60s when the British underground was a glorious melting pot of styles and ideas. But it wasn't long before a number of broadly-defined genres begin to solidify and define the musical terrain of the 1970s. Yet Hawkwind never consciously aligned themselves with any particular genre, and instead created a sound and image that was unique to themselves. They existed in a sometimes beneficial, sometimes uneasy relationship with the British rock scene – however, there are certain attributes that they shared with its key players which are worth exploring.

## From Elitism To Nostalgia

'Progressive' was originally a catch-all term for any band that didn't conform to the three-minute verse-chorus-verse format of old, but by the turn of the 70s, **progressive rock** began to refer to a specific genre of music, one characterised by multi-part songs, oblique time signatures and lyrical imagery ranging from the portentous to the ludicrous. 'Prog' quickly became the standard-bearer for the new seriousness in rock, seeing itself as the classical music of the modern age, with operatic and sometimes jazz overtones. Key bands were King Crimson, Yes, Genesis, Emerson, Lake & Palmer and Van Der Graaf Generator – with Pink Floyd shanghaied as an honorary if not entirely willing member of the club.

Some of this music was genuinely ground-breaking, demonstrating how far rock as an art form had come. But in its themes and musicianship, it quickly came to represent a new type of elitism. Technical proficiency became a prerequisite for peer respect, audience adulation and record company interest. Hendrix and Clapton may have taken fretboard wizardry to a new level, but they remained in the tradition of the gifted showman-soloist. For the leading progressive groups, every player had to be a master of their instrument.

Less cerebral than prog, but similarly prone to windiness and pomposity, was the emerging **hard rock** scene. Based on power and velocity, this amplified update of the blues had been pioneered by Hendrix and Cream, but Led Zeppelin defined the emerging form. Dismissed as brash and unsophisticated by the British media, this wailing behemoth focused on breaking America instead, which they did with indecent haste. Heavier rock & roll for harsher times, their aggressive, pyrotechnic approach struck a deep and resounding chord with their audience.

Others quickly followed the harder/faster line. Deep Purple produced 1970's definitive proto-metal album *In Rock*, the Mount Rushmore parody on the sleeve perhaps not as tongue-in-cheek as it first appeared. Uriah Heep hit paydirt with a sound combining brutal thud with cod grandiosity. And Black Sabbath have a very strong claim on being the well-spring of *all* heavy metal – but like Hawkwind, Sabbath are perhaps best considered in a genre of one…

**Glam rock** was a fascinating if often bizarre amalgam of reheated Chuck Berry riffs, thumping drums and rabble-rousing vocals, performed mainly by long-in-the-tooth rockers dressed as space-age pimps. Kickstarted by Marc Bolan's T. Rex, the field was soon dominated by Slade, The Sweet, Gary Glitter and Mud, the competition to see who could appear in the most garish costume on *Top Of The Pops* obscuring how good the songs often were.

Glam might have been anathema to the more serious rock fan, but being fun, to-the-point and unafraid of melody, it was also popular, with Slade becoming the most successful singles band since The Beatles. And glam deconstructed rock to such an extent that it sometimes became accidentally innovative: the primal stomp of the Glitterbeat is every bit as minimal and effective as Neu!'s more feted *motorik*. Both David Bowie and Roxy Music were classified as glam during the early 70s, but soon broke free of genre constraints.

The 70s is the decade when the nostalgia industry really kicks into gear, the past not only referenced and asset-stripped by younger acts, but repackaged and reproduced to be consumed all over again. And here also began the notion of the 'rock canon', with acts like The Stones, The Who, Clapton, Paul McCartney and Rod Stewart seemingly installed forever in the public's affections, living off past triumphs and former glories, yet fuelled by the uneasy feeling that rock's imperial phase was already over. With their arena-sized shows, satin tour jackets and transatlantic affectations, they epitomised a sense of complacent indulgence that would ultimately fuel a new insurgency in rock.

## Occasional Intersections

Of course, this is a much-simplified picture of the British scene during the early to mid-70s. There were plenty of bands drawing influences from folk, country, R&B etc, while other acts navigated a path between styles and transcended genre conventions. Hawkwind were clearly in the latter camp, but let's look at how they occasionally intersect with the genres above.

Rock historians often try to force-fit Hawkwind into the progressive scene, despite the fact that, particularly pre-*HOTMG*, they sound nothing like how a prog band is 'meant' to sound. For a start, Hawkwind certainly never went to music school. Their entire philosophy is antithetical to the pursuit and celebration of virtuosity. They're fuzzy and diffuse, a murky throb of sound and light looming out of the darkness, whereas prog tends to be carefully delineated. And of course there's no sense of exclusivity or elitism – they are a 'people's band', with a minimum of artifice separating them from their fans. They cater for whoever wants to listen, not just for the tastes of a more educated audience.

But what they do share is a love of the fantastical, in terms of imagery and subject matter, and also of new technology – though in the early days, Hawkwind are more interested in synths as noise-making machinery, not for adding the pseudo-orchestral flourishes of the prog bands. Of course, this changes when Simon House joins the band and an undeniably proggy flavour starts to creep in, particularly in his extensive use of the Mellotron. Hawkwind are also not averse to stretching their songs out, though they much prefer to extrapolate on a single riff rather than create pocket symphonies.

Finally, there's the 'rock theatre' connection. While prog musicians were usually too busy watching their chops to don a flower suit, a handful did dress up – notably Peter Gabriel of Genesis, who pretty much invents this stereotype. It was via narrative-based songs and concept albums that prog bands really injected a sense of the theatrical into their music, which Hawkwind also do whenever Robert Calvert gets his hands on the controls. With his literary and performance art background, Calvert is a master storyteller both on record and onstage.

Given much of their output in the 80s, it's not that surprising that Hawkwind often get lumped in with hard rock as well. But how much sense did it make in the 70s? There was certainly a cross-over audience: the long-haired freaks, greasers and bikers attracted to guitar-heavy, maximum volume music. And the success of 'Silver Machine' catapulted them into the mainstream, its cosmic boogie aligning them firmly in the popular imagination with groups like Status Quo and the denim-and-leather brigade.

But again, there are significant differences. Compare, for instance, the riff to 'Smoke On The Water' with the ones that drive 'Brainstorm' or 'Born To Go' – while Deep Purple's is full of tension and sonic machismo, the Hawkwind riffs are relentlessly propulsive and fluid, cyclical chord patterns that dissolve identity rather than affirm it. When young fans came to a Hawkwind show after catching them on *Top Of The Pops*, what did they make of the poetry readings and atonal electronics that occupied the space where "Norwich, are you ready to rock & roll?!" would normally have been? No doubt many loved it, though probably just as many retreated in horror back to their copies of *Machine Head*.

And then there's the lyrics. Proto-metal is full of wicked women doing wrong by their hard-lovin' men. There's the occasional nod to fantasy, but it's meagre fare compared to Hawkwind's science-fiction universe. Hard rock escapism is about the pursuit of sex and having a good time all the time. By contrast, references to human relationships in Hawkwind songs are rare, and even when they do appear – 'Spirit Of The Age', 'Quark, Strangeness And Charm' etc – they're decidedly tongue-in-cheek. This sometimes fuelled the accusation that Hawkwind were out of touch with rock & roll's traditional imperatives – but it also meant they were one of the few bands that weren't reinforcing the inherent sexism of the times.

What about glam? Marc Bolan applied glitter to his face, and seeing the reaction it got, other bands followed suit. Yet Hawkwind were arguably ahead of the glam game – Nik Turner had already been identified by Jimi Hendrix as "the cat with the silver face" at the 1970 Isle Of Wight festival, and he regularly wore eyeliner and face paint onstage.[1]

The glam bands looked like they'd been beamed down from the sleazy back streets of some cartoon future world, paralleling Hawkwind's own conception of themselves as starfaring reprobates.[2] Turner adopted his 'Thunder Rider' persona onstage, his costumes painted with stars and flames, while Lemmy perfected a grimy biker chic look subtly offset with Nazi regalia.[3] And in the 'Silver Machine' promo, Stacia is a painted space-age priestess leading her faithful musicnauts in an obscure Bacchanalian ritual. As *Top Of The Pops* changed to reflect the new glam look, Hawkwind fitted right in – and to most pop fans, 'Silver Machine''s squiggly, whooshing intro and faux-naif chant-along words were of a piece with the other 'novelty' rock songs now regularly in the charts.

▼　　▼　　▼

Hawkwind weren't the only band operating between genre and their own sonic universe in the first half of the 70s. There are three artists in particular, among the most influential that Britain ever produced, whose music and image intersects with Hawkwind in intriguing ways. They are David Bowie, Roxy Music/Brian Eno, and Black Sabbath.

## David Bowie: Loving The Alien

Like Hawkwind, David Bowie's music is full of science fictional ideas and imagery. In fact, his entire persona during much of the decade is that of an androgynous alien far from home. 1969's 'Space Oddity', the song that first brought him to public attention, was a canny channelling of the zeitgeist, referencing both the previous year's *2001: A Space Odyssey* and the impending Apollo 11 moon mission. Major Tom is a square-jawed hero overcome by feelings of insignificance and alienation – "*Planet Earth is blue / And there's nothing I can do.*" He could be a character from *The Black Corridor*, echoing Moorcock's sentiments that the psychological effects of going into space might be more dangerous than NASA's technocrats could ever imagine. This conflicted, fatalistic perspective is also very Hawkwind.

In 'Memory Of A Free Festival', an array of fantastical craft descend to entertain the flower children. On *The Man Who Sold The World*, Bowie salutes the Ubermensch in 'The Supermen', while a computer created to oversee humanity goes berserk with boredom in 'Saviour Machine'. 'Oh! You Pretty Things' is about the "*coming race*" of the "*Homo Superior*" about to make us all redundant. And on *Ziggy Stardust*'s 'Five Years', the apocalypse is clearly flagged: "*News guy wept and told us, Earth was really dying.*"

Bowie's career had slumped after 'Space Oddity', but the upbeat 'Starman' revitalised it, its alien saviour telling us "*not to blow it, 'cause he knows it's all worthwhile*", evoking lingering countercultural visions of a golden people in the sky ready to rescue the world from itself.[4] Bowie too seemed like an exotic creature from the stars, and dangerously in touch with his feminine side – performing 'Starman' on *Top Of The Pops*, the singer casually draped his arm around guitarist Mick Ronson, a defining moment in both pop and LGBTQ history.

Less acknowledged is that the 'Silver Machine' promo appears for the first time on the following week's *TOTP*. For all the significance attached to Bowie's performance, surely just as many heads were turned by Stacia and Hawkwind in full flight, by this startling portal to the underground.

Bowie continued to write in a post-apocalyptic SF vein – 'Drive-In Saturday' on *Aladdin Sane*, much of *Diamond Dogs*. He even resurrected Major Tom as a junkie *"strung out in heaven's high"* on 'Ashes To Ashes'. Yet there are musical as well as thematic connections between Hawkwind and Bowie. Both were early fans of The Velvet Underground, but perhaps more interesting is the shared acknowledgement and influence of Krautrock on their music.

At a time when music from continental Europe is largely viewed by the press with either suspicion or derision, Hawkwind and Bowie are two of the very few British artists who contemporaneously take on board what Can, Amon Düül II, Neu!, Tangerine Dream and Kraftwerk are doing, though neither slavishly reproduce it.[5] Hawkwind assimilate the ecstatic rhythms and deliquescent instrumentation while Bowie is more interested in the streamlined propulsion and futuristic soundscapes, most evidently on *Low*: the precision-built groove of 'Sound And Vision', the ominous synth washes of 'Warszawa'.

And then there's the Simon House connection, his recruitment to Bowie's live band in 1978 precipitating Brock's decision to temporarily dissolve Hawkwind. Bowie knew House from his High Tide days, and there weren't that many 'rock violinists' to choose from – but was Bowie aware of what Hawkwind were doing at the time? Did *Quark*'s polished sound and streamlined arrangements pique his interest – the similarities between 'Station To Station' and 'Spirit Of The Age', for example, with their slow-building mechanistic intros? At the very least, both 'Damnation Alley' and 'Hassan I Sahba' were fine showcases for House's style of violin.

And given their shared taste for SF themes and theatrical performance, Bowie and Robert Calvert were likely aware of one another – even their vocal style is sometimes similar, Estuary English moulded into a mannered alien monotone.[6] It's also possible that the Calvert-era albums *Quark* and *25 Years On* were partly a response to Bowie's own reinvention as a Europhile modernist. Rather than jumping the new wave bandwagon, Hawkwind were listening to *Station To Station* and *Low*.[7]

## Roxy Music & Brian Eno: The Art School Dance

While Bowie was a lone pioneer synthesising the ideas of others, Roxy Music were the world's first post-modern band, knowingly referencing rock & roll's past while sounding as though they'd been beamed back from the distant future. Their hybrid sound mashed up everything from doowop and cocktail jazz to garage rock and avant-garde noise into a dramatic non-seamless whole, as though challenging the listener to reconcile the different musical parts.

Roxy dressed eye-catchingly – from galactic high commander to leopard-skin caveman – but unlike other glam acts, this was a very knowing engagement with style and artifice, part-fashion spread, part-art school prank. Bryan Ferry's lyrics constantly circle around themes of mutability, fascinated by how consumer society enables individuals to construct and remodel their own worlds and personas.[8]

One obvious parallel with Hawkwind is the presence in Roxy's early line-up of an avowed "non-musician". Brian Eno was fascinated by the disruptive, alchemical power of electronics, acting as sonic provocateur to Ferry's more measured calculations. Initially 'treating' instruments from the mixing desk via home-made loops and gadgets, he quickly moved on-stage to attack his patch-board Moog with as much panache as twiddling knobs allowed. Where DikMik and Dettmar's whooshes and howls complemented Hawkwind's music, Eno's interjections came with quote marks around them, a deliberately intrusive challenge to the listener. But their effect was similar, producing a strange, otherworldly vibe and acting as a signifier of non-human agency.

When Eno left Roxy for a solo career, an even more significant overlap takes place. His 1974 debut, *Here Come The Warm Jets*, features Simon King on drums and percussion and future Hawkwind member Paul Rudolph on bass and guitar.[9] Eno set out his vision of the studio as a "unique opportunity" to engineer unlikely collaborations: "Imagine trying to get Robert Fripp [of King Crimson] together with Simon King, the drummer of Hawkwind! The concept is ludicrous, neither would agree to it".[a] But of course, it did happen, most notably on the thrilling 'Baby's On Fire', though Eno's comment tellingly alludes to an implicit high culture/low culture divide between Hawkwind and prog.

Later that year, Eno would play synth and treat instruments on Calvert's solo debut *Captain Lockheed And The Starfighters*, and the following year he produced the follow-up, *Lucky Leif And The Longships*. Their relationship was perhaps surprisingly harmonious. As Calvert commented afterwards, "I still think Eno's the best producer I could possibly have had. The recording went like a dream. We did have some friendly arguments while we were working. Originally I wanted some dialogue sketches between the tracks, to help along the narrative. But Eno advised me that dialogue and humour don't really work on an LP".[b10]

Along with Hawkwind and Bowie, Eno was another of the small group of British musicians who openly admired Krautrock – he collaborated extensively with Cluster, and the roots of his ambient work can be traced back to Germany. Eno and Hawkwind cross over musically too: Del Dettmar's 'One Change' and 'Goat Willow' anticipate *Another Green World*, while Paul Rudolph's rubbery bass on 'The Aubergine That Ate Rangoon' and 'The Dream Of Isis' recalls his former employer's art-funk inclinations.

A number of Roxy tracks occupy the same zone of driving intensity as Hawkwind at full pelt, drummer Paul Thompson doing a fine version of the King Beat on tracks such as 'Editions Of You' and 'The Thrill Of It All'. And then there's 'Out Of The Blue', a spacey and allusive track which features the exact same chord progression as 'Assault And Battery'.

The quirky phrasing and robotic wobble of Ferry's distinctive voice is also sometimes similar to Calvert's. In a live review of Hawkwind from 1977, *NME*'s Monty Smith refers to Calvert singing 'Spirit Of The Age' in "his finest Ferry."[c] The following year, Smith's colleague Andy Gill describes '25 Years' as "the best Roxy Music track that Roxy Music never recorded" – when he refers to "the disparity in fashionability" between Hawkwind and newer bands playing in a similar style, Calvert observes, "the difference really is that we grew up with Bowie and Eno."[d]

## Black Sabbath: Subcultural Parallels

Where the paths of Bowie, Eno and Hawkwind actually overlap, the links with Black Sabbath are perhaps less obvious. But there are interesting musical and thematic similarities.

For many, Sabbath simply epitomise heavy metal: grinding, woe-heavy riffs; aggressive, wailing vocals; morbid subject matter. But Sabbath were an anomaly too. Many groups during the 70s made a living from passable impersonations of Zeppelin, Purple or Heep – but the combination of Ozzy Osbourne's terrified holler, Tony Iommi's mechanically intense guitar, Geezer Butler's image-packed, socially aware lyrics and Bill Ward's surprisingly jazzy drumming proved harder to replicate.

Sonically, Hawkwind and Sabbath both existed at the heavier end of the spectrum, and were both well versed in the effects of extreme noise on an audience. There are some musical parallels too – 'Paranoid' has a Hawkwind-like relentlessness, while 'Sweet Leaf' has the hypnotic slow-motion density of space rock.[11] Listen also to similarities in their playing style. Iommi lost his fingertips in an industrial accident, which led to Sabbath's dark, down-tuned sound, but also the machine-like precision of his fretwork.[12] Brock, with his similarly clipped stun-guitar style, is equally unafraid to let an unadorned and repetitive riff do the main work of a song, eschewing the bluesy fluidity other players favoured. And Geezer Butler – like Lemmy, a rhythm guitarist turned bass player – shadows Iommi's riffs for additional heft, producing a similarly single-minded "black nightmare" of noise.

However, the most important parallel is that both groups consciously adopted the themes and imagery of a literary subculture to advance their music and ethos. For Hawkwind, this was science fiction. For Sabbath, it's horror, with Iommi's deployment of the tritone (or 'Devil's interval') flying in the face of rock's 'good time groove'. Iommi's riffs created a sense of impending doom, while Butler raided the occult fiction of Dennis Wheatley and the gothic horror of Hammer Films as a springboard for their lyrics.

Yet rather than retreat into rock & roll cliché, Hawkwind and Sabbath both used genre tropes to confront the harsh realities of the present. 'War Pigs' highlights the class violence of the conflict in Vietnam, and the threat of nuclear war is explicitly referenced in 'Electric Funeral' and 'Children Of The Grave'. And 'Lord Of This World' echoes the same sentiments as 'Master Of The Universe', the human race having lost its moral compass: "*Your soul is ill but you will not find a cure.*"

And ironically, for all Sabbath's reputation as a 'Satanic rock' band, there's just as many science fiction as occult ideas in Butler's lyrics. 'Iron Man' features a tragic but vengeful figure who once "*travelled time for the future of mankind*", but now stands forgotten, while 'Planet Caravan' is an ecstatic journey through the stars. And 'Into The Void' is practically a compendium of early Hawkwind themes, describing the flight into space from a dying Earth: "*Freedom fighters sent out to the sun / Escape from brainwashed minds and pollution.*"

Science fiction and horror were both considered lowbrow genres at the time, unsophisticated and unworthy of serious consideration – and as a consequence, critics tended to assume the same of both Hawkwind and Sabbath. Their sound was felt to have a proletarian thuggishness, to lack finesse, to be as gauche as its subject matter. And when live shows and records proved to be a major draw, they were further condescended to – just like Hawkwind, Sabbath had to contend with the back-handed compliment of being labelled a "people's band".

▾     ▾     ▾

Hawkwind never achieved the same level of commercial and/or critical success as Bowie, Roxy and Sabbath. Yet while their idiosyncratic vision and determination to do things their own way stopped them from becoming part of the rock mainstream, the 'genre of one' they created went on to exert a considerable influence on music's future, from punk and industrial to rave and modern psychedelia.

◇◇◇◇◇◇◇◇◇◇◇◇◇◇◇◇◇◇◇◇◇◇◇◇◇◇◇◇◇◇◇◇◇◇◇◇◇◇◇◇◇◇◇◇◇◇◇◇◇◇◇◇◇◇◇◇◇◇◇◇◇◇◇◇◇◇◇◇◇◇

a       'Eno Creates New Frictions' – Kathy Miller, *Creem*, August 1973

b       'Some Thoughts On The Underground From Hendon Cemetery' – Vivien Goldman, *NME*, 20/9/75

c       'Still Riding The Time-Wind' – Monty Smith, *NME*, 21/5/77

d       'Hawklords: Leisure-Wear Of The Timelords' – Andy Gill, *NME*, 16/12/78

1       Interestingly, given his adventures with make-up, other members of Hawkwind have suggested that he was also flirting with bisexuality, in the form of a French boyfriend called Pierre. Turner has denied this interpretation, however.

2       On the first page of *Shock And Awe* (2016), his overview of the glam rock aesthetic, Simon Reynolds describes Marc Bolan as resembling "a war lord from outer space". Along with the drag aspect of glam, there was a genuinely transgressive element to it, with the Lurex sci-fi gear and android glitter presenting a break from grey reality.

3       And it was just a look – Lemmy was often at pains to point out that he was neither a biker nor a Nazi.

4       For example, Neil Young's hippie homily 'After The Goldrush': "*I dreamed I saw the silver space ships... The loading had begun / They were flying Mother Nature's silver seed to a new home in the sun.*"

5       Given Krautrock's subsequent influence on modern-day alternative music, it's striking how little it seemed to impact on British bands during the 70s. Only at the end of the decade did a generation come through prepared to cite Kraftwerk *et al* as an influence.

6       This is certainly true for Calvert. Adrian Shaw [interviewed by the author]: "Bob was somewhat jealous of David Bowie's fame, he thought he was every bit as creative..." The two had something in common personality-wise as well, with both capable of unhealthy obsessions: for Bowie, fascism and ritual magic; for Calvert, terrorism and techno-paranoia.

7    Reviewing a 1977 Hawkwind gig in Paris, *NME*'s Monty Smith notes that the prelude to the show is "Bowie's *Low* (both sides) blaring from the sound system" ('Still Riding The Time-Wind' – Monty Smith, *NME*, 21 May 1977).

8    Roxy's own mutability gave them the air of sci-fi dilettantes indulging in cosplay on the holodeck, as opposed to the proletariat grease monkeys of Hawkwind in the engine room.

9    King in particular makes his presence felt on album opener 'Needles In The Camel's Eye', his relentless thud driving the song's gleeful two chord thrash, which sounds like a sugar-rushing escapee from *Space Ritual*.

10    This final comment indicates that Eno wasn't always correct, given that *Lockheed* was the better and funnier of the two albums. The fact Calvert conceded this point shows how much he respected Eno's opinion.

11    Also of interest: the strange, electro-ambient interlude of 'FX' and the synth-driven paranoia of 'Who Are You?', both of which flag an experimental side to Sabbath at odds with their lumpen reputation.

12    Iommi and Brock both admired Belgian jazz guitarist Django Reinhardt, whose unique technique was also the result of an injury that effectively left him just three fingers to fret with.

Charisma promo shot. L-R - Rudolph, Calvert, King
(source: Robert Calvert archive)

# Maybe It Was Only An Hallucination

## January–August 1976

By the end of the previous year, Hawkwind had secured themselves new management in the shape of **Tony Howard** and **Jeff Dexter**. Howard heads Wizard Artists, which looks after Marc Bolan, and has strong links to Pink Floyd and their manager Steve O'Rourke. Dexter has been one of the underground's most in-demand DJs, and until recently headed up Implosion at the Roundhouse – he will become Hawkwind's de facto tour manager over the next couple of years.

Having extricated the band from UA, Howard and Dexter's next challenge is to get them a new record contract. Hawkwind are a top 20 act with a large and loyal following, but given their general antipathy towards the music business, they've acquired a reputation for being difficult to deal with. Weighing up the options,[1] they ultimately sign to Charisma Records.

As Hawkwind's music moves into more nuanced territory, Charisma is potentially a good fit. Alongside the classically-trained House, recent recruit Paul Rudolph is a versatile, naturally-gifted musician who brings another layer of sophistication to the band's sound – he also has a strong working relationship with Calvert, now firmly ensconced as Hawkwind's lead singer. Going forward, Calvert's witty and clever lyrics will become as much a focus of their music as Brock's riffs or House's sci-fi arabesques.

▾      ▾      ▾

In February, the band begin work on their next album at Roundhouse Studios. As is now customary, they produce themselves, though Pink Floyd's Dave Gilmour is also on hand, his involvement procured via Tony Howard – his only official credit will be to remix 'Kerb Crawler', but other tracks suggest his influence. The sessions are unusually collaborative, with the songwriting more evenly split than before. Not everybody's happy about this, with Brock's long-fomenting crisis of confidence seeing him lose control of overall creative direction. Brock also judges

Rudolph's musical chops to be superior to his own, with the bassist consequently playing much of the album's solo guitar.

In March, ahead of a short UK 'college tour', Hawkwind once again face the press, Calvert quickly establishing himself as spokesperson. In a *Sounds* article that refers to a "revitalised Hawkwind", Calvert re-pledges his allegiance: "I realised that I missed collaborating with Dave Brock. In the past, the most successful things either of us have done is when we're worked together... I feel very stimulated. I think I'm going to become England's answer to Iggy Pop, I really do, a *Raw Power* type Iggy..." Clearly a little over-excited, he adds, "I've been saved from the clutches of bourgeois limbo by Hawkwind, and I thank them for it".[a]

Despite a recent unrealised stage adaptation of *Dan Dare,*[2] Calvert wants to re-energise the theatrical side of the band's shows and music, and promote their intellectual credentials. To a sceptical *Melody Maker*, he says, "I think most of the members of this band are quite articulate and very intelligent people... We get letters from art lecturers, computer analysts, insurance people – grey-suited types".[b] Hawkwind is marketable, he believes: "I think we're at the beginning of a science fiction boom, rather like the spy boom we had a few years ago".[3c]

▾        ▾        ▾

Yet even as Calvert predicts the future, the past looms back into view. April sees the release of *Roadhawks*, their first – and best – compilation album, planned prior to their departure from UA. Brock himself is credited with compiling and editing the album at Olympic Studios the previous November, with the tracks segued into each other to create a unique spin on the best-of concept.[4]

His choices are revealing. Roughly in chronological order, it opens with two tracks from the debut. By 1976, '**Hurry On Sundown**' must have sounded positively archaic, but it's an evocative reminder of countercultural idealism. However, it slides into the flipside of the hippie dream with '**Paranoia pt.2**' (referred to as an 'excerpt' in the sleeve notes), its brutal repetition and wailing electronics like the ultimate bad trip.

The main attraction for prospective buyers is an unreleased live version of '**You Shouldn't Do That**', one of the encores from the Space Ritual tour recorded at the December 72 Liverpool Stadium gig. Looser and less monolithic than *Space Ritual* itself, it captures the band's onstage energy, the crowd clapping along to Brock's militantly flanged introductory riff. While the original is hypnotic and trance-like, this is a savage, headlong rush into oblivion that climaxes with a snarling (and uncredited) snippet of '**Seeing It As You Really Are**'. Ending with wild cries of pain or pleasure, it's a visceral performance that captures the ecstatic madness of an early 70s Hawkwind show.

After that, '**Silver Machine**' is light relief and comfortingly familiar. This is a remixed version of the original, though aside from the opening burblings being cut short, it's hard to discern any major differences. It's also the only time in the 70s that this iconic chartbuster features on a Hawkwind album. Side two opens with '**Urban Guerilla**', their other charting single. Following its withdrawal, this gives fans the chance to own it if they missed out first time around. An angry slice of two-chord skronk, it feels particularly timely given that the filth and fury of punk is just about to break.

The final three tracks are the album's most impressive piece of sequencing. The *Doremi* version of '**Space Is Deep**' remains a lovely piece of pastoral/celestial music – despite the heaviness of its concept, it feels hopeful for a new tomorrow. However, his feeling dissipates as soon as its meandering 12-string outro is shattered by the blast wave of '**Wind Of Change**'. The nebulous Mellotron chords still sound magnificent, while House's beautiful violin pushes the song onto a more progressive level. From its lulling coda of solitary organ, listeners are jolted out of their skins with a dramatic smash edit into '**The Golden Void**', its high opening synth note more piercing than ever. The *bolero* section remains startlingly intense and the denouement features perhaps Turner's best sax playing on a Hawkwind record.

Housed in a gatefold sleeve, *Roadhawks* is another desirable package. The front cover illustration by Bob Searles of a truck-cum-hearse with a grinning skull at the wheel (based on a previous illustration by Barney Bubbles) is also included as a poster, while the inner gatefold is dominated by a striking photograph of the band performing at the Brixton Sundown during the Space Ritual tour. There's even a sticker of the *Doremi* shield. Best-ofs are generally looked down on, but *Roadhawks* peaks at a respectable 34 in the charts.[5]

·        ▾        ▾        ▾

Another item that flies in the face of the band's desire to move on from the past is *The Time Of The Hawklords*, a sci-fi pulp novel published in June which features a fictionalised version of the band. Initially cooked up by Michael Moorcock, and prominently featuring his name on the cover, the book is actually written by *New Worlds* contributor Michael Butterworth. It's no great work of literature, but again positions the band as the ultimate heroes of the underground, defenders of the ragged remnants of the counterculture in a post-apocalyptic world devastated by the mysterious Death Generator. Hawkwind's music is the only force powerful enough to alleviate the bad vibes it produces, with the band seemingly doomed to play a never-ending set at the world's last free festival. (For more on the *Hawklords* novels, see p. 285 of 'Cosmic Dada Nihilismus!')

It does little to support Calvert's assertion that Hawkwind are now a more sophisticated proposition,[6] but it consolidates their links to Britain's science fiction subculture.

▾       ▾       ▾

A new single comes out in July. Musically, '**Kerb Crawler**' cleaves to the boogie rock template of 'Silver Machine' and 'Kings Of Speed', albeit with a cleaner, crunchier production. But the presentation is something else. The press ads are a particularly grubby take on the currently popular '50s revivalism of *American Graffiti* and *Happy Days*,[7] the band (minus Brock) leering from an open top Chevrolet Bel Air at two provocatively posed streetwalkers. The track itself is a paean to *Autocar/Fiesta*-style 70s manhood, with the lure of an "*eight-track stereo*" and "*leopard skin upholstery*" to entice any lady "*looking for a lift*" into the backseat.[8] As it gallops along, Rudolph's prodding tumescent bass and the female backing singers get Calvert so steamed up and breathless that he can barely get his words out – and the ejaculatory guitar-solo finishes him off altogether.[9]

If the A-side is a slightly salty surprise for the average Hawkwind fan, B-side '**Honky Dory**' flags another change in their sound. It's actually an excised section from 'Reefer Madness' which highlights House's Euro porn keys as Calvert murmurs about "*hashish*" and "*bananas*". Hardly slick, there's nevertheless a squelchy funkiness to it that suggests a move into looser territory.[10]

▾       ▾       ▾

The single's release coincides with a short West Country tour, including an appearance at the Cardiff Castle Music Festival on 24 July. Mick Farren is there for *NME*, and is full of praise for his ex-Deviants bandmate Paul Rudolph, particularly when he plays guitar, though his assessment of the band is less fulsome: "There's no doubt the new model is a good deal more sophisticated than any of the previous combinations… but the content above the rhythm is still a fairly limited blur."

Nevertheless, Farren provides the sharpest visual sketch of the band at this time, noting Turner's Long John Silver tricorn and Brock in WW1 aviator goggles, affecting "the debonair grace of the first man to swim the Atlantic". He's unconvinced by Calvert's vocals – a Lou Reed monotone that's mainly inaudible – but Farren's description of the frontman will go on to be much quoted: "In black leather jodhpurs, riding boots, head scarf and flying helmet, he comes on like a cross between Biggles and Lawrence of Arabia with definite S&M undertones."[d] Completing the image, Calvert menaces the audience with a dummy Sten gun.

The band's gig itinerary is noticeably lighter this year – Doug Smith would probably have had them on another US tour by now.[11] As it is, Cardiff is the last gig the band play before the release on 27 August of their new album, *Astounding Sounds, Amazing Music*.

<hr>

a 'Have The Hawks Become Doves… Or Just A Vision Of The Future That Went Wrong?' – Geoff Barton, *Sounds*, 20/3/76

b 'Wind Of Change' – unknown writer, *Melody Maker*, 20/3/76

c 'Hawklords Taking Care Of Business' – Gary Cooper, *Beat Instrumental*, 5/76

d Mick Farren, *NME*, 31/7/76

1 Calvert: "When we left United Artists, we nearly signed with CBS, and I'm very glad we didn't because, from what I saw of them, they seemed to sum up a whole side of the music business that talks in terms of 'product', almost like selling soap powder" ('Hawkwind's Space Rock – A New Songwriting Trend?' – Gary Cooper, *Beat Instrumental*, 11/76).

2 Calvert on the *Dan Dare* project: "I wrote a whole script for the thing. Very long, it had Digby being captured on Venus and being replaced by Harold Wilson, all zany things like that. Everyone was behind it, it was just a matter of tying everything up, legally. Unfortunately, someone else stepped in with an offer for the *Dan Dare* rights, bought them up, and left me high and dry" ('Have The Hawks Become Doves… Or Just A Vision Of The Future That Went Wrong?' – Geoff Barton, *Sounds*, 20/3/76).

3 With *Star Wars* just round the corner, Calvert is absolutely right. He subsequently expands on the prediction: "I've got a feeling that, in any sort of art, realism isn't going to tell you anything

today – it's not a real world we're living in, it's a science fiction one and rock will reflect that, if only because rock music is this generation's literature" ('Hawkwind's Space Rock – A New Songwriting Trend?' – Gary Cooper, *Beat Instrumental*, 11/76).

4   Label and back cover imply Brock has remixed the entire album, though maybe this just refers to the segues between tracks. Only 'Silver Machine' is explicitly listed as remixed, but there does seem to be a subtle polish to other tracks, particularly the final three. Subsequent single reissues of 'Silver Machine' will use this version.

5   Officially unavailable since the mid-80s, due to a rights issue over the inclusion of 'The Golden Void', *Roadhawks* was finally reissued by Atomhenge in April 2020.

6   Calvert himself had written similar fantastical tracts about Hawkwind only a few years before, though probably wouldn't have made the mistake of having both Lemmy and Paul Rudolph in the band at the same time. In fairness to Butterworth, Lemmy's sacking took place while he was writing the book, and it was perhaps thought expedient to retain his character given his popularity with the fans.

7   Indeed, the ad that runs in *Music Week* has the tagline "Fifties Rock With Seventies Sound Effects".

8   'Kerb Crawler' by feminist post-punks Au Pairs (the B-side of their 1979 debut single 'You') is possibly a critique of the Hawkwind song: "*He's outside in his silver machine / Cruising along, living his dreams*".

9   The irony of this excitable tribute to the modern motorcar? Calvert couldn't drive when he wrote it.

10  An extended version of 'Reefer Madness' which includes the 'Honky Dory' section was released in 2008 on *Spirit Of The Age – An Anthology 1976-1984* (Atomhenge). It's interesting to note that 'Honky Dory' is credited to every member of Hawkwind – Brock/Calvert/House/King/Powell/ Rudolph/Mandelkau (Hawkwind and Pink Fairies associate Jamie Mandelkau, standing in for Turner for publishing reasons) – but 'Reefer Madness' itself is just credited to Brock/Calvert.

11  Smith would surely also have insisted that Hawkwind product be available in the American market. As it is, *Astounding Sounds* fails to get a US release.

# *Astounding Sounds, Amazing Music*

Released 27 August 1976

| | |
|---|---|
| *Label:* | Charisma (UK & Europe — no US release) |
| *Track listing:* | Reefer Madness (Brock/Calvert) / Steppenwolf (Brock/Calvert) / City Of Lagoons (Powell) / The Aubergine That Ate Rangoon (Rudolph) / Kerb Crawler (Brock/Calvert) / Kadu Flyer (Turner/House)[1] / Chronoglide Skyway (House) |
| *Line-up:* | Dave Brock / Robert Calvert / Nik Turner / Simon House / Paul Rudolph / Simon King / Alan Powell |
| *Recorded at:* | Roundhouse Studios |
| *Produced by:* | Hawkwind |

Hawkwind songs all sound the same, the critics would endlessly insist. Yet their 70s output is defined by its sheer diversity of styles – it's hard to think of any other band whose sound shifted quite so much year-on-year during this period. There's a core aesthetic – Brock's choppy riffs are a constant and we're never far from that metronomic beat – but already they've delivered barbarian psychedelia, propulsive space rock, and widescreen Kraut-prog. However, for many fans, here is where the real schism in style begins…

'**Reefer Madness**' begins with the sound of a steam train approaching, its engine producing a lot of smoke… Brock cuts through the fug with a nervy, highly strung riff, but something's happened to his guitar tone. Moving on from simple distortion (and his beloved wah-wah), he favours a sound here that's scrunchy and almost 'wet'. It's quite a change, but its feverish hue works well in this context, amplifying the anxiety of Calvert's mock-guardian of propriety.

Calvert's arrival as lead singer has changed the music's dynamic: his double-tracked vocals take prominence in the centre of the stereo field in a cleaner and more conventional mix, all the better to hear his words. The rhythm also feels 'straighter': drums tight and dry, Rudolph's bass little more than a pulse under the beat. But it's a catchy, funny, clever song, with Calvert in his role-playing element, warning us that, "*Marijuana monster is stalking the streets.*" Calvert turns the tables on critics who regard Hawkwind as drug-addled freaks by referencing a swivel-eyed 30s propaganda film,[2] where teenagers become crazed delinquents after just a few puffs of the demon weed. House's *Keystone Kops* piano in the chorus evokes the moral panic and general lack of intelligent debate around the subject.

The instrumental section ups the ante with House and Turner's queasy approximation of jazz fusion, duelling on synth and sax while King and Powell lay down a strident, thumping beat. It's dense, but there's a lot more air in this jam than before, anticipating the punk funk sound of The Blockheads. Calvert has evidently inhaled, warbling in the background before accusing a mysterious eleventh finger of ripping off his stash. The android doom-mongering of old has been replaced by more measured absurdity.

Yet Calvert's still a literary man at heart. '**Steppenwolf**', the longest and most impressive track here, has a sophistication to its arrangement that must have nonplussed those fans hoping for another album of acid-drenched brain-blasters. Its title and inspiration come from Hermann Hesse's 1927 novel about man's battle to reconcile savagery and civilisation,[3] and the extended, evocative lyric brims with Calvert's delight at the poetry of words and the mechanics of rhyme. The way it unfurls and develops is rather wonderful, a theatrical performance for the ears that never feels flabby or flashy, the music perfectly complementing the narrative.

With its lush, midnight-hour looseness, this could almost be a Steely Dan track if it wasn't for Brock's angular riffing. Calvert's teasing opening line – "*You can see my eyes are lupine*" – beckons us to lean in and enjoy the tale he's about to spin. Rudolph's bass is less muscular and more rubbery than Lemmy's, but its "*loping walk and slinking spine*" are just perfect here. In general, the musicianship has gone up a notch or two. Even the reliably maverick Turner blows with more control, providing the main instrumental hook over a high-end rumble of bass.

But once again, it's House who enthrals the most, his ghostly, double-tracked violin in the breakdown transporting us to the moonlit back streets of Mitteleuropa.

Calvert wanders alone, musing on his dual nature: "*I am a man-wolf / Upright on two feet in the city / Dressed sombrely as a man.*" The story of *Steppenwolf* could be drawn from Calvert's own life, and the way he makes the narrative his own is rather magical.[4] There's no grand finale, just a gradual, dream-like dissolve with twinkling guitar, as the man-wolf slips away into the night.

In fact the fade is so lulling, it's a shock when the "*da-dum!*" of Powell's snare suddenly announces 'City Of Lagoons'.[5] But it's an interruption quickly forgotten, as this is even more beautifully soporific, like lying on your back in the blazing summer sun as Rudolph languidly plays delicate, slow-motion, Gilmour-esque guitar.[6] House adds woozy clavinet and spiralling synth, further enhancing its sleek, mellow vibe. It's *Wish You Were Here* without the existential crisis – though perhaps more provocatively for hardcore fans, it also sounds a lot like the laid-back jazz funk of Herbie Hancock and Grover Washington Jr.

If 'City Of Lagoons' elegantly gets away with its diversion into leftfield, 'The Aubergine That Ate Rangoon',[7] from its daft title onwards, is pushing its luck. It starts as an argument between Rudolph's insistent bass and Powell's reverbed snare drum, before a squelchy synth loop takes us into robot funk territory. And is that *Monty Python*'s Knights Who Say Ni on backing vocals? A nod perhaps to Eno's experimental playfulness, but it's a strangely aimless way to start side two.

'Kerb Crawler', by contrast, is a meaty riff with galloping bass and drums, not unlike Alice Cooper's similarly-themed 'Under My Wheels'. Calvert coos over the engine, before exclaiming: "*Mohair motorised wolf / Looking for lambs.*" He's clearly enjoying playing the role of a predatory car fetishist cruising for sex, but however much his tongue is in his cheek, lines such as "*high heels clicking like a pair of cloven hooves*" can't help but feel slightly anomalous – Hawkwind have always previously avoided such rock & roll clichés.

But the brassy female vocals in the chorus are nice, perhaps taking another cue from Pink Floyd. There's a great sliding, overdriven solo from Rudolph or Brock (or possibly both), Calvert slips in a reference to the "*Autobahn*", and Turner swings like an R&B revue player at the end. It's high-octane raunch, and more substantial than 'Kings Of Speed' – but when did the fantasy warriors of yore turn into sleazy guys in bad sports jackets?

The wind blusters, House bangs out an upbeat, synth-embroidered piano riff, and 'Kadu Flyer'[8] takes to the air on the back of an artfully *faux-naïf* melody. Turner winkingly references a "*different kind of trip*" and wanting to "*get high*", but it's actually a song about gliding in the Himalayas: "*Never fly through a cloud if there's a mountain in it.*" It's another quirky but compelling vocal performance from Turner – you have to applaud him and Calvert for steering clear of rock's transatlantic *lingua franca*. Both favour an adenoidal Estuary English, yet another mark of otherness in the prevailing scene.

When Brock turns up in the second chorus, it's like he's crashing someone else's party.[9] A promising minor key bridge after the vocals turns into a school band rendition of 'Tomorrow Never Knows'. It's as though the 60s has leaked back through time into Hawkwind's present – creaky sitar, Turner's snakecharmer sax. Even The Incredible String Band have by now called time on this kind of exoticism. It clanks and wails aimlessly for a couple of minutes, then fades out.

There's the sound of reality being stopped and rewound, and then '**Chronoglide Skyway**' brings a flotation-tank-and-scented-candles vibe. There's a distant Mellotron, vaporous synth lines, Turner's new age lounge muzak sax – everything putters pleasantly along. The best thing here is Rudolph's guitar, wringing maximum value out of a string of long, leisurely notes, but it all feels a bit insubstantial, particularly for a House composition, and the album peters out with a shrug.

*Astounding Sounds* may be the most stoner-friendly of Hawkwind's albums, but as Brock subsequently concludes, the ship is definitely drifting off course.

◇◇◇◇◇◇◇◇◇◇◇◇◇◇◇◇◇◇◇◇◇◇◇◇◇◇◇◇◇◇◇◇◇◇◇◇◇◇◇◇◇◇◇◇◇◇◇◇◇◇◇◇◇◇◇◇

1    On the original release, 'Kadu Flyer' is credited to Mandelkau/House (Mandelkau standing in for Turner) – Calvert's name was added to the credit for the re-issue, although it's hard to discern his input. The first release (and subsequent re-releases) also erroneously credits 'City Of Lagoons' to House and 'Chronoglide Skyway' to Powell.

2    An anti-drug education film re-cut as a lurid exploitation movie, *Reefer Madness* had the tagline "Women cry for it – men die for it!" It was popular on the 70s 'midnight movies' circuit, and Calvert likely saw it at an Electric Cinema showing or similar.

3    *Steppenwolf* was a popular countercultural novel – one man's struggle against the straight world etc – but the 1974 film adaptation (starring Max von Sydow and featuring trippy, psychedelic visuals and cartoon sequences) had also recently played in London's arthouse cinemas. Calvert's lyric predates the film, having first appeared on Adrian Wagner's 1974 album *Distances Between Us*. (Though it's possible Calvert was prompted to write the lyric after hearing the film was in production.)

4     The line he repeats at the song's climax is *"Und ich weiß nicht was ich sagen soll,"* which translates from German as *"And I don't know what I should say."*

5     The title is presumably a reference to Venice, sometimes called the city of lagoons. As with the album's other instrumentals, the track was named by Calvert.

6     Despite Gilmour's involvement with *Astounding Sounds*, Rudolph has confirmed that the solo is his. However, Rudolph maintains that Gilmour's influence on the album was greater than has previously been acknowledged.

7     The title alludes to 'The Eggplant That Ate Chicago', a 1967 novelty song by Dr West's Medicine Show & Junk Band, written by Norman Greenbaum (of 1970 chart hit 'Spirit In The Sky').

8     The title is a contraction of 'Kathmandu Flyer'. The capital of Nepal was a popular destination on the hippie trail, not least because marijuana and hashish were then sold legally via government-licensed shops.

9     Brock should perhaps have sat out altogether – but after the three instrumentals, that would have made it the fourth song he doesn't play on. No wonder he isn't keen on this record.

# Maybe It Was Only An Hallucination

August–December 1976

Charisma promo. L–R – House, Rudolph, Brock, King, Turner, Powell, Calvert
(source: Michael Scott collection)

Whether it's the band's relatively low visibility, a lack of promotion, or poor word-of-mouth, *Astounding Sounds* is the band's lowest placed original album since their non-charting debut, peaking outside the top 30 at 33.

Maybe it's just not a great time to be releasing such an opulent-sounding album: 1976 is the year the tide definitively turns against progressive music. While bad reviews have never really affected sales before, a change in tone is permeating the music press, a caustic impatience with the self-indulgence of rock's aristocracy, particularly at *NME*.[1] Band of the people they may be, but Hawkwind are in danger of finding themselves on the wrong side of a cultural divide.

Yet *Astounding Sounds* is by no means universally panned, with *NME* perversely giving it the thumbs up: "Hawkwind are back on form... their music has acquired about 15 new levels since the old churn-churn days".[a] *Sounds* is more ambivalent, as Pete Makowski wrestles with his own preconceptions: "Hawkwind to me represented a certain era in a certain state of mind. A group created through environmental rather than musical circumstances. They were never built to last but gradually they began to develop a professional attitude." He describes 'Kerb Crawler' as "'orrible", but praises the production and Calvert for the new direction and energy.[b]

The sleeve is another vibrant, if slightly confusing, Barney Bubbles design, its typography lifted wholesale from *Astounding Stories Of Super-Science*, one of the earliest US pulp SF magazines.[2] But instead of bug-eyed monsters and heroic spacemen, it features an illustration by Tony Hyde of an elegantly attired lady tuning into her Bakelite radio amid a fog of dope smoke.[3] The longer you look at it, the odder this image gets: menaced by the curling cannabis leaves of a rising sun, the woman could be an Edwardian medium using a combination of radio and narcotics to channel the spirits. In a completely different style (and by Bubbles himself), the back cover features an angular metallic eagle sat atop a monumental Hawkwind logo, lit in garish shades of red and orange. The striking resemblance to some piece of Nazi iconography is slightly uncomfortable.[4]

One source of confusion is the absence on the front of the band's name – indeed, early copies have the eagle side as the front cover. The inner sleeve features enjoyable parodies of the kinds of adverts found in the pages of the pulps: "develop a stronger, he-man voice!" by sending away to the "R. Calvert Perfect Voice Institute", purchase a "manly strap-on" from Paul Rudolph, order the latest in "sheer nylon" nightwear from "Monsieur Nik Turner". Whether there's any significance in "Doctor Brock's Atomic Pile Preparations" being the smallest ad on the sleeve is a moot point.

▾          ▾          ▾

In line with Calvert's vision of Hawkwind shows as "spontaneous theatre", new staging and lights are designed to complement rather than distract from the performers. As Jonathan Smeeton explains to *Sounds*, "We had to do something totally removed from the concept of projections onto one big screen, plus a million special effects".[c] The solution, 'Atomhenge', is a series of monolithic interlocking columns that mimic molecular structure, framing three separate projection screens: at 18 feet high by 40 feet wide, it's illuminated from within by over 2,000 light bulbs.[5] Calvert calls it a "temple of hallucinations erected by a hoard of skilled devotees armed with drills, screwdrivers and faith".[d6]

Low chart-placing notwithstanding, Hawkwind are still a major live draw, and the September-October tour pulls in the crowds. Reviewing the show at the Birmingham Odeon, Geoff Barton admits he's astonished to find the venue packed. But Calvert is one of the most compelling performers of the day, stalking the stage in a variety of costumes, every song an opportunity to externalise the films playing inside his head. During the "*stole my stash*" section of 'Reefer Madness', he jabs an accusatory finger at Brock. For 'Steppenwolf', he appears in frock coat and top hat, walking cane in hand, severed head under his arm.

Calvert later describes to Barton some spontaneous theatre during 'Brainstorm': "Nik was playing this sax solo wearing a big pair of lenseless spectacles, looking totally insane. I used my megaphone like an eyepiece and examined him – I could have been a galactic psychiatric inspector or something. Then I went over to Dave who was wearing a gasmask with a big hole in it and the trunk hanging down, looking extremely sinister, and I examined him and then accused them both of brainstorm. '*Brainstorm! Brainstorm!*' I yelled into the microphone." As Barton concludes, "the audience lap it all up, eyes wide and mouths agape".[e]

Several new songs air during this tour. 'Uncle Sam's On Mars' combines the driving metronomy of 'Opa-Loka' with Calvert's acerbic vision of the colonisation of the Red Planet, complete with a roadie dressed as a shambling Martian for him to torment, and Turner as an astronaut.[7] And during the grinding eastern swing of 'Hassan I Sahba' he gives full vent to "Aubrey Dawney", as he's named his fighter ace-cum-Bedouin warrior persona.[8] A sabre in each hand, he slashes at unseen enemies before plunging both blades into the stage.

'Back On The Streets', a more swaggering take on their brand of pub rock, will be their next single. By contrast, the extended, semi-improvised **'Time For Sale'** won't be released until years later.[9] Opening with flashy, trebly bass from Rudolph, it's an undeniably funky number, but harder-edged than much of *Astounding Sounds*. Brock throws in some cosmic licks before reverting to what resembles the riff from 'Steppenwolf', while Calvert delivers his words in a proto-rap style, unsure whether he's selling us immortality or time travel. Clearly a work-in-progress, it shows a band still finding new ways to repackage its space rock essence.

The tour is deemed a success, the band genuinely revitalised on stage. *Melody Maker*: "Anyone who thinks that Hawkwind are dead, had better think again. Their music is better written and played than ever".[f] As for their relevance to the rising new music scene, *NME* now characterises the band's "one chord beat that didn't vary at all" as a "bid for the punk rock vote".[g]

▼     ▼     ▼

But trouble is brewing once again. Increasingly at odds with the band's musical direction, Alan Powell leaves soon after the *Astounding Sounds* tour.[10] And there are more ructions to come.

Dave Brock believes moves are underway to remove him from the band, with Turner as rebel leader.[11] Brock quickly launches a counterstrike, persuading the others that it's Turner who needs to go, citing his still-variable musicianship. And so at the end of October, the only other remaining member of the original line-up is ejected into space.

This departure is profoundly symbolic for all kinds of reasons. Perhaps Turner is now surplus to requirements, with Calvert usurping his crowd-pleasing role as frontman, but for many fans, he's still the person most associated with the band's role as heroes of the benefit gig, and with the freewheeling spirit of their earlier music.

As a streamlined five-piece, the formation they'll keep for the rest of the 70s, Hawkwind enter AIR Studios to record 'Back On The Streets' for release as a standalone single. They then return to Rockfield to begin demoing a new album.

▼     ▼     ▼

In December, they embark on their traditional Christmas tour. Dick Tracy[12] from *NME* reviews the Coventry Theatre gig, his extended write-up opening with a reference to the drop-in centre for unemployed teenagers across from the venue. It's a sign of the times – the economy is out of control, with sterling plummeting against the dollar. After receiving the largest bail-out loan the International Monetary Fund has ever made, £2.3 billion, James Callaghan's Labour Government has been forced to slash public spending. In a year which has seen a heatwave and drought of Biblical proportions, the social and political climate is also harshening.

Tracy's article runs under the headline 'Hawkwind Survive 1976'. But the title isn't entirely accurate, at least not for Paul Rudolph, who becomes another ex-member after the tour. The review unwittingly flags the band's divisions: as Calvert "paces and jerks around the boards decked out in a patent-leather aviator's uniform, like an evil Action Man doll," Rudolph stands with his foot on the drum riser, a "white Stetson pulled down over his face, resplendent in green tracksuit with white side stripe and running shoes".[h]

Meanwhile, a song debuted on this tour points the way forward to the next, more futuristic phase of Hawkwind's ongoing mission. Over a minimal chug that's more pulse than riff, Calvert semi-improvises lines about "*test tubes*", "*circuitry towns*" and "*the shape of things to come*," words that will soon be jettisoned, leaving just the chorus: "*That's the spirit of the age*"…

◇◇◇◇◇◇◇◇◇◇◇◇◇◇◇◇◇◇◇◇◇◇◇◇◇◇◇◇◇◇◇◇◇◇◇◇◇◇◇◇◇◇◇◇◇◇◇◇◇◇◇◇◇◇◇◇◇◇◇◇◇◇◇◇

a    Dick Tracy, *NME*, 6/9/76

b    'Weasels Ripped My Flesh, Hawkwind Stung My Brain' – Pete Makowski, *Sounds*, 04/09/76

c    'The Glow Of The Futuristic Druids' – Geoff Barton, *Sounds*, 2/10/76

d    '8 Days A Week' – Robert Calvert, *Melody Maker*, 2/10/76

e    'The Adventures Of The 10 Stone Warriors That Shattered The Earth' – Geoff Barton, *Sounds*, 2/10/76

f    Gary Cooper, *Melody Maker*, 16/10/76

g    Unknown writer, *NME*, 16/10/76

h    'Hawkwind Survive 1976' – Dick Tracy, *NME*, 25/12/76

1    A prescient opinion piece from Mick Farren epitomises this attitude. 'The Titanic Sails At Dawn' rails against the "absorption of rock'n'roll into the turgid master stream of traditional establishment showbiz" (*NME*, 19/6/76). Allegedly inspired by angry reader letters, it concludes that the 70s generation must start "producing their own ideas, [and] ease out the old farts who are still pushing tired ideas left over from the 60s". Meanwhile, punk's first rumblings can already be heard…

2    *Astounding Stories Of Super-Science* was first published in 1930. *Amazing Stories* – the first dedicated SF magazine – started in 1926.

3    A friend of Calvert's from his Margate days, Hyde also did the *Leif* sleeve.

4    Reproduced in Paul Gorman's *Reasons To Be Cheerful*, the 'Amazing' side of the album sleeve – ultimately rejected – was to have featured an illustration of a wolf-man's head with laser beam eyes looming over a city of skyscrapers (presumably inspired by 'Steppenwolf').

5    Atomhenge was built by theatrical set designer George Galitzine: "I remember that we constructed the set during the very hot summer of 1976 in a small workshop in Highgate. It took up the entire space even in pieces and was very hard work to construct, especially in the stifling heat. It could be put together and dismantled within a couple of hours for touring purposes" (Interview with the author).

6    Art rockers Be-Bop Deluxe toured in 1976 with a stage set based around strikingly similar ideas. Bill Nelson: "We had a large film projection screen in the centre of the stage, with clips of futuristic

movies like *Metropolis*, then either side of that we had two slightly smaller screens that projected pulp science fiction covers from the 1950s. The whole thing was choreographed to work with each song" (from 'Red Hot', Johnny Sharp, *Prog*, Feb 2019).

7      The Martian "[resembled] nothing as much as Frank Zappa's Gypsy Mutant Vacuum Cleaner," according to a subsequent Calvert interview: "The alien is killed for his sins by an astronaut in an American uniform. As the murderer raises Old Glory on high, Robert Calvert declaims 'Life's unsafe on Mars!'" ('Pulsating Poets of Sturm und Drang' – Chas de Whalley, *Album Tracking*, 7/76).

8      According to Geoff Barton, Calvert is at this time reading a book about a fighter ace, "one Aubrey Dawney". It's more likely it was about Aubrey Ellwood, a distinguished real-life WW1 pilot ('The Adventures Of The 10 Stone Warriors That Shattered The Earth' – Geoff Barton, *Sounds*, 2/10/76). The way in which Calvert is often lost in fantasies of being a WW1 ace recalls similar imaginings by *Peanuts*' Snoopy.

9      'Time For Sale' eventually appeared on *Atomhenge 76*, a semi-official live album recorded at Bristol's Colston Hall (27/9/76) and released on Voiceprint in 2000.

10     Powell: "I wasn't really enjoying the sort of material I was playing with Hawkwind. And I made no attempt to disguise it. On our last tour, the other lads found me listening to cassettes by Herbie Hancock and James Brown. This didn't go down too well, and helped to make my departure inevitable!" ('Hawks Lose A Drummer' – *NME*, 30/10/76).

11     The details of Brock's mooted expulsion remain murky. According to Brock, Calvert had alerted him to a decision by the other members to remove him. But Turner, Rudolph and Powell all deny plotting against Brock. Given Calvert's propensity for flights of fancy, a question must remain whether the entire situation was sparked by a misinterpretation.

12     AKA Space Ritual dancer and ex-*Frendz* writer John May.

# HAWKWIND SURVIVE 1976! EXCLUSIVE

THURSDAY NIGHT at the Coventry Theatre, and the latest mutation of Hawkwind is all set to damage the sensibilities of an 80% capacity crowd of Coventry's youth. At least half of them look like they might have spent their day at the building on the opposite side of the road from the theatre, a long, two-storeyed structure draped with a banner which reads: "THE OLD FIRE STATION CENTER FOR THE UNEMPLOYED."

Underneath in flowing, red lettering is the inscribed legend. "If you are between 16-19 why not drop in?" Yes indeed, times are hard.

After being guided through the theatre's labyrinthine innards, painted corporation blue and white, I stumble into the dressing room buried deep beneath the artists' bar.

Upstairs, I'm told, Bob Calvert is giving audience to assorted penmen who've come down on this record company coach outing. Somehow the rest of the band don't seem to be enthused with the idea of joining him, preferring instead to stick papers together and get toned up for the evening's performance.

I wander around until I find my seat in the circle. *Reefer Madness*, the classic '30s drug paranoia movie, unfolds larger than life on the backstage screen.

The band stroll on to a roar from the crowd. The Hawkbrothers version of "Reefer Madness", opening power cut from the "Astounding Sounds" album, slams out and the show begins.

Calvert is the first one you notice as he paces and jerks around the boards decked out in a patent-leather aviator's uniform, like an evil Action Man doll. Stage left stands Blackie, white stetson pulled down over his face, resplendent in green track suit with white sidestripe and running shoes. One foot perched on the drum platform, his body hunched over his bass. Later on, when he switches over to black Gibson and starts powering out some heavy metal you get a glimpse of his justifiable reputation as a good psychedelic axeman, though not nearly enough for my taste. Right now though, he's content just pushing the pace.

Numbers whizz by and then they're into "Hashishin." named after the young men at the court of Hassan I Sabbah who were drugged with weed and then dispatched to kill the sultan's rivals. For this routine Calvert has now mutated into Dune-laden Lawrence of Arabia gear. The front liners — Blackie, Brock and Calvert — scream out a hard-edged chant to the Coventry kids while the stage lighting strobes and pulses, treating the audience to a downhome version of the Star Trek energisation chamber effect. Now you see me, now you don't. It works well and provides one of the concert's highspots.

On the far right of the stage Simon House sits unobtrusively, his head immersed in a striped mask with wings, concentrating hard on his organ work, only occasionally emerging to provide some violin backup. His contributions may be good but from where I was sitting they were lost in the mix, for the most part.

"Sonic Attack", the last remnant from the Space Ritual act of some years before, draws applause from diehards in the audience. While Calvert leans out over the front of the stage reciting the Mike Moorcock instruction leaflet for surviving 'a future war, Dave Brock turns his back so the audience can grock his white lab coat painted with fluorescent patterns which shine out under the ultra-violet light. Despite all the years on the road with the band, he still retains the aggressive stance and rapid strumming technique of the busker he used to be.

Backing him Simon King, the other oldest member of this lineup, sits on his plinth laying into his kit with a will. The Hawkwind double drummer incarnation has been and gone. Alan Powell disappearing for new percussion pastures, but tonight he isn't missed. King hits his skins with good timing and attack and looks like he means it.

Nick Turner *is* conspicious by his absence, but that's another story. "Back On The Street", the new January single is the last cut before the band leave the stage, wait three minutes and then return for the obligatory encore. The patrons are going wild, writhing around like a living room full of bloodworms. It's a good bionic rock number, punk music for the space cadets who have now graduated from the Academy. It gives as good an idea as any of the new Hawkwind style.

LATER, ON the company coach, I fish around for comments but no one seems quite sure what to say. You see, Hawkwind have signed with a new label, Charisma, an outfit distributed by European giant Phonogram, and this trip is the first glimpse that the Euro execs have had of the band.

To be honest most of them have flaked out, having flown over to England that day. One lady, however, did confess to me that she had got somewhat nervous at those points in the stage act when Calvert withdrew two rapiers from scabbards fastened to his sides and proceede to plunge them into the wooden floor. Even more nervous when he unbuttoned his holster and produced a revolver which he waved in the general direction of the audience.

You know, she confided, that he has a history of mental illness.

Don't we all deaf, don't we all.

Back at the Montcalm Hotel behind Marble Arch, in an atmosphere of chocolate-brown padding and soft lights, it's time to ask the questions I came to ask. Why Nick Turner left the band.

Simon King and Dave Brock were honest enough about it. For reasons both personal and musical it was time for parting of the ways. Exit Nick Turner.

Blackie had commented some days before when I put the question to him: "One chap spoiling the fun for the rest of the chaps." That about says it. There's no ill-feeling on their parts at least, only regret and a trace of sadness. Nick is currently living in Wales and planning a trip to Egypt so they tell me. Meantime old members of the band keep reappearing. A few weeks back Del Dettmar flew over to renew contact with the lads and played with them at Hammersmith. He now has a log cabin in the Rocky Mountains where he entertains the natives with his synthesiser. Meantime Lemmy is still Motorheading and Stacia and Dikmik and all those many others who were with the Hawks at sometime in their long history are still around . . . somewhere. So it goes.

It's been a long strange trip, but right now Hawkwind are developing. Many years back the original lineup played for three days inside a huge pneumatic dome at the Isle of Wight Festival. Hawkwind were *the* benefit band. Anyhow, any way, anywhere. No matter how many miles, no matter

how many drugs, Hawkwind would do their best to outwit provincial drug squads and take the stage.

Now, many years later, one hit single and a thousand gigs on they're down to five and still going. While George Harrison agonises endlessly about his legal problems to the world's press, Hawkwind have been steadily moving on and have almost finished paying off the numerous debts incurred in the past. They have new managers and agents, still carry a light show but no dancers, and are generally still hard at work getting their act together.

Right now their strongest songs are good enough to carry them but many lose their structure and dissolve into repetitious riffing. Calvert has yet to decide how far to take his theatricals and generally the band, having stepped out of the space image, have yet to find a comfortable niche.

But the general feeling in the Hawkwind camp is one of optimism. For the first time in many, many months the business problems are beginning to sort themselves out and light is appearing at the end of the tunnel.

It will be interesting to see what universe they arrive in next.

☐ DICK TRACY

'Yes indeed, times are hard.' *NME*, 25 December 1976
(source: Wolfie Smith collection)

Atomhenge promo shot. L-R - Rudolph, Calvert, Brock
(source: Robert Calvert archive)

Brock on bass, Rudolph on guitar - Vale Hall, Aylesbury, 7 December 1976
(photo by Geoffrey Tyrell, source: aylesburyfriars.co.uk)

# Paul Rudolph

Bass and guitar
May 1975—December 1976
*Captain Lockheed And The Starfighters*, *Lucky Leif And The Longships* and *Astounding Sounds, Amazing Music*

Paul Rudolph (from 1976 tour programme)
(source: Stephen Dunthorne collection)

What set the Pink Fairies and Hawkwind apart from the rest of the scene at the time?

It was very spontaneous, starting with the outdoor concerts with the generator under the flyover in Ladbroke Grove. Both of them just wanted to play, to push the envelope and the establishment. They both did a lot of stuff in the early days with free festivals, doing benefits to get the word out there. They would just show up, support the community and play. If we were lucky, we might get some petrol money.

**What are your memories of those early gigs where they performed together?**

We tossed a coin to see who went on first. As the bands got used to doing gigs together, sometimes one or two people would get up on stage with their instruments. At some college gig, I can't remember which, everybody was on stage together, including the three drummers. It was absolutely exciting.

Everybody would start on a riff or a chord. Sometimes I would play lead guitar, then step back and nod at Dave, and he'd play. Sometimes we'd both lay back and let Nik play. [There was] never any agenda. Anytime it happened it would be totally different.

**How did you hook up with Brian Eno?**

One of the last gigs I did [under the Westway] was with a blues band called Uncle Dog. A friend of mine introduced me to Brian Eno there. Brian asked me if I'd be interested in playing on his first solo album, and I said, "I'd love to."

**Did you introduce Simon King to Eno for *Here Come The Warm Jets*?**

I think so. I knew Eno was looking for drummers, and I had mentioned Simon to him.

**You also start to work with Robert Calvert…**

My first impression was of this quirky and articulate aristocrat. But with an incredible talent, something that nobody else had. He and I bonded from our first meeting. I still credit Bob and Nik with being Hawkwind's stage presence.

Both his solo albums were co-written by Bob and me. I was a paid session musician, it never entered my mind to ask for writing credits. But if he were alive, he would certainly vouch for this. He had a few one-string ideas on the guitar, but most were refined or rearranged to go with the lyrics and to suit the ideas he had. Almost all the guitar and bass is mine.

**Eno appears on *Captain Lockheed*…**

He was interested in the project and Bob liked his stuff, his spontaneity and different approach. And it certainly stirred up interest, because part way through one session at AIR Studios, George Martin turned up and stayed for the whole thing, he was fascinated. Arthur Brown was also there that day. Initially Brown thought it was kind of crazy, but then he realised these are really interesting sounds.

Brown was very eccentric, and when he arrived everybody had to go for lunch while he meditated in the studio, to clear the air of bad vibrations. But boy, could that guy ever sing.

Eno and I had our matching EMS Synthis, [with] Calvert's voice going through the synthesiser and getting all chopped up. We plugged things in completely backwards and did a lot of experimenting. [Producer] Roy [Thomas Baker] and the engineer were worried about the mixing desk [catching fire]. Bob was so taken by Eno's contribution and presence that he wanted him to be involved in the next project.

Calvert and Eno were both 'non-musicians' making solo albums. Were there similarities?
Just the idea of let's do something different and see what happens. They were both very much art people, not just work and music people.

How did the sessions for *Lucky Leif* compare?
They didn't differ that much. Eno was a facilitator and had an incredible sense of imagination and a great set of ears. The difference was that *Lucky Leif* focused more on the music. Content-wise, it was more varied and more polished with Eno directing. He had a very good way of steering people to get the best results.

I don't know if [UA] ever recouped their money. In a way, it was an investment in art. They didn't get in the album charts, but it was incredibly creative and different.

When you got the call to take over from Lemmy, did you think it was temporary?
The phone call was basically, "Fly out to the States, Lemmy's just been busted crossing the border." I thought, 'Let's do the US tour then we'll see how it goes.'

What were the recording sessions for *Astounding Sounds* like?
I found them interesting and exciting. I think that was a turning point in collaboration. Until that point, Dave had a lockdown on writing all the songs. Everybody wanted more freedom. There was animosity brewing over Dave getting all the publishing royalties. [Plus] everybody wanted to express themselves more from a musical point of view, not just for extra royalties. When we recorded it, Dave conceded letting other people try some of their ideas, though I think reluctantly.

*Dave Gilmour is credited as just remixing 'Kerb Crawler', but did he have more input?*

He did! Some of the loops and other things happening were validated by his say-so and presence. Dave had a certain amount of respect for [Gilmour's position] in Pink Floyd, and said, "Well OK, everybody can have a track on the album, do what you want." I think [Gilmour] had a huge input and influence, even though some of it might have just been his presence there behind the mixing board.

*Brock has talked about feeling threatened by your superior musicianship…*

I don't know how relevant that is. I think Dave was more threatened by the norm changing, and [more] people being involved in writing the material.

*Do you remember why 'Back On The Streets' was released as a standalone single?*

Bob really wanted it to become a single, and people in the record company thought it had commercial potential. I liked it, though at the time I thought 'Hassan' was a better choice for Hawkwind. But 'Back On The Streets' was Bob's venture into the pop realm if you like. I would have produced it with a much edgier, raw, rough sound. But I could say that about a lot of things.

*You were initially involved in demoing Quark, Strangeness And Charm…*

There's two or three tracks I like, but the rest, you can almost hear the tension and in-fighting. It was a real grind getting it finished. Dave decided that he really didn't like the way things were going. I have a cassette tape of the original mix, and a lot of it is disjointed and lifeless compared to *Astounding Sounds*. There wasn't that freeform creativity. I was listening a few months ago, and I had trouble listening, even [to] my own bass playing. [1]

[But] I don't want to dwell on the negative. Being in Hawkwind was an honour at the time and I will always remember it fondly – except the last bit.

◇◇◇◇◇◇◇◇◇◇◇◇◇◇◇◇◇◇◇◇◇◇◇◇◇◇◇◇◇◇◇◇◇◇◇◇◇◇◇◇◇◇◇◇◇◇◇◇◇◇◇◇◇◇◇◇◇◇◇◇◇◇◇

1    According to Rudolph, demos of what became *Quark* were recorded while Powell and Turner were still in the band. But if they exist, they have yet to come to light. *Quark* demos (by the five-piece featuring Rudolph) do exist, however.

# Alan Powell

Drums & percussion
June 1974—October 1976
*Warrior On The Edge Of Time* and *Astounding Sounds,
Amazing Music*

Alan Powell (from 1976 tour programme)
(Source: Steve Readhead collection)

You initially deputised for an injured Simon King.
Hawkwind could have been a reggae band for all I knew, I'd never heard them,
I had no idea what they were like. When they were becoming popular, I was
in California doing session work. But I said, "Sure!" because you never say no.
"Absolutely, what time do you want me there?"

How did the experience compare with anything you'd done before?

It was like nothing I'd played with or heard in my entire life! For a start, there was no rehearsal. I went over to Doug's flat in a cab, and Dave was staying there. I said to him, "So, you want to run through a couple of tunes, I'll tap it out on the sofa with my sticks?" He said, "No, it's all right, we're not musicians, you'll figure it out." Fair enough! So we get to the gig in Norway, and I'm setting my kit up, and I say, "You want to run through some stuff?" "Nah, nah, don't worry about it, we're just a jam band." Nobody seemed to care!

So when we go on that night, I'm next to Lemmy, he goes one-two-three-four, we start playing, and I had no idea what the songs were like. For all I know, they could have started playing regimental marching band music! But by then I was very good at watching the guitarist or bass player, for the wink when to stop playing, or turn their hand round, faster, faster. At the end of the night, I came off and thought, "Wow, I've never heard anything like that in my life!" Not to mention the fact that Stacia was dancing around me completely nude. I thought, "That is without a shadow of a doubt the most unusual experience I've ever had in my unusual career – it sounded horrible, but who cares? They don't seem to care, so why should I?"

And when Simon King recovered it was decided to keep both of you.

Simon rejoined, but nobody said to me, "OK, thank you, go home," so I stayed on! Lemmy liked it. He said, "It makes it easier for me," and Simon was alright with it because Hawkwind were a very loud band, and when you're the drummer, you're slogging your guts out just to keep up with the volume a lot of the time, so it made it a little easier [for him]. I wasn't playing drums on every single number, I was playing as much alternative percussion as I could, like timbales and congas, and it happened to fit quite well with some of the stuff they did.

What are your memories of recording *Warrior On The Edge Of Time*?

Rockfield's an old converted farmhouse in the country, it's a nice place. We'd go in the studio mid-afternoon. Some of the songs were already written, but a lot was literally jammed out in the studio.

You have four credits: 'Opa-Loka' plus the Michael Moorcock pieces.

'Opa-Loka' was just a studio jam I'd made a demo of in my flat. Lemmy was unavailable, so Dave played bass. It's basically trance rock. In the early 90s, when raves were the big thing over here in America and everybody was taking ecstasy, 'Opa-Loka' was apparently played a lot.

*Lemmy was critical in retrospect about what he called the 'Drum Empire'. Do you remember this at the time?*
No I don't, he seemed to like it at first. I have a feeling Lemmy somehow got it into his head that Simon King and me were instrumental in him being fired, but we had nothing to do with that at all. I read later he'd started calling us the 'Drum Empire', but why that was I don't know.

*What did you think about Lemmy's expulsion?*
I was surprised, he was one of the most identifiable members. Lemmy and Nik were the two guys you thought of when you thought of Hawkwind. I just think the rest of the band had had enough at that point of Lemmy being unreliable. If you had a rehearsal arranged for three o'clock, Lemmy would get there at seven. If he got there!

*How did Paul Rudolph's bass style compare to Lemmy's?*
Paul is an excellent musician. A really good guitarist who can play bass too. And he wasn't taking massive amounts of speed or downers, so he played bang in time.

*Robert Calvert rejoined in December 1975. How did that change the dynamic?*
I'd never met the guy and had no idea what he did. He was suddenly in the band, and I was like, "How you doing? Fine by me!" Dave took care of all that sort of thing. Bob then became front man. Of course, the poor guy suffered from manic depression – there'd be times when he was just up there feeling wonderful, then plummeting into the depths of despair. I'd never had to deal with that kind of thing, it must have been very difficult.

*How do you remember the sessions for* Astounding Sounds, Amazing Music?
Paul had a lot of studio experience. I had a lot of studio experience. For me, Hawkwind in the studio was just appalling, the quality of the sound and production was at best amateurish. If I listen to *Warrior* now, it sounds like it was recorded on a Sony cassette player, it's just terrible. They'd go in the studio,

set up microphones, and start playing, and that's not how you get a good quality recording. But *Astounding Sounds* was recorded to proper standards, so it was a completely different sound. I don't think Dave liked it, he preferred it messy and ragged, so that did cause a problem.

**'City Of Lagoons' is your track.**
It was kind of a homage to Pink Floyd, the closest that Hawkwind ever sounded to Floyd. The more I listen to it, I wish somebody had used it as a film track, it would have worked great on some kind of science-fiction movie. I don't think Dave liked it at all!

**But it goes on, suggesting a certain level of democracy.**
Yes, I think so. Afterwards Dave said he didn't like the album, that for him, a track like that with decent production and playing was not what he wanted. He wanted it ragged, crude and rudimentary. I don't mean that in a negative way, it's just the way he liked to hear it. I think he felt that album was the band moving away from him, and that's why he didn't like it.

**'City Of Lagoons' is presumably a reference to Venice.**
Bob Calvert was listening very intently in the control room, and says, "Call this 'City Of Lagoons'." He seemed very particular about this! And I thought, "OK, that sounds pretty good." The pronouncement came down from on high! There's so many effects on the guitar that it's kind of watery, so that's where he got that from.

**It's been claimed there was a conscious effort by you and Paul to make the band 'funkier'?**
I was just trying to push the band to expand their horizons rather than just be a continual wall of droning sound – a Santana-meets-Pink-Floyd kind of thing, because they could have done that. There were gigs where we just jammed for 20 minutes, and I enjoyed that more than playing the tunes. I was just trying to open it up to different kinds of rhythms and feel.

You're quoted in *NME* as saying your departure was inevitable after the *Astounding Sounds* tour.

I'd put on James Brown, and Bob would turn round with a look on his face, like, "What the FUCK is this?" He just hated that kind of stuff. So it was obvious to everybody else, I was saying, "Look, I'm done with this, guys." So me getting fired was fine. If I was in charge of the band, I would have fired me, so I was perfectly OK with it. I wasn't upset, there were no harsh feelings on my part. I still think they were a great bunch of guys, there was no nastiness.

Live promo from 1977. L-R - Calvert, Brock, House
(source: Robert Calvert archive)

# Your Android Replica Is Playing Up Again

January–June 1977

With **Adrian Shaw** replacing Rudolph, Hawkwind recommence recording the new album at Rockfield in early January. A long-time associate, Shaw is a former member of free-festival stalwarts Magic Muscle, who supported Hawkwind on the Space Ritual tour. He'd once deputised on bass during the Lemmy era, and perhaps most importantly from Brock's perspective, Shaw isn't going to upstage the band's founder with any flashy guitar licks.

However, Rudolph's influence is still apparent on '**Back On The Streets**', a song he co-wrote with Calvert, which is released on 28 January as a standalone single. It's crunchy with a hint of NYC garage cool, the riff more Lou Reed than Chuck Berry, while Calvert toughens his act up to deliver a raucous, Jagger-esque lyric melody and a punchy chorus. With a stripped back arrangement, King's drums sound great, and Rudolph unleashes another explosion of a solo. Unfortunately, having been persuaded to use an external producer, Bob Potter's production is flat, the chorus especially needing beefing up.

On the flipside, '**The Dream Of Isis**'[1] is at the other end of the spectrum, a peculiar instrumental based around an organ drone and what sounds like a looped recording of a grandfather clock. Tentative drum rolls lead into a beat that never quite straightens out while Rudolph funks around on the bass. There's an old-style chant in the background, but in this context, it sounds more hysterical than hypnotic. With the potential to go somewhere interesting, it fades out too soon, an abandoned experiment.

Despite coming in Hawkwind's most eye-catching single sleeve, with full colour pictures of Atomhenge from the December 76 tour, 'Back On The Streets' fails to break into the charts, despite *NME* describing it as more punk than The Stranglers, an endorsement of sorts ("which just goes to prove once more how meaningless labelling anything punk rock is").[a] *Sounds* blames the production: "This could have been a great single… [But] all the high points end up sounding about as lethal as blank cartridges."[b]

In February, and for reasons best known to themselves, UA release their second Hawkwind best-of in less than 12 months. *Masters Of The Universe* is also chronological, but there's no segueing or remixing this time, and the debut is resolutely ignored. With (naturally) 'Master Of The Universe', 'Brainstorm' and 'Orgone Accumulator', it's a decent if unimaginative introduction, lacking the sense of light and shade Brock brought to *Roadhawks*. The main attraction for fans is the inclusion of 'It's So Easy', previously only available on the B-side of 'The Psychedelic Warlords'. Another plus point is Mark Harrison's science fantasy cover art. Possibly intended as a gatefold (until the finance department decided otherwise), it only becomes apparent in adverts that front and back work together as a complete picture.[2]

▾     ▾     ▾

There's a one-off show at the Roundhouse on 27 February to celebrate the completion of the new album, with just about every song from it played. There's also an encore of 'I'm Waiting For The Man' – either an acknowledgement of VU's influence on Hawkwind or a savvy play for art-punk credibility.[3] *Sounds* notes that Calvert has the audience "positively eating out of his leather glove" while Brock is described as looking "like a psychopathic dentist in his white coat." The show attracts "plenty of new young fans; new wave as regards their hair and their status. Acid may no longer be in vogue but Hawkwind soon may be."[c]

In March, there's a tour of the Netherlands and West Germany; in April, France – there seems to be a concerted effort to get the band back on the road this year. With Calvert at his most charismatic, it seems like a good idea, especially as a new generation of fans comes through. However, this pressure to perform will have serious ramifications for Calvert's mental health later on in the year. But for now, they're on a roll, demoing new songs at Rockfield between these tours, including **'Fahrenheit 451'** and **'We Like To Be Frightened'**.[4]

A short UK tour in June (with Motörhead supporting) culminates in a triumphant free performance at Stonehenge.[5] *Quark, Strangeness And Charm* comes out on 17 June.

a   *NME*, 5/2/77

b   *Sounds*, 1/77

c   Christopher V. Middleton, *Sounds*, 3/77


1   The title is probably a reference to 'And the Seventh Dream is the Dream of Isis' by David Gascoyne, published in 1933 and credited as the first surrealist poem in English. Isis was one of the most important deities of ancient Egypt, a magical healer closely connected to death rites.

2   If the introduction to 'It's So Easy' sounds like Popol Vuh's soundtrack for *Aguirre, The Wrath Of God*, the *MOTU* back cover resembles its opening scene: a single-file procession through misty hills.

3   It also sees Calvert enact a classic piece of rock theatre, conducting a mock drugs deal on stage during the song. What Calvert doesn't realise is that Rod Goodway – Adrian Shaw's old bandmate from Magic Muscle, who has been roped in to play the part of the dealer – has hurriedly grabbed some dry shampoo from backstage to act as cocaine. As Goodway relates, "Calvert leers at the audience with a true pantomime Dame expression of 'Mmmm, nice'... and snarfs the bloody lot up his nose!" He doesn't relate what happens when Calvert realises his error, if he ever does (ref: 'Rod Goodway on Robert Calvert', *Spirit Of The P/age*).

4   A version of 'We Like To Be Frightened' ended up on Calvert's 1981 solo album *Hype*, and a new recording of 'Fahrenheit 451' appeared on Hawkwind's 1982 album *Choose Your Masques*. It was announced in 2017 that Hawkwind's current label, Cherry Red, was to put out an album of "unreleased" tracks from 1977, including the original demos of these two songs, but at time of going to print, this has yet to emerge.

5   Roger Hutchinson witnessed this performance on 21 June: "[A] blinding set aided by a giant generator, the Atomhenge stage set and Liquid Len's light show. It was also memorable because the show drained the generator and while diesel was drained from vehicles on site, the band continued acoustically illuminated by the light of dozens of torches and car headlights" (ref: Stonehenge Free Festival 1977/www.ukrockfestivals.com).

Simon House
(source: Doug Smith archive)

Robert Calvert
(source: Robert Calvert archive)

QSAC live. L-R - King, Brock, Shaw, Calvert
(source: Doug Smith archive)

# Quark, Strangeness And Charm

Released 17 June 1977

*Label:*  Charisma (UK & Europe) / Sire (USA)

*Track listing:*  Spirit Of The Age (Brock/Calvert) / Damnation
Alley (Calvert/Brock/House) / Fable Of A Failed
Race (Brock/Calvert) / Quark, Strangeness And
Charm (Calvert/Brock) / Hassan I Sahba
(Calvert/Rudolph) / The Forge Of Vulcan (House) /
Days Of The Underground (Brock/Calvert) / The
Iron Dream (King)

*Line-up:*  Dave Brock / Robert Calvert / Simon House /
Adrian Shaw / Simon King

*Recorded at:*  Rockfield Studios

*Produced by:*  Hawkwind

With a harsh, metallic wake-up call, Hawkwind announce yet another change in sound and direction. Brock calls it a course correction on the inner sleeve, but this is genuinely a new phase, sonically and thematically. The hessian throw rugs have been chucked into the engine's furnace, and steel and plastic fittings take their place. The future is bright – but still broken. Instead of space rock as mystical onrush into the void, here comes a funnier, if more mundane vision of interstellar travel…

'**Spirit Of The Age**' begins with the insect babble of mission control, the sound of technocrats overseeing their latest socio-scientific experiment. Gradually fading up, Brock's chugging guitar is ultra-minimal. Shaw's bass is wiry and subtly propulsive, weaving and bobbing around the mix, while House's keyboards flicker like needles in a dial. The wild dramatics of *Warrior* and the lush atmospheres of

*Astounding Sounds* have been expunged in favour of an insidious mechanical pulse, with King almost (but not quite) locking into a *motorik* rhythm.

Calvert takes his time before making an entry, but his opening line is surely one of the best in rock: "*I would have liked you to have been deep frozen too.*" This musical setting is perfect for his oddly inflected monotone and sardonic lyrics, the heroics of pulp SF replaced by reflections on lost love and malfunctioning robot companions. Calvert sings with peevish resignation, though Brock's backing vocal in the chorus has a hint of proletarian bolshiness – the worker drones trying to stir themselves against the system.

In the second verse, Calvert laments this perfect future where men are flawlessly alike but robbed of free will – House's string synth evokes clones in endless chromium corridors, stretching on forever. The musicianship is uncluttered, the arrangement ebbs and flows – it all sounds as modern as the title implies. But as if to prove that human imperfection is indomitable, Calvert falters before the final pay-off: "*Oh for the wings of any bird / Other than a battery hen.*"[1]

'Damnation Alley' takes its title from another Roger Zelazny novel, about a journey across a perilous, post-apocalypse America. An early warning siren wails through a radioactive rainstorm, signalling a very different spirit of the age. It's the end of the world, but the music is upbeat, with a classic Brock riff and Calvert's gung-ho, pitch black delivery: "*No more Arizona, now Phoenix is fried up / Oklahoma City, what a pity it's gone.*" And there's another catchy chorus – "*Thank you, Doctor Strangelove!*"

The song itself is like the "*eight-wheeled anti-radiation tomb*" ploughing through the blasted terrain, the separation between the instruments making for a compact but chunky sound. The bridge into the middle section is particularly cinematic, Calvert sat at the controls reporting what he sees, repeating his *Strangelove* mantra to keep himself sane. As the machine breaks down, House appears like a master mechanic to save the day, extemporising around a block of organ chords, his keening violin combining gorgeously with the driving rhythm. 'Damnation Alley' lacks the fuzzy logic and cosmic density of their earlier output – but its sleek lines and curves are confident and purposeful. This is a band moving forward still, paralleling both punk's directness and contemporary Krautrock's growing sophistication.

After a lovely cross-faded segue, 'Fable Of A Failed Race' could be read as a sequel to 'Damnation Alley': a thousand years hence, when aliens colonise the earth, they find only a desert of radioactive sand. Calvert pushes at his range and adopts a near-conventional vocal style to fit the ballad-speed melody, spinning a compelling, allusive narrative from a few well-chosen phrases and images. Despite its arid theme, the song sounds like the calm undulation of the ocean and sees the return of the cosmic backing choir of old – and Brock's solo into the fade is the very definition of tasteful.

From the sublime to the ridiculous, '**Quark, Strangeness And Charm**' is a novelty song-cum-bar-room boogie. It sounds like everybody's having fun – House throwing in some nice garage punk organ – but the focus is again on Calvert's witty lyrics and arch, puckish performance. Who else would use the names of sub-atomic particles[2] to punningly speculate on the love lives of famous scientists: "*Copernicus had those Renaissance ladies crazy about his telescope*"?[3] There's a pleasing insolence to Calvert's crisp enunciation – though goodness knows how it affected the science education of any schoolchildren hearing it on the *Marc* show (see below). In some parallel universe, this was the theme tune to *Tomorrow's World*, as presented by Magnus Pyke and Marty Feldman.

The finger bells and quasi-Arabic violin at the start of '**Hassan I Sahba**' may be blatant exoticism, but they conjure images of Bedouin tents and veiled harems nonetheless. There's some teasing foreshadowing of the song's main theme, some villainous organ, and then its big Eastern-flavoured riff crashes in. Calvert chants frenziedly over the top, conflating an ancient Islamic warrior creed with the present day Middle East of oilfields, "*petrodollars*" and Black September. His analysis isn't exactly nuanced, but it's a potent reminder of 70s headlines about the oil crisis, the Yom Kippur War, Palestinian terrorism and endless plane hijackings – all of which retain a queasy prescience today.[4]

There's a great switch-up to a stomping middle section – the massive reverb on King's snares anticipating the gated drum sound synonymous with 80s pop rock – and a call-and-response vocal, as Shaw's rubbery bass ripples underneath. A sense of precision in the arrangements is what sets *Quark* apart from previous albums. It might feel over-engineered were it not for Calvert's gleeful role-playing and House's nervy violin, ratcheting up the tension before we slam back into the main riff.

'**The Forge Of Vulcan**' is a solo piece from House based around the striking of an anvil and the rise and fall of an arpeggiated synth line. Tangerine Dream and Kraftwerk had been exploring electronic automation for a while, while Donna Summer's 'I Feel Love' – released the same month as *Quark* – will soon change popular music forever, spending four weeks at number one in the summer of 1977. Of course, sequencing and arpeggiation brought out the Luddite in most British bands, being anathema to musicians still hung up on craftsmanship and virtuosity. Yet here on Hawkwind's most finessed album to date is a vision of another not-so-distant future, of bedroom artists liberated from the need to slavishly master an instrument before making a record… House sets his musical idea in motion and gradually builds layers of sound around it, until we're rewarded with a vivid sunburst of organ at the end.

As if to emphasise the break with the past, '**Days Of The Underground**' harks back to a world only a few years distant – though for Calvert, it might as well be another age. He casts an affectionate eye back on late 60s/early 70s Ladbroke Grove, its would-be revolutionaries and dreamers: "*In visions of acid, we saw through delusion and brainbox pollution / We knew we were right.*" Is he shaking his head in wry disbelief or sincerely lamenting the fallen heroes and failed ideologies of the past?[5] His delivery is cocky, almost sarcastic, the tone of a man who can't quite square his current outlook with that of his younger self. Perhaps his ambivalence also stems from observing another, more aggressive scene now emerging from their old west London stamping ground, the nihilistic no future of the Sex Pistols and the white riot posturing of The Clash.

'Days…' certainly has a punky chippiness to it, Brock's bright, mischievous riff underpinned by twinkling, fluting keys. It's also the first self-referential Hawkwind song – "*Now we can look back at the heroes we were then / We made quite a stir then with our sonic attack*" – though the band are past masters of self-mythologisation. For Calvert, Hawkwind were always characters in his own story, even if he appears to be consigning its initial chapters into the filing cabinet of history.[6]

Finally, '**The Iron Dream**' is a short instrumental outro fashioned atop another synthetic arpeggio hidden in the guts of 'Days…'. It takes its name from a novel by US New Wave SF author Norman Spinrad, in which Hitler is re-imagined as a pulp science fiction writer – and it's a pounding, pulsating King Beat special, Moorcock's barbarian crew gone mad after their thousand year mission and intent on destroying anything they can lay their hands on. Its bombastic, sustained crescendo could have graced some 70s current affairs show (as Mountain's 'Nantucket Sleighride' had for *Weekend World*). After the rather limp endings to the last two albums, this states in no uncertain terms that here is a band that refuses to die.

1  The words are from Calvert's poems 'The Starfarer's Despatch' and 'The Clone's Poem'.

2  Calvert: "I have a layman's understanding of it (sub-atomic science). I read about this particular thing in a book by Arthur Koestler, which was written as a general description of modern physics" (interview with BBC Radio Manchester in September 1977). This might be *The Roots Of Coincidence* (1972), which links physics and various alleged types of psi power. Curiously, the 1976 Nobel Prize for Physics went to Burton Richter and Samuel Chao Chung Ting for their discovery of the 'Psi' quark, which helped validate the existence of the 'Charm' quark.

3  In the interests of pedantry... Copernicus made his observations of the solar system with the naked eye, 50 years before Galileo first used a telescope. And Einstein had plenty of girls, and was married twice.

4  The title is a misspelling of Hassan-i Sabbāh, an 11th century Persian lord and mystic who founded the military order referred to as the "Hashshashin" ('assassins') – it's likely Calvert first encountered him in William Burroughs' *Nova* trilogy (along with his credo "nothing is true, everything is permitted"). The name "Hashshashin" means "users of hashish" in Arabic, but was probably a rival faction's slur rather than evidence of a drug-crazed death cult. "Petrodollars" refers to the system – brokered by Henry Kissinger – whereby Saudi Arabia accepted payments for oil exports in US dollars in return for American military protection of Saudi oilfields. Calvert alternates between singing "*petrodollar*" and "*petro d'Allah*". Black September were the first terrorist group to operate in discrete sleeper cells embedded around Europe, a structure later mimicked by Al-Qaeda. Their most notorious action was the killing of 11 Israeli athletes and officials at the 1972 Olympics in Munich.

5  The "heroes" include Hawkwind roadie John The Bog (thrown from the back of a van when it was hit by another vehicle) and Ladbroke Grove face Smiling Michael (who died falling from a drainpipe as he tried to access the third-floor flat above the *Frendz* office). Calvert fudges the details of both deaths.

6  Calvert had already foreshadowed this sentiment, as he described himself and Dave Brock wandering through Pinewood Studios during rehearsals for the first *Astounding Sounds* tour: "We find ourselves walking through an abandoned film set, a derelict facade that looks exactly like the streets of Notting Hill. And we look in the window of a cafe called the Reluctant Dragon. Nothing but miles of field growing inside. As we walk away from it, I glance back over my shoulder and see that our reflections are still there, peering out of the glass, scanning the deserted wind-swept streets." ('Eight Days A Week' – Robert Calvert, *Melody Maker*, 2/10/76). (This diary-style article is a wonderful piece of writing – funny, insightful and poignant – and well worth seeking out online.)

# Your Android Replica Is Playing Up Again

June–December 1977

L-R - Shaw, Brock, Calvert, King, House
(source: Michael Scott collection)

Hawkwind might still be wowing live audiences, but their chart performance continues to disappoint. *Quark* only just improves on its predecessor's placing, peaking at number 30, perhaps hurt by Charisma's curious decision not to promote it with a single beforehand.

Ironically, the reviews are all extended and mostly positive. The ever-loyal Geoff Barton at *Sounds* still misses the "magnificent mugginess" of his beloved *Doremi*. But if *Astounding Sounds* was fragmented, *Quark* is more powerful, with Calvert's lyrical contributions being particularly effective. Barton worries their venues are getting smaller, but "Hawkwind do have a place in today's music world".[a]

*Melody Maker*'s Brian Harrigan is less convinced: they're "sharper and more direct than they've been for a long time", but can still be "glaringly archaic", despite Calvert's amusing lyrics. Most tellingly, Hawkwind's commitment to long-form metronomic composition remains an issue for writers with the crash-bang-wallop of punk in their ears: "It's obvious that they've yet to grasp the essential difference between an extended riff on record and the same in a live context".[b1]

Yet it's *NME*'s Monty Smith who deems the album an unqualified success, its sound "all battering ram riffs and monoplane synthesized drones" – though there's still a hint of condescension: "…the Hawks once again bring sci-fi comic book thrills to the proles".[c] Even his punk iconoclast colleague Julie Burchill doesn't entirely hate it. It isn't the "usual idiot-dancing stuff one comes to expect from Hawkwind" but "spacey, scientific and a somewhat scary item, which proved a trifle too – uh – cerebral for my taste." She suggests that anybody who loves reading Moorcock while listening to early Velvet Underground should check it out.[d]

For the first time since *ISOS*, Barney Bubbles has no involvement in the packaging.[2] Instead, and presumably at Tony Howard's behest, the brief goes to Hipgnosis, design house of choice for Pink Floyd. Based on photographs taken inside Battersea Power Station,[3] the cover delivers a suitably scientific (if slightly grey) interpretation of the album's themes. While a technician's back is turned, energy crackles across banks of generators as the machines create a new super particle in mid-air. On the reverse, the technician is slumped in a chair, a folder over his face – in the foreground, a synchroscope seems to smile and wink, technology triumphant… Calvert is credited with 'strangeness', Brock with 'quark', House with 'charm'.

The inner sleeve contains the songs' lyrics, typed up with corrections left in by Calvert, and a blunt hand-written message from Brock assuring fans that after the "sacking" of Nik Turner, Paul Rudolph and Alan Powell, "we are <u>back on course</u>". According to Brock, 1976 was "the worst year for us, finding us in debt and out of touch with the modern world." It's a reassertion of his role as musical director, while acknowledging that *Astounding Sounds* wasn't perhaps the best record to release as punk became the new noise. Yet the message's Stalinist tone, with ex-members named and shamed, feels a little uncomfortable.

▾　　　▾　　　▾

Brock and Calvert make evident their disdain for the band's previous iteration in an interview with fanzine *Sniffin' Flowers*. Brock blames Rudolph and Powell for the band nearly folding, while Calvert accuses them of wanting Hawkwind to be a "funky soul band". He also complains about the lack of enthusiasm for the science fictional aspects of the music: "Rudolph was always carping about not doing it and it affects you".[e]

In other interviews, the band are asked to justify their position in the emerging new world order of punk, and Calvert is happy to rise to the challenge. "Hawkwind is an experimental group at a time when rock music is very conventional; very conservative," he tells *Sounds*. Punk may be refreshing compared to older bands, but its world-view is "old-fashioned" and "outdated",[f] something he reiterates to *NME*'s Julie Burchill.[g] However, he's impressed by long-time Hawkwind fan John Lydon, who is "proving that freedom of speech cannot be taken for granted in this country".[h]

Calvert is also keen to defend the band's countercultural roots. 'Days Of The Underground' isn't just hippie nostalgia, but a celebration of a genuinely creative and radical era. "Hawkwind is more than just entertainment. It's a serious band. We're in touch with the modern world… not living outside the tide of events just because we're interested in science fiction," he concludes.[i]

Charisma belatedly releases '**Quark, Strangeness And Charm**' as a single on 29 July, with 'The Forge Of Vulcan' as a B-side.[4] It doesn't make the charts, but it does lead to an incongruous slot on Marc Bolan's teatime pop show *Marc*, its foil discs and flashing lights the epitome of the sterile, artificial pop world the band has thus far shunned. While the rest of the band give a good impression of wishing they were somewhere else (and Brock actually is), a heavily made-up Calvert – who seems to have leapfrogged the punk years into the New Romantic era – pretends to play guitar and gesticulates meaningfully with a stuffed hawk on his arm, a man in his element.[5]

▼　　　▼　　　▼

Since his departure, Lemmy has surprised his peers by not only forming a band, but keeping it together despite line-up problems and record company apathy. An album recorded the previous year for UA had been declared unfit for public consumption, but in August, *Motörhead* is released on the independent Chiswick label. Calvert puts it succinctly: "Lemmy has taken the heaviness and got rid of the spaciness":[j]

it's a growling, petrol-soaked version of Hawkwind's galactic chug, featuring harder, faster versions of all the songs Lemmy wrote and recorded with them.

The bass intro to '**Motörhead**' becomes the dirty rumbling of some monstrous chopper, while Phil Taylor's drums are a frantic assault of rattling snares and pounding toms, like someone trying to hack their way out of a fume-filled garage. Guitars are turbo-charged, though the words are often lost in Lemmy's Woodbine rasp. '**Lost Johnny**' starts raggedly, until its chugging riff locks into a relentless grind, alleviated only by a spiralling solo from guitarist 'Fast' Eddie Clarke.[6] '**The Watcher**' transforms from morbid cosmic rumination into high-energy rock for headbangers. Lemmy's voice is effected, and there's a metallic phase on the double-tracked guitars, but like all the material here, it's breathless, frenetic, and resolutely earthbound.

There are other echoes of Lemmy's past – the driving low-end churn of '**Keep Us On The Road**' could be a harder version of 'The Aerospace Age Inferno' – but its collision of 60s garage rock and heavy-duty 70s blues is infused with the aggression of punk. *Motörhead* has the swing and solos of rock, but the cut-the-crap instincts of The Damned, the Sex Pistols and The Clash: '**Vibrator**' could be the Pink Fairies playing 'White Riot'.[7]

It scrapes into the charts for one week at number 43, but it's the start of a run of records that will see Motörhead become one of the most influential rock bands of their time, godfathers to both the late 70s/early 80s New Wave Of British Heavy Metal (NWOBHM) and the subsequent US thrash metal scene.

▾　　▾　　▾

August also sees the publication of *Queens Of Deliria*, part two of the proposed *Hawklords* trilogy. Featuring a new enemy in the Red Queen, as well as various band members' children, it's even stranger than the first instalment – and even further from representing the real Hawkwind of 1977. Moorcock's name is still slapped across the cover – though his only connection with it is the appearance inside of his albino anti-hero Elric of Melniboné. With tongue more firmly in cheek than ever, Butterworth's back cover blurb describes "a world stalked by decaying ghouls and policed by satanic Bulls, their amplifiers meting out the punishing music of Elton John".

▾　　▾　　▾

On 28 August, Hawkwind play the Reading Festival again, and deliver a *tour de force* performance, the Footsbarn Theatre Company joining them band onstage, to dance, fire-breathe and appear as spacemen and monsters.[8] Calvert's props include a gigantic reefer, a grotesque alien head and his swords, which he uses to cut up an American flag during 'Uncle Sam's On Mars'. He then strews the pieces about, which means The Doobie Brothers – billed as "special guests from the USA" – get to play amid the shredded remains of the Stars and Stripes.[k]

The great majority of their set during the UK tour that follows in September is drawn from newer material, and there are more unrecorded songs to keep the bootleggers busy. Calvert makes good on his promise to keep them a science fiction band: the spiky 'Robot' quotes Isaac Asimov, the elegiac 'High Rise' references Ballard, and the poppy 'Jack Of Shadows' is inspired, once again, by Roger Zelazny. For *NME*'s Paul Morley, the trademark Hawkwind sound of "throbbing insistencies" and "weird interjections" is no longer depressing or suffocating, but "persuasive, sharper, jumpier." He credits Calvert's "surprisingly strong pop persona," dubbing him the "Peter Cook of rock'n'roll".[l]

Certainly, Calvert is the catalysing centre of their increasingly focused songwriting and of their shows. There's a real physicality to his performance, as though he's acting something out that goes beyond mere showmanship. He's the snarling literary terrorist of his own imagination, the hero with a wing fighting unseen enemies, constantly on the edge of control. He certainly isn't the first frontman to channel private demons on the public stage, but he allows his characters to take over in a way that other 'theatrical' performers such as David Bowie or Peter Gabriel never do.

But with the pressures of being on the road, this all comes at a cost. Inhabiting a variety of personas night after night, he starts to lose his grip on reality. His breakdowns and tendency towards manic depression have long been a running gag within the press and the band's inner circle, especially as he's unusually open about his illness. He considers all this psychic thunder and lightning to be the well-spring of his inspiration – but if left unchecked, the storm can rage out of control. And during a second tour of France in October, this is exactly what happens.

Suffering from insomnia and hooked on books about guerrilla warfare, Calvert has taken to wearing a combat outfit both on and off stage. On 26 October, at the Palais des Sportes in Paris, he becomes convinced that the heads of various terrorist organisations are in the audience. When Jeff Dexter tries to calm him down after the show, Calvert attacks him with a sword. The band are used to his sometimes

# And you thought Hawkwind were just a bunch of old cosmic hippies

## DAVE HANCOCK FINDS SIGNS OF LIFE IN ANCIENT PSYCHEDELIC CONCEPT HELMSMAN ROBERT CALVERT

F ACT: Brian Jones and lone yachtsman Donald Crowhurst drowned about the same time. QUOTE: I'm not even sure if rock is the answer anymore. POEM: *Where dat Idi id Did dey do dat Idi in Idi in heben Or idi in hell Or idi just not feelin well Where dat Idi id id*

Quark, strangeness and charm. An entirely new sketch starring Bob Calvert.

Our legendary hero has spent the last year saving sci-fi rock band Hawkwind from the dreaded funk. Now read on . . .

"Alan Powell and Paul Rudolph who were effectively the rhythm section of the band, had distinctly different ideas to me and Dave Brock — and we're the ones who have to take responsibility for the direction.

"There was always an argument about the style of music because they wanted to play a more funky rhythm and they weren't too keen on our near obsession with fantasy and science fiction, so it came to an obvious split," says Calvert cunningly disguised as a mortal, eating melon in a Soho restaurant.

Powell and Rudolph have formed their own band, Kicks, and saxophonist Nik Turner has also left. He'll be working with Steve Hillage.

But the institution of Hawkwind continues even though Calvert admits that in 1977 they're hardly a fashionable band.

"We try to stay outside fashion and do what interests us and if people come round to liking what we do that's fine. But no, we're not as popular as we have been though we do still manage to pull a large concert audience," he says.

Point is, the last album 'Astounding Sounds, Amazing Music' was their least successful.

"It was not a very good album," concedes our hero. "Because it was made before the split and under the tension of a lack of co-operation." But the latest 'Quarks, Strangeness And Charm' is a more solid achievement.

"The musical direction is not vastly different but it's a step further from what we've done before. We seem to be able to clarify what we're doing now, whereas before it was instinctive, a bit thrown together. Nowadays more thought goes into it, I think the music is more sophisticated.

"To me Hawkwind is a way of life. Other things I've written, like poetry, I would sometimes put into Hawkwind, but it does have a clearly defined area. For instance we've never done a love song."

A N EXAMPLE of, Calvert's poetry met you on the way in to this article, as did the subject of a play the man's written about Brian Jones.

"I've researched it quite a lot," he says. "And a lot of the things that were happening to Brian Jones were happening to Donald Crowhurst. So I've written this play, an extremely controversial piece

of work actually, especially as far as the Rolling Stones parts of it are concerned.

"I don't really want to say too much about it in case it's squashed before it's even seen the light, but it's full of strange coincidences because they were both driven to a kind of suicide by inadequacy and the drive of ambition for fame. They were carried along by publicity.

"To get a thing like this staged is going to be difficult," he adds. "I don't think various members of the Rolling Stones might like the way they're being portrayed and it would be easy for someone round the Stones to stop the whole thing by not allowing the music to be used which is what they've done before.

"I understand Mick Jagger would like a film made of Brian Jones, I don't know whether it's true."

And if you thought that was a revelation how about this for a bit of science fiction gossip:

Johnny Rotten used to hang around Hawkwind. (Gasp).

"Yeah I knew him vaguely from some time ago, but I don't want to blow his image for him," maintains Calvert.

dangerous piece of work actually.

"It was about urban bombing and just after we released if the IRA had a really concentrated attack all over London, so the record was quickly withdrawn.

"United Artists quite rightly got cold feet about it because it would have been very likely they'd have made themselves a target for a bomb attack."

A ND YOU thought Hawkwind were just a bunch of old cosmic hippies.

"Hawkwind is an experimental group at a time when rock music is very conventional; very con-

servative," claims Calvert.

"That's the thing that puzzles me about the 'new wave' actually. It's produced by kids who have grown up with the media at their disposal and yet still their view of the world is so old-fashioned. Their political ideals seem to be based on really outdated ways of thinking; influenced by George Orwell. They still believe that a 1930's vision of paranoia for the future applies for our time.

"Big Brother is watching you is nothing to the subtle techniques that are already being used.

"The 'new wave' is the most conventionalised influence I've ever noticed in any art

form at all."

Hawkwind presumably defy convention.

"To my mind the psychedelic era was the most creative with new adventures in lifestyle and music style; pharmaceutical experiments.

"I tend to be against trends," (which is why he's dressed like a solicitors' clerk), "because it's a denial of individuality. There are people now who are so trendy they can't like anything unless it's been OK'd by the trend, and they end up being unable to form an opinion.

"During the acid rock period there was a new ap-

proach to the music but now it's all gone back to the three-minute pop format, even the current avant-garde use it.

"I'm really not even sure if rock is the answer anymore."

Calvert, like his band, thrives on being unfashionable; calculatedly enjoys going against the grain. From his house in Devon he doesn't view modern urban society as the frightening picture painted by Ob Noxious from his tower block flat.

But he also warns that Hawkwind "are not a joke".

"Hawkwind is more than just entertainment. It's a serious band but people don't take it seriously, they think it's a joke. But that's starting to change.

"It's certainly more than the common misconception of us being a bunch of Ladbroke Grove hippies into science fiction. In fact I suppose Nik Turner was the nearest we got to a hippy.

"In many ways Hawkwind is unique; there's no other band like it. We're in touch with the modern world as people and we take an interest; we're not living outside the tide of events just because we're interested in science fiction."

S CIENCE FACT: Physicists now believe that the atom is not the smallest particle of matter. It is in fact a quark.

> 'Big Brother is watching you is nothing to the subtle techniques that are already being used... The new wave is the most conventionalised influence I've ever noticed in any art form at all'

"I don't want to suggest that he might not be 20 years old.

"He came to see us when we were in Camden Town and I knew his face . . ."

But Calvert refuses to be drawn anymore although he denies rumours that Rotten was once a Hawkwind roadie!

In fact he admires much of the punk rock scene: "Johnny Rotten is proving that freedom of speech cannot be taken for granted in this country."

But "while they're saying decadence is to be despised they're manifesting another sort of decadence just as much, in the same sort of star syndrome.

"We've done punk kind of things," owns up our hero. "In fact back in 1972 I think, just after 'Silver Machine' we wanted to follow it up with 'Urban Guerilla', a very

'Hawkwind is more than just entertainment.' *Sounds*, 16 July 1977
(source: Wolfie Smith collection)

impetuous and demanding behaviour, but this feels like a full-on psychotic episode. The final straw comes when Dave Brock's hotel room is raided by armed police, who find the replica pistol that Calvert plays Russian roulette with on stage.

After extricating himself from this situation, Brock tells the rest of the band that enough is enough. The remainder of the tour is cancelled and they're leaving – without Calvert. Discovering them mid-escape, Calvert pursues their car on foot through the Paris traffic in full combat gear – but despite his efforts to wrench the doors open, the band make it to the airport without him.

Bizarrely enough, once Calvert is returned to England by the long-suffering Dexter, relations are patched up in time for his wedding on 5 November to his second wife Pamela Townley. Not only are past and present members of the band in attendance, but Simon King is his best man. Long-time Hawkwind associate Jamie Mandelkau is also there, and files a report for *NME* in which Calvert says: "Dave Brock convinced the others that I was having a nervous breakdown. What nonsense! They dumped me and my bags on the street in Paris. If I had been ill, what kind of mates are they to leave me?" He attributes the incident to "high spirits", but when he later starts talking to Mandelkau about being interrogated by the KGB, it's apparent that Calvert is still hovering a few feet above terra firma.[m]

▾　　▾　　▾

With no Christmas tour planned for once, Brock and Calvert both retreat to north Devon, where the latter has rented a cottage a few miles away from the former's farmstead. Brock is a well-known face on the local music scene, and friendly with a band called Ark, who have previously supported Hawkwind around Devon and Cornwall. Keen to develop a local side-project to play free festivals, he rehearses with Calvert and three of Ark's members: bassist **Harvey Bainbridge**, drummer **Martin Griffin** and keyboardist **Paul Hayles**. A show at Barnstaple's Queens Hall is organised for 23 December, billed as 'Dave Brock's Sonic Assassins with Bob Calvert', with support from 'Nick (sic) Turner's Abluhla'.[9] His marriage already on the rocks, Calvert is showing signs of another breakdown – but after initially refusing to appear, he turns in a truly compelling performance.

Alongside crunching versions of stalwarts 'Brainstorm' and 'Master Of The Universe', both 'Magnu' and 'The Golden Void' are resurrected from *Warrior*. But it's the new music that offers clues to Hawkwind's future.[10] **'Free Fall'** pivots around two bass riffs from Bainbridge, one spacey and serene, the other stark and gloomy, over which Calvert improvises a lyric about falling through the sky as "*an airborne projectile*" before making it to the ground, murmuring "*the earth is rising up to greet me*." It's as much performance art as song, and an effective metaphor for Calvert's trips through his own internal weather. '**Death Trap**' is the opposite, a manic slab of garage psych, faster and punkier than anything Hawkwind have previously done. With shouts of "*Death trip!*", "*I don't care!*" and "*Come and take me!*", Calvert turns into the English version of Iggy Pop he'd previously threatened to become.

But it's an inspired improvisation that will become known as '**Over The Top**' which demonstrates Calvert's quicksilver thought processes in real time. After an amusing discussion about the quality of the microphone stands[11] and a request to "cut the gypsy music", the singer begins to feel his way into the spiralling soundscape of synths constructed by Brock and Hayles. After fitting the words of 'The Awakening' around the gradually building track, he rails against unseen forces "*telling me that you know just when to stop*". This in turn becomes an anti-war tirade filled with WW1 imagery, from the comic ("*Hey Kitchener, don't you know that moustaches went out with the Beatles?*") to the impassioned ("*Give me white feather!*") It's at once riveting and disturbing – an insight into the raw logic of a mind where all channels are open.[12]

By accident or design, this show marks another turning point in Hawkwind's evolution, with Brock in particular attracted to the possibility of working locally and creating a new type of group.

a       'Strange But Charming' – Geoff Barton, *Sounds*, 9/7/77

b       'Hawks Get Back In Gear' – Brian Harrigan, *Melody Maker*, 25/06/77

c       'Hawkwind Back On Course' – Monty Smith, *NME*, 9/7/77

d       'Mindless Aggreshun On Hippy Farm' – Julie Burchill, *NME*, 28/10/77

e       *Sniffin' Flowers* no.2, 1977

f       'And You Thought Hawkwind Were Just A Bunch Of Old Cosmic Hippies' – Dave Hancock, *Sounds*, 16/7/77

g       Julie Burchill, same source

h&i     Dave Hancock, same source

j       *Sniffin' Flowers* no.2, 1977

k       Thanks to fan Steve Readhead for this recollection

l       Paul Morley, *NME*, 1/10/77

m    'Hawklord in KGB wedding affair' – Jamie Mandelkau, *NME*, 12/11/77

1    Calvert responded directly to Harrigan's review in a piece entitled 'Structural Defects: Why The New Wave Lose Out', printed in the following week's *Melody Maker*: "The long intros and fade-outs that Mr Harrigan refers to are, in fact, passages of musical texture and effects essential to and expressive of the lyrics…"

2    Bubbles was at the time providing art and design for punk and new wave artists such as The Damned, Elvis Costello and Ian Dury and The Blockheads. Though compare the electrical circuit logo he designs for Clover's 1977 *Unavailable* album, with *Quark*'s Hawkwind logo…

3    Just a few months before, Hipgnosis had used the exterior of Battersea Power Station as the backdrop to the notorious inflatable pig photoshoot for Pink Floyd's *Animals*.

4    In Germany, 'Quark' is coupled with 'The Iron Dream'. In Italy, an edit of 'Hassan I Sahba' is released as a single instead, with 'Damnation Alley pt. 2' as the B-side.

5    With Bolan introducing them as "my best friends, Hawkwind!" this is their second and last appearance on British TV in the 70s. It's brokered by Tony Howard, though it later emerges that Calvert and Bolan had genuine plans to collaborate – but Bolan died in a car crash just a few weeks after this recording. Brock's absence is explained either by a long-standing grudge against Bolan (for having once thrown him out of a party) or (as Adrian Shaw suggests) simply not wanting to travel from Devon to Manchester to film it. This meant Shaw had to record Brock's guitar parts for the show – a music union requirement at the time was that bands appearing on shows like *Top Of The Pops* and *Marc* nevertheless had to record a new backing track to mime to. And the stuffed hawk? This is likely an allusion to Moorcock's Jerry Cornelius character, who appears in a Mal Dean illustration from *The Final Programme* with a hawk similarly affixed to his arm (and goggles pushed back on his head). Calvert had previously posed with a stuffed hawk on his arm for the *Captain Lockheed* press ad, though this may also have been a reference to his (at the time) former band.

6    Though perhaps the best version of 'Lost Johnny' (also from 1977) is by Mick Farren & The New Wave, a buzzing punkoid dash through the song like Bob Dylan backed by a hyper-stimulated Hawkwind.

7    No surprise, as Motörhead's first guitarist Larry Wallis, who wrote it, was once a Pink Fairy.

8    The Footsbarn Theatre Company were based out of Cornwall, and had hooked up with the band via Roche Studios, a Cornish facility run by Ark and future Sonic Assassins/Hawklords/Hawkwind drummer Martin Griffin. Tony Davies, who performed with Footsbarn at the time, recalls: "The 'alien' head was from an old production called *Giant* (based on a Cornish legend). I remember having loads of plates to smash on the stage. We also did a show at the Hammersmith Odeon, which was chaotic. We were slipping around on paraffin that was all

over the floor from soaking a 12-foot high cross covered in linen material. It was then lit and I walked on stage with it. The fire officer was having fits. Two other members of our group had been fire spitting over the audience, and he was threatening to drop the fire curtain and stop the show. Great times" (interview with the author, 2019).

9    There's some confusion about who played support at the Sonic Assassins gig. Paul Hayles claims it was a local band of ex-Ark members called Osmosis. Other attendees maintain that Abluhla played, but without Nik Turner. Acoustic singer songwriter Reg Meuross is also said to have appeared.

10   It's hard to be precise about certain musical aspects of this show. An edited portion of the set initially appeared in 1980, on the first of Dave Brock's *Weird Tapes*, while 'Over The Top', 'Free Fall' and 'Death Trap' were released as a 12" EP by Flicknife in 1981. However, both releases feature significant overdubbing (partly because one of Paul Hayles' keyboards broke down during the first number). For example, the *Weird Tapes* version of 'Angels Of Death' (referred to as 'Angels Of Life') is full of ecstatic synths over a throbbing rhythm track, reminiscent of such contemporary German bands as Harmonia and La Düsseldorf. Yet a bootleg recording of the song from the gig itself is dominated by an aggressive guitar riff and crashing drums, much more like the version recorded on 1981's *Sonic Attack* album. The sinister electronic pulse at the beginning of 'Over The Top' was also added in post-production.

11   Calvert seems to have taken his own 'he-man' voice training course here, his masculine banter sounding like more role playing: "'Ere, Dave, where d'yer get these stands from? They're really heavy... So are you."

12   When Bainbridge was dispatched to Calvert's cottage to persuade him to do the show, he found the singer dressed in a WW1 military uniform, which clearly had a bearing on the following night's performance.

Poster for Sonic Assassins gig, 23 December 1977
(source: Philip Tonkyn archive)

# Adrian Shaw

Bass and vocals
January 1977–March 1978
*Quark, Strangeness and Charm* and *PXR5*

Adrian Shaw
(source: Doug Smith archive)

When did you first encounter Hawkwind?

I'd lived in Maida Vale, round the corner from Clearwater Productions in Great Western Road. I hung out there a bit and got to know High Tide, Hawkwind and Doug Smith. So when [singer] Rod Goodway and I formed Magic Muscle, I came to ask Doug if we could get any gigs with Hawkwind. This was at the time 'Silver Machine' was in the charts, and he got us on the Space Ritual tour.

Very shortly after, when I was living in Bristol, Nik and I think DikMik came to visit and said that they wanted to get rid of Lemmy – a really good move! – and would I join? With great regret I turned them down, out of loyalty to Magic Muscle.

How did the next call-up to join happen?
It was the end of 1976. I used to play tennis with Simon House – always chemically assisted to make it more interesting! – and he got in touch saying they wanted me to join. They'd fallen out with Paul and Alan and Nik, so the idea was for me to go and overdub all the bass parts.

How was the situation presented to you? As a new beginning?
Pretty much, yeah. Up until *Quark*, I think the band was a band. Dave was the most important member, because he'd been there right from the beginning and was very creative, and had a view of what they should be. But it was pretty democratic, amazingly so really. If you had a decent song, it would go on the album.

What was the atmosphere like when you joined?
It was really good, fun. Everyone was on good form. Calvert was coming out with spectacular stuff, full of ideas. Dave was very personable. I got on very well with Simon King, he was great to work with. And Simon House was an old friend. Rockfield was a lovely environment to work in, very laid back. I have very fond memories of it.

How does your style compare with Paul's, particularly overdubbing his tracks?
We have very different styles of playing. I don't think any of my parts had any relation to what he had done, they were completely rewritten. His were quite straight ahead, whereas I like doing stuff that's not obvious. He uses a pick, I use my fingers. Not disrespecting his playing at all, but Paul is a lead guitarist playing bass.

How did the *Quark* tour compare with Space Ritual? Were the audiences comparable?
The audiences were still very good. But it had changed a lot, much slicker and more musical. We were largely playing songs off *Quark* and what would become *PXR5* – we were recording a lot of the basic tracks for *PXR5* on that tour. The songs were shorter with more structure, it wasn't that overwhelming thing with

the audio generators. Very cut-down and tight, a good stage show, and Bob at the height of his powers.

**Did Bob have set routines?**
Pretty much so, with a touch of improvisation depending on the number. On 'Hassan', he'd throw his swords so they'd stick in the stage. I read how he nearly cut my head off with one of them, but that is so not true. It's just a myth.

**What's the story behind your appearance on *Marc*?**
It came about through Tony Howard. I read Dave didn't want to do it because it involved miming, but I don't think it was that. He basically couldn't be bothered, as I recall. He was in Devon and just didn't want to do it. He thought we couldn't do it without him, but we could and did. Bob in particular really wanted to do it. Bob was somewhat jealous of David Bowie's fame, he thought he was every bit as creative. He really wanted to be a star, I don't think there's any question about that.

**He was working himself up to peak mania on the French tour…**
I'm afraid he was. He couldn't sleep, he had this chemical imbalance, his mind was racing with creative ideas. I remember him knocking on my hotel door in the early hours. He had black foam flecking his mouth, desperate to talk about this idea for a song he had. I'm afraid he got short shrift!

**Then there's the notorious Paris gig…**
The next day, there was a band meeting without Bob. Dave said, "We can't do this, I think we ought to go home." The plan was we'd meet downstairs at 10am and go straight to the airport, and Jeff Dexter would get Bob home. So we packed, no one argued. We met up in the lobby, and Sod's Law, Bob walked in at that moment, and said, "Oh, are we going? I'll just get my bag." We skedaddled to the car. I'm really ashamed of this. So we drive off just as he appeared, bag in hand, and of course run straight into a traffic jam. Bob took off up the road after us, banging on the window, pleading to be let into the car. And everyone just stared straight ahead, and ignored him. It was horrible. Then the traffic cleared, and we just drove off and left him there, in full combat gear. It's tragedy and farce, but not something I'm proud of. I didn't do enough to stop that, and I really should have done. You don't leave sick friends behind.

How were the Rockfield sessions for *PXR5*?

The *Quark* sessions were fun, but it's weird looking back on the *PXR5* ones. Various members had problems. Bob had his mental problems, and Simon King had issues, though he was performing well and was perfectly affable. I think it bothered Dave more than anyone. But I think it's a good album, some tracks are considered classic Hawkwind.

Bob wanted to called it *PXR5*. He just plucked it out the air. It sounded a bit spaceshippy, but there's no significance to it at all. I never thought it was a good title, and I always remember Dave saying it was terrible, like *Thunderbirds Are Go* or *Fireball XL5*. But Bob got his way.

I definitely played on 'Death Trap', but I was not doing what Dave wanted, he wanted it very punky and he subsequently overdubbed his own bassline. And when Cherry Red reissued *PXR5* with bonus tracks, there was a version of 'Jack Of Shadows' with me singing that I have no memory of at all! But it's definitely me.

What was your experience of the March 1978 US tour?

Touring America is every musician's ambition, I had a wonderful time. It was unfortunate that Simon House was in the process of leaving to join Bowie. He'd phoned me up to say that he'd been offered the gig, and said, "What should I do?" I said, "Do it." It was a real drag losing him, you can't really replace Simon, but he was a mate and I would have done him a disservice [not saying go].

Paul Hayles has suggested that Brock had plans for Hawkwind to become the Sonic Assassins…

I certainly wasn't privy to them! I knew nothing about that. I knew that the band had a three-album deal with Charisma, and that Dave was desperate to get out of it one way or another, and the Hawklords was a way of circumnavigating the Hawkwind contract. Maybe that's why I and Simon King weren't asked [to join], because if you want a different name to start afresh, you can hardly have the same members.

# Cosmic Dada Nihilismus!

## The Hawkwind Mythos And The Space Age Re-Enchanted

*There's a Hawkwind cult now that's almost as vital to their gigs as the music. No matter which part of the country they play in the audience is basically the same. Every gig is a stage for local fantasies. Bottled up extrovert tendencies explode into fancy dress and painted faces, as if some messiah had given the sign... This ability to plant their myth in to popular imagination has played a large part in their making.*
Melody Maker, 1972[a]

One of the most fascinating aspects of Hawkwind's story is the mythology which grows up around the band, locating them in some parallel, science fictional version of reality. Variously portrayed as time-travelling astronauts, rakish superheroes, starfaring buccaneers and the last band on Earth, a central idea emerged of Hawkwind as the (sometimes grudging) saviours of humanity, reincarnated demi-gods fulfilling the prophecies of an ancient millenarian saga.

Mythologisation – explaining the world via stories rather than facts – was rife in the 1970s. The 60s had seen a collective eye-opening happen within society, a "revolution in the head".[1] But as the post-imperial mindset was slowly dismantled, all manner of belief systems – some radical, some reactionary – rushed in to fill the vacuum.

A growing distrust of traditional institutions was paralleled by a rising passion for anything occult or paranormal – from ghosts and UFOs to past lives and telepathy. The floodgates of credulity and conspiracy had burst open. What if we weren't being told the whole truth by the authorities – the government, the military, the scientists? A paranoid society faced with economic, ecological and nuclear apocalypse could only bear so much reality,[2] and the desire to retreat into a mythopoeic worldview became overwhelming.

The Hawkwind mythos was another way in which the band reflected the spirit of the age. Complementing the radical escapism of their music and multi-sensory shows, a web of self-mythologising fictions appeared in sleeve notes, tour programmes, the alternative press, and finally novels, which functioned as a fantastical allegory for their rise through the underground to deliver their fans from the tedious oppression of the straight world.

## A New Iconography

Of course, Hawkwind weren't the first band to indulge in self-mythologising. Since the dawn of popular music, acts have been portrayed as larger-than-life figures living a fantasy existence. By the 70s, exaggerating for effect had become an essential part of winning an audience over. Serious bands might have scorned the pre-rehearsed moves of pop groups and soul troupes, but the 'wild man' antics of Hendrix and Townsend created a new iconography of rock. And the media loved it, writing about the stars of the day as though reporting the affairs of a new pantheon of gods.

Some artists used costumes and props to ramp up the theatricality of their shows. Arthur Brown was an early pioneer, his face daubed in corpse paint, wearing ceremonial robes and a flaming headpiece for his 1968 hit 'Fire'. Genesis's Peter Gabriel dressed as a fox-headed debutante, a flower, and the horribly deformed Slipperman. Alice Cooper's show featured snakes and dwarves, and ended with him hanged from a gallows, while Kiss hid their identities behind outlandish make-up, breathing fire and spitting fake blood in an orgy of dry ice and pyrotechnic explosions.

The theme of deliverance from space inspired a number of artists. Jazz visionary Sun Ra and his Arkestra created an AfroFuturist mythology that envisioned black liberation among the stars. In the 1974 film *Space Is The Place*, Ra has established a colony free from white people in outer space. Returning to Earth to spread the gospel, he emerges from his spaceship in Oakland, resplendent in the golden finery of an Egyptian god – and blows the minds of the assembled crowd with a blast of atonal electronics. More tongue-in-cheek, George Clinton's Parliament ran with the AfroFuturist concept, with characters including the Starchild, Dr Funkenstein and Sir Nose d'Voidoffunk locked in a battle to bring funk to the people of Earth. The Parliament concept included an ambitious live show, complete with a flaming disco-ball spaceship landing on stage.

The French band Magma created a ritualistic form of progressive jazz they termed 'Zeuhl' based around an apocalyptic saga of refugees from Earth colonising the planet Kobaïa. It's hard to be more precise given that their songs are all in Kobaïan, a phonetic language that ranges from harsh, guttural barks to ethereal wailing. Magma would often appear live and in publicity shots dressed in black with giant metal pendants around their necks, looking like a particularly whacked-out branch of The Process Church (see later). More whimsical, but no less cosmic,

Gong – also based in France – made a series of albums inspired by a convoluted allegorical mythos featuring Pot Head Pixies, flying teapots and Radio Gnome Invisible transmissions from Planet Gong…

As the home of *Barbarella* and *Métal Hurlant*,[3] France also produced Space, whose opaque astronaut helmets and hit single 'Magic Fly' helped inspire the cosmic disco scene, and Rockets, a glam synth rock band who shaved their heads and painted themselves robot silver. Over in Los Angeles, Zolar X played a mix of hard rock, glam pop and prog dressed as extras from *Star Trek,* complete with giant shoulder pads, matching haircuts and antennae – they also had their own alien language, which they used both on and off stage.

## A Mutual Mission

When Moorcock saw Hawkwind for the first time, he described the experience as "like being aboard a generational starship whose crew had gone totally raving barmy". [b] Hawkwind embodied their mythos from the start – it wasn't a record company-driven initiative to shift product, but self-generated and controlled, something owned by both band and audience.

But that's not to say it was entirely without an author. It was Robert Calvert who first developed the narrative, forging the band's creation myths, and mixing the mystical and profound with the surreal and absurd. When Nik Turner described Hawkwind's noisy post-psychedelia as 'space rock', Calvert saw a conceptual seed, a confluence with the science fiction poetry he was writing.

In May 1971, when he first took to the stage with the band to recite 'Co-Pilots Of Spaceship Earth', Calvert effectively created a framing device for Hawkwind.[4] Many a psychedelic happening had involved poets and non-musical performers, but to 'interrupt' a rock gig with a reading was unusual: it instantly turned the show into something more akin to performance art. The words themselves are striking, essentially announcing a regime change:

> "*We are all co-pilots of spaceship Earth.*
> *Your captain is dead.*
> *Your captain is speaking.*
> *Your captain is dead.*
> *This is your captain speaking.*
> *Your captain is dead.*"

The "*we*" is everyone on the planet, but spoken from the stage, it also implies a pact being made, between the 'we' of the band and the 'we' of the audience. It's the start of a mutual mission: "*Let us all take off together / Let us all fly together / Let's all get back on course together / Let's get this ship together.*" It also combines science fiction's 'sense of wonder' with the still-warm ecstatic utopianism of the hippie movement: "*Switch all channels through to the void and fill your heads with peace and fire your flesh rockets with the fuel of love... let us ride together on orgasmic engines to the stars*".[5]

If no more had been heard from Calvert after this, Hawkwind would still have plotted a course into deep space – though possibly without co-ordinates or bearings. But Calvert did continue to perform with the band – 'Co-Pilots Of Spaceship Earth' (retitled 'Technicians Of Spaceship Earth') became Hawkwind's intergalactic mission statement, while poems such as 'The Awakening' and 'The Starfarer's Despatch' suggested an emerging narrative that underpinned the band's songs, especially new tracks like 'Master Of The Universe'.

Calvert had inhabited roles – from thwarted fighter pilot to underground Dadaist poet – all his life, so it was natural for him to use Hawkwind as a new canvas for his fervid imagination, transforming them into something far beyond a mere group of musicians.

## The Immaculate Void

Released in October 1971, the packaging alone of *In Search Of Space* showed that – thanks to the visionary design work of Barney Bubbles – Hawkwind had taken a huge conceptual leap forward. The interlocking sleeve is like a glorious artefact from some countercultural galactic empire, with a quote from 'Technicians Of Spaceship Earth' on the back. And within its folds is the first sacred text of the Hawkwind mythos: printed as a 24-page booklet on flimsy newsprint style paper, *The Hawkwind Log* is surely the strangest set of sleevenotes ever included with an album.

Written/compiled by Calvert (though it's very likely that Bubbles also contributed), it purports to be extracts from the log of the "two-dimensional" spacecraft Hawkwind, discovered during an expedition to the South Pole by "Captain RN Calvert of the Société Astronomae (an international guild of creative artists dedicated in eternity to the discovery and demonstration of extra-terrestrial intelligence)."

It's a record of a journey through space-time, and the philosophies that inform its voyage – a dense screed of text and imagery, with a non-linear narrative, full of apparently random digressions and allegorical allusions to band and album. Travelling through space is a disorientating process, and in cryogenic sleep, the mind is prone to wander and dream: "Hallucination is no rare occurrence in outer space… We decided, as usual, to ignore the apparent evidence of our senses until complete investigations had been made by our instruments".[6]

On the inside cover is a retelling of the Judeo-Christian creation myth, where God ('the Supreme One') broods in darkness with "only the thick, deep sable night in which to fumble and find nothing." With a gigantic effort of will, He imagines the universe into being, creating "a stern reality of dreams, a reality so contrived that it would persist for all time".[7] This chimes with 'Master Of The Universe', particularly the line, "*It's all a figment of my mind*".

The *Log* then describes the discontinuous adventures and thoughts of the crew, beginning with a ceremony in which their vessel – a "celestial edifice" and "great silvership" – is lifted from a sacred lake.[8] The *Log* states: "For you must journey the unmeasured expanses of this Universe to take the sound of these spheres, the sound of the Supreme One, to a tiny solar system and there you must fill the emptiness" – this won't be the last time the band are portrayed as enlightened beings tasked with saving the earth. References are also made to both Brinsley Le Poer Trench and Joseph Goodavage, real-life ufologists convinced that many of the ancient world's monuments were built by a race of extra-terrestrials – the implication being that Hawkwind and crew are remnants of such a race, returning to the world they left behind centuries before.[9]

Here, the *Log* reflects a growing belief in the 70s that Man's history had been shaped by contact with beings from other worlds, the previously accepted view of the past becoming clouded by pseudo-science. As society began to doubt its own agency and judgement, it began to question whether ancient civilisations could really have created the pyramids, the Nazca lines or the stone heads of Easter Island on their own. Perhaps the wisdom of the ancients came from somewhere else – as the *Log* itself notes, "we may be merely remembering old lessons learned long before our collective amnesia."

Certainly it has little good to say about the immediate future. As the Hawkwind prepares to land in 1978, "We played Hendrix. Third stone from the sun. It seemed to be appropriate. Earth is already become nothing much more than a stone. Piles of wrecked cars to the sky; rusting industrial waste accumulating in a landscape of crumbling concrete." The ship returns to space in 1987: "There was hardly any point in hanging around this burnt out version of mother Earth. We could always

Stills taken from film made by Cynthia Beatt, mid-1973. Some of this footage was used in the 'Urban Guerilla' promo. Line-up: Calvert, Stacia, Brock, Turner, Dettmar, Lemmy, King. (stills by and courtesy of Cynthia Beatt)

*Astounding Sounds* tour, 1976 – Nik Turner in his astronaut suit, King, Brock, House
(source: George Galitzine archive)

Robert Calvert and dancers, Hawklords tour 1978 (source – Keith Kniveton collection)

Robert Calvert, Bracknell Sports Centre, 18 December 1976
(source: Keith Kniveton collection)

Robert Calvert,
Hawklords tour
1978(source :Keith
Kniveton collection)

Blake, Lloyd-Langton, Bainbridge, Oxford New Theatre, 23 November 1979
(source: Keith Kniveton collection)

come back later, in the future, when her wintering is done. Or come back earlier in the past before the industrial madness began." Both entries echo the sentiments of 'We Took The Wrong Step Years Ago', and suggest their mission – to counter the emptiness of Man's existence with the music of the spheres – has been a failure.[10]

The *Log* spins head over heels through various ages and philosophies, its pages adorned with cosmic, astrological and mystic images, from pictures of Stonehenge and Glastonbury Tor to pulp-style illustrations. There are quotes from Carlos Castaneda's *The Teachings Of Don Juan* and Sioux holy man Black Elk, and much paraphrasing of esoteric Eastern religious tracts regarding 'thought forms' and the Tao. Other unattributed quotes address the notion of the pioneer spirit and the quasi-mystic allure of unspoiled landscapes.[11]

But the ship's occupants have become unmoored in time – "We journey on through space, in search of the present, leaving a trail of abandoned futures in our wake" – and the *Log* 'ends' its story in Ladbroke Grove on 5 May 1971: "Space/time indicators near to zero. Our thoughts are losing depth, soon they will fold into each other, into flatness, into nothing but surface. Our ship will fold like a cardboard file and the noises of our minds compress into a disc of shining black, spinning in eternity."

The *Log*'s final entry states: "And now I believe in the supreme and mystic darkness of nothing, in the deepest reaches of the immaculate void." For Hawkwind, this will be a recurrent theme – the cosmos as a site of vast unknowingness. To escape into space is to embrace absolute possibility, a place to begin again, but there's also the prospect of being lost forever, of being subsumed by eternal night.

## Space Age Mysticism

The *Log*'s conflation of space travel and mysticism might read like leftover mumbo-jumbo from the 60s, but Hawkwind certainly weren't alone in thinking of space in this way. There's a surprisingly strong connection between utopian visions and the early days of the space race.

The US government had intended the moon programme to be a monument to America's technological supremacy over the USSR, a muscle-flexing display of one-upmanship at the height of the Cold War. But for many astronauts, visiting space and the moon would be a life-changing experience. As they gazed back at Earth – this small blue marble in an ocean of darkness – they found themselves grappling with ideas of both existential insignificance and universal consciousness.

Edwin 'Buzz' Aldrin, the second man on the moon, found it difficult to come to terms with his cosmic experience, and succumbed to depression. Yet for Edgar Mitchell, the sixth man on the moon, it led to a spiritual epiphany, or as he described it, a feeling of 'samadhi', a yogic term denoting a union with the divine. In 1973, he founded the (still-extant) Institute of Noetic Sciences, which promotes Eastern practices said to raise consciousness and lead to higher perceptions of reality.

The US space programme often felt like an extension of America's creation myth, the pioneer spirit upon which the nation was founded. In *Of A Fire On The Moon* (1970), Norman Mailer wrote that mankind had made a profound leap forward on reaching its nearest celestial neighbour, escaping the restraints of Earth and daring to look God in the face. For respected physicist (and rejected astronaut) Gerard K. O'Neill, the moon landings were merely a first step towards the colonisation of space – his 1975 book *The High Frontier* again evokes America's pioneer mythos.

Things get stranger further back. It's well known that rocket scientist Wernher von Braun – the man who enabled America's post-war dreams of space conquest – began his research as a willing member of Hitler's Nazi regime. But less well known is the colourful backstory of Jack Parsons, who invented the first rocket engine to burn a composite, containerised fuel. A committed occultist and science fiction fan obsessed with space exploration, Parsons was prominent in Aleister Crowley's Ordo Templi Orientis and also a close associate of L. Ron Hubbard.[12] During rocket tests, Parsons could be found fervently reading aloud Crowley's poem 'Hymn To Pan'. As his biographer George Pendle puts it, Parsons "saw both space and magic as ways of exploring these new frontiers – breaking free from Earth literally and metaphysically".[c]

However, the space race's mystic foundations stretch back further still, to 19th century Russia and Nikolai Fedorov's philosophy of Cosmism. This was the belief that science would one day fulfil God's promise to resurrect the dead to eternal life. As Earth would be unable to sustain its undying population, Man's ultimate destiny was to leave the planet and colonise the stars.

Cosmism would probably have been forgotten had Konstantin Tsiolkovsky – one of Russia's first proponents of rocketry – not been a keen disciple. His Cosmist tract *The Will of the Universe: The Unknown Intelligence* sets out his vision of the human race's expansion into the Milky Way. Tsiolkovsky inspired a group of 'space activists' called the Cosmopolitans, who staged the world's first exhibition dedicated to space travel and exploration in 1927. Tapping into the utopian impulses of the Russian Revolution itself, a Cosmist-derived space evangelism became embedded in the national consciousness, with hundreds of articles and books published on the subject in the 1920s alone.

More practically, Tsiolkovsky's ideas about rocketry influenced Sergei Korolev, the man who built the R-7 rockets that propelled both the Sputnik satellites and Yuri Gagarin into space. The atheistic Soviet authorities produced a propaganda poster showing the happy cosmonaut floating above the slogan "There is no God" – and yet the Soviet space art produced in the wake of Gagarin's historic flight is imbued with a cosmic utopianism, Fedorov and Tsiolkovsky's visions of Man taking his rightful place among the stars brought to glorious technicolour life.

## The Pop Apocalypse

Two further items promoting *ISOS* expand on the Hawkwind mythos.

The first is a set of 21 'Galactic Tarot' cards published in *IT* (18 November 1971). Another Calvert/Bubbles co-creation, their "divinatory meanings" are as cosmic and arcane in tone as the *Log*: "The Galactic Tarot does not speak of the future or the past, for all galactic time is contained in the present."

Band members are listed, albeit with obscure non-musical credits – Dave Brock for "slow alchemic anatomy", DikMik for "Banes Bridge Bingo Hall Theatre of Satanism". We're assured that the "pop Apocalypse is coming" and that Earth remains in deep trouble: "Prepare for upheaval. Lord Chaos is coming. And Warlord Disorder. Followed by disaster unless something is done NOW to prevent it."

The cards have the words to as-yet unreleased songs – 'Born To Go', 'The Black Corridor', 'Silver Machine' and 'Infinity' – split across them. 'Born To Go' in particular is an anthemic statement of intent, the inclusive "we" once again bringing band and audience together on the same mission: "*We're breaking out of the shell / We're breaking free / We're hatching our dreams into reality*". Again, it pushes the idea of the band as cosmic avatars tiring of Earth and yearning for escape into some esoteric version of the universe.

The second item is altogether more tongue-in-cheek compared to the *Log* and Galactic Tarot, a two-page comic strip entitled 'Codename: "Hawkwind" – The Sonic Assassins'. Written by Michael Moorcock, illustrated by James Cawthorn and published in *Frendz* (29 November 1971), it wants to raise a smile rather than debate profundities. But it adds another layer to the mythos, positioning the band as superheroes ready to battle danger on behalf of the underground whenever they're needed.

First panel of Sonic Assassins strip, *Frendz*, 29 November 1971
(source: John Coulthart collection, courtesy of Michael Moorcock)

As with 'Sonic Attack', Moorcock bases the strip on the idea that sound waves can inflict terrible mental pain and discomfort – in this instance, the "audiopollution" of middle-of-the-road, saccharine pop music. It dramatises the keenly-felt musical conflict between the mainstream and the underground, where to be a head or freak is to be in opposition to the sounds of straight society. The strip is peppered with examples of contemporary audiopollution: The Piglets' contrived 'Johnny Reggae'; Daniel Boone's sickly 'Daddy Don't You Walk So Fast'; Tom Jones' overwrought 'Till'; Frank Sinatra's ubiquitous 'My Way'.[13]

Cawthorn – who also designed T-shirts and a backdrop for Hawkwind – draws in the 'underground comix' style of Robert Crumb and Gilbert Shelton, though his likenesses of the band are actually rather good. His vibrant panels are packed with intriguing detail. Void City, the community under attack, is populated with various 'freaks' – a yelling John Trux represents the denizens of Ladbroke Grove, but other characters include Dracula, Frankenstein's Monster (plus Bride), King Kong, the Invisible Man, The Thing, Jane and her dachshund Fritz, and Snoopy. On Trux's T-shirt, Moorcock's anti-hero Elric screams "Arioch!"

In the story, such as it is, Hawkwind (or "the Seven", including new recruits "Cap" Calvert and "Lem") are summoned from a secret HQ to combat this threat. Terry Ollis ("Boris Skin") throws a cocktail of calming pills down Trux's throat. When DikMik finds a plastic "Tony Blackburst" grin on the ground, "Del 'Dynamo' Detmar" (sic) exclaims, "It's worse than we thought!" As Blackburst and cohorts reappear, in MOR-spewing aircraft with BBC insignia,[14] Hawkwind create a "sonic wall" by firing their instruments at the sky, repelling the bad vibes and forcing a retreat. If audiopollution strikes, the strip concludes, there is "a band of dedicated men pledged to find it, fight it and destroy it! … Remember the code name. It could save you. That name is – Hawkwind!"

Moorcock might take the band less seriously than Calvert, but Hawkwind are still presented as superhuman beings helping the enlightened few to resist the forces of oppression. What's new is the way they take the fight to the enemy, muscled warriors now rather than mystical soothsayers. In the last panel, we see a post-battle group shot of a triumphant army – in his visored helmet, Nik Turner in particular looks tooled up and ready for further action.

## Millenarian Visions

By some cosmic coincidence, the next step in the mythos appears in the pages of *Frendz* on 14 July 1972, the day after the 'Silver Machine' promo first airs on *Top Of The Pops*. In just over half a year, Hawkwind have gone from being heroes of the underground to bona fide hitmakers – and here to celebrate is an in-depth feature by Nick Kent, 'Gone With The Wind', while Del Dettmar graces the cover reading *The Dandy*.

Alongside Kent's article is a piece by Calvert, generally referred to as 'Fly As A Kite'.[15] It's another Hawkwind creation story, and surprisingly flippant in tone, even wacky. The band is once again "a supernatural, extra-terrestrial, alien thing" from "the deepest reaches of outer time" – but rather than returning demi-gods from some advanced galactic civilisation, they're an "embryonic blob of consciousness" that's somehow found its way into Notting Hill's drains. This seed of "pure potential" waits in "suspended animation, dreaming all the shapes it might assume." (Another idea gaining currency at the time was that life on Earth had been kick-started by alien spores from a comet.)

This Hawkwind star-seed has the "power to assume the form and the essence of the first thing it saw".[16] First it takes form as 'Dave Brock', an alien simulacrum of a busker who recruits other members of the band. DikMik plays the "electronic integration box" and lives in a "cybernetic castle by the sea";[17] Turner is a "great honking hawk-beaked being" who plays the "saxoscope" and appears in a "great whirl of wind". Together, they create a "weird space language" that nobody understands.

There's no mention of John Harrison or Huw Lloyd-Langdon, gone before Calvert got involved with the band, but Dave Anderson appears as a "Venusian space bassist", while Ollis (whose family were scrap-metal merchants) is a "door-to-door scrap wind hawker" who wears cast-off bits of iron. Dettmar is the "longest haired building labourer in the world", his "sympathiser" a "bleeping, chirruping, wherping, blaspheming machine". With the *ISOS* line-up complete, the band look out of the window, only to discover they've already taken off: "Their name went before them throughout the Universe and huge crowds gathered to watch their ritual of noise and light."

As in real life, the ship's crew now changes. Anderson "slowly vanished into the sun", while DikMik points out that Ollis "has OD'd and slipped the dimension". Lemmy makes a grand entrance as a "dark stranger", man-with-no-name style, though Calvert slyly notes: "No-one understood what he said, but all were deeply impressed by the speed with which he said it…" Calvert himself is a "tall red-bearded" sage who has foreseen the coming of Hawkwind in his "ominous dreams". But for all his magickal airs, he politely asks to join, adding rather sadly that, "The Orgone Glade is a lonely place."

Simon King, the final member (as of July 1972) then arrives, an "Elfin stick-beater, the tallest they had ever seen" who plays "a cloven-hoofed machine of perpetual motion". (With his long, thin face and rangy demeanour, King does indeed resemble some Moorcockian elemental). Thus assembled, "the seven" take to their "vehicles of whirling blue" (Ambulances? Police vans?), to begin their next adventure.

It's a curious, decidedly mock-heroic piece compared to what's gone before, but again presents the band as fantastical, larger-than-life characters with special powers.[18]

Unfortunately, the key supporting apparatus of the underground's own mythology was about to crumble. 'Fly As A Kite' appeared in one of the last issues of *Frendz*, with the magazine closing in August 1972 – and both *IT* and *OZ* would close by the end of 1973. The countercultural press had played a vital role in propagating the love & peace, anti-establishment spirit of the late 60s, but just a few years later, idealism and enthusiasm had given way to disillusionment and the financial realities of running a magazine.[19]

"We seem to be back where we started," *OZ* had written in November 1971. "Rock music, which once seemed to hold such hope as a social tool" had been taken from the underground and corrupted by money. But *OZ* still urged a philosophy of personal liberation as the way forward, however difficult that might be – "to all practical purposes to be a freak is to be an outlaw… to be constantly harassed by the law, to be the subject of dislike and hatred from the majority, to be some kind of instantly identifiable alien…"[d]

This harsher, less romantic worldview increasingly shapes the direction of Hawkwind's own mythos, a more militant edge displacing the cosmic mysticism. There's still humour and wordplay in the next instalment of their story, which appears on the back cover of *Doremi*, but Calvert's tone has changed again. 'The Saga Of Doremi Fasol Latido' takes place in the year 12753 during the "terrible age of the machine logic god, Eye See Eye".[20] The piece is written as cod-scripture, like a science fantasy version of the Old Testament or a Norse myth, with Hawkwind as the starfaring prophets of a quasi-religious narrative.

The album is a "collection of ritualistic space chants, battle hymns and stellar songs of praise" which recount how the "Lords of the Hawk" escaped into space in the distant past of 1972 to begin their "epic journey to the fabled land of Thorasin". In line with the underground's siege mentality, the band are now forest-dwelling Robin Hoods, renegade outlaws fighting "a desperate but losing guerrilla battle against the Bad Vibes squads." Their decision to abandon Earth and "set course in their silver ships into the unknown" is depicted as a glorious Dunkirk-like action, retreat (into fantasy) as radical escape.[21]

To flee oppression for a promised land (or an elevated state of existence) is common to many religions. But there's more, as *Doremi*'s inner sleeve makes plain: "And in the fullness of Time the Prophecy must be fulfilled and the Hawklords shall return to smite the land. The Dark Forces shall be scourged, the Cities razed and made into Parks. Peace shall come to everyone. For is it not written that the Sword is key to Heaven and Hell?" It's not enough to escape persecution; when the 'end times' arrive, enemies and non-believers must be defeated. The apocalypse is both the revenge of the righteous and the harbinger of a new age of Heaven on Earth.

"I don't think we ever wanted to be stars, but to be at the head of a small cult would be enough," Calvert once joked.[e] And there's plenty of fans who would attest that seeing Hawkwind in the 70s was akin to a religious event or experience, the pounding shamanic music and the consciousness-expanding visuals producing feelings of liberation and ecstasy.[22] Yet Calvert's growing fascination with the millenarian language and iconography of terrorism was also spilling over into the mythos.

## Dissonance And Disillusionment

The more esoteric philosophies of the counterculture had already combined with an extremist utopianism in strange, sometimes dangerous new ways. For some on the political fringes, the terrorist actions of the Weathermen and the Baader-Meinhof gang were the way forward. For others, returning to the land was still the model for an ideal society – even as the Khmer Rouge prepared to commit genocide in the service of a similar 'great leap forward'. Charles Manson's cult murdered nine people in 1969, intending to trigger a 'race war' that only they would survive, in a secret city beneath Death Valley... Some of Manson's ideas came from the Process Church Of The Final Judgement, a Scientology offshoot that became a Swinging London-based doomsday cult, complete with glossy magazine (*The Process*), branches in several US cities, and a 24-hour Mayfair coffee bar called 'Satan's Cave'.[23]

The counterculture might have been in retreat by the early 70s, but as the crisis of confidence in traditional institutions grew ever more serious, the desire for new mythologies had passed from the pages of the underground press into the mainstream media. Newspapers ran stories about UFO sightings and the Loch Ness Monster side-by-side with reports on IRA bombings or the latest industrial action. It created a strange kind of dissonance, as rival versions of reality vied with one another.

The UFO in particular was a dominant symbol of this new age of willed re-enchantment. Erich von Däniken's tales of ancient astronauts had already caught the public imagination, as had Stanley Kubrick's *2001: A Space Odyssey*, which portrayed a superior intelligence guiding mankind's development from the dawn of time. David Bowie created a pop cult out of the notion that a 'starman' was waiting in the sky to solve all our earthly problems, and in 1977 came Steven Spielberg's *Close Encounters Of The Third Kind*, the ultimate celebration of UFO contact.

Yet as we watched the skies for flying saucers and alien salvation, enthusiasm for our own space age was dwindling. Writing in *OZ*, Bob Hughes described the moonshot as the "most expensive public relations exercise in the history of man," and decried the spending of billions "so that our Faustian technocrats might leave behind them the culminating traces of several million years of evolution" – "plastic bags of urine" and "a plaque inscribed with a cliché".[f] How many lives, he angrily wondered, might have been saved if these billions had been spent instead alleviating famines or fighting poverty?[24]

For Robert Calvert, it was all a big anti-climax: "It was so farcical, the moonshot, so military-minded. When I was a kid I was really into rocketry, sci-fi, I really thought that the moon landing would be a momentous occasion, there would be dancing in the streets, people would be leaping about, kissing each other... but it wasn't like that at all".[g][25]

## Another Bloody Crusade

As the military/industrial adventurism of the space race ground to a halt, Hawkwind offered an alternative account of mankind's quest for cosmic omniscience. Apollo 17, the final mission to the Moon, took place in December 1972 – just as the band were undertaking their most ambitious tour yet performing the long-mooted Space Ritual show.

Every member of the audience received a free joss stick and a fold-out programme-cum-lyric sheet. Entitled 'An extract from the Saga of Doremi Fasol Latido', this followed on directly from the *Doremi* sleevenotes: returning from Thorasin to Earth to fulfil their prophecy, the band have suffered "collective amnesia", with only Nik Turner entrusted by "the priests of Ilbrahim" to have the information imprinted on his brain.

Pitched somewhere between the mock-heroism of 'The Sonic Assassins' and the irreverent fantasy of 'Fly As A Kite', it's another insight into group dynamics from Calvert's perspective, with his old friend Turner cast as captain of the ship and main protagonist. The band are battle-hardened warriors in military regalia, Lemmy and DikMik depicted as foppish cavaliers bored by missionary work for a "race of superstitious natives". With his "fresh face" and "well-muscled body", Brock is a simple Devonshire yokel, homesick for farm and wife. King is a rowdy womaniser, the long-suffering Dettmar a dwarf with thinning hair.

These toughened-up roles are in line with their strident and increasingly intense music, Hawkwind as unruly soldiers sorting out the Bad Vibes squads. Barney Bubbles may still be talking about the Space Ritual as channelling the music of the spheres, but the description here of "people standing and screaming and a band playing loud shrieking metal music" captures the Hawkwind live experience more accurately.

Returning as representatives of the "Galactic Union", they've come to issue their home planet a familiar ultimatum: "Your ambitions are causing an imbalance to the Galaxy... suspend immediately all traffic in arms... please show our emissaries unrestricted powers of investigation." While Turner urges "restraint... bring peace with honour," Lemmy responds, "Honour my arse, give me a good wenchling and some cocaine".[26] And DikMik is spoiling for a fight: "I didn't get these scars by wailing to my gods when things got difficult."

A pre-battle ceremony takes place, finally giving Stacia a role within the mythos, as a "woman of proud bearing with a painted silver face of the prime sorceress caste." She's also on the programme's front cover, defiant before a looming alien skull and crossbones. As the Hawkship descends towards Earth, the question is posed, "Will these people accept us... or must there be another bloody crusade...?"

With its seamless meld of music and spoken word, bedazzling visuals and dancers, the Space Ritual performances were absolutely key in establishing Hawkwind as purveyors of something far beyond average rock show entertainment. And as fans entered the band's mythological narrative, they also bought into its brand. Every Barney Bubbles logo, poster, advert and record sleeve reinforced Hawkwind's image as sci-fi freedom fighters inhabiting a technicolour version of the underground. They were also one of the first bands to sell their own merchandise via mail order, with ads for branded T-shirts, singlets, posters and patches regularly appearing in the back pages of *IT*.

Yet the Space Ritual tour also marked the peak of the band's self-mythologisation. By the end of 1973, some members were expressing a desire to step away from their overtly science fictional image, and with Calvert concentrating his creative energies on developing a solo career, further tales of the Hawklords were not forthcoming.

The notion of Hawkwind as a band engaged in an epic struggle with the forces of darkness persisted however, in a series of Michael Moorcock-penned spoken word pieces recited at their live shows and recorded on *Warrior*. While separate from the Calvert-derived mythos, Moorcock's tales of soldiers on the edge of time and veterans of the psychic wars complemented its general vibe, and could be seen in some ways as a continuation of the story, Hawkwind locked in a never-ending and perhaps unwinnable battle.

## The Mythos Resurrected

The Hawkwind mythos was given an unexpected second wind in 1976 with the publication of *The Time Of The Hawklords*, an entire novel inspired by it. Attributed to both Michael Moorcock and Michael Butterworth, it was in fact the sole work of Butterworth, a young writer for *New Worlds* whom Moorcock had taken under his wing. Moorcock's sole editorial direction was "Hawkwind rocking in the ruins of London", but Butterworth took inspiration wherever he could find it, specifically the Sonic Assassins strip and the Saga of Doremi Fasol Latido.[27]

From such slender elements, Butterworth constructed a post-apocalyptic scenario, Hawkwind versus Major Mephis, the crazed leader of the devastated straight world, intent on wiping out the Children of the Sun, who are re-building a community amidst the ruins of Notting Hill. Hawkwind are the last band standing, their live performances the only thing that can stave off "the Horrors", a feeling of psychic and physical torment from which both band and Children increasingly suffer. At the same time, Hawkwind's music induces nausea and a loss of bowel control in the straights, who can only repel its effects by listening to the soothing sounds of John Denver, Paul McCartney, and Simon and Garfunkel.[28]

The band discover that their music's restorative power comes from the "Delatron Processor", a semi-magical sonic box bequeathed to them by the departed Dettmar.

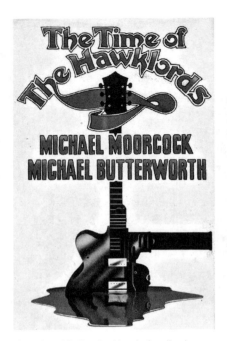

*The Time Of The Hawklords* hardback,
1976, artwork by Mike Little
(source: Michael Butterworth archive)

Michael Butterworth, 1976, from *The
Radcliffe Times*
(source: Michael Butterworth archive)

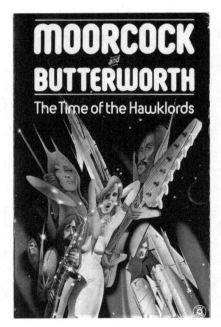

*The Time Of The Hawklords* paperback,
1976, artist unknown
(source: Michael Butterworth archive)

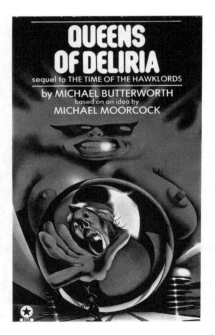

*Queens Of Deliria* paperback, 1977,
artist unknown
(source: Michael Butterworth archive)

They also learn of their destiny as the Hawklords from the *Saga Of Doremi Fasol Latido*, an ancient book that "Moorlock the Acid Sorcerer" happens to have kicking around his house. They discover that the Horrors are caused by the "Death Generator", an alien device at the Earth's core responsible for corrupting the minds of men down through the ages and leading the world to its current state. As the reincarnation of the Hawklords, the band must destroy the Generator and free humanity from its malign influence…

*The Time Of The Hawklords* is an oddity to say the least. The fact it was commissioned in the first place reflects the band's popularity at the time, but for anybody not already fully invested in the Hawkwind mythos, it probably seemed downright bizarre. And even hardcore fans might have thought twice about taking on 250 pages of the stuff. Written quickly to order, it was Butterworth's first novel, and reads like a strange cross between exploitation pulp, New Wave fever dream and a fan review of their favourite band.

Still, it zips along at a decent pace and the setting is vividly imagined, if never explained, though climate breakdown and collective madness are hinted at. Some of it could be from a Jerry Cornelius novel – the rat-infested Brighton amusement arcades, and Moorlock's sentient Blenheim Crescent house 'Victoria', with whom the Acid Sorcerer seems to be having an improper relationship. One of the more intriguing scenes takes place inside a virtual-reality tower, where the minds of Britain's middle classes are stored, in an early example of a shared cyberspace environment.

The story itself may be faintly risible: Hawkwind shooting music guns at an army of darkness, while running round London under their *noms de plume* – Turner is the 'Thunder Rider', Lemmy is 'Count Motorhead', Simon House is the 'Sonic Prince' etc.[29] But it's rarely written for laughs. In fact, it's quite violent in places and by the end (spoiler alert) just about everybody except the band is dead. While its 'hippies vs straights' motif was outmoded by 1976, its evocation of a ruined urban environment and world on the verge of destruction was entirely of a piece with the 'No Future' vibe of mid-70s Britain.

After an initial hardback run, it came out as a Star Books paperback – in both cases, Moorcock's name appears prominently on the cover. Reviews were mixed, to say the least. At *NME*, Charles Shaar Murray called it an "almost terrifyingly bad novel", adding "If I was any of the past or present members of Hawkwind caricatured in this book, I wouldn't leave the house for six months".[h] Writing in *The Guardian*, Brian Aldiss goes easy on his friend Moorcock, but admits that the "aggrandisement of a real rock group may make the unfaithful uneasy".[i] Keith

Seddon at *Vortex: The Science Fiction Fantasy* pays it the backhanded compliment of being "fun to read, and a pleasant way to cure insomnia."[j] And Steve Pinder in *Time Out* is almost positive – he's reminded of "the 'Ladbroke' feel of Moorcock's 'Jerry Cornelius' works… yet this is more doom-laden and pessimistic".[k]

Unsurprisingly, the band were ambivalent. Brock called it "a sort of joke really" though admitted, "some of the characters do behave vaguely like we do." Calvert dismissed it as being "aimed at young people".[l] Moorcock too was keen to distance himself from it, wanting to be seen as a more serious writer. But despite a lack of support, *The Time Of The Hawklords* still managed to rack up worldwide sales of around 50,000 copies.[30]

*Queens Of Deliria*, the second part of a projected trilogy, appeared the following year, but while Moorcock's name was still on the cover, this one came entirely from Butterworth's imagination. Set 150 years later, the immortal Hawklords are still going strong, while the remnants of the Children of the Sun have established 'Earth City' on Hampstead's Parliament Hill (which inevitably gets razed to the ground early on). The plot involves the rescue of the Complete Orgasm Band, whose line-up includes Turner's daughter Patti, Paul Rudolph's son Lord Jefferson, and (for some reason) Terry Ollis. The COB have disappeared inside one of the 'Time Zones' that now dot the surface of the Earth, portals to other ages and dimensions. Venturing within, the Hawklords discover their musical offspring are being held captive by the Red Queen, an agent of the Death Generator ruling over a nightmarish alternate version of America, with plans to expand it into the Hawklords' world…

There's a frenetic, Biggles-on-bad-acid feel to it all – at one point the Hawklords are trapped inside a giant pinball table, as depicted on the paperback cover – but despite a cameo from Elric of Melniboné, it's more an exercise in low-grade, nightmarish surrealism than an extension of the Hawkwind mythos.[31] With no reviews and sales of just 15,000, Star Books declined to commission *Ledge Of Darkness*, the final part of the trilogy.[32]

Hawkwind themselves were unlikely to have been distressed by this cancellation, having just released *Quark, Strangeness And Charm*, its arch SF modernism entirely at odds with the madcap scenarios of Butterworth's *Boy's Own* fantasy.

## Embracing The Unknown

*Quark* itself featured Calvert's own comment on the band's tendency towards self-mythology in the song 'Days Of The Underground', both a lament for the scene that spawned them and a rueful admission that idealism and fantasy only gets you so far. In just a few short years, the musical climate had grown too cynical to tolerate the notion of a band as starfaring saviours from another world, and while Calvert continued to deploy various larger-than-life personas on stage, the Hawkwind mythos itself was quietly laid to rest...

Except not quite. It wasn't long before Hawkwind were trading as Hawklords, having very nearly become the Sonic Assassins. And Calvert couldn't resist creating another alternate identity for the band, this time as Pan Transcendental Industries, a corporation committed to fabricating Heaven on Earth. Calvert was also canny enough to cater for the new mythologies of mainstream culture: 'Psi Power' was the perfect rejoinder to a nation obsessed with the spoon-bending antics of Uri Geller, its chanted Zener card symbols now passing into common parlance.[33]

As the 70s drew to a close, the counterculture's distrust of science, with its anti-nuclear/back-to-nature stance, was a sentiment now shared by many people within mainstream society. The disillusionment with the space programme – captured brilliantly by Calvert on 'Uncle Sam's On Mars' – and a backlash against increased automation in the workplace had led popular culture to question the technocratic and embrace the unknown, a desperate need to believe in the other. *Tomorrow's World* found itself competing with *Arthur C. Clarke's Mysterious World*, where such 'unexplained phenomena' as Bigfoot, poltergeists and the Loch Ness Monster were treated with the same gravitas as the latest scientific discovery.[34]

In his piece for *OZ* on the Apollo missions, Bob Hughes had argued that "science fact was frustrating after the science fiction to which, from childhood, we were all used." He was prophetic too: "Nothing had happened on the screen which could not have been done in a television studio for £30,000. The special effects were so far below Kubrick level that they seemed unreal".[m] As the decade ended, these seeds of doubt about the moon landings were blooming, particularly on screen. In *Capricorn One*, NASA kidnaps its own astronauts and films them enacting a faked landing on Mars – then tries to kill them when the cover-up threatens to become public. And in *Alternative 3*, its UK TV equivalent, the moonshots are a PR hoax, while a terraformed Mars is about to be colonised – but only by a global elite.

This notion of space being controlled by secret government agencies and shadowy forces is also present in *Close Encounters Of The Third Kind*, with the authorities covering up an international project to contact extra-terrestrials. Steven Spielberg said, "I wouldn't put it past this government that a cosmic Watergate has been underway for the last 25 years... Eventually they might want to tell us something about what they've discovered over the decades".[35]

## A Harsh New Age

The 1970s was the decade when a healthy scepticism towards authority tipped over into full-scale paranoia. An innate distrust of the establishment had been a defining characteristic of the counterculture, but now this feeling had spread throughout the whole of British society. Did our leaders really have our best interests at heart? Perhaps the post-war social consensus was just another myth, one which might cease to exist as soon as people stopped believing in it.

Change was in the air. The Labour government faced off against the trade unions, triggering 1978-79's Winter Of Discontent – hospitals were picketed, petrol stations closed, and mountains of uncollected rubbish filled the streets. And unemployment kept rising, particularly among the young. Frightened and exhausted, Britain put Margaret Thatcher in charge of the country, little realising how toxic the new mythology she offered – neoliberalism plus 'traditional' family values – would turn out to be.[36]

A popular perception of the 60s had developed: at best, a time of woolly-headed naivety; at worst, the point when everything started to go wrong. The countercultural values that Hawkwind themselves embodied were regarded as being at the root of the country's current malaise. The nanny state and appeasing "the enemy within" was out; aggressive self-reliance and "no such thing as society" was in.

As this harsh new age dawned, Hawkwind found themselves in the wilderness. Without a record deal or Calvert to inspire them, their prospects looked bleak. 'PXR5' saw them back aboard a spaceship, but it was just a thinly veiled metaphor for the ejection of Turner, Rudolph and Powell three years before.

And yet it was the enduring appeal of the Hawkwind mythos that saw their 1979 winter tour sell out, paving the way for further success in the 80s and beyond. Generations of fans had bought into the band, to the point where the mythos had taken on a life of its own. Album sleeves and lyrics were sacred texts to be pored over, their meanings to be divined. Fan-produced artwork, stories and poems filled the fanzine pages of Brian Tawn's *Hawkfan* and Trevor Hughes' *Hawkfriends*. And every year, the people's band returned, and the faithful paid homage. Hawkwind had become the immortal Hawklords of their own legend...

a     'Hawkwind – The Joke Band That Made It' – Andrew Means, *Melody Maker*, 12/08/72

b     Interview with Michael Moorcock – Klemen Breznikar, *It's Psychedelic Baby*, April 2015

c     'Occultist father of rocketry "written out" of NASA's history' – Olivia Solon, *Wired*, 23/4/14

d     *OZ* 38, November 1971

e     *Sniffin' Flowers*, 1977

f     'Did You Feel The Moon Move, Little Rabbit?' – Bob Hughes, *OZ* 23, September 1969

g     'Have the Hawks become Doves… or just a vision of the future that went wrong?' – Geoff Barton, *Sounds*, 20/3/76

h     Charles Shaar Murray, *NME*, 24/7/76

i     Brian Aldiss, *The Guardian*, 22/7/76

j     Keith Sedden (writing as John Grubber), *Vortex Science Fiction & Fantasy*, April 1977

k     Steve Pinder, *Time Out*, 22-28/10/76

l     *Sniffin' Flowers*, 1977

m     Bob Hughes, same source

1     As Ian MacDonald memorably described the 1960s in his book of the same name about The Beatles.

2     Alternatively, the population was suffering from 'future shock' – from Alvin and Heidi Toffler's 1970 book of the same name – caused by "too much change in too short a period of time." As Dominic Sandbrook observes in *State Of Emergency* (2011), for Britain's middle class, the early '70s were characterised by "a revulsion from technology and modernity" and a retreat into an idealised mythological past (ref: p195).

3     *Métal Hurlant* ('Howling Metal') is the French science fiction comic book founded by Jean Giraud (Mœbius) and Philippe Druillet, both influences on Barney Bubbles.

4     The expression 'Spaceship Earth' was popularised by social theorist R. Buckminster Fuller in his *Operating Manual For Spaceship Earth* (1969). This eco-awareness tract describes Earth as a ship flying through space, with finite supplies on board. "We are all astronauts," writes Fuller.

5     This poem features the line "Cosmic Dada Nihilismus!" and Calvert's street theatre group was called Street Dada Nihilismus. Both are presumably references to Leroi Jones' 1964 poem 'Black Dada Nihilismus', which has a similar violent tone to Jerzy Kosiński's *Steps*, from which Calvert recites 'Wage War' at the 1973 Wembley Empire Pool show.

6     "There is now significant evidence that space travel has mind-altering effects. One of the most common experiences are frequent hallucinations… caused by cosmic rays" ('Isolation And Hallucinations: The Mental Health Challenges Faced By Astronauts' – Vaughan Bell, *The Observer*, 5 October 2014). Both Calvert and Bubbles were William Burroughs fans, so the

cut-up and randomised narrative is probably deliberate – many copies of the *Log* were likely slipped back into the sleeve after an initial baffled perusal, there to remain. Calvert and Turner are the only band members mentioned by name (in the version of 'The Awakening' in the *Log*, the words become "Turner stared from the trauma of his birth").

7    This is the most blatant example (of several) of other people's writing being lifted wholesale for the *Log* without attribution. This creation myth is actually 'Sole Solution' (1956), a short story by British SF writer Eric Frank Russell. Calvert and Bubbles were both voracious magpies and synthesists, though this clearly verges on outright plagiarism.

8    The illustration on pages 18-19 of the *Log* presumably depicts this scene.

9    It's interesting that Calvert chooses to cite Le Poer Trench and Goodavage rather than similar claims by UFO populist Erich von Däniken, whose bestselling *Chariots Of The Gods?* (1968) kick-started a popular fascination with all kinds of unexplained phenomena. Le Poer Trench, the 8th Earl of Clancarty, had argued in *The Sky People* (1960) that Noah's Ark was a spaceship fleeing Mars – its crew established Atlantis before escaping back into space. Goodavage was a contributor to the rebranded *Astounding Science Fiction* (now *Analog*) and a keen proponent of Immanuel Velikovsky, whose controversial books (beginning with *Worlds In Collision* in 1950) explain various Biblical events in terms of planetary upheaval within the solar system – mankind's "collective amnesia" regarding the true nature of these events (an idea quoted in the *Log*) is a popular Velikovsky trope. Goodavage would go on to write a book entitled *Seven by Seven: Your Life's Rhythmic Energies* (1978).

10   The *Log* also reports that, "back on earth the Nova Mob still play games of governmental roulette". The Nova Mob first appear in William Burroughs' 1964 novel *Nova Express*, virus-borne criminals capable of mind-control, and the personification of the idea that 'bad vibes' can influence people's behaviour, a notion that will continue to crop up in the Hawkwind mythos.

11   For example: "Thine alabaster towns will tumble, thine engines rot into dust" (the words of the skeleton astronaut) are from Jerry and Renny Russell's *On The Loose* (1967), a hippie-era meditation on the great outdoors; "And still, men who by guts and skill had mastered the farthest wilderness" (on the inside last page) is from Bernard DeVoto's *The Course Of Empire* (1952), this particular passage referring to Lewis and Clark's expedition through the American west in the early 1800s (intriguingly, DeVoto's opening chapter is entitled 'The Children Of The Sun').

12   Hubbard, who had written for the SF pulps, founded in 1952 the Church of Scientology, which would come to epitomise the cult-like 'new age' religions of the 70s.

13   All these songs were hits on the UK chart when Moorcock wrote the strip. Hawkwind will subsequently record a track entitled 'Void City' on their 1982 album *Choose Your Masques*.

14    Blackburst is of course anodyne Radio 1 DJ Tony Blackburn, and BBC here stands for Blackburst's Bomber Command. Ironically, Blackburn's support of 'Silver Machine' just a few months later would help to make it a major hit.

15    The chemical yellows, reds and blues of 'Fly As A Kite' were presumably meant to look nice against the clouds, because they certainly didn't help its legibility. As Tony Vesely remembers: "I designed and laid out the *Frendz* Hawkwind edition. This was – literally – designed to be cut up and reassembled as a kite. Not sure it ever flew, but it looked good – the hippie ethos. I remember the printers complaining mightily as all the copy, photos and illustrations were weird shapes and took 'em about 20 times as long as usual to print" (interview with the author). 'Fly As A Kite' was re-printed in the programme for Hawkwind's May 73 Wembley Pool show, under the title 'Once Upon A Space…'

16    As featured in *Invasion Of The Body Snatchers* (1956), the original SF 'body horror' movie.

17    The "cybernetic castle" may be a reference to the Dreamland amusement park in Margate. DikMik hung out with Calvert and Turner in Margate, and Calvert had worked at Dreamland in his youth.

18    There's a curious piece of mythic ephemera printed in the programme for Hawkwind's show at the Rainbow on 13 August 1972. Under the title 'Cosmic Stuff', and written in 40 short, numbered paragraphs, it describes a meeting between "the Brock" and "the King", and includes a namecheck for Brock's pregnant wife Sylvia MacManus ('Silver Machine' was credited to Bob Calvert & S. MacManus, Brock using his wife's name for publishing reasons). Stylistically, it's a strange mix of mock-courtly banter and references to a Hawkwind show at Watford Town Hall (13 March 1972?), where Stacia apparently had some trouble with a Hells Angel. Possibly written by Mick Farren – the programme was produced by *Nasty Tales*, which Farren co-edited – it's another depiction of Hawkwind as knightly warriors, but doesn't add to the 'official' mythos.

19    The underground press were particularly hit when record companies stopped advertising in their pages, concentrating instead on *NME* and *Melody Maker* etc. *OZ* published its last issue in November 1973, having accrued unsustainable debts as its readership dwindled; *IT* ceased publication in October 1973 after being convicted of printing gay contact ads – it re-started sporadically throughout the 1970s, but its glory days were over. When writer Francis Wheen turned up at the offices of BIT, and announced he had dropped out to join the counterculture, he recalls, "This boyish enthusiasm was met by groans from a furry freak slumped on the threadbare sofa. 'Drop back in, man,' he muttered through a dense foliage of beard. 'You're too late… It's over'" (p7, *Strange Days Indeed* (2009), Francis Wheen).

20    ICI was the largest manufacturer in Britain at the time.

21     The songs on *Doremi* can be reshuffled to create a concept album with narrative sequence. In story order, 'Brainstorm' and 'Time We Left This World Today' address the oppression of the Bad Vibes society, 'Lord Of Light' and 'Down Through The Night' describe the mystical ceremony prior to departure from Earth, 'Space Is Deep' sees them travelling into the void and 'The Watcher' suggests what befalls the world they've left behind.

22     As fan Paul Eaton-Jones recalls: "Attending a Hawkwind concert was something akin to attending a religious service. The sense of expectation of something truly amazing about to happen was always palpable. I became short of breath, my hands sweated and my mouth became dry. For many years I was filled with an overwhelming feeling of joy, my entire body was suffused with happiness and I often found myself crying. Not tears running down my face but actually crying with love and joy." In 1982, the band released an album entitled *Church Of Hawkwind*.

23     Sign of the times: originally dressed in forbidding black robes, declaring the apocalyptic return of Christ and Satan, the Process Church were offering classes in astrology, tarot and astral travel by the mid-70s.

24     The final cost of the Apollo programme was reported to the US Congress as being $25.4 billion in 1973, or roughly $150 billion today. Bob aka Robert Hughes went on to become a renowned art critic, best known for his book and TV series *The Shock Of The New* (1980).

25     "During the course of the Apollo program, and despite its repeated and favorably publicized successes, the proportion of Americans who favored further government expenditures on space activities remained fairly steady at about two out of ten. Meanwhile, those opposed gradually increased from about three out of ten to five out of ten" ('Public Attitudes Toward The Apollo Space Program, 1965-1975' – Herbert E. Krugman, *Journal Of Communication*, December 1977).

26     However tongue-in-cheek, references to "the wenching room" and "femchiks" remind us that feminism was at best a distant rumour in the 70s provincial underground.

27     The exact genesis of the *Hawklords* books is now unclear, but at some point Moorcock had pitched WH Allen the idea of a "rock and roll sci-fi" trilogy based on the fictionalised exploits of Hawkwind. However, he then found himself too busy and sub-contracted them to the cash-strapped and grateful Butterworth, who knew little about the band and its history. On the back cover of *Queens Of Deliria*, the series idea is credited to Piers Dudgeon, then-editor of Star Books. Calvert and Bubbles also have a claim to inspiring the books – the prophecy from *Doremi* is quoted at the start of the first book (and referred to throughout), and one key scene is clearly inspired by an illustration on *Doremi*'s inner sleeve. And let's not forget those marathon sessions the band played in 1970 at the Isle Of Wight, both Canvas City and their seemingly non-stop

live performances also perhaps an inspiration. Also of interest is Mick Farren's post-apocalyptic novel *The Texts Of Festival* (1975), where the music of the counterculture has become the basis of a religion in a future version of Britain, and the capital city of Festival is under threat from marauding tribes of anarchic speed freaks – the 'texts' of the title is a scratched copy of the *Woodstock* soundtrack album. The book would lend its name to *The Text Of Festival*, a bootleg-quality collection of Hawkwind radio sessions and live tracks released in 1983.

28 10cc and Yes also provide succour to the dark forces, while the Hawklords nearly come to a sticky end via a sustained blast of Elton John's 'Daniel'.

29 Butterworth notes that this fictionalised version of the band is "based on roles used by members of Hawkwind on stage and recorded performances", but it's interesting how he portrays the individual members. Turner and Brock are presented as the nominal leaders of the band, yet we see things more from Turner's hippiefied point of view, while Brock's general demeanour is more belligerent. Simon House is by far the most proactive member in terms of combatting the Death Generator (with help from a renegade scientist called Hot Plate), while Stacia is inevitably lumbered with the role of caring for the dying Children, and also used as the bait in a honey trap. In a neat twist, Captain Calvert helps defeat the dark forces by being projected from what sounds like a present day sanatorium into the post-apocalyptic future.

30 In Butterworth's own estimation. As well as being published in the UK and the US, there was also a Spanish edition/translation, entitled *El Tempo de Los Señors Halcones*.

31 Butterworth also makes the mistake of foregrounding Turner, Rudolph and Powell, as all three had been ousted by the time of publication. Other examples of 'death music' this time round include Queen's 'Bohemian Rhapsody' and The Moody Blues' 'Nights In White Satin', confirmation if it was needed that these choices reflect Butterworth's personal tastes rather than Hawkwind's, as Dave Brock is a fan of the Moodies.

32 *Ledge Of Darkness*, the third instalment, finally appeared in 1994, as a graphic novel illustrated by Bob Walker – and then only as part of a CD box set in the US. (According to the inside back page of *Queens*, this concluding volume was originally to be called *The Quest Of The Life Sword*.) Sniffy at the time, the band have since returned to the Hawklords books for inspiration on a number of occasions. The 30th anniversary shows in 1999/2000 (plus an album) were originally to be based around *Ledge Of Darkness*. And the original title of 2005's *Take Me To Your Leader* was *Destruction of the Death Generator*.

33 Zener cards were used for testing ESP. There are five symbols in a standard pack: circle, square, wave, cross and star (but no triangle).

34 With his 'invention' of the communications satellite highlighted at the start of each show, Arthur C. Clarke conferred scientific credibility to the topics explored, though a strand of intergalactic mysticism also runs through much of his work.

35 Spielberg made these comments in a syndicated TV interview, and also said similar to *The Washington Post*. Another popular conspiracy theory holds that *Close Encounters Of The Third Kind* was made to prepare mankind for the arrival of real aliens.

36 Mick Farren knew that the Conservatives offered no bright future. He recalled his shock when Alan Powell announced his intention to vote for Thatcher in 1979: "If Al from Hawkwind could make such a statement, Britain as a nation had clearly become so demoralised and collectively depressed that it would run, lemming-like, to any self-proclaimed authoritarian who promised an illusion of strength, order, and a return to some greetings-card past that had never really existed" (p402, *Give The Anarchist A Cigarette*, Mick Farren).

*Hawkfan* illustration by Steve Lines
(source: Brian Tawn archive)

Hawklords promo shot outside GCHQ CSO Morwenstow, a satellite station & eavesdropping
centre in North Cornwall. L-R - Bainbridge, Swindells, Griffin, Brock, Calvert
(source: Robert Calvert archive)

# Give Yourself To Gravity

## January–October 1978

In January, the band return to Rockfield to record the follow-up to *Quark*. The previous year's sessions had yielded a crop of fresh material, but the main focus this time is on producing studio versions of songs that have already been in their live set for months. However, it's decided that live versions of 'Robot', 'High Rise' and 'Uncle Sam's On Mars' will be overdubbed instead.

It's possible this dip in creativity is due to Calvert finally coming down from the manic high of the past few months, with the singer now taking his medication. Another factor is the knowledge that Simon House, the man responsible for bringing colour to Brock and Calvert's blueprints, is leaving the band to play violin on David Bowie's upcoming world tour and album.[1]

To complicate matters further, Hawkwind have their own American tour lined up for March, their first since May 1975. With *Quark* having been picked up by Sire, the band are keen to re-connect with their US fanbase. House agrees to play the first few dates, and Brock drafts Paul Hayles in from the Sonic Assassins to cover the rest.[2]

Inevitably, House's departure casts a pall over the band. Calvert is often disengaged, reading a newspaper at the side of the stage during extended instrumental sections, while King is struggling to kick a heroin habit. Plus the venues are smaller than the last time, and crowds are in the hundreds rather than the thousands. As a punter shouts out at the start of the first show, at New York's Bottom Line Club, "Where have you been for the last three years?"[a]

Brock in particular has been mulling over the band's future, with the recent Sonic Assassins experience a catalyst to his thinking. By the final gigs in San Francisco, Brock has come to a decision. At their last show, he sells his guitar to a fan[3] and tells their management team that Hawkwind are finished.[4]

⌄    ⌄    ⌄

As Hawkwind self-destruct in America, Nik Turner has been preparing his re-entry onto the public stage. In April, his album *Xitintoday*, credited to Nik Turner's Sphynx, is released on Charisma. Featuring various members of Gong, including producer Steve Hillage and future Hawkwind keyboardist Tim Blake, plus Alan Powell on congas, it's an album so audaciously hippiefied that it's almost a radical statement in 1978. After leaving Hawkwind, Turner had travelled to Egypt, where he'd been allowed to record his flute inside the King's Chamber of the Great Pyramid of Giza.[5] These recordings form the basis of this record, with further instrumentation and vocals overdubbed at Rockfield.

On the one hand, *Xitintoday* is a mystically inclined meditation on ancient gods and the Egyptian Book of the Dead that taps into the emerging genre of new age ambient music. On the other, it's a loopy piece of self-indulgence that Charisma have been persuaded to fund and release, with a full page ad in *NME*: "It's logical. It's square. It sits on the ground like a triangle… and Nik Turner played inside it." Either way, it confirms Turner as a charismatic maverick within what's left of Britain's counterculture, even if his ambitions sometimes exceed his abilities.

The album starts promisingly enough: a monolithic hammering, like a tomb being excavated, gives way to drifting flute and the natural reverb of the King's Chamber on opening track 'The Awakening (Life On Venus)'. Heraldic sax echoes the flute, with distant synth creating an almost Debussy-esque atmosphere – and then Turner's vocal enters, an awkward double-tracked invocation that torpedoes all suspension of disbelief. This pattern is repeated throughout: pleasant enough flute improvisations – plus tablas, bells, harp, and frustratingly short bursts of guitar and synth – interrupted by heavily mannered readings and ruminations on Anubis, Thoth and Horus.

Of course, there's a seam of ritualistic, quasi-occult weirdness beneath the surface of many early Hawkwind tracks, which *Xitintoday* also seeks to channel. And it does pick up as more rhythmic elements are introduced, becoming increasingly Gong-like – however, it's debatable whether the space-jazz jam of final track 'God Rock (The Awakening)' is worth the wait.[6]

▾      ▾      ▾

Back in Britain, Brock considers his options. With Hawkwind disbanded, the album they've just recorded is shelved. In June, Brock does some home recording with Simon King with a view to releasing a solo album,[7] but he's also still keen to create a new group from the ashes of the old. On the plane over to the US, the band had run into Doug Smith again. Smith agrees to work with Brock once more, persuading Charisma to release an album by Brock's new band in lieu of

Hawkwind product. But instead of the Sonic Assassins, they'll be the Hawklords – not so different from the old name, and one that longstanding fans will hopefully get behind.

The next task is putting a group together. Calvert may not be the easiest person to be around, but Brock recognises his talents as a writer and performer, and the two are soon working together on new songs and a new concept, one that deviates significantly from the Hawkwind of old. Harvey Bainbridge is recruited on bass, **Steve Swindells** (formerly of pop rockers Pilot, but with a free festival background) on keyboards. Neither Hayles nor Shaw are approached.

On 18 June, Calvert and Brock attend the Bohemian Love-In, a free concert organised by Turner at the Roundhouse to promote *Xitintoday*. Also involved are Moorcock's Deep Fix and Tanz Der Youth, the band formed by ex-Damned guitarist Brian James and Alan Powell. The show is dogged by technical issues, and for many commentators it's the last enfeebled hurrah of the original 60s underground. But Calvert and Brock are impressed by the concert's staging, particularly the dancers from the Ballet Rambert encased in bandages and blindfolds, as choreographed by Barney Bubbles. The Hawklords need someone to design a new show, and Bubbles is the obvious choice.[8] After some persuasion from Turner, he agrees to work with Calvert and Brock again.

Establishing a base at Langley Farm near Barnstable, the band begin recording an album in July using Ronnie Lane's Mobile Studio. King plays on the initial sessions, and will be credited as drummer on half of the subsequent tracks, but soon leaves, disgruntled that it's essentially "Bob and a backing band".[b9] Keeping things local, he's replaced by Martin Griffin, another recruit from the Sonic Assassins. House, back in the country after the UK leg of Bowie's world tour, plays violin on three tracks.[10]

The album is mixed at Wessex Studios in Highbury, London. Giovanni Dadomo from *Sounds* interviews Brock, trying to get to the bottom of the Hawkwind/Hawklords conundrum. Brock merely confuses matters: "We haven't changed it to that yet, I mean, the album's called *The Hawklords*, and that's what we are for this tour." So, an alter ego rather than a complete change?

Clearly enthused by the new stage show, Brock talks about tearing things down to start afresh. However, his description of this new piece of "rock theatre" sounds like some nightmarish play from the fringe: "It's about a factory... There's the foundry, then there's the sales, and there's a production line, and what happens is there's various scenes, and at the end these people fuck off with wings into the sky!"[c] But he's clearly re-energised, his old gloom gone: "Usually I dislike going out on the road, having done it so many times before, but now I've found new enthusiasm".[d]

The full production includes film, professional dancers and hundreds of projected images cued to the set's running order, and final rehearsals take place at Shepperton Studios.[11] With staggering co-ordination, *Hawklords/25 Years On*[12] is released on 6 October, the tour starting on the same day.

◇◇◇◇◇◇◇◇◇◇◇◇◇◇◇◇◇◇◇◇◇◇◇◇◇◇◇◇◇◇◇◇◇◇◇◇◇◇◇◇◇◇◇◇◇◇◇◇◇◇◇◇◇◇◇◇◇◇◇◇◇◇◇◇◇◇◇◇◇

a    Roman Kozak, *Billboard*, 3/78

b    'The 'Wind Of Change' – Steve Gett, *Melody Maker*, 5/1/80

c    Giovanni Dadomo, *Sounds*, 21/10/78

d    Steve Gett, *Melody Maker*, 10/78


1    Bowie knew House from years before, High Tide having played with Bowie's short-lived band The Hype. Brian Eno, Bowie's collaborator at this time, was also familiar with House from his work on *Lucky Leif*.

2    House claims to have left after the first two New York dates; Hayles says that he stayed on for the following Milwaukee show, with Hayles taking over on keyboards and House playing violin. The exact nature of House's departure is another grey area – as Ian Abrahams notes in *Hawkwind: Sonic Assassins* (p119), House was "contractually on 'sabbatical'" and it seems that he intended to rejoin Hawkwind after completing his Bowie commitments, only to discover that 'Hawkwind' no longer existed. House later rejoined the band, 1989-1991 and 2001-2003.

3    The fan was Marc Sperhauk, who will subsequently appear on 'Some People Never Die' from 1982's *Church Of Hawkwind*. Jello Biafra of the Dead Kennedys, who attended one of the Old Waldorf San Francisco shows, recalls: "It was a strange, transitional show for them. It was in a major label, stiff showcase club with tables all the way to the stage and grubby waitresses trying to force people to buy drinks they didn't want. It was the kind of venue that's practically died out now. But it's where everybody from The Ramones to the Dead Boys to Iggy to The Stranglers would get booked into. It wasn't as well attended as I wish it was – there was one guy off on the side trying to dance dressed in total freak flag (gear), who was kind of an anomaly there…" (interview with the author).

4    Hayles maintains it was Brock's intention to retire the Hawkwind name and replace it, and presumably the band, with Sonic Assassins instead. This isn't the first time this name change was mooted – as far back as April 1972, an Aylesbury Friars newsletter notes,

"Actually Hawkwind are in the process of changing their name to the 'Sonic Assasins' [sic]", presumably inspired by Moorcock's comic strip from the previous year. A series of UK dates had been pencilled in for after the US tour, but Tony Howard and Jeff Dexter had already decided to end their relationship with Hawkwind. Neither Hayles nor King were aware at the time of Brock's decision to split the band, and Shaw only found out via Howard.

5   Turner was perhaps inspired by the example of jazz flautist Paul Horn, who had done similar a year before, and released the album *Inside The Great Pyramid* in 1977.

6   Members of Sphynx – Turner, Hillage, Harry Williamson and Mike Howlett – recorded and released a more contemporary-themed single later in the year as Fast Breeder & The Radio Actors: 'Nuclear Waste'/'Digital Love' is perhaps most notable for the A-side being sung by The Police's Sting.

7   Two songs from this session will later be added to the running order of *PXR5*: 'Infinity' and 'Life Form'.

8   Bubbles had also designed the sleeve for *Xitintoday*. Doug Smith says it was his idea to approach Bubbles about the stage show, as was switching the band name to Hawklords.

9   Shaw too has suggested Brock wanted the new band simply to be hired hands on a wage, with Brock in overall control.

10   House's violin also features on Bowie's live album *Stage*, released on 8 September. *Stage* is not highly regarded within Bowie's catalogue, and House's contribution is largely textural. But he steps into the limelight a few times, notably during the opening 'Warszawa', where he plays spiralling arabesques against the main theme.

11   *Alien*, Ridley Scott's iconic sci-fi horror, was being filmed at the same time in the next-door studio.

12   Confusingly, the first 25,000 copies of the album are credited on the label as *25 Years On*, while subsequent copies drop this title and refer just to *Hawklords*.

Robert Calvert prose piece that may have inspired 'Psi Power':

(source: Robert Calvert archive)

"This is a secret between me and this page. If you are reading these words, please don't feel that you are prying. The trouble is that I see too clearly into people, and see them for what they are. This can be a bad thing. This seeing more of people than they are aware of revealing. I do not for one minute consider this a privilege.

You see, I think I can say it now, after all if you are reading this, it isn't likely that you will know who I am or my whereabouts.

I didn't come forward and declare myself a telepath and (unknown) in myself in the usual way, because, well because of some (unknown) reasons. Of course, I've known for a long time now.

When I was a child, I thought it was completely normal. To know what my parents were thinking before they spoke. No one told me that there was this special gift that only a few had. My parents never mentioned the psi-class in my presence. And I'm sure never dreamed that they could have spawned one, with no background history of psi-powers traceable to their ancestors.

My teachers put me down as a flippant child. They found some of my remarks a little uncomfortable."

# Hawklords / 25 Years On

Released 6 October 1978

*Label:*        Charisma[1]

*Track listing:*    Psi Power (Calvert/Brock) / Free Fall
(Calvert/Bainbridge) / Automoton (Calvert/Brock)
/ 25 Years (Brock) / Flying Doctor (Calvert/
Brock) / The Only Ones (Brock/Calvert) / (Only)
The Dead Dreams Of The Cold War Kid (Calvert) /
The Age Of The Micro Man (Calvert/Brock)

*Line-up:*      Dave Brock / Robert Calvert / Steve Swindells /
Harvey Bainbridge / Simon King ('25Y', 'TOO',
'(O) TDDOTCWK' & 'TAOTMM') / Martin Griffin ('PP',
'FF', 'FD' & 'TOO') / Simon House ('TOO', '(O)
THDDOTCWK' & 'TAOTMM')

*Recorded at:*    Langley Farm, Devon (using Ronnie Lane's
Mobile Studio)

*Produced by:*    Robert Calvert & Dave Brock

If *Quark* tempered its pessimism with humour and irony, then *Hawklords/25 Years On* is a much bleaker take on the technocratic society, the individual as a cog in an automated assembly line. Where *Quark* was precise and controlled, *Hawklords* is stark, even austere. Yet the various psychodramas that Calvert enacts here are more intimate, giving the album a sense of humanity that its predecessor sometimes lacked.

'**Psi Power**' gets straight to the heart of the action. A tightly wound acoustic riff underpinned by simple organ chords, bass and drums rising and falling uneasily, it's the sound of being under pressure and under surveillance, the ticking of the guitar like the clock in an interview room. And Calvert's opening lines put us right inside that room: "*When I was a kid in school / They showed me* *symbols on a card / Then they sent them from a locked and bolted room / I had to fake that it was hard."*

That last line is a brilliant kicker, establishing the protagonist's dilemma with admirable concision. Uri Geller notwithstanding, Calvert supposes that anybody with genuine extra-sensory powers would want to hide them away, to avoid being exploited or becoming an outcast. The clean, lucid production magnifies both the sense of alienation and the struggle to keep his "gift" under control, while the glorious rush of the chorus suggests those powers unbound.

Brock's more assertive *"I can read your mind like a magazine!"* casts a sinister shadow over the song, while his Morse Code guitar chips away like a telepathic message trying to penetrate the skull. Steve Swindells' synth line has an incongruously perky plastic triumphalism that recalls low-budget TV sci-fi, as does the stern trumpet fanfare that follows,[2] both heralding some harshly lit dystopian future. An outro of overlapping, colliding voices gradually swamps the music, *"like a radio you can't switch off"*. In terms of songwriting, arrangement and lyrical sophistication, 'Psi Power' is perhaps Hawkwind's finest track of the 70s, or of any decade.

After the nervy tension of the opening track, '**Free Fall**' floats into view on a wave of serene synth and Harvey Bainbridge's soothing, undulating bass – it's like being dropped into a pillow of clouds, tumbling softly through the air. Swindells is a more textural, less painterly player than House, and his sound palette a little colder, but his swooping arcs here in shades of blue and grey are just perfection. Martin Griffin's spare, almost jazzy drumming adds to this feeling of weightlessness.

But when Bainbridge switches up to a faster, more urgent bass line, our eyes are snapped open to the vertiginous reality of the situation. The drums start to roll, the synth shoots away from us, and now we're plunging downwards, at the mercy of the sky. It's the aural equivalent of a panic attack, something Calvert was no doubt familiar with. He channels his anxiety into terse, cold-sweat poetry, and one of his best double-rhyming couplets: *"The wind will take your frightened face / And force your mouth to smile / While destiny is on your case / The gods look up your file."*

There's a taut yet spacey post-punk vibe to the overall sound here, somewhere between Joy Division's *Unknown Pleasures* and Public Image Ltd's *Metal Box*.[3] And then, like waking from a bad dream, we're back to the sonic balm of the opening section, meandering happily along as if nothing had happened. It's a strange dislocation, as though we've just taken a sedative designed to erase sudden mood swings or inconvenient moments of clarity.

The strange clockwork we hear next could be the whirring of conveyor belts laden with these soma tablets. '**Automoton**' (a misspelling of 'Automaton'?) is more contraption than song, its mechanism being gradually wound to its limit. Since the dawn of the Industrial Revolution, machines have threatened to take our jobs – but the 70s saw an upsurge in concerns about robots in manufacture, skilled labour sidelined in favour of pre-programmed assembly.

As 'Automoton' is about to blow a fuse, '**25 Years**' crashes in to save the day. It's yet another iteration of the 'Silver Machine' riff, but Brock's swaggering block chords are more charged than ever against some straight-ahead rock drumming from King. An odd bounciness fits well with the assembly-line concept, almost approaching the new wave robot boogie of Devo. Unusually, Calvert is singing a Brock lyric, and ramps his neurotic android delivery up to the max.

The words are blunt but strangely affecting, the hapless protagonist spat out by both the education system and the workplace: "*I started out one day / And I worked in a factory / My mind went blank / I needed a battery*." It replaces punk's anger with a bemused fatalism – "*Didn't do me no good*" – but still captures the sense of futility now felt by many, with UK unemployment at 1.5 million. While dropping out might once have been a lifestyle choice, British youth were now faced with enforced idleness.

Consumed by the machine, Calvert's voice is strangulated and processed. Through gritted teeth, he chants the title – and soon all the disaffected workers in their underground hives are joining in and stomping along, the humans rising up against their mechanical masters like a scene from Fritz Lang's *Metropolis*, with a final show of defiance in the last verse: "*25 years of social reform / Ain't gonna make me change or make me conform*."

The album's title, *25 Years On*, refers to the founding in 1953 of the quasi-mystical corporation Pan Transcendental Industries (PTI) mentioned on the sleeve. But it also conjures images of the social and economic planning undertaken by Britain in the post-war period – from high rise estates to the managed decline of traditional industries – which by 1978 was widely felt to have failed in delivering a better future.

But before things get too serious, here's a clever/stupid drug song from Calvert and another character for him to play. Steaming in on an abrasive and downright punky riff, '**Flying Doctor**' is a cross between a rejected *Monty Python* sketch and a football terrace chant. Calvert sings the entire song in a cod-Australian accent for comic effect, with popular perceptions of Down Under in the 70s coloured almost entirely by Rolf Harris, Rod Hull & Emu, and *Skippy the Bush Kangaroo*.[4]

Supposing that a doctor in the outback might explore the recreational possibilities of his medicine cabinet, Calvert concocts a ludicrous scenario reinforcing various Aussie stereotypes – he even plays a wobble board and a "Didgereedon't". It's incredibly daft but also irresistibly funny, musically as well as lyrically – Griffin clatters on tin cans while the seemingly endless "*cabinet key*" chant is performed with gusto. It might not fit with the rest of the album, but its manic, feverish edge suggests a venting of tension if nothing else.[5]

The sound of a small plane gunning through the sky heralds '**The Only Ones**', the third song on *Hawklords* to reference flight. Sonically, it harks back to 'Psi Power', but the acoustic riff here is driving and less constrained. Brock would later disparage this album as "armchair Hawkwind" – and certainly there's an air of melodic maturity to tracks like this. But what's striking is the clarity of the mix compared to the impressionistic fog of earlier albums – the sound is a balm for the ears rather than an assault on them.

The song is another attack on technocratic thinking – just as new modes of production crush the human spirit, the space age is driven by capitalist colonialism: "*In chariots of fury and flame / We head for above to stake out our claim.*" It's a recurring Hawkwind theme, expressed here in quasi-religious terms: mankind may have become convinced of its own godhood, but there are higher and more powerful forces at work in the universe.

Brock's earthier tones on the chorus contrast well with Calvert's cooler voice, and there's magic when the two hold the word "*free*", punctuated by the dramatic thump of the drums. 'The Only Ones' really emphasises the freshness and vitality of *Hawklords*' sound, less knowingly antiseptic than *Quark*'s production. Plus, we're treated to the return of Simon House's violin, arcing gracefully over the coda like vapour trails in a summer sky.

'**(Only) The Dead Dreams Of The Cold War Kid**' brings to life various scenes of derring-do ripped straight from the pages of *Boy's Own*, only to be undercut by the chorus. This solo composition from Calvert is almost childlike in its simplicity, yet it's more sophisticated than it first appears. He strums a basic rhythm on guitar, but there's plenty of subtle embellishment – House's pizzicato violin plays a vaguely Oriental melody which Swindells weaves around and mirrors in the background.

Calvert laments how the nuclear stand-off has robbed a generation of the joys of playing Dick Barton in the schoolyard, the fate of the earth no longer dependent on secret-agent heroics, but the push of a button. Or perhaps Calvert himself is the Cold War Kid, reflecting on the innocent games of his childhood, and using role-playing as a strategy against depression. And lines such as "*Deep in his trenchcoat, secret papers are hid*" can't help but evoke images of the post-punk bands currently assimilating this romantic-noir vision of Europa.

And now, almost in a parody of an adult-oriented rock album, the final song is a piano-driven ballad with a magnificently portentous fade up. **The Age Of The Micro Man**' encapsulates the alienation and disenfranchisement of living in a technocratic society, doomed to see "*the detail but never the plan.*" This slow-burning lament nails the creeping anomie of a world where ideas such as the dignity of labour and a job for life will be relentlessly eroded over the coming years. Calvert's ennui-laden verses end with an ambivalent cry, "*25 years of social research,*" but the track has nowhere else to go. House's violin motif could have stood some expansion, but this is ultimately an end credits track, and it fades down the way it came in.

<hr />

1    This is the only Hawkwind album that Charisma itself releases in both UK/Europe and US.

2    Performed by noted trumpeter Henry Lowther, whose credits range across jazz, classical, rock and pop, and who played at Woodstock.

3    *Hawklords* is ahead of this particular cold-wave curve, since both these albums belong to 1979.

4    This is ironic, given the role that people like Germaine Greer, Clive James, Robert Hughes and Richard Neville played in British intellectual life in the late 60s/early 70s. By 1978, all but James had left Britain.

5    Calvert sneaks another William Burroughs reference into the lyric – "*A Sheila in the bush by a coolabah tree needed an urgent appendectomy / The Flying Doctor like a true Australian, performed the operation with a saltine can / He made a rough incision and tried to chew it out…*" is inspired by the amoral Dr Benway in *The Naked Lunch*, who says, "Did I ever tell you about the time I performed an appendectomy with a rusty sardine can? And once I was caught short without instrument one and removed a uterine tumour with my teeth." (A "*coolabah tree*" is a common type of Australian eucalyptus, and features in the words to 'Waltzing Matilda'. A "*saltine can*" refers to an old tin container for saltine crackers.)

# Give Yourself To Gravity

October—December 1978

Hawklords live
L-R: Swindells, Bainbridge, Calvert, Griffin, dancer, Brock
(photo by Peter Zabulis)

Not everyone gets that Hawklords are just Hawkwind in disguise, and the album barely scrapes into the top 50 at number 48. And once again, there's no promotional single ahead of its release.

It's also possible that Barney Bubbles' daring sleeve design has an effect. Shot in stark black and white, the front cover features the oiled torso of ex-Ark percussionist Alistair Merry — staring down into his shoulder, he grips a fluorescent tube, which flares as it approaches his groin. With 'Hawklords' roughly spray-painted across the picture in neon pink,[1] it's a strikingly ambivalent image with homoerotic overtones, like a sci-fi appropriation of a Robert Mapplethorpe shot. If Bubbles, Brock and Calvert want to break with the past, they certainly do so here.

Top left corner, in tiny writing, is the name 'Pan Transcendental Industries Inc'. Diagonally opposite, bottom right, is a flaming hand motif and the slogan 'Reality you can rely on'.[2] The back cover is just as perplexing: a still life of cube, cone, sphere and ruler, along with a small abstract illustration, all drolly titled 'Metaphysical View of Factory', suggesting the influence of Kandinsky or El Lissitzky. The inner sleeve features more cryptically posed monochrome shots of Merry, now in the proletarian attire of the Chinese revolution, his face obscured by bandages.

The surreal background to the album is included in a booklet-cum-manifesto (available on the tour) which satirises the technocratic mindset.[3] PTI is depicted as a vast conglomerate, its ultimate aim being the "industrialisation of religion." Calvert's text parodies the high-powered, pseudo-scientific business speak increasingly being pedalled by neo-liberal thinkers and politicians, with "voluntary prisoners" working in vast "metaphactories" in pursuit of "the reduction of culture to commodity."

As ever, reviews are mixed. *Record Mirror*'s Steve Gett is positive, despite worrying that the band is veering "towards commercialism with a capital 'C'," surely the first time a Hawkwind album has ever been accused of this. He finds it "fresh and vital", likens Calvert to Peter Hammill and Bowie, and suggests that newcomers might easily imagine the Hawklords to be a "new wave band".[a] At *NME*, Bob Edmands also picks up on this, but as a stick to beat them with. He accuses them of stealing from XTC – as well as Pink Floyd, Spirit and Roxy Music – and bafflingly claims that, "After all these years… a distinctive style has eluded them".[b4]

Already into a two-month UK tour, the Hawklords stage presentation – promoted as the "Heavy Street-Punk Show" – is harshly confrontational compared to the playfulness and colour of Atomhenge. The stage is lit by prison-camp watchtowers and the band – all wearing industrial overalls – enter to a film of workers filing through a tunnel, in the style of *Metropolis*.[5] They play alongside a troupe of drably dressed dancers, who sweep the floor and perform other mundane tasks. Slides are projected in rapid succession behind the stage, ranging from anatomical diagrams to Situationist cartoons.[6]

A review from Brunel University's student magazine is evocative: "The four spotlights mounted on the roof-high towers blazed into light, and with agonising slowness, played on the back of the hall, then down onto the audience and finally the stage, where Bob Calvert stood in his urban guerrilla costume, empty bandolier over his shoulder, and megaphone hanging at his side".[c78]

Dystopian rock theatre is risky, as *NME*'s David Housham warns: "Angry young futurism and Fritz Langerama are dangerously fashionable and a target both sitting and much sat upon." But he finds the show "overpowering with impressive consistency",[d] even if the fans sometimes seem bemused. The set leans heavily on new material, but there's still room at the end for such classics as 'Brainstorm', 'Master Of The Universe' and 'Silver Machine'. The band's delivery is tight and terse, the songs chopped out with a punk-fuelled single-mindedness.

Hawklords live — Bainbridge, Calvert, Brock and dancers
(photos by Peter Zabulis)

Hawklords live
Top - Calvert and Swindells. Bottom - Brock, Calvert and Bainbridge.
(photos by Sandy Cameron)

In *Melody Maker*, Mike Davies – writing in response to a negative gig review the paper itself had run – addresses the band's ongoing perception problem: despite an audience largely in the 14-19 age bracket, here again was the "tired old cliché of 'faded hippies'". Interviewed later in the feature, Calvert insists on their continued relevance: "The early band was expressing what was going on, with the whole space programme, and the concern with communication and industry. That's what people living now should be concerned about… In spite of the new wave, people are still singing about problems with their girlfriends. That's not enough. William Burroughs was right when he said that if man is going to become a space-age creature, he has to drop a lot of ties. The punk thing didn't do enough".[e]

▾      ▾      ▾

A week after the album comes out, Charisma releases an edited version of '**Psi Power**' as a single, with '**Death Trap**' from the January Rockfield sessions on the B-side.[9] It doesn't chart, though it can't help that UA re-release '**Silver Machine**' on the very same day. 'Psi Power' is the better song, but 'Silver Machine' has become a 'rock classic', and a new generation of fans propels it into the charts again, where it peaks at 34.[10] It might generate new royalties – and Hawklords are performing it on tour – but this implicit rejection of the band's new aesthetic must be a little galling for someone as anti-nostalgia as Calvert.

Three weeks into the tour, and despite well attended shows, reality descends. They can no longer afford to stage the show in its full format. Following the show at Bradford's St George's Hall (25 October), the dancers are sacked. For Bubbles, this is the final straw – having already seen much of his proposed staging changed or ignored, he vows never to work with the band again.[11] It's also the last tour that Jonathan Smeeton is involved with.

In another surprisingly thoughtful and even-handed article, this time in *NME*, Calvert explores where to go next, proposing, "an album which is musically much more daring, less tied to recognisably traditional song formats." He also discusses a possible solo or band project about teenage schizophrenia with the radical psychologist R.D. Laing. Whether Hawkwind fans actually want more experimentation is a moot point, but Calvert acknowledges the duty he feels towards their audience: "In a completely dead town, it's quite a responsibility to provide an exciting and colourful two hours. That's why I think rock music is so popular, because it's the only way – short of forming terrorist cells or something

– that you can actually find a sort of collective excitement without causing anyone any harm".[f]

There's talk of taking the *Hawklords* show to America, but once again, there are already cracks in the line-up, with Martin Griffin finding his services no longer required.

◇◇◇◇◇◇◇◇◇◇◇◇◇◇◇◇◇◇◇◇◇◇◇◇◇◇◇◇◇◇◇◇◇◇◇◇◇◇◇◇◇◇◇◇◇◇◇◇◇◇◇◇◇◇◇◇◇◇◇◇◇◇

a     Steve Gett, *Record Mirror*, 21/10/78

b     Bob Edmands, *NME*, 10/78

c     Andy Thompson, *Le Nurb*, 30/11/78

d     'Strike a light! It's the Lords of the Universe: The Hawklords' – David Housham, *NME*, 14/10/78

e     'The Hawklords Riddle' – Mike Davies, *Melody Maker*, 13/11/78

f     'Hawklords: Leisure-Wear Of The Timelords' – Andy Gill, *NME*, 16/12/78

1     Brian Griffin, photographer and regular Bubbles collaborator, suggests that the *Hawklords* sleeve pays homage to the front cover of *Neu! 2*. Yet neon pink against monochrome is a Bubbles theme in 1978: see the back cover of Iggy Pop's 'Kill City' single and an advert for *Do It Yourself* by Ian Dury and The Blockheads.

2     Chris Gabrin, who took the photographs for the sleeve and worked closely with Bubbles on the *Hawklords* stage show, designed this logo based on 'Mr Therm', a character from 1930-60s Gas Council adverts.

3     The booklet was supposedly to have been included with the album, but wasn't printed in time.

4     This was a game that older bands could never win: update your sound and you're a bandwagon jumper, don't and you're a dinosaur.

5     This film was shot by Chris Gabrin, as "an experimental piece without sound, because we were going to try and get the band to soundtrack it, but that never happened. It had all kind of weird images of people in those costumes doing robotic movements at night in front of fires. I used the very first sort of computers, big reel-to-reel tape machines, in one sequence" (interview with the author).

6     Many of the cartoons come from Christopher Grey's *Leaving The 20th Century: The Incomplete Work Of The Situationist International*.

7     An audio recording of the Brunel set is currently available as *Hawklords Live '78* (Atomhenge). This show was also professionally filmed, but other than fleeting clips – such as a few seconds aired on Channel 4's *Top Ten: Prog Rock* in 2001 – it has never been broadcast or made available

in the UK. However, fans in Australia recall seeing footage of '25 Years' on the late-night Channel 7 music programme *Night Moves* in mid-1979, which coincided with the release of this song as a single in the UK – perhaps it was also mooted for release in Australia, with this footage intended as a promo? Other fans recall seeing the entire concert. In 2017, it was announced that the film would finally be made commercially available, but at the time of going to print, it has yet to emerge.

8    In pictures from this tour, Calvert sometimes bears an unfortunate resemblance to suburban guerrilla Wolfie Smith from *Citizen Smith*. A surprisingly popular BBC1 sitcom that ran 1977-80, it did much to colour popular perceptions of what remained of the revolutionary/left-wing underground at the time, with Wolfie depicted as a feckless, ineffectual layabout. Its writer John Sullivan went on to create British sitcom institution *Only Fools And Horses*.

9    This is the version of 'Death Trap' that appears on *PXR5*, despite claims to the contrary. In early adverts for the *Hawklords* tour, 'The Age Of The Micro Man' is advertised as being the B-side of the 'Psi Power' single. Charisma sent promotional postcards to the press in support of the single bearing the slogan, 'Imagine A Revolution'.

10    In 1976, the *NME* Readers All-Time Top 100 Singles poll had 'Silver Machine' at number 36; it also featured the following year in the Nation's All-Time Top 100 singles, as voted by BBC Radio 1 listeners. And apparently warming to Hawkwind again, John Peel plays both 'Death Trap' and 'Silver Machine' on his show in October, though of 'Death Trap' he opines, "It's more interesting than anything on the album."

11    Chris Gabrin: "I went to the first rehearsal and came away rather annoyed, and left them to it. It was just a shambles, after the amount of work that Barney and I had done, we felt cheated I think. Also, all the principles behind the imagery had been completely ignored."

# Pamela Townley

Married to Robert Calvert 1977–1980

Pamela Townley
(source: Pamela Townley archive)

**How did you first meet Robert?**

My sister was doing PR for Charisma, and invited me to the Hammersmith Odeon for my thirtieth birthday (October 5 1977). It was standing room only, and when we walked into the back of this great big room, [the audience] were all shouting "Calvert, Calvert!" and the place was rocking. And then he raunched on stage, huge charisma and massive presence, dressed in long black boots and leather flying jodhpurs, bandana round his head and a Biggles flying helmet. He tore round the stage, so tall and lean, a great performer. We met backstage – I clinked a glass of champagne and it was Robert.

**What were your first impressions?**

He'd just done an incredible gig, but I felt a massive amount of detachment and sadness. I never thought I'd fall in love, but I really wanted to. When we met, he said, "I need you to marry me, because I need somebody to look after me, love me and be there." And I said, "Alright then."

**That really is a whirlwind romance…**

Well, yes! I thought, 'OK, I'd rather marry him than anyone else.' I'm not going to fall in love, but if somebody needs me – I know it sounds stupid now – perhaps I can make him well. I felt his sadness and his need, and I thought probably I could be his strength. [Charisma boss] Tony Stratton-Smith said, "You do know what you're doing by marrying him? He's very unwell, he's just got back from Paris, and my advice would be you do not marry him." I said, "No, he needs me, that's what he wants." "I advise against it." I said, "Rubbish, I'm listening to Robert."

**The wedding must have been quite something…**

I come from a very old-fashioned family. We got married at Caxton Hall, which was quite the thing, and then went up to my father's house in Hampstead, with its cream carpets and antique furniture, and had a little do. The maiden aunts were all assembled, trying to pretend it was a normal wedding, with a reception and canapés. But then in came stomping all these guys like Simon King and Johnny Rotten, in their leathers and biker boots, with my family looking at them in absolute horror. My stepmother had taken off all her very valuable jewellery and left it in the bedroom, and somebody nicked the whole lot, so I was in real trouble. And it wasn't insured, oh my God! Then Robert said, "Right, we're going," and off we went to Devon, where he had a cottage.

**Had you colluded with him in his role-playing?**

Yes, I bought into the role-playing, very much so. I was doing my twinsets-and-pearls [look], swishing through the fields in boots and long skirt. We had a Great Dane called Quark that dragged us through all the lanes, an immensely strong dog. I completely romanticised being with this guy who was so wild, but could be so poetic and quiet.

When he got back from Paris, we were living between the cottage in Devon and my flat in Conduit Street. He was very crazy when he came back. I didn't realise he wasn't well, I thought maybe that's just the way he is. But he was storming around saying, "There's a CIA plot. The steam coming out of the gutters in the road is because they're down there and nobody seems to realise this but me." And then there was a black-out, which he immediately said, "See!? I'm right, they're down there, and they've created a black-out!" So we huddled down waiting for the CIA to destroy the streets outside.

But Robert kept just going up. He got hold of a plastic gun and knives he bought in Paris, really exploding to that top level of mania. He'd lost two or three stone, his eyes were circular, and he was talking nonsense, spitting with foam.

It must have been incredibly difficult living with somebody like that... Five weeks [after the wedding] we separated. It was so intense, I dashed back to London and spent Christmas with my mother, completely shell-shocked, because he was at his most manic. But then I thought, "I've got to give this marriage another go." But when he came back from Devon, he was absolutely cartwheeling. He took off down to Margate, booked himself into a hotel, got on the rooftop waving his plastic guns and said more about the CIA plots, Russian plots, American plots, that only he knew about. [The police] wrestled him to the ground because obviously they thought he was very dangerous. I didn't believe he was.

The police said to me, "We're sectioning him". So they shut him up, I think in Horton Hospital. By the time I got to see him, he'd put his fist through a glass door. They honestly thought he could kill somebody, so they'd put him on E Wing with all the murderers. His hair was standing up on end, his eyes were wild, foam was coming out of his mouth, his hand was wrapped in bandages, and the whole seat of his trousers was torn where he'd been man-handled. They'd drugged him to the gills, and all he could say was, "Please get me out of here, I'm not a murderer."

But they said, "You can't have him. He's a paranoid schizophrenic, a manic depressive, and completely irrational. You cannot have an argument with him, and tell him he's misbehaving, because he won't get it. He's on a completely different track. All you'll do is hurt each other. You should turn him over to us, we can give him drugs to keep him calm." Which I knew Robert would hate, because the whole beauty of Robert was his amazing imagination.

I'm there at a table with 20 doctors and nurses, and he's sitting there looking desperate, the poor thing, and they said, "Give us reasons why you can look after him." I talked the talk and got him back to Conduit Street.

*He lived with you ahead of recording the Hawklords album…*

I couldn't get divorced in under three years, as you had to have grave grounds for divorce, and he hadn't done anything awful, so I wasn't going to go there. I spent another year with him getting him well, feeding him lithium and getting him off all the other drugs. He lived in my flat and composed every day, living a very quiet life. I gave him his drugs at regular intervals, but only minimal amounts so that he could be creative. He used to sit on the stairs, and ask could I sing the backing tracks with him?

Creatively I did help where I could, but I was as much trying to wean myself off him as he was trying to wean himself off drugs, even though they were helping. They were right, you can't rationalise with someone who's mad. After a year of that, I said, "Right, I'm off."

*Was Hawkwind good for him?*

No. Because he was a poet, and it was an extreme sort of life. People were coming in and out of the band, but they were all of a type, lots of drugs and drinking, loud people crashing about, there was no gentleness in it at all. It went with the music and the times. I think if he'd lived in a gentler environment, he would have had the chance to blossom. But he was very much a lost soul.

[Imagine] performing that night at the Hammersmith Odeon – you have to drag up all that energy and make it explode, but the other side of that is going to be an absolute downer. And if you're mentally ill, you're going to go very far down. It's very exciting, you're wearing crazy clothes and make-up, the lights are flashing and people are screaming your name – that's got to be pretty exhilarating. Then suddenly, you have to go home, and the silence is singing at you. You're all alone, where's that big crowd? People like Dave and the others were very grounded and were able to deal with it. But Robert was absolutely not like that, he was super-charged.

*What are your lasting impressions of him?*

Robert was an exceptional human being. Being married to him was one of the highlights of my life. We can all play-act, but he could transport himself. He believed he was the person who was going to save the world. He believed he was an extraordinary person in our midst, and we needed to take advantage of this person Robert Calvert. And everybody just thought he was crackers!

# New Worlds And Dangerous Visions

## Hawkwind As The Ultimate Science Fiction Band

Hawkwind's defining feature above and beyond their unique brand of deep space psychedelia is their strong association with science fiction. Their 70s output in particular tackles many of SF's big ideas head on. They weren't the only people inspired to marry music and SF – David Bowie kick-started his career with it, while bands as diverse as Magma and Parliament built an SF-inspired mythology around themselves.[1] But Hawkwind's embrace of science fiction went beyond just conceptual showmanship.

What is it then that sets Hawkwind apart? With Robert Calvert at the ship's helm, alongside vital collaborators Michael Moorcock and Barney Bubbles, science fiction became both vehicle and metaphor for the band's music: forward-facing and implacable, otherworldly and mysterious, imbued with the terror of the present, charged by the energy of the future. Their engagement with SF at its literary source, with many songs inspired by specific works, is also key to Hawkwind's position as the ultimate sci-fi band.

### Inventing The Future

With the space age and the teenager created at roughly the same time, it's no surprise that early rock & roll songs are full of rockets, flying saucers and alien invaders. High energy and youth-oriented, rock & roll presented a transformative, disruptive vision of the future in much the same way as science fiction did, twin heralds of the shape of things to come in the post-war period.

In the US, the 50s were SF's 'Golden Age', with pulp magazines *Amazing Stories* and *Astounding Science Fiction* publishing Isaac Asimov, Robert Heinlein, Ray Bradbury and Arthur C. Clarke. A generation raised on *Flash Gordon* and *Buck Rogers* were now watching Hollywood sci-fi such as *The Day The Earth Stood Still* (1951), *Forbidden Planet* (1956) and *This Island Earth* (1955) plus SF chillers including *Invaders From Mars* (1953) and *Invasion Of The Body Snatchers* (1956), the threat of alien possession reflecting paranoia about the 'Red Menace' of communism.

Growing up in the aftermath of WW2, Hawkwind's future members would probably have been exposed to some if not all of the above, an injection of garish American technicolour into the drab reality of their young lives. But it was home-grown SF that perhaps made more of an immediate impression on them.

Stories of wartime derring-do still dominated British books and comics, but SF was creeping in at the edges. *Eagle*'s 'Dan Dare, Pilot Of The Future' was serialised on Radio Luxembourg (1951-56), while BBC radio drama *Journey Into Space* (1953) had over eight million listeners following the adventures of various stiff upper-lipped types trying to get to the Moon, with a further serial (1958) featuring a mission to Mars.

The critical establishment might have regarded such serials as essentially juvenile, but British TV featured some surprisingly serious SF. The three *Quatermass* serials (1953-59 on TV, filmed 1955-67), scripted by Nigel Kneale, were intelligent treatments of fantastical subjects, exploring the dangers of spaceflight, alien conspiracies and genocidal mass hysteria. In *A For Andromeda* (1961) and *The Andromeda Breakthrough* (1962), a decoded alien transmission leads to the construction of a malevolent super computer, while stories by writers including Asimov, John Wyndham, Philip K. Dick and J.G. Ballard were dramatised in the anthology series *Out Of This World* (1962) and *Out Of The Unknown* (1965-71).

The most enduring British SF TV show was *Doctor Who*. Launched in 1963 as a BBC1 teatime serial for children, it quickly became must-see viewing for all age groups. Each week, the Doctor and his companions faced alien foes such as the fascistic Daleks or the emotionless Cybermen, though neither were as scary as the show's howling, unearthly theme tune, created by Delia Derbyshire for the BBC Radiophonic Workshop.

The other series to dominate SF TV viewing habits was *Star Trek* (US TV 1966, UK after 1969). Whereas *Doctor Who* inhabited a shadowy, monochrome universe in line with contemporary BBC production values, *Star Trek* had state-of-the-art special effects and a wide-eyed colonial optimism – space became "the final frontier", and every episode promised "to boldly go where no man has gone before".

## The New Wave

But as with all culture in the 60s, science fiction was changing. Space was no longer just there to be explored and colonised; science didn't always make things better. Instead, SF started to ask questions about what living in the future might be like in psychological terms – how might technology change us as a species? A 'New Wave' of science fiction emerged that challenged old assumptions and tackled controversial topics, using SF as a vehicle for social comment, satire and subversion.

Michael Moorcock played a key role in the New Wave's development. Having become editor of British SF magazine *New Worlds* in 1964, he soon changed its focus from hardware-obsessed geekery to what was happening in the present day. Science fiction, he argued in a series of polemical editorials, didn't have to be set on far-flung worlds populated by exotic aliens – the technocratic march of progress on our own planet provided more than enough material for a new type of 'speculative fiction' that dealt with inner as much as outer space.

If Moorcock was the New Wave's prophet, J.G. Ballard was the word made flesh. Fascinated by surrealism and psychology, his early novels – including *The Drowned World* (1962), *The Drought* (1965) and *The Crystal World* (1966) – explore how his repressed protagonists discover internal liberation via external disaster. But increasingly, Ballard's central theme was the psychic dislocation of the modern age, epitomised by a series of novels starting with *The Atrocity Exhibition* (1970). Others followed suit, as *New Worlds* became a platform for experimental literature on both sides of the Atlantic – key British voices included Brian Aldiss, Christopher Priest and M. John Harrison, while American writers such as Thomas Disch, John Sladek, Norman Spinrad and Judith Merril moved to London to be closer to the action.

Not that the New Wave was a completely British invention. In the US, Philip K. Dick had been using science fiction as a means of interrogating the nature of reality for years. Like Ballard, Barry Malzberg was obsessed with the dark side of the space programme, and such era-defining events as the assassination of John F. Kennedy. And Harlan Ellison published the first *Dangerous Visions* anthology in 1967, a collection of taboo-busting SF stories which caused quite a stir.[2] The New Wave also acknowledged a debt to the fractured, hallucinatory fiction of William Burroughs – alongside Salvador Dali and Sigmund Freud, one of Ballard's key inspirations.

US writers also embraced the quasi-mystical, mind-expanding potential of SF, with Robert Heinlein's *Stranger In A Strange Land* (1961) and Frank Herbert's *Dune* (1965) – both concerning the coming of a revolutionary messiah – concomitant with counterculture favourites such as Tolkien's *The Lord Of The Rings* (1954-55, first single volume edition 1968), Carlos Castaneda's *The Teachings of Don Juan* (1968), and John Michell's *The View Over Atlantis* (1969).

Cover of *New Worlds* 191
(artwork by Mal Dean, 1969. Courtesy of Michael Moorcock)

Inevitably, the psychedelic experience itself fed into New Wave SF. Besides editing *New Worlds*, Moorcock continued to write prolifically, with the figure of Jerry Cornelius emerging as one of his most enduring creations. The narcotic-enhanced, ambisexual anti-hero of Moorcock's 1968 novel *The Final Programme*, Cornelius would become the louche flag-bearer for the New Wave's often cynical take on the modern world. Moorcock depicts a dystopian London on the cusp of the Swinging Sixties, yet already succumbing to the slow death of entropy, his inventions including hallucinatory man-traps and the Needle Gun.[3]

Other New Wave novels are more explicit in their use of drugs as a plot device. Aldiss's *Barefoot In The Head* (1969) is set in the aftermath of an 'Acid Head War' fought with hallucinogenic chemicals, leaving the population in a state of ongoing psychosis. And in Ballard's *The Crystal World* (1966), time itself has begun to solidify into a dazzling canopy of fractal shapes, a description of reality through the perceptual lens of LSD.

## Set The Controls

In 1962, 'Telstar' by The Tornados celebrated the launch of the first communications satellite, its faux-cosmic Clavioline melody speaking of an optimistic future where technology might bring us closer together rather than lead to our destruction. But as the decade wore on, pop music's take on the space age became darker and more science fictional in tone. Bowie's 'Space Oddity' is the obvious example, but The Rolling Stones had already used space as a metaphor for alienation on the brooding '2000 Light Years From Home'. There's also Zager And Evans' 1969 hit 'In The Year 2525', an urgent litany of future woe – from thought-controlling pills to test tube babies – which topped both the UK and US charts.

Some songs were inspired by literary SF itself. Hendrix's 'Purple Haze' had tenuous origins in Philip José Farmer's *Night Of Light* (1957), where sunspots (with a "purplish haze") cause a planet to experience a morphing of reality. The title of Pink Floyd's 'Set The Controls For The Heart Of The Sun' was inspired by Moorcock's *The Fireclown* (1965), where a messiah figure on a future earth does exactly that. And early Bowie track 'We Are Hungry Men', with its themes of overpopulation and cannibalism, has been connected with Harry Harrison's *Make Room! Make Room!* (1966), later filmed as *Soylent Green* (1973).

The most on-the-nose effort was The Byrds' 'Space Odyssey', a musical version of Arthur C. Clarke's 'The Sentinel' (1951), the short story that inspired *2001:*

*A Space Odyssey* (1968). The band had heard that Kubrick wanted music for the soundtrack - suffice to say, they didn't make the final cut.[4]

## Space Rock Takes Off

Hawkwind formed in 1969, and played their first gig just a month after Apollo 11 touched down in the Sea Of Tranquillity. In parallel, New Wave SF was at its peak, and its epicentre – Moorcock's *New Worlds* – just happened to be in the same place as the band's own base: Ladbroke Grove. The term 'space rock' had already been applied to Pink Floyd – it's why the BBC invited them to live soundtrack some of the Apollo 11 mission – but Hawkwind's electronic-enhanced post-psychedelia, like the whirring and whooshing of star-bound machinery, gradually made its claim on the title. By the time of *Hawkwind*'s release, 'space rock' was how they described and promoted themselves – and this was the spark that fired Robert Calvert's imagination.

Calvert had been publishing SF-influenced poetry in *Friends*,[5] and leapt at the chance to do a reading as part of a Hawkwind gig, his performance catalysing their music into a formal alliance with science fiction. Various band members read the popular authors, including Moorcock, but it was Calvert who had the literary chops to transform and assimilate SF themes and ideas – Golden Age *and* New Wave – into words and lyrics, and to fashion a group mythology around them.

By *ISOS*, Hawkwind had fully embraced the role Calvert had created for them, with invaluable visual and conceptual support from Barney Bubbles. In particular, *The Hawkwind Log*'s interleaving of Eastern philosophy, astrology and mysticism with SF-flavoured commentary[6] is entirely in keeping with the countercultural-friendly science fiction of the aforementioned *Stranger In A Strange Land* and *Dune*, plus the writings of Roger Zelazny (see below). With its lift-off drones, rocket ship rhythms and alien distress calls, the music itself also now explicitly evokes both the vastness of the void and the means to traverse it.

But one song in particular crystallises the band's new direction, the Turner-penned '**Master Of The Universe**', their first overtly science-fictional track. It taps into a long-standing SF idea, that of the alien race so advanced they may as well be gods, with the word 'master' suggesting an active if admonitory interest in the affairs of man. For instance, in Arthur C. Clarke's *Childhood's End* (1953), the Overlords stage a 'benign invasion' of Earth to guide us towards the next stage of evolution. More starkly, *The Day The Earth Stood Still* (1951) features an alien emissary who warns mankind to cease development of atomic weapons, or face obliteration to protect the rest of the universe.[7]

However, it's just as likely that Turner took inspiration from similar figures in superhero comics. All-powerful cosmic entities included Marvel's The Watchers, and also Eternity, who featured in *Doctor Strange*, a favourite title among countercultural readers. Turner was particularly enamoured with the latter, at one point asking Bubbles to design an Eternity-based costume for him.

## Dystopias And Inner Space

The idea of Hawkwind as pilots of a boogie-propelled spaceship flying "*sideways through time*" was cemented in the popular imagination by the success of '**Silver Machine**'. But there's evidence of harder SF input on the album that follows. *Doremi's* artwork features space pirates, cosmic angels and fantastical warriors, but its lyrical content is often dystopian in tone. '**Brainstorm**' and '**Time We Left This World Today**' both paint a picture of an oppressive society, with "*brain police*" spying on its fearful citizens, who hope not to "*turn android*".

SF is rife with sterile utopias and technology-controlled future states, with Aldous Huxley's *Brave New World* (1932) and George Orwell's *Nineteen Eighty-Four* (1949) being the most well-known examples. A more contemporary version was the enclosed society of *THX 1138* (1971), by future *Star Wars* creator George Lucas, where a daily regime of emotion-repressing drugs ensures that love remains outlawed between its citizens, who are kept in line by chromium-plated police robots.

In 'Brainstorm' and 'Time We Left', the solution is to get the hell out and set the controls for the heart of the void, but that presents its own issues.[8] Hawkwind significantly enhanced their SF credentials by having Michael Moorcock do occasional readings at their gigs, and his novel *The Black Corridor* (1969) seems to have been an influence on '**Space Is Deep**'.

One of Moorcock's rarer excursions into space-based SF (and part-written by Hilary Bailey, his then-wife), *The Black Corridor* is a quintessential New Wave take on space as a site of alienation and existential despair. Escaping a world spiralling into anarchy in a stolen spaceship, the protagonist Ryan attends to the cryogenically frozen bodies of his friends and family – but the isolation and responsibility drive him mad. 'Space Is Deep' recalls the fractured log entries that Ryan makes: "*Space is dark, it is so endless / When you're lost, it's so relentless*". If the song itself isn't as bleak as the novel, it certainly captures the sense of a universe without end, and of our insignificance against this infinite backdrop.

The gloomiest song on *Doremi* is Lemmy's acoustic blues 'The Watcher'. Likely inspired by Marvel's The Watchers – the oldest race in the universe, sworn to observe the progress of other civilisations – this is a thematic sequel to 'Master Of The Universe'. The all-seeing demi-god turns their back on mankind and condemns us to our fate: *"Human greed destroys your sphere / And there's no room for you out here."*

By contrast, Brock's 'Lord Of Light' is the album's most upbeat track. It's also the first of many Hawkwind songs to lift its title directly from an SF novel – even if the lyrical content bears little relation to its source. Published in 1967, Roger Zelazny's *Lord Of Light* was SF's most ambitious melding yet of the religious and the scientific, and with its references to Hindu deities and Eastern philosophies, was tailor-made for the late 60s counterculture. On an alien world, a far-future group of Earth colonists have turned themselves into gods by using technology to transfer the 'soul' from one body to another, a type of reincarnation that makes them immortal.[9] Brock's song on the other hand is about ley lines forming a mystical power grid across the earth's surface, though reincarnation is touched on: *"A day shall come, we shall be as one / Perhaps the dying has begun / From the realms beyond the sun / Here our lifetime has begun."*

Calvert had envisioned the *Doremi* tour as a rock space opera, its storyline based on the dreams and fantasies of a crew of starfarers in suspended animation. However, the Space Ritual concept got mangled along the way – the tour programme portrayed the band as unruly sword-wielding spacelords, while Bubbles was more interested in turning the stage into an audience-powered starship via the Pythagorean theory of the music of the spheres.[10]

But the original idea is still discernible on *Space Ritual*, particularly in the spoken-word pieces. On 'Born To Go', the Hawkship achieves escape velocity, blazing *"a new clear* [ie nuclear] *way through space"* and leaving a "burning track". This reflects the reckless, atomic-powered optimism that characterised many early SF adventures, Earth's complexities jettisoned in favour of a new beginning among the stars.

'The Awakening' is a much darker take on the pioneer impulse, where *"one man stares from the trauma of his birth / Attending to the hypno-tapes, assuring him / That this was reality, however grim"*.[11] The scenario is stark, with Calvert's clinical, near-robotic delivery adding disquieting layers to one of Hawkwind's most condensed hits of pure SF. Suspended animation – the body in a state of ageless near-death, to be revived in the future – has been a popular SF device since H.G. Wells' *The Sleeper Awakes* (1910), though often just as a convenient way to get star-travellers from galactic point A to B. But surprisingly few works had dealt with the effects of waking from such a prolonged hibernation, let alone the *"thousand years of dreams"* that may have occurred.[12]

Calvert's other two poems on *Space Ritual* are of an even stronger New Wave bent. '10 **Seconds Of Forever**' counts down the last moments of a man's life, each second a fragment of his unravelling consciousness, from the intimate and personal (*"I saw your mouth whispering something I could not hear"*) to blown-out, cosmic omniscience: *"I thought of the vermillion deserts of Mars, the jewelled forests of Venus"* (like an *Amazing Stories* cover). As the details accumulate – a *"plastic fragment of a child's toy"* and the *"pair of broken shades lying on the tarmac"* – this flight through inner space could be the immediate aftermath of a fatal road accident, very much in Ballard territory.

'**Welcome To The Future**' is a short but bleak vision of ecological breakdown, of *"dehydrated lands"* and *"oceans in a labelled can"*. Ballard is again salient, his 1965 novel *The Drought* describing the sea rendered toxic with industrial waste. The parlous state of the environment was big news in the early 70s, with SF quick to respond to the poisoning of the land – for example, John Brunner's novel *The Sheep Look Up* (1972), plus eco-apocalyptic films *No Blade Of Grass* (1970) and *Silent Running* (1972).[13] Here, the planet is less imperilled by alien invaders than by doomsday scenarios of man's own making.

Two other spoken-word pieces, both Moorcock's, help make *Space Ritual* the ultimate space rock/SF album. Not written specifically for the band, '**The Black Corridor**' is essentially the opening lines of the novel, a haunted meditation on the void, the abyss that Nietzsche warned us against gazing into: *"Space is a remorseless, senseless, impersonal fact."* Ballard too saw space exploration as a "symptom of some inner unconscious malaise afflicting mankind"[a] – though the undisputed *enfant terrible* of early 70s cosmic angst was Barry Malzberg, whose *The Falling Astronauts* (1971) and *Beyond Apollo* (1972) dealt specifically with the dehumanising effects of the space programme. Condensed in style and relentlessly pessimistic, they caused outrage among more traditional SF fans – but they reflected the growing mood of the times.

'**Sonic Attack**' remains one of Hawkwind's most iconic tracks, painting a chilling picture of citizens caught up in some terrible future conflict: *"metal, not organic limbs, should be employed wherever possible."* Its tone is cynical and unsentimental, the caring veneer of the 'nanny state' stripped back to reveal the cold, Darwinian

Moorcock watches Stacia perform on the set of *The Final Programme* (1973)

logic of self-interest: "*Survival means every man for himself*". It's an entirely New Wave take on how the powers-that-be perceive the mechanics of modern warfare, where civilian casualties become mere collateral damage. "*If you are making love, it is imperative that all bodies reach orgasm simultaneously*" is also invasively prurient, the future state seeking to dominate both the body and the mind.

## Entropy At The Movies

Perhaps the strangest of all the dystopian SF movies from the early 70s,[14] and certainly the only one to feature Hawkwind, is *The Final Programme* (1973), a freewheeling adaption of Moorcock's first Jerry Cornelius novel. Originally optioned by Sandy Lieberson, with the team that worked with Nic Roeg on *Performance* (1970) producing, the role of Cornelius was first offered to Mick Jagger. But in the end, Moorcock's friend Jon Finch took the leading role, with Robert Fuest directing.[15]

*The Final Programme* is incoherent if sporadically entertaining, its plot revolving around a top secret project to scientifically create a new messiah. Yet it often looks fantastic, an eye-catching vision of pop-art decadence and

The Star-farer's Despatch.

I would have liked you
to have been deep
frozen and waiting still
as fresh as your flesh
for my return. But you
rather refused outright
to sign the forms.
Let's see, you'd be, what,
about sixty now.
And long dead by the time
I return to earth.
In my cold-storage sleep
my dreams were full
of you, as you were
when I left, still underage.
an android replica
as my wife. It's no joke
when the times moving

An early draft of 'The Starfarer's Despatch'
(source: Robert Calvert archive)

entropy: Trafalgar Square piled high with car wrecks; nuns playing fruit machines; a disco from the imagination of Hieronymus Bosch. It's in this latter scene that it's possible to very briefly spot Hawkwind playing (inaudibly) in the background – Stacia swirls around in a fetching green cape, part-obscured by rollerskating majorettes.[16]

Moorcock's plan was for Hawkwind to soundtrack the entire movie, but this was nixed by Fuest – in the end, the music was provided by pioneering electronic duo Beaver & Krause and jazz saxophonist Gerry Mulligan. Moorcock described on-set reactions to the band: "When Hawkwind started playing, the crew moved visibly backwards as if pushed by a wave of sound. They said, 'Could you turn it down a bit, lads?' and Dave Brock said, 'We are turned down'".[b]

Fuest had directed episodes of *The Avengers*, and clearly saw Cornelius as some kind of countercultural secret-agent figure – so while the film captures the New Wave SF aesthetic visually, its tone is more camp irony than Moorcock's intended black humour: "[Fuest] didn't get it at all, he was crap".[c] It's debatable whether more Hawkwind would have made the movie any better, but it's apt that they at least play a small role in the early 70s' upsurge of apocalypse-themed SF cinema.

## Flirtation With Fantasy

With Calvert on an extended sabbatical, the band stepped back a little from science fiction, although the crashed spaceship and alien planetscape of *HOTMG*'s sleeve could have adorned the cover of a Golden Age paperback. As for the content, the title of Turner's '**D-Rider**' may have been inspired by *Dragonriders Of Pern* (1967- ), Anne McCaffrey's SF fantasy series about humans telepathically bonded to genetically modified dragons to defend their planet against the deadly 'Thread' that falls from space every 400 years. This melding of the scientific and the mythical would point the way forward for both Hawkwind and the SF genre itself.

By the mid-70s, 'hard' SF was in relative decline, with fantasy – or 'sword and sorcery' as it was often referred to – increasingly taking up shelf space in bookstores. As the author of the Eternal Champion series, Moorcock was a prime mover in this field, dashing titles off in days to fund *New Worlds*. However, when he quit the editorship in 1971, he continued the series, exploring humanity's battle against the eldritch races in twilight versions of Earth's distant past and future.[17]

*Warrior* drew on these books, particularly on the spoken word tracks '**The Wizard Blew His Horn**' and '**Warriors**'. The music had also changed, no longer evoking the cryogenic hallucinations of interstellar travel, but instead the epic sweep of a magical narrative depicting the struggle between order and chaos. The album does end with a throwback to New Wave SF though – 'Kings Of Speed' has lyrics that refer to *"Mr C"* (Jerry Cornelius himself) along with his brother Frank and the monstrous Bishop Beesley. A souped-up take on the 'Silver Machine' template, it reminds us that combining rock & roll with SF is itself a very New Wave notion, with veiled versions of Hawkwind cropping up throughout Moorcock's novels as avatars of anarchy.[18]

## From Alienation To Damnation

Returning at the end of 1975, Calvert set about re-establishing Hawkwind as the world's pre-eminent SF band. The interplanetary light-projections of their live shows hadn't gone away, and 'Master Of The Universe' and 'Brainstorm' still remained part of the set – but Calvert realigned Hawkwind towards a brand of satirical SF more engaged with the day after tomorrow than the far-flung future.

*Astounding Sounds* is a transitional album, its title and cover referencing SF's early days as pulp entertainment. The title and mood of the instrumental 'Chronoglide Skyway' hint at the futuristic cityscapes that adorn SF book covers, but only Calvert's 'Steppenwolf', an interpretation of Herman Hesse's 1927 novel, is relevant lyrically. The book's focus on urban alienation anticipates many New Wave SF ideas – but while Hesse intended the lupine manifestation of his protagonist as a metaphor for inner turmoil, Calvert mashes the idea up with the legend of the werewolf, a man who physically transforms into a beast at full moon.[19] The terror of being 'taken over' or turned into something non-human is a recurrent theme in SF, particularly in films such as *Invasion Of The Body Snatchers* (1956), *The Quatermass Xperiment* (1955) and *The Fly* (1958).

But Calvert's desire to fashion rock into science fiction theatre was fully in evidence on the *Astounding Sounds* tour, the impressive Atomhenge lighting set creating an on-stage molecular temple from which to preach his version of the SF gospel – 'Time For Sale' is an example of this evangelism, Calvert playing a cosmic huckster selling us the secrets of time travel and immortality.

On *Quark*, Hawkwind hit their SF stride again. The first half of 'Spirit Of The Age' is Calvert's poem 'The Starfarer's Despatch', a blackly skewed take on suspended animation and time dilation, with its brilliant opening line: *"I would have liked you to have been deep frozen too."* According to Einstein, a few years in deep space travelling at near-light speed may be the equivalent of over 100 years back on Earth. Novels such as Joe Haldeman's *The Forever War* (1974) explored this idea – an army conscript fighting aliens in a distant galaxy has to deal with the culture shock of returning to Earth many years in the future.

In Calvert's scenario, the starfaring protagonist rues the fact that his young lover will be long dead by the time he returns, and her "*android replica*" no longer recognises him during sex (or worse, thinks he's someone else). In just a few lines, this vignette sums up both the reality and the bathos of Einsteinian space travel – as well as the notion of robots as lovers.[20]

The second half of 'Spirit Of The Age' is 'The Clone's Poem', which tackles non-sexual reproduction. Cloning has featured in SF since *Brave New World*, and would be popularised in such mainstream films as *The Boys From Brazil* (1978), where Hitler's DNA threatens to birth a master race of homicidal tyrants. But in the New Wave period, its wider societal implications were investigated, culminating in Kate Wilhelm's *Where Late the Sweet Birds Sang* (1976). After nuclear war and environmental breakdown, an infertile mankind is dying out, but an isolated community learns to clone itself. As we follow the ensuing generations, the clones bond as a single psychological entity, leading to a fatal decline in adaptive creativity. This is also the theme of Calvert's poem, the cloned protagonist lamenting his lack of free will, destined forever to reproduce the same words and thoughts as his "*test-tube brothers*", the pulsing, programmatic music a glimpse into a vacuum-packed future.

'**Damnation Alley**' is Hawkwind's second close encounter with Roger Zelazny, and their most fully-realised interpretation of a SF work. As novella and then novel (1967-69), the book is a pulpy action-adventure with post-nuclear apocalypse America as backdrop. Its anti-hero is the last Hells Angel, one Hell Tanner, convicted murderer and rapist, pardoned for his crimes on condition he drives from Los Angeles to Boston in a specially adapted vehicle to deliver a plague vaccine. The journey is a suicide mission though a radioactive, hurricane-wracked wasteland full of mutated monsters – though the tone mainly coming through in Calvert's re-telling is Tanner's studied insouciance. *Dr Strangelove* (1964), Stanley Kubrick's blackly comic take on the end of the world, is also referenced in the song's jaunty chorus.

'**Fable Of A Failed Race**' is a short story in lyric form about the doomed colonisation of another world, while the irreverent '**Quark, Strangeness And Charm**' refers to the sub-atomic particles associated with quantum theory. And the title of the final dramatic instrumental, '**The Iron Dream**', comes from a 1972 parallel reality novel by Norman Spinrad,[21] in which Adolf Hitler immigrates to America to become a pulp SF writer, rather than Führer. Most of it consists of Hitler's own novel, *Lord Of The Swastika*, a luridly written science fantasy adventure fuelled by Nazi ideology highlighting the fascistic and racist overtones of much early SF. Alternative history novels were a popular stand-by for SF writers, with Philip K. Dick's *The Man In The High Castle* (1962), set in an America where Germany and Japan won the Second World War, being perhaps the most renowned.

Just a few months after *Quark*'s release, a wayward adaptation of *Damnation Alley* (1977) opened in US cinemas.[22] While the impressively realised "*eight-wheeled anti-radiation tomb*" had expanded to 12 wheels, Tanner is now an army lieutenant involved in the nuclear exchange that destroyed the world – though in a ludicrously happy ending, the earth tilts back on its axis, and the film's surviving protagonists are greeted by a hippie community in upstate New York.

Tanking at the box office, *Damnation Alley* marked the end of 70s Hollywood's run of dystopian SF. A poor script and troubled production didn't help, but more significant was the release in the same year of the film that would go on to redefine mainstream science fiction…

## No One Can Hear You Scream

*Star Wars* (1977) turned the clock back completely, rebooting the heroic space opera of *Flash Gordon* and *Buck Rogers*. After years of depicting mankind on the brink of annihilation, here was a much less depressing SF movie. Worlds might get blown up along the way, but crucially, they weren't our world. Essentially a fairytale – "A long time ago in a galaxy far, far away" – it quickly became the global blockbuster against which all subsequent screen SF would be judged, particularly in terms of the increasingly important 'special effects'.

*Star Wars* showed that movie SF didn't have to be entirely pessimistic – but it wasn't the only late 70s film that shook up the genre. With its memorable tagline "In space, no one can hear you scream", the publicity campaign for Ridley Scott's 1979 *Alien* harked back to *The Black Corridor*, the void as a place of isolation and psychological terror, the creature itself a manifestation of space as a "*remorseless, senseless, impersonal fact*".

British science fiction TV also continued to mine a surprisingly dark seam of inspiration. *Doctor Who* was more culturally engaged than ever, and more frightening. The Doctor remained an enigmatic, mercurial character, and the programme no longer attempted to imbue a 'sense of wonder' in its viewers, preferring instead

Mal Dean illustration of Jerry Cornelius from *New Worlds* – an
inspiration for Robert Calvert?
(Courtesy of Michael Moorcock)

to scare the living daylights out of them. Plots revolved around environmental meltdown, eco-fascism, insane supercomputers, mutant maggots, lethal showroom dummies, and full-on body horror. The sense that *"we took the wrong step years ago"* – that the capitalist establishment can't be trusted – was implicit throughout.

ITV's big-budget 70s SF series *Space: 1999* (1975-77) was similarly dark, despite trying to emulate *Star Trek*'s format. Flung out of orbit by a nuclear explosion, Moonbase Alpha hurtled through the cosmos, encountering new worlds and alien dangers. But in contrast to *Star Trek*'s swaggering colonial confidence, *Space: 1999* was far less cocky, the Alphans technologically and psychologically unprepared for their 'mission'.[23]

Yet the clearest contrast with *Star Wars* came from the BBC series *Blake's 7* (1978-81). Both followed the adventures of a band of rebel freedom fighters resisting a brutal galaxy-wide regime. But instead of well-drilled squadrons of X-Wing fighters and a 'good empire' in waiting, the crew of the Liberator are a rag-tag bunch of criminals fighting a terrorist war, with varying degrees of commitment. Blake himself is an idealist often blinded to the consequences of his actions, convinced the end justifies the means. Undiluted heroism is thin on the ground and the insurgency is ultimately doomed to failure.

## Man Vs Technology

Calvert's take on SF and the future was similarly ambivalent, as a number of new songs aired on the *Quark* tour demonstrated. '**Uncle Sam's On Mars**' in fact dated back to the first Atomhenge shows, and had gone through various iterations, including an unused studio recording during the *Quark* sessions. By the autumn of 1977, it was a throbbing juggernaut of sound perfectly reflecting its theme, of Man preparing to blithely despoil Mars the same way as Earth.

Mars was topical at the time, with NASA's Viking probes transmitting images from the Red Planet since the previous summer. From H.G. Wells' *The War Of The Worlds* (1898) to Ray Bradbury's *The Martian Chronicles* (1950), our nearest neighbour has fired the imagination. And it's from Bradbury's book that the song drew its initial inspiration: in the story '– And the Moon Be Still As Bright', an explorer declares, "We Earth Men have a talent for ruining big, beautiful things".[24] The song captures this imperialistic belief in our destiny – our right to spread our values and psychoses among the stars – along with the anger felt in some quarters that money spent on space exploration should be used instead to fix some of our own world's problems.

In 'Robot', with its forbidding, mechanical riff and melodramatic organ, Calvert equates the lives of suburban-dwelling, middle-class city workers with that of machines – not original perhaps, but rarely so brilliantly expressed, with a pay-off line, "*You're very nearly human you're so well disguised*," that adds a sinister edge. The idea of Man creating life as an "*automated homunculus*" goes right back to Mary Shelley's *Frankenstein* (1818), as do the practical and ethical problems that arrive with robots. How do you control beings potentially much stronger and more intelligent than yourself? When does an android effectively become a man?

'Robot' explicitly invokes Asimov's "Three Laws of Robotics", as made famous in the short story collection *I, Robot* (1950). These are designed to stop robots from harming people or allowing themselves to be damaged – but the point of these stories is always the loopholes. New Wave writer John Sladek produced a number of satirical novels around the theme of robots in human society – for instance, in *The Reproductive System* (1968), a new breed of self-replicating robots threatens to inadvertently take over the world.

The title of '**High Rise**' may well have come from the 1975 J.G. Ballard novel of the same name – in which the tenants of a luxury tower block descend into tribal barbarism as services start to break down – but Calvert's lyric was based on his own experience of living in a Margate flatblock, and reflects the growing belief that 'council estates in the sky' were a failed experiment that encouraged only vandalism and anomie.[25] Nevertheless, *High-Rise* the novel also drew on similar perceptions, and was the third part of a trilogy of books from Ballard that targeted the alienating effects of a built environment increasingly designed to accommodate technology – the car in particular – rather than people, starting with the hugely controversial *Crash* (1973), followed by *Concrete Island* (1974).

Finally, '**Jack Of Shadows**' is the third of Hawkwind's Roger Zelazny-referencing songs. Published in 1971, and again drawing on ancient mythology in its telling, *Jack Of Shadows* is essentially a rather convoluted revenge story, but interesting for being set on a planet where one side is perpetual day (where technology predominates), and the other is eternal night (where magic holds sway). The song is poppy and upbeat, with the most straight-forwardly heroic of Calvert's SF lyrics, describing the superhuman powers of the novel's titular protagonist.

## Voluntary Prisoners

Calvert would claim to be more interested in SF's heroic and fantastical elements than in the possibilities of the New Wave. But the concept he constructed for *Hawklords* could have come straight from the pages of *New Worlds*. It's built round Pan Transcendental Industries (PTI), a mysterious conglomerate dedicated to the re-modelling of reality. Its manifesto outlines PTI's successful 25 year plan, in a text that parodies and cuts up corporate jargonese and pseudo-scientific dogma.[26] The result – funny, surreal and disturbing – resembles the 'condensed novels' in Ballard's *The Atrocity Exhibition*. We learn that PTI's purpose is to entice angels down to Earth, where their wings can be replaced by car doors – the "Assembly Rooms" are "staffed by car crash victims whose function is to generate new forms of social behaviour through the transformation of private into public fantasies".

Calvert would berate the sloganeering 'No Future' generation for fixating on Orwellian dystopias – instead, he imagines a world where the citizens "escape into PTI in an impulsive exodus… to become its Voluntary Prisoners". Much like the workers of 'Robot', we are its willing slaves… It's a pre-emptive attack on the materialistic consumer philosophy that will define the 1980s: "Our true ambition is to create a heaven totally fabricated by man."

*Hawklords'* songs have a chilliness to them that suggests futures derailed and lives unfulfilled. And opening track '**Psi Power**' addresses a core SF theme head on, in what may be Calvert's finest lyric. It's a deeply humane depiction of what it's like to be genuinely different, the protagonist struggling to hide his powers from the world and block out the psychic noise in his head – a metaphor perhaps for Calvert's own struggles with his mental health.

SF had long embraced ESP, rebranding telepathy, telekinesis and precognition as 'psionics', although many stories dramatised the same problems as Calvert's protagonist faces, with characters hiding their special powers out of fear of how 'normal' people might react. Classics include A.E. van Vogt's *Slan* (1940) and Olaf Stapleton's *Odd John* (1935), which coined the phrase "homo superior"[27] to describe this next stage of human evolution. In Theodore Sturgeon's *More Than Human* (1953), damaged individuals with psychic powers gather together as a potent gestalt, while John Wyndham's *The Midwich Cuckoos* (1957, filmed as *Village Of The Damned* in 1960) gives us reason to fear such an entity, as a hivemind of alien children wreaks psionic havoc in the English countryside.

'Psi Power' channelled a mainstream fascination with ESP, particularly in the cinema: movies from 1978 included *The Medusa Touch* (telekinesis), *Eyes of Laura Mars* (precognition) and *The Fury*, in which a young man with psychic powers is kidnapped by the CIA to be trained and used as a weapon.[28] Calvert's line, "*It's like a radio you can't switch off / There's no way to get peace of mind,"* also chimes with David Cronenberg's *Scanners* (1981), its protagonist a tortured vagrant unable to stop the voices in his head.

'The Age Of The Micro Man' is the one song on *Hawklords* that explicitly takes up the PTI theme. Under its Kafka-esque neoliberalism, the Voluntary Prisoners are condemned to lives of meaningless button-pushing – the slaves may not be so willing once they realise what they've given up. The 1978 Hawklords stage show continued this theme, explicitly referencing the oppressive class system of German SF classic Metropolis (1927).

Frustrated with group politics, Calvert quit Hawkwind for the final time at the start of 1979. Just before leaving, he declared: "I don't like SF that much... There are much more interesting sources of inspiration to be found outside the field altogether, in newspapers and magazines like *Scientific American*... Most SF is trash, actually".[d] And while much of the music that Calvert produced post-Hawkwind was still concerned with the impact of technology on man and society, it steered clear of any hard SF references.

Released in June 1979, *PXR5* contained overdubbed live recordings from the autumn 77 tour of 'Uncle Sam's On Mars', 'Robot' and 'High Rise', plus a studio recording of 'Jack Of Shadows'. It also featured a Brock solo take of the Calvert poem '**Infinity**'. With its reference to *"crystallised eternity"*, it's tempting to make another Ballard connection – for instance, to his short story 'The Garden Of Time', a favourite of Calvert's, or *The Crystal World* – with its immortal protagonist frozen in time.

Calvert left one other SF-referencing song behind, an homage to Ray Bradbury's *Fahrenheit 451* (1953), set in a future where books are banned and any found are burnt, sometimes along with their owners. A 1977 demo, '**Fahrenheit 451**' wouldn't be properly recorded until 1982's *Choose Your Masques*, its lyrics derived from a Calvert poem entitled 'Centigrade 232'.[29] Also in 1977, Calvert claimed to be writing a science fiction novel entitled *Eye Of The Falcon* – "a curious tale dealing with Arabs, First World War pilots and oil-drinking Martian machines"[e] – but no more was heard of this.

## New Apocalypses

Looking back over Calvert's tenure as Hawkwind's SF poet in residence, it's easy to see why Moorcock describes him as a great "synthesist" of other people's work. But he was also a fiercely creative and original thinker, with a unique voice and perspective on many key SF themes.

Hawkwind continued to mine science-fictional imagery and ideas, but often struggled to recapture Calvert's imaginative spark. The Brock-penned 'PXR5' returns to the language of the early pulps – "*Two years ago, our Nova-drive failed and we drifted in space*" – but is merely a veiled reference to the three 'crew' (Turner, Rudolph and Powell) whose "*life supports could not take the strain and so they died!*" And Tim Blake's '**Lighthouse**' on *Live Seventy Nine* is even more simplistic, with a benevolent, new age vision of the cosmos conspicuously absent from previous Hawkwind songs: "*Far away in outer space, a lighthouse guiding star / It's there to guide you, human race, and show you where you are.*"

*Levitation*'s cover featured an airbrushed Hawkship cruising over an arid landscape, and contained various allusions to SF. The instrumental '**World Of Tiers**' takes its title from a science-fantasy series by Philip José Farmer. '**The 5th Second Of Forever**' references the "*Venus/Mars*" line from '10 Seconds Of Forever', but has no other connection with it. '**Dust Of Time**' has a solid SF theme at its core, depicting a dystopian world with "*queues of sterile mothers waiting for inspection.*" The possibility of the world ending not with a bang, but in a whimper of mass infertility has been tackled a number of times in SF, with Brian Aldiss's *Greybeard* (1964) being one of the most lauded, while David Cronenberg's first film *Crimes Of The Future* (1970) also examines this apocalyptic scenario.

As the Cold War began to hot up again following the Soviet invasion of Afghanistan in December 1979, '**Who's Gonna Win The War?**' was Brock's most pertinent lyric on *Levitation*. It taps into 80s nuclear dread with its stark imagery of a "*radiation wasteland*", the "*creeping sickness*", and a world where "*only death is lurking*". On its release as a single in 1980 (with 'Nuclear Toy' on the B-side), it was one of the first of many subsequent songs to address the nightmare of the Bomb.[30]

Long a topic of horrified SF fascination, nuclear war and its aftermath were considered so inevitable during the 60s that by the time of Zelazny's *Damnation Alley*, an irradiated earth had become merely the backdrop for a pulp thriller. But with the return of superpower sabre-rattling, more serious works began to address the topic again. In Russell Hoban's *Riddley Walker* (1980), post-atomic humanity lives a bleakly primitive future existence sustained by myths and traditions derived from misremembered fragments of the pre-war past, with even language itself becoming fatally corrupted.

The last song of this era that directly references SF is '**Dangerous Visions**', a Keith Hale composition played on the 1980 *Levitation* tour (though unreleased until 1983's *Zones*). The title comes from Harlan Ellison's controversial anthology, but the lyrics don't appear to have been inspired by its contents.

## Despised Art Forms

In October-November 1979, the fourth and final instalment of Nigel Kneale's *Quatermass* quartet provided a suitably apocalyptic TV finale to the decade. Previously portrayed as a headstrong yet resourceful man of science, Quatermass is now shown as an older, almost beaten figure, dejected by the ruined urban environment and decadent culture of a world going rapidly to the dogs. His granddaughter has fallen in with the Planet People, a feckless mass of chanting hippies who assemble at stone circles hoping to be rescued from Earth by the perennial golden sky people. When a group of them vanishes in a blinding flash of light, it becomes all too clear that, far from achieving celestial oneness, they've been incinerated and harvested as food by a malevolent alien intelligence.

Kneale had originally written this story in 1973, back when Hawkwind ruled the underground – and the notion of a New Age Traveller-type group turning their backs on the broken modern world to seek salvation among the stars could have come from one of their early albums.[31]

Speaking in 2006 to Alan Moore, Michael Moorcock called science fiction and rock & roll the two great despised art forms of the 20th century,[f] their coming together in the counterculture having confounded and even angered many commentators, Nigel Kneale among them. Hawkwind were the ultimate expression of this union – and often the focus of this ire. And yet, undaunted by any pre-existing 'canon', as Moorcock points out, they created a visionary body of work, an alternative sonic universe that stretches from space opera to dystopian satire.

Simply put, Hawkwind *are* science fiction…

◇◇◇◇◇◇◇◇◇◇◇◇◇◇◇◇◇◇◇◇◇◇◇◇◇◇◇◇◇◇◇◇◇◇◇◇◇◇◇◇◇◇◇◇◇◇◇◇◇◇◇◇◇◇◇◇◇◇◇◇◇◇◇◇◇◇◇◇

a    From 'A Question Of Re-Entry', J.G. Ballard, 1963

b    Q&A with Michael Moorcock after a screening of *The Final Programme*, 10/8/10, BFI, London

c    'Episode 235 – *The Final Programme*', *The Projection Booth* (podcast), September 2015

d    'Leisure Wear Of The Hawklords' – Andy Gill, *NME*, 16/12/78

e    'Making Waves – Hawkwind', *Melody Maker*, 16/7/77

f    Moorcock and Moore were filmed talking at the Vanbrugh Theatre, London in January 2006. YouTube, 2018 – *Michael Moorcock And Alan Moore Savoy 2006*

1    There are many others, including several space-based concept albums. *To Our Children's Children's Children* by The Moody Blues was inspired by the 1969 moon landing, and may well have influenced the early Hawkwind. Flaming Youth's *Ark 2* (1970), which featured a young Phil Collins, certainly didn't, despite its theme of evacuation from a dying Earth. *A Time Before This* (1970) by Julian's Treatment tells the story of the last man on Earth travelling to Alpha Centauri (band leader Julian Jay Savarin went on to write the *Lemmus: A Time Odyssey* trilogy). Nektar's *Journey To The Centre Of The Eye* (1971) features an astronaut imparted with alien wisdom (like Hawkwind, Nektar had their own liquid lights and slides team).

Bands including Van Der Graaf Generator, Genesis, Ramases, Black Sabbath and Rush also leaned in an SF direction, while the pop charts featured such songs as the Carpenters' Klaatu cover 'Calling Occupants Of Interplanetary Craft' and Sarah Brightman & Hot Gossip's 'I Lost My Heart To A Starship Trooper', the latter inspired by *Star Wars* and perhaps the best known song from the late 70s sci-fi disco boom (risqué lyrics include *"Take me, make me feel the Force"* – plus a reference to 1977's other big SF film: *"What my body needs is close encounter three"*).

Other French artists using SF themes include Heldon, Spacecraft, Pulsar, Space and Jean-Michel Jarre.

With Sun Ra's AfroFuturism in their DNA, Parliament spawned an entire sub-genre of space-inspired black funk. Early pioneers of house and techno music such as Juan Atkins, of Cybotron and Model 500, were also big SF fans.

2    *Dangerous Visions* is practically a compendium of New Wave/Hawkwind SF writers, including Brian Aldiss, J.G. Ballard, Philip K. Dick, Philip José Farmer, John Sladek, Norman Spinrad and Roger Zelazny.

3    The Cornelius novels are full of references to Jerry's favourite bands: "Jerry reached into his pocket. He turned on his miniature stereo taper. Hawkwind was halfway through *Captain Justice*; a VC3's (sic) synthetic sounds shuddered, roared and decayed" (*The English Assassin*, 1972).

4    Hendrix was one of rock's most high-profile devotees of SF, as songs like 'Third Stone From The Sun' and '1983 (A Merman I Should Turn To Be)' clearly attest.

The Byrds' 1966 hit 'Mr Spaceman' is a light-hearted song about a night visit by aliens: *"Won't you please take me along for a ride?"* the singer asks, but they don't. An aerospace obsessive like Calvert, songwriter Roger McGuinn hoped its transmission via AM radio signals would reach extra-terrestrial ears. Its description by the press as 'space rock' is one of the first uses of the term, though the sound is their familiar jangly pop.

Also worthy of note is the track 'Universes' (1968) by The Liverpool Scene, the poetry/jazz/free rock collective fronted by Adrian Henri. Divided into sections, it includes '4 Love Poems For Ray Bradbury' and 'Poem For Gully Foyle', the latter taking its name (and first few lines) from

Cover of *Gnawing Medusa's Flesh*
(source: Robert Calvert archive)

Michael Moorcock - illustration from *Hawkfan* by Pete Knifton
(source: Brian Tawn archive)

the protagonist of Alfred Bester's SF pulp noir classic *The Stars My Destination* (1956). There's a fantastic extended version of 'Gully Foyle' available online, taken from a 1969 Granada TV performance; the same show also features the track 'We'll All Be Spacemen Before We Die'. While it's unlikely that The Liverpool Scene were a direct influence on Hawkwind – though Calvert would almost certainly have been aware of Henri as one of the 'Liverpool poets' – both songs' combination of gloomy, SF-themed verse over brooding space jazz make for an intriguing parallel. Liverpool Scene guitarist Andy Roberts would later play on Calvert's *Lucky Leif And The Longships*.

5    Calvert also contributed poetry to *New Worlds*. 'Ode To A Time Flower' (*New Worlds* 5, 1972), which he performed on-stage with Hawkwind, quotes Ballard's 'The Garden Of Time'. In the extended essay *Gnawing Medusa's Flesh: The Science Fiction Poetry of Robert Calvert* (1999), Steve Sneyd (a noted SF poet himself) identifies in Calvert's work a tension "between the Sense of Wonder… for escape, liberation, a rebirth free from past constraints of space and the future, and the dystopian possibilities of… loss of nature and planetary ecology, threatened by many aspects of technological advance."

6    The way in which Hawkwind become unmoored in time in *The Hawkwind Log* recalls Kurt Vonnegut's *Slaughterhouse-Five* (1969).

7    *Brother John*, a Sidney Poitier film from 1971, updated this idea for the times, with a divine – or possibly alien – messenger condemning mankind to destruction before it can reach the stars.

8    Another album that embraces this idea is 1970's *Blows Against The Empire* by Paul Kantner & Jefferson Starship, a concept album about countercultural revolutionaries hijacking a spaceship and exiting the solar system. Musically there's little comparison (other than the driving, garage-y opening track 'Mau Mau (Amerikon)'), but it came with a full-colour booklet featuring lyrics and poetry. Kantner (who also wrote Jefferson Airplane's 'Have You Seen The Saucers?') cited Robert Heinlein's *Methuselah's Children* (1958) as an inspiration for *Blows*.

Ursula Le Guin's *The Dispossessed* (1974) also has as its backstory a group of anarchist revolutionaries fleeing their planet and setting up home on a new world.

9    Possibly due to its complex and sometimes confusing structure, *Lord Of Light* hasn't proved to be as enduring as *Stranger In A Strange Land* or *Dune*. However, it did form the basis of the 'fake film' that was used as a cover for the rescue of American hostages from Iran in 1979, as depicted in the 2012 movie *Argo*.

10   The back of the Space Ritual programme also cites a variety of SF inspirations, including Moorcock, (M.) John Harrison, Frank Herbert, Robert Heinlein, Lin Carter (a prolific American SF/fantasy writer and editor – he wrote a novel entitled *Tower at the Edge of Time* in 1968) and Philip José Farmer.

11   'The Awakening' is the first half of Calvert's poem 'First Landing On Medusa' – in the concluding section, when the starfarers venture out onto the surface, they are turned to stone.

12    Although James White's *The Dream Millennium* (1974), again about a spaceship escaping a
      dystopian Earth, does address this idea.

13    Based on John Christopher's *The Death Of Grass* (1956), *No Blade Of Grass* begins with a
      protracted sequence surveying a despoiled world. Roger Whittaker's themesong rams the point
      home: "*We've circled Mars, and we've walked on the Moon… / But no blade of grass here and no
      blue above / No you and me, it's the end of life.*" In *Silent Running*, the last of Earth's vegetation
      has been blasted into orbit in a series of gigantic bio-domes.

14    And boy, were there a lot: along with the aforementioned *THX 1138*, *No Blade Of Grass* and
      *Silent Running*, other dystopian movies included *The Omega Man* (1971), *A Clockwork Orange*
      (1971), *Z.P.G. (Zero Population Growth)* (1972), *Soylent Green* (1973), *A Boy And His Dog* (1975),
      *Rollerball* (1975), and *Logan's Run* (1976).

15    Learning the book was to become a film, Calvert had turned up on Moorcock's doorstep and
      asked, "What do you think?" As Moorcock remembers, "When I didn't immediately reply, he
      enlightened me. 'I'm him,' he said. 'I AM Jerry Cornelius.'" (From Moorcock's introduction
      to 2008's *The Fluxus Paradigm – A Jerry Cornelius Compilation*, a fan-fiction collection.) Finch
      had already played a prototype Cornelius in the BBC's short-lived alien-invasion serial
      *Counterstrike* (1969). Fuest also directed the memorably sadistic *Dr. Phibes* films (1971-72),
      starring Vincent Price.

16    Though according to Moorcock: "You can see them, and me, in the DVD version where I walk
      in front of the nightclub stage and exchange a word with Jerry." From 'Hawkwind Collectables'
      – Ian Abrahams, *Record Collector*, March 2009.

17    A more intriguing Moorcock character from this period is Oswald Bastable, protagonist of *The
      Warlord Of The Air* (1971) and *The Land Leviathan* (1974), scientific romances in the vein of
      Jules Verne, and since acclaimed as founding texts of 'steampunk'. Calvert referred to *Warlord*
      in interviews, and Bastable may be another inspiration for his 'Biggles Of Arabia' persona.

18    For example, Turner appears as Turning Nikhe in *The Quest For Tanelorn* (1975): "He was bearded,
      red-haired, with a quiet, wry manner… he was covered all over in jingling talismans, in beads,
      decorated leather, embroidery, charms of gold, silver and brass." Moorcock also dedicates various
      editions of his books to Hawkwind, starting with *An Alien Heat* in 1972. The 1993 reissue of
      *The Black Corridor* is dedicated "To the memory of Bob Calvert, a rare talent."

19    Steve Sneyd goes further in *Gnawing Medusa's Flesh*, pointing to "the low-key, never-explicit
      suggestion that the beast is in some way made, like Frankenstein's monster, rather than born…"
      and highlighting "futuristic imagery" such as "*It echoes like a cave of chromium / To vacuum up
      my soul when I die*".

20    While literary SF made a decent fist of addressing time dilation, screen SF tended to sidestep
      it via 'warp drives' and 'hyperspace' – however, time dilation proves to be a vital plot point in

*Planet Of The Apes* (1968). Unsurprisingly, page and screen both embraced sex-robots: the "pleasure models" in Philip K. Dick's *Do Androids Of Electric Sheep?* (1968) and film adaptation *Blade Runner* (1982); the sinister suburban replicants of *The Stepford Wives* (novel 1972, film 1975); the theme-park fantasy droids of *Westworld* (1973); and *Barbarella*'s comic-strip robot lover Diktor.

21    Spinrad's most well-known novel is his scabrous media satire *Bug Jack Barron* (1969), partly because a question was asked in Parliament about why public money was being used to publish obscene material when it was serialised in the Arts Council-funded *New Worlds*.

22    *Damnation Alley* didn't make it into British cinemas until January 1979. Whether Calvert wrote the song knowing that the film was in production is up for debate.

23    Prior to *Space: 1999*, Gerry and Sylvia Anderson (*Fireball XL5*, *Thunderbirds*, *Captain Scarlet* etc) had created another surprisingly dark live-action SF show – *UFO* (1970) addressed the flying saucer craze, its faceless aliens harvesting human organs ahead of a full-scale invasion. After writing the *Hawklords* books, Michael Butterworth's next job was novelising *Space: 1999*'s second series.

24    Hammering the point home, *The Martian Chronicles* was published as *The Silver Locusts* in Britain, and Calvert would refer to "*silver locusts*" in the song's live improvised middle section. 'Uncle Sam's On Mars' had evolved from Calvert reading his poem 'Vikings On Mars' over 'Opa-Loka'. He was no doubt amused that NASA had named its Martian probes after a bunch of marauding pirates in longships.

25    J.G. Ballard: "Someone told me that Hawkwind based a song on my novel *High-Rise*, but I doubt that myself" (Jon Savage, *Search & Destroy*, No. 10, 1978). Despite having practically no interest in music, Ballard was certainly aware of Hawkwind – not least because his friend and confidante Moorcock kept performing with them. Moorcock has described an awkward Ballard visiting Ladbroke Grove: "The gulf between Hawkwind and Jimmy was enormous… Nik's saying 'Yeah man, I really like your stuff,' and Jimmy not entirely comfortable with it. And rolling up a joint and offering it to Jimmy as a matter of common decency, and Jimmy saying, [does harrumphing voice] 'Oh no, I'm a whisky man myself'" (from the online 'An Interview with Michael Moorcock (2010)' by Hari Kunzru, published in edited form as 'When Hari Kunzru met Michael Moorcock' – *The Guardian*, 4/2/11).

26    Calvert's PTI manifesto was partly inspired by iconoclastic architect Rem Koolhaas, specifically his books *Exodus, Or The Voluntary Prisoners Of Architecture* (1972) and *Delirious New York* (1978). Certain passages are found in both manifesto and Koolhaas (for instance, "these institutes together form an enormous incubator of the World itself; they are breeding on the Globe"). Barney Bubbles was also a fan of *Delirious New York*, which is perhaps how Calvert encountered Koolhaas. Alternatively, as with *The Hawkwind Log* and *Space Ritual* sleeve notes, Bubbles may have had a hand in writing the manifesto.

27    By the 1970s, this expression had wormed its way into popular culture via Heinlein's *Stranger In A Strange Land*. It appears in Bowie's 'Oh! You Pretty Things' and in children's sci-fi series *The Tomorrow People* (1973-79).

28    Also in 1978, the US Army initiated the Stargate Project, a secret military investigation of psychic phenomena such as 'remote viewing' and killing by the power of thought. This inspired Jon Ronson's 2004 book *The Men Who Stare At Goats* , which was subsequently filmed in 2009.

29    451° Fahrenheit / 232° Centigrade is the temperature at which writing paper burns. *Centigrade 232* was also the title of Calvert's first poetry collection (published by Quasar Books in 1977). Confusingly, this includes a poem entitled 'Fahrenheit 451' bearing no relation to the song lyrics.

30    The 1979 programme for the 'Masters Of The Universe' tour, where this song was first played live, has an entire page dedicated to "Nuclear Facts", newspaper clippings about near-disasters at nuclear power stations and the proliferation of nuclear arms.

31    Written directly after *The Stone Tape*, Kneale's hair-raising techno/occult chiller for the BBC (shown at Christmas 1972), *Quatermass* wasn't made at the time because the BBC didn't have permission to film at Stonehenge, then decided it would be too expensive to produce. The 1979 production was made by Euston Films for ITV. A contemporary Hawkwind article is titled 'Send For Quatermass!' and sub-headed "Britain in grip of time-warp as thousands flock to Hawkwind rites" (John Gill, *Sounds*, 8/12/79).

Bronze promo shot. L-R - Brock, Bainbridge, King, Lloyd-Langton, Blake
(source: Doug Smith archive)

# I Hope You've Brought Your Credit Card With You

January–June 1979

If Hawklords was intended as a new dawn, it seems more like a failed experiment by the start of 1979. Despite a good turn-out on the tour, it hasn't made any money, and Charisma decides not to extend their contract. Penniless and without a record label, they once again decamp to Rockfield in January, holing up in the Mill House rehearsal facility where conditions are little better than a squat.

So it's no surprise when Calvert cracks and leaves the band for good. *Sounds* reports that, "Calvert left the Hawklords in a state of advanced paranoia, at one point even believing that Brock had a contract out on him".[a] But lack of income may also account for the decision – Calvert responds: "The story of Hawkwind is one of dominance. Brock over all the others who float in and out." Brock replies, "You can say what you like, Calvert... but this time you aren't getting back in",[b] which rather supports the ex-frontman's point.

**Mick Smith** (of Hawklords support band The Softies) briefly sits in as replacement drummer for Martin Griffin,[1] but it's ultimately decided to get Simon King back on board. King has been playing in a power trio called Jawa, with former Hawkwind guitarist Huw Lloyd-Langton and bassist Nic Potter, ex-Van Der Graaf Generator.[2] But Potter has other commitments with Peter Hammill, and King is happy to return, especially now that Calvert has gone.

▾     ▾     ▾

Once again, the band looks for a new direction. Having previously released a solo album, Steve Swindells is tapped for ideas, and two of his songs are demoed. **'Shot Down In The Night'** is a hard rock song with pop overtones, yet retains the driving intensity of classic Hawkwind – with a catchy, rabble-rousing chorus, it will subsequently be included in the band's live set. **'Turn It On Turn It Off'** is less polished, with an American new wave edge, a crunching riff and a sneery Swindells vocal.[3]

Two other recordings will appear on future releases. '**Who's Gonna Win The War?**' begins with a furious salvo of guitar and drums before dropping into a menacing slink. There's a blasted relentlessness to it, matching its grim, post-apocalyptic subject matter, sparse synth vamps and whistling electronics evoking a world destroyed by nuclear fire. By contrast, '**Valium 10**' is a joyous, pumping slab of cosmic Northern Soul propelled by an insistent organ riff from Swindells. Brock's chanted vocal is pretty much indecipherable, the sound of a man begging to have a good time by any means necessary.[4]

There are also less-formed recordings, which later feature on various semi-official releases. '**Time Of**' references the book they'd previously been keen to disown, its sinister rumble of bass and crazed Moog soloing having more than a hint of the Death Generator about them. '**British Tribal Music**' is a high energy instrumental sketch that later mutates into the middle section of 'Levitation', its title as fine a description of Hawkwind's output as has ever been coined. Then there's '**Douglas In The Jungle**', a Residents-esque slice of musical Dada that's little more than a nervy bass pulse and a series of non sequiturs: "*give us a feasibility study*", "*who's paying for all of this?*" and most memorably "*the chimpanzees are on their knees!*" It's a disturbing and rather unpleasant listen.[5]

But despite all this activity, there's no obvious way forward. Swindells is the next member to bail, leaving the remaining trio – Brock, Bainbridge and King – to consider their next move.

▾      ▾      ▾

April sees the re-emergence of Del Dettmar, who plays EMS Synthi and 'electric axe'[6] on *Stranger In Mystery*, the debut album from Melodic Energy Commission, a Canadian collective of experimental musicians based out of Vancouver. Dettmar had met Commission leader Don Xaliman en route to planting trees in the wilderness. The album resembles a spacey new age Gong, its songs drifting in and out of focus in the cosmic ether. It even features a track called 'Song Of The Delatron', a reference to the magical Death Generator-repelling device from *The Time Of The Hawklords*.

On 18 May, David Bowie's *Lodger* album is released, which features Simon House's violin on the tracks 'Yassassin', 'Red Sails' and 'Repetition', and on the album's two top 30 hit singles, 'Boys Keep Swinging' and 'D.J.'

▾      ▾      ▾

Meanwhile, Charisma has mysteriously decided to give the *Hawklords* album one last plug, and also on 18 May releases '25 Years' as a 7" single and 12" EP, the latter pressed on Orwellian grey vinyl. Both versions have '(Only) The Dead Dreams Of The Cold War Kid' on the B-side, while the EP additionally adds 'PXR5' (credited to 'Hawkwind') from the 1978 Rockfield sessions. It's a different, shorter version of '25 Years', with a cleaner sound that emphasises the vocal and relentless *motorik* drumming, while the "*25 years*" chant dissolves into a more user-friendly guitar solo.[7]

The EP's sleeve, designed by Rocking Russian, brings a new perspective on the totalitarian aspects of the Hawklords project. The front features a rough pencil drawing of an oppressed proletariat, their trudging progress spotlit from Vulcan bombers flying overhead. On the back, the workers have risen up to strike a revolutionary pose, a crashed bomber behind them. The designers put their own spin on the title, with "1979" printed front top-right corner, and "2004" on the reverse.[8]

On 15 June, Charisma releases *PXR5*, described in press ads as the "legendary 'lost' tapes".

◇◇◇◇◇◇◇◇◇◇◇◇◇◇◇◇◇◇◇◇◇◇◇◇◇◇◇◇◇◇◇◇◇◇◇◇◇◇◇◇◇◇◇◇◇◇◇◇◇◇◇◇◇◇◇◇◇◇◇◇◇◇◇

a    'Send For Quatermass!' – John Gill, *Sounds*, 8/12/79

b    Both quotes from Pete Frame's 'Hawkwind Family Tree', 1979

1    Mick Smith drums on 'Valium 10' from the Rockfield Hawklords sessions.

2    Jawa demoed Lloyd-Langton's 'Rocky Paths', subsequently recorded for Hawkwind's 1981 *Sonic Attack*.

3    With Jawa's (temporarily reformed) aid, 'Shot Down In The Night' and 'Turn It On Turn It Off' were re-recorded by Swindells as solo demos, and ultimately appear on his 1980 album *Fresh Blood* (which also features King and Lloyd-Langton).

4    The Hawklords version of 'Who's Gonna Win The War?' initially appeared on the first *Weird Tapes* cassette (1980). Its first vinyl release was on *Hawkwind, Friends And Relations* (1982), with an edited version released as a single the same year. Both were on the Flicknife label, an archival and contemporary source of Hawkwind music during the 80s. 'Valium 10' first appeared on the second *Weird Tapes* cassette (also 1980). Its first vinyl release was as a Flicknife single in 1981, paired with an alternate take of 'Motorhead' from 1975. It too appeared on *Hawkwind, Friends And Relations*. Its spoken word introduction ("*Now, I don't want you to panic*") was sampled by electronica pioneers Autechre on 'Cavity Job'.

5    'Time Of' first appeared on the second *Weird Tapes* cassette (1980). Its first vinyl release was as the B-side to the Hawklords/Flicknife 'Who's Gonna Win The War?' single in 1982. 'British Tribal Music' first appeared on the *Anthology* collection (1985). 'Douglas In The Jungle' first appeared on the second *Weird Tapes* cassette (1980). Doug Smith, its inspiration, was not impressed when he heard it.

6    An instrument of Dettmar's own invention, the 'electric axe' is essentially an amplified wire strung between the head and handle of a wood axe.

7    Clearly fonder of this incarnation of the band, John Peel also spins '25 Years' on his 24 May show.

8    Rocking Russian's Alex McDowell was strongly influenced by Barney Bubbles' work, particularly his interest in the Russian Constructivist artists (hence his company's name). In fact, the deliberately unfinished look of the '25 Years' sleeve is the type of thing that Bubbles might have produced during his tenure with Stiff Records. The Vulcan bomber spearheaded Britain's nuclear strike force during the 70s and beyond, and was an iconic symbol of the Cold War.

# *PXR5*

Released 15 June 1979

| | |
|---|---|
| *Label:* | Charisma (UK & Scandinavia only) |
| *Track listing:* | Death Trap (Calvert/Brock) / Jack Of Shadows (Calvert/Shaw/House) / Uncle Sam's On Mars (Calvert/Brock/King/House) / Infinity (Calvert/Brock) / Life Form (Brock) / Robot (Brock/Calvert) / High Rise (Calvert/House) / PXR5 (Brock) |
| *Line-up:* | Dave Brock / Robert Calvert / Simon House / Adrian Shaw / Simon King |
| *Recorded at:* | Rockfield Studios ('DT', 'JOS' & 'PXR5') / Week Park Farm ('I' & 'LF') / De Montfort Hall, Leicester, 29 September 1977 ('R' & 'HR') / Hammersmith Odeon, London, 5 October 1977 ('USOM') |
| *Produced by:* | Calvert/Brock ('DT') / Calvert/House ('JOS') / Hawkwind ('USOM', 'R' & 'HR') / Brock ('I', 'LF' & 'PXR5') |

Here's where the chronology gets twisted. 'Psi Power', the menacing but melodic *Hawklords* opener, is what fans heard next after *Quark*, when it should have been '**Death Trap**', an even greater sonic leap from what came before. Where *Quark* was controlled but lustrous, this is wired and aggressive, King's snares like a hard stab in the kidneys. Brock's riff is fast and robotic, full of stop/start energy and delivered with a punkish sneer. It's repetitive and relentless, but far distant from the hypnotic mantras of yore – instead, it's like having your head rammed up against a car alarm.

If 'Kerb Crawler' was a man/car love affair, this is hysterical auto-phobia, Calvert undergoing an existential crisis trapped inside "*a shell of steel and plastic*".[1] It's a wide-eyed, foam-flecked performance that features some of his most vivid lyrics: "*I feel like a hero heading for extinction!*"[2] Perhaps this is what it felt like to be inside his head during a manic phase, both exhilarating and terrifying, staring life and death in the face as a "*monkey on elastic*" bobs furiously in the rear view mirror.

Brock plays with similar abandon – having overdubbed Shaw's bass line with something more direct, he launches into his solo on a slash-and-burn mission. Dating from 1977, but released too late to be heard as first-wave punk, there's nothing tokenistic about 'Death Trap' – it's a taut, riff-heavy version of the year-zero sound that may well have inspired hardcore punk bands like Discharge. The media that still considered Hawkwind members of the 'old guard' failed to grasp the stylistic changes the band had rapidly progressed through.

'**Jack Of Shadows**' is a lush and airy contrast to the brittle claustrophobia of the opening track, and perhaps a less surprising progression from *Quark*. Borne aloft by a phasing, semi-acoustic riff and nimble bass, it's a sci-fi pop song, and would have made a great single. Calvert's vocal is upbeat, the melodies are strong, there's even a rattle of castanets. The title is from Roger Zelazny again, though Calvert is more interested in the heroics of the magical protagonist rather than the novel's backstory. There's a real vigour to the arrangement too, a classic slice of House synth wizardry condensed into a short middle eight before cutting back to the foot-tapping riff and teasing "*la la la la*"s.

The sky rips apart as '**Uncle Sam's On Mars**' arrives with another change of mood. Originally an evolution of 'Opa-Loka' (plus Calvert's 'Vikings On Mars' poem), the source material is just about discernible – pulsating bass line, metronomic King Beat – but it's very different tonally, now the entrance music to a fantastical carnival arriving into town, House's twinkling keys promising marvellous sights inside the big tent. Alternatively, it's like walking through a contemporary amusement arcade, the *Space Invaders* craze in full swing.

"*Shoals of dead fish float on the lakes / But Uncle Sam's on Mars!*" is another extraordinary opening line from Calvert that immediately establishes the song's theme of a broken, despoiled Earth vs the flag-waving colonialism of a technocratic elite.[3] The idea of the 'greenhouse effect' was already starting to gain traction, but Calvert still sounds disturbingly up to date: "*Layers of smoke in the atmosphere have made the earth too hot to bear.*" He also makes ironic play of the search for life on other planets, concluding that we'll just destroy it as we've done with life on Earth.

It also skewers the consumerism that America has exported around the world (and potentially into space). As Richard Nixon congratulates the astronauts of

Apollo 11,[4] Calvert blurts out "*McDonald's hamburger!*" like a snarky schoolboy unable to contain himself – but at a time when they only had a few outlets in Britain, he correctly identifies McDonald's as a key bridgehead of homogenous globalisation over the coming decades. The world outside the UK was still a mysterious place in the mid-70s, and the signifiers of the American Dream he tosses out – credit cards, highways and intersections, drum majorettes – would have a certain transatlantic exoticism for much of his audience. The attack isn't subtle, but he's accurately calling out the neoliberal economy that the UK will soon have to embrace.

One other musical note: the pagan *motorik* of 'Opa-Loka' found ways to undulate and swing, but 'Uncle Sam's On Mars' has a more single-minded groove, its fast pounding drums and rumbling bass frequencies pointing towards the repetitive beats and synthetic textures of modern electronic dance music. Radical for its time, though possibly a little headache-inducing.

There's something of the splitting migraine too about the piercing but shaky synth lines of '**Infinity**'. Originally intended for a Brock solo album, it takes an old Calvert poem about falling in love with Time herself, and turns it into an electronic ballad. Yet there's something a little uncomfortable about the queasy sonic rub of the fizzing keys against Brock's nasal vocal. Tune out the higher frequencies and there's some nice folky guitar picking and piano – and a familiar descending chord sequence appears at the end. But its unpolished, demo-like quality is a let-down after the high energy zip of the preceding tracks.

'**Life Form**' is another Brock solo piece, a buzzing cyborg vignette that's more sound design than song. An early Tangerine Dream album compacted into a minute and a half might sound like this. Some of its ideas would be developed by industrial and electronica artists, but its most striking feature is a frantic alien chant towards the end, which sounds worryingly like "*Sieg Heil.*"

After side one's more modern take on the Hawkwind aesthetic, side two opens by harking back to the crunching sci-fi rock of the early 70s, albeit with a steelier edge. '**Robot**' fades up on a gnarly, biting riff from Brock before House's *Phantom Of The Opera* keys prepare the way for another outstanding performance from Calvert. There's something of the educated yob about his delivery here, poking fun at suburbia's white collar workers in his yowling monotone like an older, more theatrical Johnny Rotten. It's another song that worries at the schism opening up in British society between traditional industries and the faceless City institutions that will shape its future – but Calvert isn't entirely without sympathy for the Reginald Perrins stuck on the corporate treadmill.

The slow ratcheting up of tension in its instrumental centre is superb, House's violin fed through effects until it becomes almost unrecognisable, a distorted alien glossolalia against Brock's grinding, shape-shifting riff. Against a constant rumble of sub-bass, King hits his drums with evident relish – this is probably the closest that late 70s Hawkwind get to the immersive head trippery of *Space Ritual*. Calvert appears as a robot undergoing a personality crisis, the way he haltingly quotes Asimov's Three Laws of Robotics suggesting that if only the desk jockeys of the world threw off their corporate shackles, bloody emancipation could be theirs – as ever, a key theme for Calvert is breaking free from pre-written scripts and defying fate. By the end, he's calling out the letters of 'r-o-b-o-t' like an incitement to revolution.

After the manic conclusion of 'Robot' comes the twinkling synth arpeggio and plunging bass of '**High Rise**'. House's funereal organ and the track's languid tempo immediately establish a tone of introspection and melancholy, not qualities you'd normally associate with Hawkwind, but increasingly present during the Calvert years – his vocal here is unexpectedly earnest compared to his usual semi-detached, in-character delivery.

The title nods to Ballard, but the words are inspired by Calvert's experiences of living in a Margate tower block. His depiction of boredom-fuelled vandalism amid brutalist architecture could have come from a contemporary Sunday supplement, where high rise estates were routinely condemned as spirit-sapping "slums in the skies." For Calvert, they're the epitome of a dehumanised future, where dignity is sacrificed to the cold bureaucracy of central planning. This isn't *Quark*'s sci-fi satire, but angry social comment – "*It's a human zoo / A suicide machine*" – with savage, if slightly overwrought, imagery – "*The tentacles of human gore / Spread out on the pavement from the 99th floor*".

'High Rise' is full of melodic pathos, and its chorus delivers a genuine emotional punch, harmony backing vocals bristling with Calvert's "*caged up rage*". The huge wall of organ that follows is impressive, as is the slow Floydian dissolve into a downbeat instrumental section – though Brock's solo feels perfunctory, as does the big swell of phased guitar under the final chorus.

The album ends with the fun, if slightly daft, '**PXR5**' itself, and another stab at being self-referential. But whereas 'Days Of The Underground' did it with a certain ironic elan, Brock delivers his tale of ejecting former bandmates into space with a none-too-subtle glee, the song galloping along on the back of a rubbery bassline from Shaw. The breakdown from the chorus into the middle eight is also undeniably exciting, particularly when it shifts into a manic polka and House recycles his furious fiddle reel from 'Hassan I Sahba'.

And yet, this is exactly the type of track that epitomises one of the critics' favourite charges against Hawkwind, that there's something juvenile about the band's sci-fi aesthetic. What was once an awe-inspiring cosmic trip, and latterly a vehicle for satire and social comment, sounds merely banal here. The task of presenting SF-inspired rock music in a way that doesn't invite, at best, condescension, at worst, ridicule, will become ever more challenging as the band enter their second decade.

<hr>

1 Calvert had been involved in a car accident in Devon in 1977, which had seriously injured his female passenger, and was presumably the inspiration for this lyric.

2 This line is perhaps the ultimate expression of Calvert's kamikaze tendency towards glorifying self-annihilation.

3 In terms of theme and metre, it also bears a strong relation to Gil Scott-Heron's 'Whitey On The Moon'.

4 Nixon says, "For one priceless moment in the whole history of Man, all the people on this Earth are truly one."

# I Hope You've Brought Your Credit Card With You

June–December 1979

Bainbridge, Brock, Lloyd-Langton, Blake & King – Masters Of The Universe programme
(source: Steve Readhead collection)

Stitched together from various live and studio sources, Brock describes *PXR5* as a "bodge-up of bits and pieces – a final flushing of the toilet at Charisma".[a] Yet it contains some of their best Calvert-era material and deserves better than its lowly chart placing of 59. The band remains in limbo, with fans unsure whether 'Hawkwind' even exists anymore, which hardly boosts sales – and a cryptic message on the back of the album ('This Is The Last But One') – doesn't help.[1] At the best of times, Charisma never knew how to promote them effectively, and now they're essentially clearing the decks.

Still, it's an amusingly packaged album, illustrated by artist Philip Tonkyn.[2] On the front, band name and title appear on a punch-card through which electrical wires worm, while the back features a wrongly-connected plug with a spoof HM Government warning: "This wiring can seriously damage your health". Various tabloids decry this as dangerous and irresponsible – the most publicity the album gets – and later copies come with a red sticker over the offending image which reads "Warning: This Sticker Must Not Be Removed".[3]

There's a voucher inside for a free copy of a Hawkwind Family Tree poster by former *ZigZag* editor Pete Frame.[4] The poster is reproduced in *Sounds*, where Giovanni Dadomo's review of *PXR5* is positive if unspectacular. Of 'Death Trap', he says, "You could programme it amongst a bunch of hard-nose 'punk' items and it'd sound quite right there," while 'Robot''s "hypnotic, percussive pulse, wailing guitar and synth" is tagged as "pretty much summing up the live Hawkwind experience".[b]

▼　　▼　　▼

*PXR5* must seem like an artefact from a former life to current members, but its release kick-starts them back into action. Reverting to Hawkwind, they set about re-building the band. Doug Smith contacts **Tim Blake**, a former Portobello Road scenester who had moved to France to play synth in Gong. With solo albums *Crystal Machine* (1977) and *Blake's New Jerusalem* (1978) recorded for French label Barclay, his one-man show with lasers had recently closed the 1979 Glastonbury Festival.[5] But performing solo is getting him down and he happily agrees to play with Hawkwind, though remains officially contracted to Barclay.

Rehearsals and songwriting begin again at Rockfield, but it's soon agreed that another lead instrumentalist is needed. King calls Huw Lloyd-Langton, who agrees to return when he finds a much less drug-oriented band than the one he left in 1970. Having forged their sonic identity throughout the 70s without a traditional lead guitar player, the addition of Lloyd-Langton to the line-up will have a major impact on Hawkwind's sound going forward, steering the band in a direction that, after the Calvert years, focuses on instrumental firepower rather than rock theatre.

Just a few days after Lloyd-Langton's return, Hawkwind finally return to the public eye on 9 September, headlining the second day of Futurama in Leeds. Billed as the "World's First Science-Fiction Music Festival", Futurama is a who's who of the current post-punk/electronic scene. John Lydon's Public Image Ltd headline the first day, with other bands including Joy Division, The Fall, Echo & The Bunnymen, The Teardrop Explodes, Orchestral Manoeuvres In The Dark, and Cabaret Voltaire. Hawkwind may be a different generation, but they have plenty of secret fans among these groups – and a science fiction music festival is hardly complete without the genre's foremost proponents.[6]

Also present at Futurama is Nik Turner, who guests with Hawkwind on 'Brainstorm' and performs with his new band Inner City Unit, self-described purveyors of "high energy future shock horror rock".[c] Coinciding with this appearance, ICU release their debut single on their own Riddle Records label, the rock & roll pastiche '**Solitary Ashtray**'.[7]

▾    ▾    ▾

Robert Calvert is also billed to play Futurama, but doesn't appear. Instead, he's been busy with various oddball projects since leaving Hawklords, a couple involving Adrian Wagner. A conversation about a doomed love affair between "leisure androids" leads to '**Connection Disconnection**', a quirky electronic dance track with Calvert doing his best Bryan Ferry-as-uptight-robot impersonation. Wagner has plans to cash in on the cosmic disco craze that's been in full swing since *Star Wars* became a global phenomenon,[8] and the track appears on his pseudonymous album *Disco Dream And The Androids* – Calvert is credited as 'Doréme Fasöla Latèdo 491A series type MAP'.

Another visit to Wagner's home studio leads to the resurrection of the aborted 1974 single 'Crikit Lovely Reggea'. Re-titled '**Cricket Star**' and credited to Robert Calvert And The 1st XI, this tweaked and partially re-recorded version of the original is released in July as a green 7" flexidisc on Wagner's own Wake Up label. Pressed with a picture of Calvert wielding a bat in full cricket whites, it's the epitome of a novelty record, and sounds like one too. Over a passably sunny faux-reggae backing, Calvert sings, "*Kiss me Ma and say goodbye / I'm going to bowl a googly-eye*" in a cod-Jamaican accent.[9]

There's also a *Melody Maker* report[d] of a project entitled *Lord Of The Hornets*, involving Lemmy, Lloyd-Langton, King and Swindells. Two songs will subsequently be released. '**Lord Of The Hornets**' itself is a jerky and deliberately mechanical take on Hawkwind's stun-riff template, with a knowingly 'new wave' vocal. It's a little under-powered, but the chorus is irresistible and it's full of brilliant imagery: "*Queen's a machine on a larva production line.*" '**The Greenfly And The Rose**' is a deceptively pretty ballad about the world, and ultimately the universe, being consumed by "*aphids*", which could be by a pre-ambient Eno. No further insect-themed tracks emerge, but Calvert is evidently still active in the margins, buzzing with ideas and mischief.[10]

▾    ▾    ▾

Towards the end of the year, Brock hints at a signing with Automatic, a new subsidiary of Warner Bros set up by Nick Mobbs, ex-boss of EMI's progressive label Harvest.[11] But before that, the band decide to self-finance their tenth anniversary UK winter tour. It's a risky proposition, yet all but four of the shows sell out, a testament to the commitment of their fanbase.

*Sounds* describes the Liverpool Empire gig with some incredulity, as an audience of "early/mid teenies… garbed in regulation counter-culture togs… go absolutely wild," fans shinning up drainpipes to reach the band's dressing room and obtain autographs. Brock is in a trenchant mood: "Everybody has missed the point of this band. We are the only revolutionary band in the country, because we have complete change all the time. We build up to a point and then it's got to be pulled down and started again… [The fans] come because they know we do something different every time we do a tour".[e]

Old numbers such as 'Brainstorm' and 'Master Of The Universe' are taken at ferocious speed, with Lloyd-Langton's metal cosmique lead dominating a high energy set. Shows open with a spirited version of 'Shot Down In The Night', and other new tracks are aired, including 'Who's Gonna Win The War?', 'Motorway City', 'World Of Tiers', and 'Levitation'. As stipulated by Barclay, there's also a solo spot from Tim Blake, performing 'New Jerusalem' and 'Lighthouse' accompanied by lasers.[12] The St Albans City Hall gig on 8 December is recorded for possible future release.

Almost down and out at the start of the year, Hawkwind end the 1970s in a triumph of resilience, if nothing else. They play their final gig of the decade at Camden's Electric Ballroom on 29 December, with Lemmy putting in a guest appearance.[13] Brock concludes: "I haven't enjoyed myself so much for at least three years".[f]

a    'Warriors Into Extra Time' – Dave Brown, *Sounds*, 7/11/80

b    Giovanni Dadomo, *Sounds*, 6/79

c    'Warriors Into Extra Time' as above

d    The 'Wind Of Change' – Steve Gett, *Melody Maker*, 5/1/80

e    'Send For Quatermass!' – John Gill, *Sounds*, 8/12/79

f    The 'Wind Of Change' as above

1     Intending to reference the fact that *PXR5* was recorded before *Hawklords*, it reads instead like a suicide note to the future.

2     Tonkyn was an old friend of Harvey Bainbridge, and produced book cover illustrations in the 80s for SF writers including Brian Aldiss, Robert Heinlein and Frederick Pohl.

3     In the rush to be offended, the papers overlook that this particular combination of wires never appeared in any real-world plug, since it mixes a pre-1977 red live wire with post-1977 blue neutral and green/yellow earth wires.

4     While the press ad for the album clearly states "First 5,000 albums contain leaflet for Hawkwind 'family tree' poster", some fans are certain their album came with the poster already included. Perhaps posters were inserted around the same time the back cover was stickered.

5     According to Hawkwind legend, it's actually Tim Blake who informs Group X they can perform at the All Saints Hall in August 1969 (he was Simon House's roadie at the time). His Glastonbury set included a version of 'Spirit Of The Age'.

6     The Leeds Queen's Hall is a suitably Ballardian concrete venue, but the science fiction aspect of Futurama amounts to some stalls and a few people dressed as robots, while the echoey acoustics reduce much of the music to a dull boom. The *NME*'s review is entitled "Set The Controls For The Squalor Of Leeds". Hawkwind's Futurama performance was filmed, but the footage remains uncut in Doug Smith's garage.

7     Originally titled 'Solitary Astrid' after Baader-Meinhof member Astrid Proll, who was standing trial in West Germany for bank robbery and falsifying documents. Money from sales of the single was donated to her defence fund, but its title was changed to avoid controversy.

8     'I Lost My Heart To A Starship Trooper' by Sarah Brightman & Hot Gossip may be the best known song from the sci-fi disco boom, but there were many, many more. Titles included 'Future World' by Ganymed; 'Automatic Lover' by Dee D Jackson; 'Galactic Reaction' by Milkways; 'Spaceship Crashing' by Bamboo; and 'Space Fever' by Cosmic Gal. More established disco acts such as Labelle and Boney M also joined in the fun – coincidentally, the latter's *Night Flight To Venus* included a track entitled 'Steppenwolf'.

9     The plan was to sell 'Cricket Star' outside Lord's to capitalise on another tour by the West Indies team – but once again, the tour was cancelled and Wagner had to dump 8,000 unsold copies on his local rubbish tip. 10cc's white fright toe tapper 'Dreadlock Holiday', which also conflated cricket and reggae in the same song, had got to number one the previous year.

10     These tracks were released as a single on Flicknife in April 1981. Lemmy only plays on 'Lord Of The Hornets' – bass on 'The Greenfly' is played by Calvert's then literary agent Gary Cooper. Both songs were re-recorded for 1981's *Hype*, the album which accompanies Calvert's novel of the same name – 'Lord Of The Hornets' in particular benefits from a crunchier, more direct sound.

11    This is perhaps why Automatic's Doll By Doll supported Hawkwind on their 1979 winter tour.

12    The lasers were a source of dispute. Brock was annoyed that they were used only during Blake's solo performances, while some local councils expressed health and safety concerns – at one show, an over-zealous official was locked in a cupboard to enable the band to play.

13    By 1979, Lemmy could afford to be magnanimous. With *Overkill* and *Bomber* reaching 24 and 12 in the charts respectively, and UA having just released the previously rejected *On Parole* (like their debut, featuring high-octane interpretations of 'The Watcher', 'Lost Johnny' and '**Motorhead**'), Motörhead were on the brink of a major breakthrough. Lemmy's time in Hawkwind had left its mark, though – for example, in the relentless conclusion of 'Bomber', with its droning, two-chord riff.

# Countdown To Year Zero

## Never Mind The Bollocks, Here's Hawkwind

### Hawkwind: punk masculinity

"THE essential balm is 30p and the mini incense is 25p," said the girl selling things in the foyer of Hammersmith Odeon on Sunday night. And so think — all I wanted was a bar of chocolate.

Still, I should have known better and worn a headband. This was a Hawkwind affair.

You could tell it as soon as you entered the theatre, with hordes of grey-dressed, unsmiling fun-seekers out for a Sunday night turn-on, replete with grubby Afghan jackets and carefully dirtied-down sneakers. No one looked especially happy, and since they were going to have to wait two solid hours for their dose of sci-fi, who could blame them? It was a weird kind of compulsion that packed the hall with thousands of devotees to whom attendance at a Hawkwind gig seemed as mandatory as a vicar going to church at Christmas.

First on stage, though, came Alberto Y Lost Trios Paranoias, a sort of underground Bonzo Dog Doo Dah Band for those with memories. Always suspect artists who appear to rely on name-dropping and spoofing for audience rapport — this band shouts out "Hendrix!" and scores heavily, and does a Captain Beefheart imitation which doesn't stand up. Their satirical act is fumbling and messy, but they pass as a bit of immature fun. They'll forever be an OK support band.

On with the show: here's Andy Dunkley, one of the underground's rent-a-low-key-voices, acting as your compere in his space-suit, and playing suitable tracks from the Virgin and you'd expect Hawkwind next. But no, enter an acoustic guitarist from the USA, Al Matthews. His set was boring, he seemed to be getting desperate with an audience that was

**HAWKWIND:** secret society

understandably fidgetty, and he was invited to leave the stage near me in the balcony. "Gerroffff!" "Get back to New York!" "Drop dead!"

When Hawkwind eventually reached the stage, unanmany times by the vocal ones nounced, just after 9.30, the otherwise sane guy in the seat near me leapt in the air several times and gave the V-sign. His girl friend remained impassively in her seat, expressionless, perhaps numbed by the long wait but absolutely disinterested in what was on stage or what her man was getting-off on. In that moment, it became totally clear that Hawkwind was a masculine preserve.

The light show behind Hawkwind's very loud sound was relevant and attractive and complemented the music very well. It consisted of all the imagery necessary to visually project the story of Machines coming from Outer Space to gobble us all up, and the lights relied entirely on the old policy of hypnosis to render the viewer thoughtless and mentally accessible. Dave Brock's lead vocals were excellent, and Stacia's dancing was-er-evocative.

The dialogue which preceded each song was loud enough, but the clarity wasn't good, so much of the story was lost unless you had heard it before. Yet there's no denying Hawkwind's carefully honed act, and the allegiance of their audience positively puts them on a very special plane. Their music sounds like good, solid punk rock to me, but their hit numbers — "Sonic Attack," "D Rider," "Master Of The Universe" and of course "Silver Machine" — have a fire and discipline, and it must be recorded that Hawkwind is one of the biggest concert attractions in the land right now.

Hawkwind exist on a level different from that of any other rock band. What's great for the scene about the Hawkwind happening is that they are creating an intensely private event and that they are members of a secret society. It was like that once, remember, with the Who at the Marquee. Anyway, for me, last Sunday will be remembered as the night when I was the only one in the audience at Hammersmith wearing a tie. If we all got to be taken over by men from space, I don't see why I shouldn't go down fighting. — RAY COLEMAN.

'Punk Masculinity', *NME*, 15 February 1975

By the mid-70s, both media and fans were becoming disillusioned with the pyrotechnic spectacle that rock & roll had become. As venues got bigger, performances became more bombastic and overblown. The 60s' surviving big hitters (The Stones, The Who, Pink Floyd etc) still attracted large audiences, as did their prog successors (Yes, ELP, Genesis etc) – but younger music fans felt increasingly alienated by this vision of rock as either consumer entertainment or pseudo-classical puffery. At best, it was a bore, at worst, it was cynical and elitist.

Resistance began in the back rooms of pubs, with bands like Dr. Feelgood, The Count Bishops and The Gorillas delivering songs that were shorter, rawer and less mannered than the arena rock gods of the day. But regime change arrived with a youthful gaggle of harder-edged bands fuelled by speed and anarchy: the Sex Pistols, The Clash and The Damned. Loud, crude and wilfully obnoxious, punk had come to serve notice on the dinosaurs that still lumbered across the stage of Earl's Court.

It was time for a music that voiced the anger and disconnection from mainstream society that many young people felt. It was year zero.

## Incubating Punk

Punk wasn't a new word – US writers had long used it to describe music that was street-level, scuzzy and unsophisticated. Hawkwind had already been paid this back-handed compliment a few times by the British press, the assumption being that their audience were all greatcoat-wearing Neanderthals who didn't get that the 60s were over.[1] Yet Hawkwind gigs were predominantly attended by teenagers and students, and acted as an incubator for many of the punk generation's key figures.

One such presence was occasional acid dealer and future Pistols frontman John Lydon, who hung out backstage during the *Quark* tour at the height of his notoriety as Johnny Rotten. Lydon has described his stage persona as part-Richard III, part-pantomime dame – but isn't there a little Calvert in there too, in the posturing and the ranting monotone? And isn't the brutal, leering "*No future!*" at the end of 'God Save The Queen' the logical conclusion of Hawkwind's own cosmic nihilism?[2]

Mick Jones of The Clash saw Hawkwind several times at the Roundhouse's Sunday night Implosion shows (though his main memory is of ogling at Stacia). And of course, Hawkwind provided an ever-present soundtrack to the mid-70s squatting scene in Ladbroke Grove – aka the Free Republic of Frestonia – which birthed The Clash as well as Joe Strummer's earlier group The 101ers. When The Clash first tried covering Junior Murvin's 'Police & Thieves', Strummer suggested they do it in the style of Hawkwind.

Brian James and Ray Burns aka Captain Sensible of The Damned were also both fans, with the relentless velocity of their early singles 'New Rose' or 'Neat Neat Neat' perhaps owing something to 'Brainstorm'.[3] Other Hawkwind heads among punk's prime movers include Pete Shelley, Jean-Jacques Burnel, Tony James, T.V. Smith and Gaye Advert.

## A Sense Of Communion

None of this should come as a surprise. If you didn't want reheated blues rock or endless keyboard solos, your options were limited in the early 70s. But if noise and simplicity were your thing, with a dash of electronics and Krautrock thrown in, then Hawkwind were literally the only show in town – particularly outside of London. They took the underground on the road, and for many gig-goers,

Hawkwind shows became a regular way of life. There were many fans – and not just hippies – who recognised the value of a grassroots, music-based community that turned the audience into participants rather than spectators.

As Barney Bubbles biographer Paul Gorman, a Hawkwind fan in this pre-punk period, recalls: "What's not really appreciated now is that, at the time, Hawkwind were very, very popular. They'd had a massive single in 1972, and played Wembley Empire Pool in 1973 – they weren't fucking about. They were a big band and were part of the mainstream in terms of media coverage, sales and profile. So it wasn't just a hip cult thing to do. Mick Jones, John Lydon, Jah Wobble, they all saw Hawkwind, and one of the reasons they remember them was because there was a sense of communion."

John Wardle – aka Jah Wobble, bassist and founder member of Public Image Ltd (PiL) – was "absolutely besotted with Hawkwind – *In Search Of Space* really grabbed me… It had a darkness to it as well. In 1974, I went to Kingsway College of Further Education, and met John Lydon there, and the one thing we had in common was a love of Hawkwind. And so we went to see them together at the East Ham Odeon – it was a terrific, evocative show."

Stephen Morris, drummer with Joy Division and subsequently New Order, was similarly affected: "It was actually my first gig, Manchester Free Trade Hall, March 1972. What an introduction that was… I just loved the racket that they made! All the synthesisers, the fact it was just a wall of bloody noise… Hawkwind was my first gig, and David Bowie was my second, and within months they were both on *Top Of The Pops*, which was brilliant".[4]

An early live encounter with Hawkwind was also sometimes a first experience of the underground ethos, as Colin Newman of Wire recalls: "I remember going to see them at Aldermaston, the free festival that was in the grounds of the nuclear plant. I remember being in a field, we were quite young, probably no older than 16." Gorman recalls a less pastoral setting, at the 1974 free festival in Harlow New Town: "There's Michael Moorcock intoning this *Doctor Who*-style camp sci-fi, Stacia naked, Liquid Len's amazing lights, Nik Turner in his frog suit… and the Windsor [Hells Angels] chapter chucking bottles of piss at the stage. When you're 14 and in that kind of atmosphere, you're wondering what the fuck is going on!"

This multimedia dimension helped them stand out, not least as the ideal soundtrack for chemical experimentation: "The concerts I went to in the mid-70s were just amazing," says Cabaret Voltaire's Richard H. Kirk. "One of them was on the Atomhenge tour, and it was truly psychedelic. I just remember the stage looked like it was melting at one point because of the way they'd done the films – I was thinking, whatever I've taken, it's stronger than I thought!" Adds Stephen Morris: "The stage presentation was amazing. If you see it now, it's probably a bit twee and cardboard-y, a bit like an early episode of *Doctor Who*, but then it was absolutely staggering. All the images zooming backwards and forwards, it was mind-blowing!"

Yet Hawkwind on vinyl could be just as intense, as punk's definitive historian Jon Savage remembers: "I turned 18 in 1971 and started smoking dope – at the end of that year, the three records I listened to were *Teenage Head* by the Flamin' Groovies, *Surf's Up* by The Beach Boys, and *In Search Of Space*. That's a big record for me, and I particularly liked 'We Took The Wrong Step Years Ago'. It's got a very deep, far back sound, with the synth just coming in, it's quite restrained. Everybody thinks of Hawkwind as a bish-bash-bosh group, but it's not the case on that. It's a really terrific song, and still relevant."

Daniel Miller, electro punk pioneer as The Normal and founder of Mute Records, was similarly enthused by *In Search Of Space*: "I'm a huge fan of that record, it was important and quite influential for me at the time. I think it caught a lot of people at a certain age. I'd say to people, you've got to hear this record, and they totally got it when they heard it."

Hawkwind stood out as being markedly different from the rest of the British music scene, an existential protest band flying in the face of convention. Kirk again: "They were fascinating, and proof that the 60s counterculture was still alive and kicking in the 70s. They seemed very druggy and anti-establishment." Miller: "The term punk wasn't around in 1972, but it felt like they were very different from other British bands of the time. It felt quite rebellious and trying to do something different. They were anti-music establishment." Gorman: "What Hawkwind were doing was stoutly 'fuck you', whereas other bands were crowd pleasers." And he adds: "[Malcolm] McLaren said that punk wasn't about safety pins through the nose or two chord ramalama – it was about anti-authority, non-conformity, anti-corporate, and DIY. Those four corners of the frame that contained punk, Hawkwind absolutely anticipated."

Hawkwind offered a noisy alternative to a well-mannered consensus. "It wasn't polite," says Wobble. "There was a feeling of trying to break out and really say something. I think Hawkwind were the first band I heard that didn't make polite little songs, that were actually avant-garde. It was underground and there was something a bit spiky about it. It was genuine and had that outsider

A headlining attraction: 1970-72

'Silver Machine' - Japanese picture sleeve    'Kings Of Speed' - Japanese picture sleeve

'Urban Guerilla' - Japanese picture sleeve

'Urban Guerilla' - German picture sleeve    'Back On The Streets' - UK picture sleeve

(source: Johan Edlundh collection)

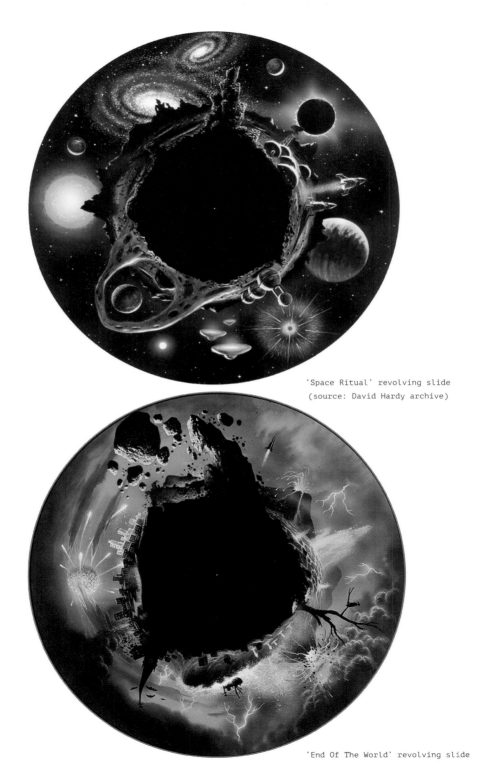

'Space Ritual' revolving slide
(source: David Hardy archive)

'End Of The World' revolving slide

*Hawkwind* promo poster by Alan Tanner

*Let It Rock*, December 1972

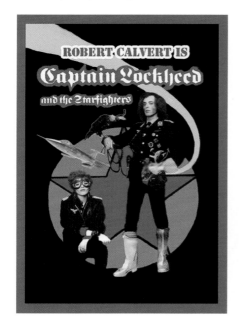

*Captain Lockheed* promo poster – Calvert with
Yugoslavian friend Yamilla
(source: Brian Tawn collection)

*Disc* – 2 September 1972

Light crew t-shirt design (source: Wolfie Smith collection)

Embroidered jacket made for Doug Smith by Tim DeWitt, whose other customers included Jimi Hendrix, Miles Davis, Janis Joplin and Neil Young (source: Doug Smith archive)

Ticket - Guildford Civic Hall, 2 July 1972
(source: Doug Smith archive)

Space Ritual ticket - Edmonton Sundown,
29 December 1972
(source: Stephen Dunthorne collection)

Stage pass - Kiel Auditorium, St. Louis,
16 March 1974
(source: Doug Smith archive)

Ticket - Malvern Winter Gardens, 9 March 1976

WITH A FAST
BREEDING MUTATER
WE'RE FACING THE FUTURE
IT'S A SURGERY FOR DREAMS

YOU'LL BE ALONE IN YOUR SYNTHETIC GLOOM
COSMETIC DREAMS IN YOUR CONCRETE ROOM

YOU'RE JUST A MANIC MUTATION
YOU SHOULD'VE MOVED SOONER
A RADIOACTIVE CREATION, NO EARTHLY RUMOUR

Illustrated poem by Harvey Bainbridge from Masters Of The Universe tour programme, 1979
(source: Steve Readhead collection, courtesy of Harvey Bainbridge)

*In Search Of Space* acetate – note the
different running order
(source: Brian Tawn collection)

Unused cover for *Church Of Hawkwind* album by Philip Tonkyn
(source: Philip Tonkyn archive)

art thing." And they weren't prog rock: "Even when they did very long songs," says Gorman, "it wasn't like *Tales From Topographic Oceans*. Instead, they had this very appealing insistent rhythm, whereas the prog guys thought, 'If it's a long song, we've got to have time changes,' which is really annoying when you're trying to get into a song!"

## Against Virtuosity

Some nascent punks spotted that Hawkwind's music and attitude aligned with the avant-rock bands coming out of Germany. Kirk: "They were probably the nearest we got to Krautrock in England, in terms of musical style, because they were very trance-y and they used a lot of electronics, which is one of the other things that got me interested in them." Miller: "I loved the hypnotic, repetitive music they played, and the experimental element as well, with the synths, the treated saxophone, and weird effects on the vocals. There's a lot of connections between Krautrock and punk in a way, and I think the same with Hawkwind as well."

Their presentation as 'barbarians with electronics' appealed to fans frustrated by the stultifying emphasis on virtuosity, as Miller affirms: "I was especially taken by all the electronic stuff because people who played synths at that time were people like Rick Wakeman and Keith Emerson. I loved the idea of electronic music, but I didn't think that was a very good use of it. [Hawkwind] were just making noise, and I thought that was much more inspiring." Morris: "I had the idea that a synthesiser was like an organ, where you'd make Chicory Tip noises. But then you'd see DikMik or Del Dettmar hunched over something which looked like a cash register at a supermarket, making all these *wheeeeoooo* noises – ah, that's a synthesiser! They were using electronics for atmosphere." Kirk: "It wasn't poncey, serious electronic composition, it was just part of what they did."

The electronics gave Hawkwind's music a harsh sci-fi edge – and this too was attractive to this section of their audience. Savage emphasises this connection: "I always thought of punk as science fiction, in the early days anyway, before it got this really tedious social realist gloss. I didn't approve of that, I didn't think it was just about tower blocks, and if it was, it was about the [J.G.] Ballard version of tower blocks, not the 'I'm-so-miserable' version."

Ballard's take on the psychotic nature of consumer society would be key to post-punk. Miller was a big fan, The Normal's 'Warm Leatherette' being directly inspired by *Crash*, and Wobble is particularly effusive: "J.G. Ballard was the man, I've read everything he's done. What amazed me was you had this guy who was really straight, but while everybody else was trying to grow their hair and be far out, he was genuinely fucking weird."

Morris: "I was a bit nerdy, read a lot of science fiction, and was into Michael Moorcock. That connection definitely helped – it's what you'd call a USP, the fact there was a *bona fide* science fiction author attached to the band." Playing truant, Morris hung out in Manchester's House On The Borderland, "a grubby little place between two pet shops" co-managed by none other than Michael Butterworth, which specialised in SF, leftfield literature and under-the-counter pornography.[5] Ian Curtis was also a regular visitor, buying Ballard, Burroughs and back copies of *New Worlds*.

A problem for many budding musicians in the mid-70s was the exclusivity of the music scene, where only the highly proficient could succeed. Hawkwind showed that this didn't have to be the case, that you could create a compelling sound and reach an audience without musical training or virtuosity. Morris says, "More than anything, Hawkwind had that, 'Sod it, we'll do the show right here' thing. 'Fuck everybody, we don't need a record, we're just doing it for ourselves,' which was a large part of punk for me. Simon King just went *blamma blamma blamma blamma*, and I thought, 'That was alright, I could probably do that'."

Miller agrees: "It felt like I could be a member of Hawkwind, just as I felt I could be a member of certain punk bands, because it was more about the ideas and the energy rather than the actual musicianship."[6] As does Newman: "Yes, that was actually key to Wire as well, it's about ensemble playing. It's not about the brilliance of the individual parts, it's about the way the parts all fit together. Someone just playing one note – if it's the right note in the right place, it's way better than 27."

## Hating The Mainstream

Crucially, Hawkwind tapped into the same vein of dissatisfaction with the music establishment as punk would do. As Savage recalls: "Me and my friends wanted to be little hippies, we were very much into the whole idea of the West Coast, playing for the people, free concerts and festivals. And of course, it was ruined by seeing the Grateful Dead at the Empire Pool. They were completely boring. I wanted proper bloody space rock, I didn't want them doing 'Johnny B. Goode', for fuck's sake!"

Gorman: "I saw Led Zep in 1975 at Earl's Court, and during the literally half-hour drum solo, I went for a walk around the back, and I remember seeing 14-17 year old kids wandering around bored. Then the Stones played in 1976, an absolutely dire series of shows. I couldn't identify the first few songs because the sound was so bad, and again there was just people walking about. Hawkwind never let you down like that, they weren't Mick Jagger poncing around. That's one of the reasons they survived."

Wobble remembers exactly why Lydon wore a Pink Floyd T-shirt with "I hate" scrawled across it:[7] "It was the soundtrack when we were at Kingsway: *Money... dum dum dum dum*". It was on all the jukeboxes everywhere you went.[8] And *Tubular Bells* had been massive before that. They're not bad records, but there was a feeling of restlessness, thinking, 'Oh for fuck's sake, this is so boring, something's got to change.' In 1974, we were already fed up with the mainstream. We were already shaping up to hate mass consumerism and punk was the zeitgeist in a way."

Some claimed to have stopped listening to Hawkwind by the time of punk. "The whole thing with punk was that it was year zero. Everything had to be new," says Savage. "I always found punks slagging off hippies really tedious, because most of these punks had been wannabe hippies who were just slightly too young to get involved." But not Kirk: "It was a guilty pleasure. Because punk came along and you weren't supposed to like hippies. Probably a lot more people were listening to Hawkwind than would let on."

Martin Glover – aka Youth of Killing Joke – clearly sees a connection between the old west London counterculture and the newly insurgent scene: "[By 1978, Killing Joke] were squatting in Ladbroke Grove, and Hawkwind came up quite a bit. They were very much part of Notting Hill mythology. We were sharing a rehearsal room with Motörhead in Frestonia, while The Clash had a room upstairs. We were influenced by Motörhead's volume, we wanted to be as loud as them! There were actually quite a lot of psychedelics around in the late 70s in the punk scene as well. When we started playing big shows at places like the Lyceum, there were always people selling LSD when you went to the toilet, and there was a fair proportion of people tripping at the shows. In a lot of ways, we were an acid band. I mixed our second album on acid."

Consciously or not, punk adopted a philosophy that Hawkwind already followed: "I subliminally knew that with PiL, you could do something that wasn't polite, you could break out into another area," says Wobble: "It's because of what you've heard, you know you don't have to stick to a formula." Morris again: "When you start writing songs, you're after a feeling. It's not about chord progressions, it's like, 'Oh, that's good, that sounds like 'Sister Ray', or that's a bit like 'Silver Machine'!'"

And Hawkwind's sound and approach did sometimes rub off. Kirk: "On *Space Ritual*, they'd have these wonderful moments where they'd be no drums, and you'd just hear electronics and somebody delivering a monologue over the top, and that was very similar to the early Cabaret Voltaire recordings, cut-up dialogue over strange synth backing." He adds: "If you listen to a lot of the guitar stuff, there's that kind of whooshing sound, played through a wah-wah or a filter of some kind, which wouldn't be out of place on a Hawkwind record".[9]

Brock's choppy, rhythmic guitar is echoed on several early punk tracks: 'Submission' by the Sex Pistols; 'News Of The World' by The Jam; 'Mirage' by Siouxsie & The Banshees; 'War Dance' by Killing Joke. But it's perhaps Joy Division that best channel Hawkwind's sci-fi nihilism – with Morris and bassist Peter Hook both being long-standing fans, there's definitely a musical cross-over at times, for instance, on 'Twenty Four Hours', with its hypnotic bassline and insistent King Beat.[10]

## Influencing The US Scene

As the UK's biggest 'cult band', Hawkwind had real presence here, live and in the charts. In the US – despite a series of tours and a few albums scraping into the *Billboard* Top 200 – they were far from a household name. Which makes their impact on a number of the punk and new wave acts that came out of America in the late 70s all the more surprising.

Jello Biafra of the Dead Kennedys is one of their most fervent US fans. Describing himself as a "culturally isolated teenager in the country rock mecca/ hellhole of Boulder, Colorado," he subsisted on second-hand records until a copy of *Space Ritual* turned up at his local store: "It grabbed me immediately, it blew me through the fucking wall... It was something new, it was trippy, but real pile-driving and heavy at the same time. Kind of like the ultimate psychedelic air raid... Prog and some of the jammier Krautrock stuff was head music – Hawkwind is so primal, it's head and body music."

"No 'Holiday In Cambodia' without Hawkwind," he insists, telling how the Dead Kennedys slowed this song down into a "spooky kind of space punk". Robert Calvert's 'Ejection' was also the inspiration for a driving, melodic punk song that would become 'Kill The Poor'. Biafra met Calvert backstage after Hawkwind played San Francisco in March 1978, and asked him about the *Captain Lockheed* album, which came out two years before the Lockheed scandal hit the US press. How did he know about it? "He kept his own files of rogue corporations and that kind of corruption. It was only years later when I started to do spoken-word shows and needed to keep a lot of facts straight about world and domestic affairs that it occurred to me that I should be doing what Calvert was doing and filing this stuff."

Another American band that Biafra believes Hawkwind had a major effect on is the Wipers, a new wave power trio led by guitarist Greg Sage, who themselves would inspire key US alt bands such as Hüsker Dü and Nirvana: "They were very Hawkwind influenced, extremely so, to the point where songs like 'Youth Of America', their signature balls-out space rock song, are constructed in such a way that they can be played from three to twenty minutes, depending on what Greg wants to do with all those guitars and effects."

Jon Savage identifies other US disciples: "If ever there was a group that was influenced by Hawkwind, it's Pere Ubu. Hawkwind are an inner city group, they're 'not getting it together in the country', and it's the same with Pere Ubu. They called themselves urban pioneers, and they deliberately went back into the decaying inner city. I was very friendly with Jim Jones, who was in the Electric Eels and roadied for Pere Ubu on their first British tour in May 1978, and Jim would always talk about Hawkwind and the impact it had on those people in Cleveland".[11] Allen Ravenstine's atonal electronics certainly owe much to DikMik and Del Dettmar, while '30 Seconds Over Tokyo' channels the nihilistic sci-fi energy of *Space Ritual*.

And then, as Savage also notes, "you've got people like Chrome." Formed in San Francisco in 1975, Chrome are the epitome of a band steeped in science fiction, particularly the avant garde works of Burroughs and Ballard. With its heavily effected guitar drones, cut-up arrangements and disembodied found voices, their breakthrough album *Alien Soundtracks* (1977) sounds like nothing so much as an interpretation of Ballard's *The Atrocity Exhibition*. Guitarist Helios Creed would later collaborate on various projects with Nik Turner.[12]

### Rave New World

Hawkwind continued to be influential in the wake of punk and post-punk. The acid house and techno boom of the late 80s/early 90s became the soundtrack for a new chemical generation who'd abandoned traditional venues and were dancing through the night at warehouse parties and illegal outdoor raves. It was the underground reborn, and as Jon Savage notes, there were also parallels within the music: "The thing about Hawkwind's early stuff is that it was spacey and brutal, and quite simple. That's a great combination, and you get that in early house music."

Peter Hook – who would help to pioneer electronic dance music alongside Morris in New Order – shares this opinion: "If you listen to a lot of house music now you hear influences from Hawkwind, you hear a lot of that drive, that percussive synth sound that you find in acid house. It's kind of like pre-acid house".[13] Daniel Miller hears the same thing: "For me, 'You Shouldn't Do That' was the track. Structurally, it's like a dance music track, the way it builds up and breaks down, the drop sections, you can really hear that influence."

Post-Killing Joke, Youth would reinvent himself, moving from Brilliant's funk-pop and Blue Pearl's techno-soul to become an in-demand dance producer and remixer. But Hawkwind remained relevant: "'Silver Machine' was massive for me and [Killing Joke guitarist] Geordie, and later on with [Brilliant and KLF member] Jimmy Cauty – 'Silver Machine' is his favourite record ever.[14] Whenever we were doing stuff with Brilliant, and then early KLF and Orb stuff, there was always this 'Silver Machine' spectre in the room that we referred to, which was great." For Youth, Hawkwind exemplify a pagan psychedelic ethos, "a direct legacy from the Stonehenge free festivals to the rave era, from the free parties in the late 80s to the birth of psychedelic trance in the 90s. It's all the same culture, an underground counterpoint to the mainstream. [Hawkwind] kind of went rave in the 90s, and I thought that was really cool how they managed to move with the times".[15]

### A Hint Of Pique

Hawkwind's own response to punk was ambivalent, and sometimes defensive. "Although it is very energetic," said Calvert in 1977, "and I find it a lot more refreshing to hear than what older bands are doing, [punk] doesn't have as much actual creativity as we had when we were that age and we were a new wave".[a] He goes further in a piece written for *Melody Maker*, referring to punk as a "hyped-up re-hash of Iggy Pop impersonations and pseudo-anarchistic posturing", opining that a genuine new wave in rock music must be "accompanied by new concepts of structure… If you look back at the history of authentic artistic (and social) revolution – Dada, Surrealism, Expressionism, Psychedelicism etc – you'll notice that structure was the first thing to be exploded. And re-defined."[b]

In a face-off with *NME*'s representative punk Julie Burchill, Calvert goads her with his opinion of The Clash as "the most orthodox band I've ever heard… They just play three minute pop songs and throw in a few slogans!"[16] But there's more than a hint of pique when he complains, "A new wave band plays a free gig and it makes the front pages! We play free all the time!" And Calvert is easily wound up by Burchill: "You think we're some kind of tax-exiled dinosaur like Yes – that's what you think, isn't it? Well, we don't have any money!"[c]

Still, punk's two fingers at the musical establishment clearly appealed to Hawkwind, with its spiky directness rubbing off onto tracks like 'Death Trap', '25 Years' and 'Flying Doctor'. And by 1979, even Nik Turner had done his best to throw off the crochet blanket of hippiedom and reinvent himself as the leader of cartoon space punks Inner City Unit.[17] When Hawkwind and ICU played Futurama, the "World's First Science-Fiction Music Festival", they were part of a gathering of the post-punk tribes that included PiL, Joy Division, The Fall, Cabaret Voltaire and Orchestral Manoeuvres In The Dark.[18]

Brock is unequivocal about Hawkwind's influence: "So many of those guys have come up to us and said, 'Oh, we used to come and see you all the time and get really out of it. If we hadn't got into Hawkwind, we'd never have started getting bands together'… And all the singers say they modelled themselves on Calvert. Especially Johnny Rotten".[d]

Michael Moorcock was also fascinated: "I knew early on that punk was just another form of dandyism and I'm a great fan of dandyism".[e] He was friends with Siouxsie Sioux and Glen Matlock, and even fronted a documentary about the early 80s 'positive punk' (aka Goth) movement.[19] He also wrote the short novelisation of *The Great Rock 'N' Roll Swindle*, turning it into another Jerry Cornelius adventure with a guest appearance by Lemmy.

▾    ▾    ▾

Punk didn't change everything – but while the stadium bands continued to sell millions of records, they were made to look out of touch and out of date. Yet despite the best efforts of the press, Hawkwind were almost totally unscathed by punk's culture wars, and in fact remained a secret totem for many.[20]

Richard H. Kirk sums up: "If you talk to a lot of people in the post-punk scene, they'd say the same as me, that they liked Hawkwind and were probably influenced by them." And Stephen Morris goes further: "I think punk rock started because in every small town there was somebody who liked Hawkwind".[f]

<><><><><><><><><><><><><><><><><><><><><><><><><><><><><><><><><><><><><><><><><><><><><><><>

a *Sniffin' Flowers*, issue 2, 1977

b 'Structural Defects: Why The New Wave Lose Out' – Robert Calvert, *Melody Maker*, 2/7/77

c 'Mindless Aggreshun On Hippy Farm' – Julie Burchill, *NME*, 28/10/77

d 'Brock's Fireworks' – Chas De Whalley, *Kerrang!*, 7/1/82

e 'Michael Moorcock on Politics, Punk, Tolkien, and Everything Else' – A *Corporate Mofo Interview* by Ken Mondschein, January 2002

f 'Bakers Dozen: Joy Division & New Order's Stephen Morris On His Top 13 Albums' – Ben Hewitt, *The Quietus*, 7/12/10

1 For instance, in a live review entitled 'Punk Masculinity' (Ray Coleman, *Melody Maker*, 15/2/75).

2 Lydon attended Calvert and Pamela Townley's wedding reception. But before this Calvert had taken him "to a party at a solicitor's house. A really lush place, with all the country set swanning around… He got off with a debutante who looked like a horse" ('Mindless Aggreshun On Hippy Farm' – Julie Burchill, *NME*, 28/10/77).

In CD magazine *Volume 3* (1992), Lydon told interviewer Mr Spencer that he was "always much more into Hawkwind than reggae." When the Pistols re-reformed in 2002, they opened their Crystal Palace set with a rendition of 'Silver Machine', and continued to play it on tour.

Lydon's friend Simon Ritchie (aka Sid Vicious) also had a soft spot for Hawkwind, and in fact lived in Lemmy's flat for a couple of months. When he told Lemmy he'd got the Sex Pistols job, the bassist laughed: "Great, as part of the road crew? You can't even play the bass, you're hopeless" (from 'An Epic Interview With Lemmy' – John Robb, *Louder Than War*, 31/10/11).

3 There are various Hawkwind/Damned connections. Lemmy was an early friend of the band, depping on bass after Brian James left (and Captain Sensible had switched to guitar). James then formed Tanz Der Youth with Alan Powell. Chris Millar (aka Rat Scabies) played drums in Calvert's very short-lived band promoting *Hype*.

4    In Tim Burgess's *Tim Book Two: Vinyl Adventures from Istanbul to San Francisco*, Morris recalls that his parents, who had accompanied him to the show, weren't so pleased: "There was a topless dancer and a whiff of marijuana… They were dressed like they were going to a meeting at the Masonic Hall. We definitely didn't fit in, but it meant I got to watch Hawkwind."

5    Butterworth is Mancunian by birth – perhaps why the climactic scene in *The Time Of The Hawklords* happens in Manchester. When he quit Ladbroke Grove, he returned to his home city to found Savoy Books with David Britton, and to help run his shop, House On The Borderland.

6    Miller didn't get to join Hawkwind, but he did secure the services of one of its members. After releasing The Normal single and setting up Mute Records, his next project was the Silicon Teens, an imaginary group of teenagers playing kitsch electronic cover versions of rock & roll standards. For his version of Chuck Berry's 'Memphis Tennessee', he made a video set on the Titanic. The ship's captain is none other than Robert Calvert, a friend of the director.

7    Lydon has since recanted: "You'd have to be daft as a brush to say you didn't like Pink Floyd" ('John Lydon Wants To Re-Record *Dark Side Of The Moon*' – John Doran, *The Quietus*, 17/2/10).

8    'Money' was never released as a single in the UK – though jukebox suppliers may have acquired import copies from Europe – but it would have been regularly played in clubs.

9    Hawkwind's influence on the industrial/electronic music scene is more controversial. Throbbing Gristle's Genesis Breyer P-Orridge was certainly a fan: they performed 'Silver Machine' on-stage with Nik Turner, and played 'Hurry On Sundown' with Psychic TV. But TG's Chris Carter has categorically denied Daniel Miller's claim that he or TG were influenced by Hawkwind's first two albums. Still, there was some overlap: Carter was a member of a travelling multimedia show in the early 70s, and Hawkwind "played a few sets to our light show" while "Liquid Len once pointed out we had a power cable drum that wasn't unreeled and under the strain of the lights was beginning to go nuclear and melt apart." TG predecessor COUM Transmissions also supported Hawkwind at the Bust Benefit Concert in St George's Hall, Bradford in 1971. Cosey Fanni Tutti: "I was dressed as a schoolgirl with a starting pistol, batting 'COUM penee' ping pong balls at the audience. We also brought bags of polystyrene granules which we threw about and got inside Hawkwind's pedals. It was a mad gig and Hawkwind were really cool about the mayhem we brought. They just thought we were out of our heads on something, and then confused when they heard we weren't" (interviews with the author).

10    Crispy Ambulance, one of Joy Division's contemporaries, first formed to play Hawkwind and Magazine covers (the latter's Howard Devoto was another punk-era singer who owed something to Robert Calvert's phrasing and delivery).

11    The Pere Ubu live album *Apocalypse Now* features a brief snatch of 'Master Of The Universe'. And Cleveland's Mirrors played Calvert's 'Ejection' in their live set. Conversely, Hawkwind were sometimes accused of ripping off art-punk pranksters Devo from nearby Akron. Mike

Davies was so incensed when this accusation was levelled in *Melody Maker* (the paper he worked for) that he wrote an entire article in response, insisting that the band had "been involved with industrialisation and technology for far longer than Devo have been wearing surgical masks". Davies notes that Hawkwind had played Akron back in 1973-74, and wonders did the influence flow in the other direction? ('The Hawklords Riddle' – Mike Davies, *Melody Maker*, 13/11/78).

12    Another North American band deserving mention here is Ontario's Simply Saucer, who pre-date punk, but made a hell of a racket anyway. *Cyborgs Revisited*, their one album, fuses the avant-garage of The Velvet Underground and The Stooges with the raw space rock of Hawkwind and Barrett-era Floyd. Recorded in 1974-75, it wasn't released until 1989.

13    From 'Peter Hook's Field Recordings – Favourite Live Tracks' – *Q*, 23/4/13. Hawkwind co-headlined Glastonbury with New Order in 1981, though Brock was less complimentary: "They were so boring. I do that sort of thing at home. And they were out of tune!" ('Brock's Fireworks' – Chas De Whalley, *Kerrang!*, 7/1/82).

14    Working under the name Infected By The Scourge Of The Earth, Jimmy Cauty remixed 'Silver Machine' for the 1999 Hawkwind anthology *Epocheclipse*.

15    In 1999, Colin Newman was commissioned by Liquid Records to remix 'Master Of The Universe' for an album that was ultimately released semi-officially as *The Hawkwind Remix Project*. Newman sped the track up and overdubbed a new vocal from comedy actor and writer Graham Duff. He describes airing his version during a Wire tour the following year: "One of the shows was at the Metro in Chicago. Downstairs was a bar where they asked me to DJ. I put this remix on and people started going completely bonkers, jumping around on the dance floor doing heavy metal poses. Now I could see why people liked it!"

16    Nick Kent echoes this sentiment: "[Hawkwind] were ready to show up for virtually any alternative community cause you could throw at them. In this respect, they were more authentic ambassadors of Ladbroke Grove's bohemian demographic than The Clash, who in the late 70s used the Westway as nothing more than a handy photo-op backdrop for their own further self-glorification" (p57, *Apathy For The Devil*, Nick Kent).

17    Turner further burnished his punk credentials by touring with Sham 69 and playing on Sham's *The Game* and Jimmy Pursey's solo album *Imagination Camouflage* (both 1980). For a full account of ICU's shows with Sham 69, a tour memoir by bassist G.P. Wayne, *Too Late To Be A Viking*, is available online: https://gpwayne.files.wordpress.com/2016/11/viking1.pdf

18    OMD's Andy McCluskey: "I saw Hawkwind twice in the 70s. They were great" (from OMD's online forum, 27/3/06).

19    'Positive Punk', *South Of Watford* (1983) for ITV/LWT. Moorcock: "When Linda [Steele, his wife] and I went to the gigs of punk friends in the eighties, people with Mohicans and black

finger nails would ask us if we wanted a chair or if they could get us a cup of tea" ('Michael Moorcock on Politics, Punk, Tolkien, and Everything Else' – A *Corporate Mofo Interview* by Ken Mondschein, January 2002).

20 Hawkfan Steve Readhead recalls, "Punks picked up on Hawkwind early, and I know a few of my punk mates actually liked Hawkwind before punk. Everyone got on, which didn't happen very much at the time because there was very little, if any, cross-pollination. So I believe Hawkwind and punk had an immediate affinity not achieved by other bands for several years."

## QUEENS HALL, LEEDS, SAT. 8th., SUN 9th SEPT
### SWINEGATE — 663252

**The World's First Science Fiction Music Festival 1979**

FUTURAMA

**SAT. 8th SEPT** (Commencing Noon)
Punishment of Luxury
FISCHERZ
JOY DIVISION
ORCHESTRAL MANOEUVRES IN THE DARK
CABARET VOLTAIRE
A CERTAIN RATIO
SPIZZ ENERGI
THE EDGE
THE EXPELAIRES
THE TUNES
STRANGER THAN FICTION
THE VOID
VINCENT UNITS
PARAAD
Special guests
TONY WILSON
THE SONNY HAYES MAGIC FANTASY
and TYMON DOG

**SUN. 9th SEPT** (Commencing noon)
**HAWKWIND**
The ONLY ONES
THE FALL
MONOCHROME SET
SCRITTI POLITTI
THE TEARDROP EXPLODES
ECHO AND THE BUNNEYMEN
NIGHTMARES IN WAX
MANICURED NOISE
AGONY COLUMN
SCREENS
TEENAGE WEREWOLVES
REVELATIONS
TWIST
E2R

*SPECIAL GUESTS:—*
ROBERT CALVERT
NIK TURNERS INNER CITY UNIT
ROGER RUSKIN SPEAR
& SURPRISE GUEST

SCI FI FILMS 1.00 a.m. till Early Morning. STALLS — SIDESHOWS — STREET THEATRE — PIN TABLES — LASER DISPLAYS ETC.
TICKETS £5 per day from Virgin, Scene and Heard. Jumbo, Molgary — LEEDS. Pearsons — BRADFORD. Impulse-Revolution — SHEFFIELD. Feelgood, Red Rhino — YORK, Virgin, Manchester Probe — LIVERPOOL (or from John Keenan, P.O. Box HH9. Leeds 8, LS8 1AN.

Advert for the 1979 Futurama Science Fiction Music Festival

# BUST BENEFIT CONCERT
### (TO AID BUSTED PEOPLE)

# HAWKWIND

### COUM TRANSMISSIONS
**Wilde Oats Stumble (Ex Medusa)**
**Gentle Revolution And "Things"**
**By Jeff Nuttall**

#### AT

# St. George's Hall
### (BRADFORD)

## FRI. 22nd OCT. 7 30 P.M.

Tickets; 50p, 75p FROM ST. GEORGE'S HALL
PEARSON'S DISC A GOGO, UNIVERSITY SHOP

Nik Turner, from the early days of Inner City Unit (photo: Mark Kennedy)

Hawkwind and COUM Transmissions on the same bill in 1971

# PENETRATION

**.13.** Exclusive interview **20p**
with
## Dave Brock

Hawkwind on the cover of punk-era fanzine *Penetration*
(source: Steve Readhead collection)

Hammersmith Odeon, November 1980. L-R - Baker, Lloyd-Langton, Bainbridge, Brock
(source: Keith Kniveton collection)

# No Cause For A Deviation

January–July 1980

If the previous year had been defined by the band's absence from the music scene and the relative paucity of product, 1980 brings forth a veritable cornucopia of Hawkwind-related releases.

First off the blocks is Nik Turner's Inner City Unit, with their debut album *Pass Out*. Its black and white Barney Bubbles-designed sleeve depicts the band in various poses of wild abandon against Soviet-style iconography.[1] To a great extent, it reflects the contents inside, all scratchy guitar, yelped vocals and an atmosphere of barely-contained hysteria.

Turner was recording his flute inside the Great Pyramid when UK punk first hit the headlines, but he's determined to ride the still-peaking second wave – even if it means that ICU sound more like the cartoonish Spizzenergi or Splodgenessabounds than the Sex Pistols. It's territory Hawkwind have already visited – on 'Death Trap' and 'Flying Doctor' – and a lot of *Pass Out* sounds parodic and throwaway in comparison. Some songs are worthwhile though, including the driving **'Cybernetic Love'** and the bizarre glam stomp of **'Cars Eat With Autoface'**. And **'Watching The Grass Grow'** will be played live by Hawkwind when Turner rejoins in 1982.[2]

*Pass Out* also includes versions of Turner's most famous Hawkwind tracks. **'Brainstorm'** is done as a novelty garage pop song, complete with reggae toasting from Turner, and is best left unheard. But **'Master Of The Universe'** shows he isn't entirely bent on trashing his legacy. Taken faster than even Hawkwind's current live version, the riff pummelling and urgent, it adds a horn-like keyboard motif and builds to a properly freaked-out climax. Turner also changes the focus in the first verse ("*It's all a figment of your mind*"), and delivers an entirely different second verse.

▾    ▾    ▾

In February, UA releases the 'Rock File' version of *Hawkwind*.[3] Its cover features a green and orange version of the *Doremi* shield, perhaps hoping to attract new punters with a sleeve image that doesn't scream 'drug-crazed hippies' quite as hard as the original crocodile leaf men.

Meanwhile, Brock has decided it shouldn't just be former record labels making money from the band's old material, and in March, he puts out the first of the *Weird Tapes*, a series of archival cassettes. It features highlights from the December 77 Sonic Assassins gig, including 'Over The Top' and early versions of 'Free Fall', 'Death Trap' and 'Angels Of Death', plus the Hawklords version of 'Who's Gonna Win The War?' and a set of Brock solo demos from 1979.[4]

Produced in limited qualities with basic card inlays,[5] and only available by mail order, these tapes will nevertheless cause much controversy in the years to come. Former members will complain they never gave permission, while record labels will worry about their impact on official sales. Yet again, Hawkwind – or certainly Brock – refuses to abide by the industry's rules of engagement, even though the days of the underground[6] are well and truly over as far as the media are concerned. Yet the countercultural spirit still survives in various pockets around the world, as evidenced by the release in March of the second Melodic Energy Commission album *Migration Of The Snails*. Del Dettmar and the band are pictured on the front cover inside what looks like a giant conch shell. Dettmar's track '**Escargot**' is a nice piece of quirky, jazzy psych, while Paul Rudolph also appears on the album. In addition, Dettmar releases a whole album (on cassette) of sci-fi cosmotronica in collaboration with MEC bandmate Gerald Toon entitled *Synthesis*, which bears comparison with Hawkwind's spacier, more abstract explorations.

▾          ▾          ▾

Despite last year's successful tour, Hawkwind remain in limbo for the first half of 1980. "We all went home," says Brock later: "Nothing happened – an unprecedented occurrence in the history of the band".[a] He develops a sideline in restoring vintage cars, Bainbridge returns to teaching, and King and Lloyd-Langton reunite with Nic Potter at Sawmills Studios, Cornwall to record Steve Swindells' next solo album.

The band are still without a contract, but luckily, there's something in the can: the recording of the St Albans gig from December. Doug Smith takes the live tape to Bronze Records – the label responsible for Motörhead's meteoric rise – and they agree to put it out with an option on a further album.

▾          ▾          ▾

On 27 June, the first fruits of the Bronze deal emerge with the single version of **'Shot Down in the Night'**.[7] A trebly, punkish attack on establishment paranoia, it sits surprisingly well with the sound of the NWOBHM, as spearheaded by Iron Maiden, Saxon, Girlschool – and Motörhead.[8] Competent promotion combines with a genuine desire for new Hawkwind product, and the single peaks at 59 in the UK charts. Aside from the 1978 re-release of 'Silver Machine', it's their most successful 7" since 'Urban Guerilla'.

By coincidence or design, the B-side is the band's live update of **'Urban Guerilla'**. Resurrected during the 1978 Hawklords tour, it now includes an extended middle section based around a chant of *"You've gotta stay cool"*, with further declarations semi-improvised on the night. Brock works himself up into a Calvert-esque state of excitement, climaxing with, *"A machine gun in my hand / I wanna blow up all the fucker, man!"* Musically a little clunky, it does feature some nice slide guitar from Lloyd-Langton. However, with the IRA still very much active, eulogising terrorism remains a risky promotional strategy, and this recording is left off the upcoming album.

The band play a handful of shows, two of them at London's Lyceum Theatre,[9] and debut more new material, including 'Space Chase' and 'Dust Of Time'. On 21 July, the St Albans recording is released as the imaginatively titled *Live Seventy Nine*.[10]

---

a    'Warriors Into Extra Time' – Dave Brown, *Sounds*, 7/11/80

1    ICU on this album include Trev Thoms on guitar, who will play on Calvert's *Hype* album (1981), and Philip 'Dead Fred' Reeves on keyboards, who will later play with both Hawkwind and Krankschaft, Calvert's live band from 1986.

2    As heard on the album *This Is Hawkwind: Do Not Panic* (1984).

3    Motörhead's *On Parole* is also part of the short-lived 'Rock File' series. *Hawkwind* had previously been re-issued on Sunset in 1975, presumably because Liberty Records no longer existed – the other albums had remained on UA's catalogue.

4    These include 'Nuclear Toy', a version of which will appear as a B-side later in the year (while its chorus will be adapted for 'Nuclear Drive' on 1982's *Church Of Hawkwind*), plus 'Assassination' (aka 'Some People Never Die') and 'Satellite' (aka 'The Phenomenon Of Luminosity'), versions of which will also appear on *Church Of Hawkwind*.

5    The card is light blue, and each tape features a science fictional cover image, some attributed to Les Cox, others of unknown origin.

6    "A drug-based 'alternative society'" as Ian Pye, writing about Hawkwind for *Melody Maker*, feels the need to explain to younger readers, before describing the band as, "pursuing an improvisational form that went out with Timothy Leary, incense and ethnic clothing" ('The Everlasting Trip' – Ian Pye, *Melody Maker*, 15/9/80). In fact, a new DIY underground scene was thriving in the aftermath of punk, as a myriad of independent labels and private releases prove, the *Weird Tapes* being just one example.

7    Steve Swindells' studio version of 'Shot Down In The Night' was released as a single on the same day. Featuring King and Lloyd-Langton, it's almost a Hawkwind version by proxy, but the most noticeable difference is Swindells' Bruce Springsteen-esque vocal – as with the Hawklords demo, he sings the first verse an octave lower than the Hawkwind/Brock version, which makes it less punchy over the vital opening bars. Swindells' album *Fresh Blood*, featuring both this and 'Turn It On, Turn It Off', is released later in the year.

8    The influence flowed both ways. Vardis, one of the early leading lights of the NWOBHM, went on to support Hawkwind on the 1980 *Levitation* tour, and released a cover of 'Silver Machine' as a single the following year.

9    Support at the Lyceum came from a confrontational Inner City Unit, who had just released the '**Paradise Beach**'/'**Amyl Nitrate**' single.

10    The vinyl label refers to it as *Live 1979*, the spine as *Live '79*.

# *Live Seventy Nine*

Released 21 July 1980

*Label:*            Bronze (UK & Europe)

*Track listing:*    Shot Down In The Night (Swindells) / Motorway
                    City (Brock) / Spirit Of The Age (Brock/Calvert)
                    / Brainstorm (Turner) / Lighthouse (Blake) /
                    Master Of The Universe (Brock/Turner) / Silver
                    Machine (Brock/Calvert)

*Line-up:*          Dave Brock / Huw Lloyd-Langton / Tim Blake /
                    Harvey Bainbridge / Simon King

*Recorded at:*      St Albans City Hall, 8 December 1979

*Produced by:*      Hawkwind & Ashley Howe

If *Space Ritual* came from the depths of the cosmic void, *Live Seventy Nine* is much more of this earth – a winter's evening in the commuter belt to be precise, the Hawkwind faithful out in force. There's cheering, a burbling elevator effect, and then a big crash into '**Shot Down In The Night**', Steve Swindells' parting gift to the band. It's a confident, up-and-at-'em opening, Brock's windmilling chords a change from his usual style, even if Blake's tootling keys are a little cheesy. It's a catchy tune, with a forceful, melodic vocal from Brock and a great shout-along chorus. And lyrically, it harks back to the paranoid themes of the band's early days, the nebulous heavy vibes of Ladbroke Grove updated to Cold War anxiety: "*Superpower looks down on you / Someone's watching every move.*"

But this is definitely a new iteration of Hawkwind, which once again seems to be moving with the times – this song in particular captures the high energy hard rock vibe of the NWOBHM. And sonically, this is light years distant from the sound of *Hawklords* – for example, Bainbridge's deep, smooth bass is replaced by a buzzy, metallic rattle. Even making allowances for a rough and ready live recording, there's not much room for subtlety here.

The most obvious change is the return of Lloyd-Langton. He's moved on considerably from the generic psych-blues playing on *Hawkwind*, and now favours a wailing, supercharged tone swathed in sustain and reverb. His first entry here is genuinely exciting, as is the pumping bassline that heralds the song's extended instrumental section. But while it generates plenty of heat, it feels a little directionless. Lloyd-Langton's original departure was a major catalyst in the development of Hawkwind's unique sound during the 70s – bringing him back is a significant aesthetic decision, and not one that always pays off. This isn't to denigrate him as a player – though he's not exactly a subscriber here to the 'less is more' principle – but over-reliance on his guitar to provide instrumental colour will become a recurring issue.

After this upbeat opening, the album drops down a gear with '**Motorway City**', a second new song. It opens with some pleasantly trippy, arpeggiated synth – Blake's arrival has changed the band's electronic palette as well, which now feels cleaner and sharper than before. Primarily a synthesist rather than a keyboard player, the sound he produces sometimes lacks warmth, and even anticipates the artificial sheen of digital synths, which will rapidly replace analogue keyboards over the next few years.

Based around a busy, phasing riff, with some tasteful accompaniment from Lloyd-Langton and King on toms, there's a ragged grandeur to the song's arrangement, even if Brock's vocal has the cadence of a nursery rhyme. However, it's clearly still a work in progress,[1] so we should perhaps overlook Blake's wayward playing. A pleasingly predatory riff emerges, but it's undermined by the horrible thudding of King's bass drum, which alongside Lloyd-Langton's piercing power drill guitar, sounds like a wall being knocked down. It drifts off into the distance, faintly unresolved.

The most telling indication of the new sound is the interpretation of older material, and '**Spirit Of The Age**' is the most interesting song in this respect. Blake turns on the random wave generator, then adds an insistent synth arpeggio, a sound that everyone from Tangerine Dream to The Human League will mine in the early 80s. There's no chugging guitar, but Brock's first verse – over just this minimal electronic backing – is actually quite effective. His take on Calvert's dense satirical screed also works surprisingly well, tapping into a vein of angry bewilderment. As Brock voices it, he's no longer an alienated member of the technocratic middle class, but a space-travelling everyman ruing his lot in life.

Similarly, the chorus is no longer imbued with stoic resignation, but swells instead into full-on outrage at a future world where science hasn't freed us, but just created new problems. By the second verse, Brock is positively maniacal, and the song becomes a rabble-rousing call-to-arms. Everybody has crashed in by now, with Lloyd-Langton's trebly tendrils invading every nook and cranny like sonic knotweed. The rhythm is hammering and oppressive, but they take it down and bring it up again, and there's even what sounds like a 'Radio Ga Ga'-style clapalong happening in the crowd.

Not exactly subtle in the first place, '**Brainstorm**' has become an even blunter instrument, now played harder and faster, the riff more punctuated than ever. It's an undeniably spirited version that bounces along with punkish vigour, even if Brock's shouted, slightly strained vocal misses the lysergic aloofness of Turner. The chanted breakdown still works well, and gives King room to assert himself properly for the first time, with some impressive tribal drum rolls, in fact, almost a solo. We still have to contend with Lloyd-Langton's fretboard logorrhoea and Blake's bibbling synths though.

'**Lighthouse**' is the album's other 'new' song.[2] It starts promisingly enough, a slow pattern of hard radiophonic pulses over a rippling arpeggio. But then it veers into cheap sci-fi TV territory: there's a string synth, plus spoken-word references to a "*Captain's Log*" and "*the outskirts of Galaxy Nine*". When Blake sings, his cramped, over-fussy voice advises us to "*light the lasers in your heart*" and watch out for the "*crystal people*". Similar to 'PXR5', it peddles a juvenile and over-literal version of space rock that panders to preconceptions of Hawkwind as *Star Trek*-addled hippies making music for nerds. A sinister bass building to a cyclical synth/guitar motif offers some redemption towards the end, but this may well be the low point in Hawkwind's recorded output from this period.

If further proof is needed that this album is a product of the denim and leather-clad times, listen to how the sprawling supernova of '**Master Of The Universe**' is collapsed into a red dwarf. It's certainly exhilarating: Bainbridge gallops along like Iron Maiden's Steve Harris, and Brock's snarl tells us this particular cosmic overlord intends to bang some heads together. The old dynamics are just about there still and the drop-down to the riff never fails to excite – but by now, Lloyd-Langton is white noise that the ear subconsciously blocks out.

Cue raucous cheering from what sounds like a young crowd – perhaps their older siblings have told them Hawkwind aren't allowed to leave the building until they've played '**Silver Machine**'. However, it's subtitled 'Requiem' here, and blown to oblivion halfway through the first verse.[3] Which is a shame, because the metallic sound of the album actually suits the track, Brock knocking the riff out with brutal aplomb compared to the sludge boogie of the original. Unfortunately, what's perhaps intended as a sardonic kiss-off to an old albatross comes across more as a "fuck you" gesture.

<><><><><><><><><><><><><><><><><><><><><><><><><><><><><><><><><><><><><><><><><><><><><><><>

1    'Motorway City' is more effectively showcased on *Levitation* a few months later.

2    'Lighthouse' had already appeared on Tim Blake's modestly titled 1978 solo album *Blake's New Jerusalem*. Given its awkward sci-fi stylings, *Blake's 7* might have been more appropriate.

3    This habit of ending songs with an explosion has become Hawkwind's equivalent of *Monty Python*'s giant stamping foot.

# No Cause For A Deviation

July–October 1980

# WARRIORS INTO EXTRA TIME

### The Hawkwind saga
### by DAVE BROWN

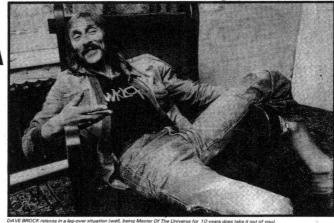

IT WAS inevitable that one day the rest of the world would catch them up.

For years they had carried on regardless of the criticisms and cries of "uncool" and continued unswayingly along their predestined route.

Then suddenly there was much gnashing of teeth and wailing of guitars as heavy metal once more joined the ranks of what is considered to be hip. And there was a further renewal of interest in the world of psychedelia (which had been stored in suspended animation since the 'sixties).

At last the time seemed right and the world was ready for them. Those who had at one time turned away now turned their heads in amazement.

*DAVE BROCK relaxes in a leg-over situation (well, being Master Of The Universe for 10 years does take it out of you).*

'It was inevitable that one day the rest of the world would catch them up.'
*Sounds*, 8 November 1980
(source: Paul Windle collection)

Proving once again that Hawkwind are far from a spent force, *Live Seventy Nine* reaches number 15, the band's highest placing since *Warrior* in 1975. Whatever the reason – an implicit rejection of the Charisma years, or better promotion and distribution by Bronze – the album catches a mood of resurgence, both in the band's following and in the hard rock/heavy metal music scene in general.

The Day-Glo visual assault of its front cover also makes it impossible to miss in the racks. Created by Steve Joule, one of Bronze's regular designers, it features not one but two hawk illustrations against a headache-inducing background of yellow and black lightning bolts. The name 'Hawkwind' also appears twice, a prosaic logo clumsily inserted at the top in case the more stylised one is illegible.[1] It's no triumph of graphic design, but the back cover is worse, an out-of-focus live shot presented at an angle along with the text.

*Record Mirror*'s Malcolm Dome likes it, opening his review with the sage observation, "There is a certain magical element incorporated into the Hawkwind psyche that I don't believe even the band members themselves fully appreciate".[a] But the usually reliable *Sounds* gives it just two stars, Phil Sutcliffe complaining that it's even more rambling than their studio albums: "thrashing bedlam rock, lacking even the relief of Robert Calvert's imagination and English eccentric persona".[b] But Brock & co have been here before, and vindicated in their new direction, shrug such criticism off to begin work on their next studio album.

▾        ▾        ▾

The band return to Bronze's Roundhouse Studios in Chalk Farm, recently upgraded to become one of the UK's first digital recording facilities. Brock is keen to exploit the new technology and inject more precision into the band's music – but this leads to another line-up change.

Brock has become increasingly frustrated with Simon King's inability to play to an exact tempo, and following an argument over potentially using a drum machine, King walks out of the studio and out of the band.[2] Brock aside, he is the last link to the *Space Ritual* era, and his departure has another effect on the band's sound, not least because of who replaces him.

Urgently in need of a new drummer, Lloyd-Langton's wife Marion suggests ex-Cream man **Ginger Baker**, who she has recently worked with as a press officer. Baker has a reputation for being difficult, and has spent the 70s burning through a succession of bands and large sums of money. But he readily agrees – initially as a session player to complete the album, which he does in a matter of days, and then as a full-time member of the band: "I found the atmosphere during the sessions so fantastic that I immediately decided to stay with Hawkwind. For me, it's not just my umpteenth group, I'm determined to give it everything I've got".[c3]

However, not everybody's overjoyed by this development. Amid arguments about budgeting for the upcoming winter tour, Doug Smith decides he can't work with Baker's eccentric manager Roy Ward, and leaves once again. Marion Lloyd-Langton effectively takes over the band's back office, while Ward stays on as 'personal manager'.

▾        ▾        ▾

More Hawkwind product appears in September when Charisma releases best-of compilation *Repeat Performance*, its main selling point being the inclusion of non-album single 'Back On The Streets'.[4] And in October comes the second and third of the *Weird Tapes*, the former featuring live tracks from 1977 and more Hawklords demos from 1979,[5] the latter consisting of live tracks from Watchfield 75 and Stonehenge 77, plus a couple of studio jams.

Ahead of the release of the new album proper, Hawkwind talk to *Melody Maker*'s Ian Pye. The resulting feature has a retrospective focus common to other articles on the band at this time. There's a recognition of tenacity in the face of formidable odds, plus a sense of wonder at their longevity: in a rapidly evolving music scene, 12 years seems like an eternity. The critics may never love Hawkwind, but they've developed a grudging respect, Pye referring to them as "acid rock's ship of state".

Whereas Robert Calvert would use interviews to emphasise the band's relevance to a modern audience, demanding they be seen in a contemporary context, Hawkwind are now regarded as an anachronistic link back to some semi-mythical psychedelic past, required to relive former adventures for the entertainment of a readership that barely remembers the counterculture. As Bainbridge ruefully notes, "the media and the system in general has this amazing capacity to absorb threatening movements… repackaging them and selling them back to people".[d]

Hawkwind may not be given the chance to articulate their vision of the future, but Calvert – an "unusual", "clever", but "over-excited" man, according to Brock – and his ever-evolving activities crop up in Pye's article, with their ex-singer noted to be writing a novel about the vagaries of the music business called *Hype*.

▾     ▾     ▾

Hawkwind's annual autumn/winter UK tour kicks off on 10 October at Manchester Apollo. With a world-renowned drummer on board to propel the mothership, spirits are high. But in just a week, the façade crumbles. Tim Blake is distracted, spending long periods on the phone to his French girlfriend who, unbeknownst to the band, has just miscarried the couple's baby. Following a bust-up after the Victoria Hall gig in Hanley on 17 October, Blake quits and returns to France.

His immediate replacement is **Paul "Twink" Noble**, Blake's roadie and former synth player in free festival stalwarts Here & Now.[6] But Noble is injured a few days later when one of the band's vans overturns. **Keith Hale**, singer and keyboardist in post-punk proggers Blood Donor, is now drafted in, taking over at the Newcastle City Hall gig on 22 October.[7]

On 27 October, Hawkwind release *Levitation*, their first 'proper' studio album since *Hawklords*.[8]

〜〜〜〜〜〜〜〜〜〜〜〜〜〜〜〜〜〜〜〜〜〜〜〜〜〜〜〜〜〜〜〜〜〜〜〜〜〜〜〜〜〜〜〜〜〜〜〜〜〜〜〜〜〜〜〜〜〜〜〜〜〜〜〜〜〜〜〜〜〜〜〜〜〜

a    Malcolm Dome, *Record Mirror*, 19/7/80

b    Phil Sutcliffe, *Sounds*, 12/7/80

c    'With Ginger Baker Aboard, Hawkwind Is Now A Totally Legendary Band' – Dutch music magazine *Joopie*, 28/12/80

d    'The Everlasting Trip' – Ian Pye, *Melody Maker*, 15/9/80

1    Steve 'Krusher' Joule later worked for *Kerrang!* and became a key DJ on the UK metal scene. A version of this sleeve is used for the 'Shot Down In The Night' picture bag.

2    Co-producer Ashley Howe doesn't recall this particular dispute, saying the album was pretty much completed when King left, and the drum tracks already recorded to, in his opinion, a decent standard (interview with the author). Brock attributes King's problems to continued heroin use, while King himself concedes dangerous levels of drinking. King would briefly rejoin Hawkwind in 1982, with a view to drumming on the *Choose Your Masques* tour, but after problems in rehearsals, he left the band and the music industry for good.

3    Given the circumstances of King's departure, the irony is that Baker's difficult behaviour was largely a result of heavy drug and alcohol abuse. Baker later revised his opinion of Hawkwind, describing them as, "fucking appalling. Atrocious" (*Classic Rock* – March 2010).

4    The cassette version of *Repeat Performance* also includes 'The Dream Of Isis', the B-side to 'Back On The Streets'. Other compilations in this (short-lived) series included Van Der Graaf Generator and Lindisfarne.

5    On the second *Weird Tape*, 'Valium 10' is misspelt as 'Vallium 10' and 'Douglas In The Jungle' is subtitled 'Ode to a manager!'

6    Not to be confused with Twink from the Pink Fairies, Paul Noble was integral to Here & Now's mid-70s line-up, though ousted before they released any material. As a spacey psychedelic band with an anarchic outlook and origins in the Ladbroke Grove squatting scene, Here & Now are arguably the UK band closest in sound and spirit to Hawkwind during this period.

7     Brock may have first heard Blood Donor when they played Nik Turner's Bohemian Love-In in June 1978. 'Rubber Revolution', the first of Blood Donor's two singles, sounds remarkably like something Hawklords or Steve Swindells might have made. Their last hurrah was recording the B-side to a *Doctor Who* novelty single. Hale had previously played with spooky folk proggers Comus. After Hawkwind, he went on to work closely with Toyah, writing her biggest hit 'It's A Mystery'.

8     Motörhead's 'Ace Of Spades' is also released on 27 October. A defining song of the NWOBHM, it will stay in the singles charts for 13 weeks, peaking at number 15. The *Ace Of Spades* album is released two weeks later – reaching number four, it confirms once and for all that the balance of power between Hawkwind and Motörhead has shifted definitively in Lemmy's favour.

# *Levitation*

Released 27 October 1980

| | |
|---|---|
| *Label:* | Bronze (UK & Europe) |
| *Track listing:* | Levitation (Brock) / Motorway City (Brock) / Psychosis (Bainbridge) / World Of Tiers (Bainbridge/Lloyd-Langton) / Prelude (Blake) / Who's Gonna Win The War? (Brock) / Space Chase (Lloyd-Langton) / The 5th Second Of Forever (Lloyd-Langton/Brock) / Dust Of Time (Brock/ Bainbridge/Lloyd-Langton) |
| *Line-up:* | Dave Brock / Huw Lloyd-Langton / Tim Blake / Harvey Bainbridge / Ginger Baker |
| *Recorded at:* | Roundhouse Studios |
| *Produced by:* | Ashley Howe / Dave Brock / Harvey Bainbridge / Huw Lloyd-Langton |

With their tenth studio album and first of the 80s, it's worth reflecting on how far Hawkwind have come, and how much they've stayed the same. One of the first LPs to be recorded digitally (and proudly described as "A Headphone Album"), *Levitation* showcases a modern rock band confidently integrating the latest technology into their sound. Sonically, it's a world away from the fuggy caveman psych of their debut. Yet most songs are still based around Brock's blocky guitar riffs and robotic vocal melodies, while the band continue to be thematically and visually defined by science fiction. There's still no other band quite like Hawkwind – over the past decade, they've assimilated elements of psychedelia, prog, Krautrock, punk and metal to create a sub-genre with a membership of one. This uniqueness will be key to their ongoing success, or at least survival, but is also a factor in their increasing estrangement from mainstream rock culture.

If *Live Seventy Nine* was a rough prototype for their 80s sound, *Levitation* perfects the template – with one wildcard. Ginger Baker makes his presence felt from the outset, his busy but unfussy backbeat bolstering the predatory guitar that heralds 'Levitation'. The switch-up to a gnarly, Eastern-ish riff is handled smoothly, and there's a nice balance between Lloyd-Langton's chiming, brighter sound and the rhythm section's bump and grind. Brock's vocal follows the jerky cadence of the riff, adding to the slightly off-kilter vibe, and the barked chorus is exciting and memorable. He also remains the master of delivering faintly daft lyrics with a winning conviction: "*Although I sit upon this chair / I rise and float up in the air.*"

There's a pleasing heft and solidity here, the dense mantric riffs of old re-tooled for a new era. Baker really drives things along, and Lloyd-Langton shows admirable restraint, playing a slow-motion solo over a sinister iteration of the riff, while someone rifles through the insides of a piano. Blake is also more integrated, his synth noodling at the service of the song rather than vice versa. There's even some urgent panting from Brock, a reminder of when Hawkwind music was animated by space chants and cosmic ululations. Older fans may miss that magical fusion of avant-garde raw power and sci-fi poetry, but this is undeniably an invigorating opening.

The studio recording of 'Motorway City' is a big improvement on the previous album's live version, with Brock's semi-acoustic guitar and Lloyd-Langton more sympathetically mixed. Baker injects a little vim into the song's trundling undercarriage, and the chorus genuinely evokes a sodium-lit urban highway at night, driving with the windows down, breathing in exhaust fumes. The vaguely atonal build to Lloyd-Langton's flanged riff and solo is interesting, and the call-and-response between Blake and guitarist more clearly defined in the big instrumental hook. But it's the arrangement that makes this track – like much of the material here, there's a progressive mentality in evidence, with parts played but not repeated, and tonally contrasting sections spliced together.

'Psychosis' is a short instrumental vignette of the type that will start to regularly appear on Hawkwind albums, spoken words set against abstract drones and oscillations, like eavesdropping on the digital ether. Here, there's a dirty rumble of synth and Bainbridge's muffled voice, before it gradually transitions into a hypnotic arpeggio. It's a strange bit of industrial electronica that works precisely because it's unclear what's going on or even what its purpose is – it hints at the future without giving away its exact co-ordinates.

That arpeggio morphs into copter blades and alien bird cries before 'World Of Tiers'[1] comes slamming in like a muscular update of Fleetwood Mac's 'Oh Well', the marching beat and propulsive bass giving it some serious oomph. There's a drop-down to a mellow prog reverie, with some tasteful fluting synth, and then back into the riff and the inevitable Lloyd-Langton solo. It's an exciting chunk of dexterous interplay, Hawkwind seemingly determined throughout *Levitation* to shake off the perception that they're musically second-division.

Only Hawkwind could have a track halfway through an album called '**Prelude**',[2] but Blake's short, reflective instrumental eases us nicely into the second side. With its new age Euro-topian sensibility, this could easily be an extract from a Jean-Michel Jarre album.

It segues into '**Who's Gonna Win The War?**', Bainbridge's melancholic bass riff harking back to the controlled but uneasy sound of *Hawklords*. While the 79 Rockfield take on this song was angry and bombastic, here it's much more sombre, the sensitivity of the music counterpointing the bleakness of Brock's lyric: "*Lonely figures waiting, shadows on the hill / Looking into valleys where everything is still / Only death is lurking, the creeping sickness waits.*"[3] The recent Soviet invasion of Afghanistan and the imminent arrival of US cruise missiles on UK soil had raised Cold War temperatures again, so these words are timely and chillingly effective.

The chorus is as rousing and indignant as ever though, with Baker's marching drums again. Lloyd-Langton plays a lovely chiming motif after the second chorus, before taking another solo. But the song feels scrubbed clean of any grit, perhaps an error given the subject matter. In particular, its instrumental coda meanders, lost in a featureless, post-apocalyptic landscape until it peters out. But maybe that's the point.

Still, there's always the cutting edge of 80s consumer entertainment to distract us from the spectre of mutually assured destruction. Video game arcades were now appearing in every town in Britain, and '**Space Chase**' (another instrumental) opens with the type of 8-bit chirruping that filled these temples to *Space Invaders* and *Pac-Man* – indeed, 'Space Chase' could be the name of the latest must-play slot machine. It's a fast, twisting duel between Lloyd-Langton and Blake, their pseudo-Arabic riffing anticipating a new wave of technology-enhanced psychedelia in the future. Fun if insubstantial, it works well thanks to Baker's super-tight, powerhouse rhythms.[4]

'**The 5th Second Of Forever**' (mischievously sub-titled 'From The Film' on the back cover, despite no such film existing) doesn't seem to have anything to do with Calvert's '10 Seconds Of Forever' – but it *is* the first Hawkwind track to feature classical guitar, Lloyd-Langton picking out a contemplative medieval theme as water trickles in the background. It's a peculiar but pleasant departure for the band, perhaps in response to the contemporary popularity of John Williams,[5] and another nose-thumb at those critics who accuse them of lacking sophistication.

It's also a tease – because with the roar of a plane overhead, it switches up to another driving, busy rhythm track with a tense, minor-key riff. Brock sings with a distorting effect on his voice, a reflection perhaps of his lyrics, which are at best allusive, at worst nonsensical: "*Track your finger in the cluster / You've found the cause which is called must.*"[6] After Calvert's clever and cogent wordsmithing, Brock's increasing lack of attention in this area is a little irking. Equally underwhelming is the way this section merely fades down to the classical guitar part again. The individual elements are good, but this is more a novelty hybrid than a song proper.

The opening to '**Dust Of Time**' is one of the album's best moments though, its pile-driving jump-cut into Brock's stun riff and Lloyd-Langton's wailing guitar raising the hairs on the neck. But the lyric melody is pedestrian, a barely modulated trudge, like 'Brainstorm' on depressants. The song addresses the possible future effects of genetic engineering, and in fairness to Brock, features the striking image: "*Queues of sterile mothers waiting for inspection*". The chorus is a bit of an afterthought, though the return of that riff-lead combo almost makes up for it.

But now it pulls the same trick as 'World Of Tiers' and 'The 5th Second Of Forever' – a section of rolling piano building towards a tastefully restrained motif from Lloyd-Langton that's really an entirely new song. Where Hawkwind once drew you along claustrophobic black corridors reverberating with the music of the void, we're now climbing towards some shining pyramid of light, with Blake's crystal people beckoning us on. It's airy up here, and the view's nice, but it's a bit bedazzling after all those years in the cosmic gloom… We get the riff one more time, a perfunctory outro, and then that's it.

◇◇◇◇◇◇◇◇◇◇◇◇◇◇◇◇◇◇◇◇◇◇◇◇◇◇◇◇◇◇◇◇◇◇◇◇◇◇◇◇◇◇◇◇◇◇◇◇◇◇◇◇◇◇◇◇◇◇◇◇◇◇◇◇◇◇

1    This title comes from a series of novels by Philip José Farmer, which feature a similar idea to Moorcock's multiverse concept.

2    Actually, Judas Priest had already pulled this trick on their 1976 album *Sad Wings Of Destiny*.

3    'Who's Gonna Win The War?' also marks the start of Brock re-contextualising old lyrics in new songs, or more straight forwardly, ripping himself off – the lyric "*Already weeds are writing their scriptures in the sand*" originally comes from 'We Took The Wrong Step Years Ago'.

4    'Space Chase' is the track that (allegedly) defeated Simon King during the initial sessions, precipitating his departure. Baker nailed it immediately.

5    Williams had a couple of big hits around this time: 'Cavatina' (aka 'Theme From *The Deer Hunter*') and a version of Bach's 'Toccata' with the band Sky.

6    These lyrics had also recently featured (overdubbed?) on the track 'Circles', from the *Weird Tape* featuring part of the 1975 Watchfield Festival performance.

# No Cause For A Deviation

October–December 1980

Lloyd-Langton, Bainbridge, Brock, *Levitation* tour 1980

With initial copies pressed on blue vinyl, *Levitation* continues Hawkwind's chart renaissance, peaking at number 21. And it comes in another striking if unsophisticated cover, a hawk-headed spaceship cruising over a barren landscape that on closer inspection resembles caramel ice cream.[1] On the reverse, there's a colourful heraldic design by *PXR5* artist Philip Tonkyn, based on a poster he designed for the December 77 Sonic Assassins gig.[2]

Bronze also fund three promotional videos for 'Levitation', 'Who's Gonna Win The War?' and 'World Of Tiers', the band filmed playing in a studio, with Brock in the Arthur Brown-style corpse paint he's taken to sometimes wearing on stage.[3]

*Record Mirror*'s Malcolm Dome is hugely impressed by *Levitation*, contrasting it favourably with the "very eccentric and far too safe" Charisma era. This is a return to "intensity and imagination", with "blistering sci-fi imagery as an angry searchlight focusing on alternative thought, leaving The Fall and their ilk still in their cots." Five stars, and "an album of the year".[a]

Many fans share this view of the album as a 'return to form', especially those with a taste for the harder-edged sounds of the NWOBHM. Brock also seems to agree that reversing into the future is the way forward: "With *Levitation*, we've come full circle back to the style of… *In Search Of Space*."[b]

▾     ▾     ▾

On the road for much of November and December, including dates in Belfast and Dublin, the *Levitation* tour is their most extensive for years – and almost inevitably, there's dissent in the ranks. Baker has taken to playing an extended solo in the middle of 'Brainstorm', to the disgruntlement of some fans, and also an impatient Bainbridge, who incurs the drummer's wrath at the Hammersmith Odeon when he comes in on bass before Baker has finished his paradiddles. Baker also suggests the band could make more money if they reduced their outlay on the light show, which causes further bad feeling.

On 7 November, Bronze issues an edited version of '**Who's Gonna Win The War?**' as a single. Unfortunately, the picture bag somewhat obscures the anti-war message: the album's Hawkship illustration, superimposed over a WW2 scene of aerial bombardment, appears to be dropping bombs itself. The single is also notable for the non-album B-side '**Nuclear Toy**', which means it contains two similarly-themed protest songs.

'Nuclear Toy' originally started life as a Brock solo demo on the first *Weird Tape*, but the Kraftwerk-esque electronica of that version is replaced here by a no less quirky slice of proto-industrial pop, dominated by Brock's heavily vocodered vocals and an insistent syndrum. More lyric-intense than any of the tracks on *Levitation* – including such stark couplets as "*Strontium-90, cancer in the blood / Who's gonna pay for the radiation flood?*" – it's an indication that Hawkwind are still willing to experiment outside the bounds of their 'classic sound'.

▾     ▾     ▾

Another indication that the band remain keen to try new approaches comes right at the end of the year, when they demo a handful of tracks at Battle Studios in Hastings. '**Zones**' is a short piece of sound design similar to *Levitation*'s 'Psychosis'. But the other two songs that emerge from these sessions are altogether more intriguing.

'**Dangerous Visions**', a track the band had started to play on the last tour, is a Keith Hale composition that the new keys player also sings. Based around a mid-tempo descending riff, it's a little unimaginative the way the main instrumental line mimics the vocal melody, and Hale's voice isn't strong enough for the tune. And lyrical references to "*the child of the Third World*" verge on the mawkish, not a quality previously associated with Hawkwind. But for all that, it's an affectingly angry ballad, almost a distant cousin of 'High Rise'.

'**Running Through The Back Brain**' is a compelling piece of paranoid stream of consciousness from Michael Moorcock, which features some decidedly Calvert-esque lines: "*My brother and my sister joined the army / They promise that they do not mean to harm me.*" More measured than usual, it's perhaps Moorcock's best vocal performance on a Hawkwind song. The music itself is minimal but effective, based around a Rhodes piano vamp and subtle guitar work from Lloyd-Langton, while Baker patiently drives the track forward. It's clearly still a work in progress, but as it picks up pace towards the end, it's the closest they get for some time to the hypno-drone vibe of their earlier years.[4]

◇◇◇◇◇◇◇◇◇◇◇◇◇◇◇◇◇◇◇◇◇◇◇◇◇◇◇◇◇◇◇◇◇◇◇◇◇◇◇◇◇◇◇◇◇◇◇◇◇◇◇◇◇◇◇◇◇◇◇◇◇◇◇◇◇◇◇◇

a      Malcom Dome, *Record Mirror*, 10/11/80

b      'With Ginger Baker Aboard, Hawkwind Is Now A Totally Legendary Band' – *Joopie*, 28/12/80

1      The illustration is by Linda Curry, who also produced a series of sleeve images for Girlschool, another Bronze act.

2      Tonkyn thought his illustration would be on the front cover. A stylised version of it is in fact being beamed out of the Hawkship.

3      These videos were shot at Ewart Studios in Wandsworth, as part of a Bronze job lot with Motörhead and Girlschool.

4      The Battle Studios tracks eventually appeared on *Zones* in 1983, with 'Dangerous Visions' listed as 'Dangerous Vision'. Both 'Dangerous Visions' and 'Running Through The Back Brain' were based on backing tracks recorded live at the Lewisham Odeon on 18 December, with 'Running…' originally being an instrumental jam. Moorcock had made guest appearances on the previous two tours at Preston and Lancaster and had also recently released the '**Dodgem Dude**'/'**Starcruiser**' single, rejected by UA in 1975, on Flicknife – he was actually the first member of the Hawkwind diaspora to work with the label. 'Dodgem Dude' sounds like The Glitter Band if they'd come from Germany, 'Starcruiser' like a barbarian Roxy Music. Both are more vital and raucous than *The New Worlds Fair* material, which makes it all the more perplexing that they weren't released at the time.

Advert for Robert Calvert's *Hype* album and book
(source: Doug Smith archive)

# Harvey Bainbridge

Bass, synth and vocals
Sonic Assassins: 1977–1978
Hawklords: 1978–1979
Hawkwind: 1979–1991
*Hawklords*, *Live Seventy Nine* and *Levitation*

Harvey Bainbridge (from 1980 tour programme)
(source: Stephen Dunthorne collection)

**You were in a band called Ark with Paul Hayles and Martin Griffin…**
Dave and Bob were living in North Devon when I met them. Dave got in touch with us as a band and asked me, Martin and Paul to join him and Bob to play free festivals. The rest of the band don't want to play free festivals anymore, that was the gist of what he was saying.

He rang me up and said, "Why don't we put a gig on, put a band together called the Sonic Assassins, just do the odd gig here and there?" That sounded like a good idea, attack people with sounds and then get away! We spent four or five days rehearsing in a little village hall putting the set together.

Then I had a phone call from Dave literally the day before the gig: "Bob's on one, he's dressed as a First World War officer, and he's decided not to do the gig." And I thought, 'Oh God.' The posters were up, everybody had bought tickets. So he said, "Why don't you go round and talk to him". I went round to Bob's place, and he absolutely was on one. I spent most of the night listening and talking to him, and at the end he said, "I will do the gig." And I thought, 'Thank God for that!'

**What kind of stuff was he talking about?**
All these different projects in his head were getting muddled up. I think he was finding it hard to prioritise which he wanted to do next. Basically, he was in First World War mode, quite bizarre really. At the gig, in the middle of the set, he went into this big long poem about going over the top, and it was just a question of following him. It was outrageous lyrical brilliance I thought. And he dressed for the occasion in his First World War officer's uniform.

**What happened next?**
After the Sonic Assassins, Hawkwind went off to America with Paul Hayles. When they came back, Paul told me Dave had sacked everybody and sold his guitar. Then the next thing I know, Bob phones me up and says, "We're recording an album as the Hawklords, we want you and Martin Griffin to come and play on it." Doing that album, I realised you had to be musically productive in this band. You have to put stuff forward, otherwise you don't exist. You're not just a backing musician, you have to have some kind of personal input as well.

**People depict the Hawklords as Brock just wanting a band on wages, but you're saying it was still more of a collaborative effort?**
Oh yeah, you still had to put things forward. I heard a quote around that time that Hawkwind were one of the best collections of one-man-bands in the business, and I think to a certain extent that's true, because you didn't last long if you weren't a character, or didn't have some kind of musical persona.

**Was there a deliberate move away from the old Hawkwind sound?**
As the first proper album I'd recorded professionally, I didn't think it was any different. But when the test pressings came back, I remember Dave phoned me and said, "I've just thrown the album out the window!" He played it, picked it off his record player, opened the window and literally flung it into his garden.

I said, "Why?" and he just said, "Well…" And that was it, he didn't have to say why really!

There was a professional sound engineer helping out with the recording, and Dave was saying, "This is like adult music now, it's grown-up music." I've a feeling he probably thought the fans wouldn't like it because it was too AOR. I have a cutting which says, "This is Hawkwind like you've never heard before, with four-part harmonies," and it had "AOR" at the end of it. Dave probably thought it was getting too smooth, that it should be a bit more raw.

Design-wise and musically, it feels post-punk, but I'm guessing you weren't influenced by that…
Not really. The whole packaging was Barney Bubbles, of course, almost industrial. The live show was like industrial trance music at times. Barney had all these wonderful ideas about scaffolding and dancers, but as the tour progressed we thinned the dancers out. I wore industrial overalls for a while, then I got rid of them. I had them for years after, useful for fixing the car.

You played the post-punk science fiction festival Futurama the following year…
Talking to John Lydon there, he said Hawkwind had influenced him. He was almost starstruck in fact. It was quite bizarre, it should have been the other way round. I liked Public Image Ltd actually, I thought Jah Wobble's bass playing was brilliant.

But you were out of contract by then…
Yes, there was no record company at that time, until after we'd done the 1979 tour. We paid for the recording [of the show)] at St Albans and for some reason we didn't think it was a very good gig, even though it was jam-packed and the place was literally jumping. There was as many people outside as there were inside. We didn't think about it until the tour was over, then Doug Smith sent us rough mixes on cassette, and I thought, 'Bloody hell, this is almost punk!'

Hawkwind were still pulling in a new wave of fans…
It's intriguing watching over the years how the audience doesn't change, you've still got the teenagers down the front. That went on for years, and you're thinking, these people should be getting older. But basically the age range stayed the same.

*Why do you think* Live Seventy Nine *charted higher than any of the Charisma albums?*

Some very astute marketing by Bronze. They put it out when there wasn't much else being released. That's why it charted, it seems to me.

*Why did Simon King leave during the* Levitation *sessions?*

He's totally clean now, but he had a habit, and Dave would accuse him all the time of slowing down. We were in Roundhouse Studios going through newer stuff and Dave was getting increasingly frustrated. He stormed out, saying, "I'm going to get my drum machine." I said, "Why don't you let me and Simon put drums and bass tracks down, give us an afternoon to see how it goes?" "No, no, it's wasting time, we'll use the drum machine." So Simon left. Huw's wife [Marion Lloyd-Langton] was doing PR for Ginger Baker, who was touring England at the time, and she said, "I'll ask Ginger if he'll drum."

*What did you think about that, given his reputation?*

As a teenager I followed Jack Bruce around the place, he was my bass-playing hero, and Ginger was the drummer with Jack and Cream. So I thought, 'Wow, I'm going to play with a legend.' We had to offer him double session money, but he came and did it. We all seemed to get on OK, so we asked him, would he like to do the tour? He said yes, but halfway through, we had a bust-up. He wanted to get rid of the lightshow: "Then we can all have more money." No one said anything, and then I said, "That's ridiculous, because the whole point of a Hawkwind show is the event, the lights, the spectacle of it." From then on, he never really liked me very much!

*Then you came in too soon on his drum solo…*

Oh God, yes, at Hammersmith Odeon. He had a drum solo in the middle of 'Brainstorm' and we used to go off stage. And I remember a lot of the fans used to say, "What is the point of that?" But it kept Ginger happy. This particular night, it was going on and on and we were saying, "I wish he'd end." I recognised one of his trigger points, for when he was going to go back into the groove again, and I thought, 'Right, that's where the first beat is, this'll get him.' I joined in, doing the "*bam bam*" on the bass – his look of shock and horror! We all fell about laughing. Anyway, he called me the worse bass player in the world after that.

# Looking In The Future

Selling a stereotype -
advert for 1984 reissue of their first album

Of course, Hawkwind just kept on going. The 1970s is the decade that defined them, but they've continued to produce innovative and exciting music right up to the present day.

Ironically, the point where this book stops is actually around the time when I first started to seriously get into the band. As a pre-teen, I had been entranced (and a little frightened) by my older brother's copy of *Warrior*. A few years later, I was getting *Space Ritual* out of the local record library[1] and buying Hawkwind's contemporary releases, the trio of albums they recorded after *Levitation* for RCA Active: *Sonic Attack* (1981), *Church Of Hawkwind* and *Choose Your Masques* (both 1982).[2]

Their 'classic' years might have passed, but Hawkwind were still uniquely themselves. In fact, it was easy to overlook just how original they continued to be – for instance, both *Church* and *Masques* anticipate the late 80s sound of electronic and industrial rock.

The RCA Active albums would be their last for a major label. A series of Brock-sanctioned archival releases on Flicknife had tried the patience of a traditional record company that demanded complete control over when material came out, though the label had never really 'got' the band anyway. With none of the other majors minded to take a chance on Hawkwind, despite those last three albums all going top 30, Flicknife became the band's main label by default.

While this undoubtedly affected their cash flow, and would have been the death of most bands, being on an independent label probably suited Brock. Now in his forties, and very much the captain of Hawkwind, the desire to be master of his band's destiny must have been greater than ever. They went through a succession of smaller labels from the 90s onwards – including their own Emergency Broadcast System – and their profile waxed and waned. But Hawkwind never went away – they were always out there somewhere, refusing to compromise yet happy to assimilate the prevailing musical climate into their sound as it suited them.

The fans too have never gone away. But it's Hawkwind's status as a genuine subcultural phenomenon that has kept their name alive, and seen their reputation continue to grow over the past few years. Not as 'elder statesmen of rock', invited at last to sit at the music industry's high table, but in recognition of the sheer depth of their influence, and their position as a constant rallying point for the alternative-to-the-alternative.

As I write this, Hawkwind are in the 50th year of their existence. To this day, they continue to embody the spirit of the underground, an implicit rejection of the mainstream's easy logic. The 1970s may have birthed the modern era, and eventually crushed the original counterculture, but Hawkwind remained as a wellspring for future generations, and for a multitude of radical escapisms to come.

◇◇◇◇◇◇◇◇◇◇◇◇◇◇◇◇◇◇◇◇◇◇◇◇◇◇◇◇◇◇◇◇◇◇◇◇◇◇◇◇◇◇◇◇◇◇◇◇◇◇◇◇◇◇◇◇◇◇◇◇◇◇◇◇◇◇

1    Bizarrely enough, the same library also had a hardback copy of *The Time Of The Hawklords*, which I consumed with perplexed enthusiasm.

2    Actually, the first 'contemporary' Hawkwind release I bought was Flicknife's *Friends & Relations*.

# Hawkwind And Related UK Discography:1970—1980

| Artist | Title | Released |
|--------|-------|----------|
| Hawkwind | 'Hurry On Sundown'/'Mirror Of Illusion' 7" | 31 July 1970 |
| Hawkwind | *Hawkwind* | 14 August 1970 |
| VA inc Hawkwind | *All Good Clean Fun*[1] | August 1971 |
| Hawkwind | *In Search Of Space* | 8 October 1971 |
| VA inc Hawkwind | *Greasy Truckers Party* | 28 April 1972 |
| VA inc Hawkwind | *Glastonbury Fayre* | 3 June 1972 |
| Hawkwind | 'Silver Machine'/'Seven By Seven' 7" | 9 June 1972 |
| Hawkwind | *Doremi Fasol Latido* | 24 November 1972 |
| Hawkwind | 'Sonic Attack' 7" (promo only) | May 1973 |
| Hawkwind | *Space Ritual* | 11 May 1973 |
| Captain Lockheed and the Starfighters | 'Ejection'/'Catch A Falling Starfighter' 7" | 13 July 1973 |
| Hawkwind | 'Urban Guerilla'/'Brainbox Pollution' 7" | 3 August 1973 |
| Robert Calvert | *Captain Lockheed And The Starfighters* | 10 May 1974 |
| Hawkwind | 'The Psychedelic Warlords (Disappear In Smoke)'/ 'It's So Easy' 7" | 2 August 1974 |
| Hawkwind | *Hall Of The Mountain Grill* | 4 September 1974 |
| Hawkwind | 'Kings Of Speed'/'Motorhead' 7" | 7 March 1975 |
| Hawkwind | *Warrior On The Edge Of Time* | 9 May 1975 |
| Michael Moorcock & The Deep Fix | *The New Worlds Fair* | May 1975 |
| Robert Calvert | *Lucky Leif And The Longships* | September 1975 |
| Hawkwind | *Hawkwind* (Sunset reissue) | September 1975 |
| Hawkwind | *Roadhawks* (compilation) | 9 April 1976 |

| Artist | Title | Released |
|---|---|---|
| Hawkwind | 'Kerb Crawler'/'Honky Dory' 7" | 16 July 1976 |
| Hawkwind | *Astounding Sounds, Amazing Music* | 27 August 1976 |
| Hawkwind | Back On The Streets'/ 'The Dream Of Isis' 7" | 28 January 1977 |
| Hawkwind | *Masters Of The Universe* (compilation) | 25 February 1977 |
| Hawkwind | *Quark, Strangeness And Charm* | 17 June 1977 |
| Hawkwind | 'Quark, Strangeness And Charm'/'The Forge Of Vulcan' 7" | 29 July 1977 |
| Motörhead | *Motörhead* | 21 August 1977 |
| Nik Turner's Sphynx | *Xitintoday* | April 1978 |
| Hawklords | *Hawklords/25 Years On* | 6 October 1978 |
| Hawklords | 'Psi Power'/'Death Trap' 7" | 13 October 1978 |
| Hawkwind | 'Silver Machine'/'Seven By Seven' 7"/12" (reissue) | 13 October 1978 |
| Hawklords | '25 Years'/'(Only) The Dead Dreams Of The Cold War Kid' 7" + 'PXR5' 12" | 18 May 1979 |
| Hawkwind | *PXR5* | 15 June 1979 |
| Robert Calvert & The 1st XI | 'Cricket Star' 7" flexidisc | July 1979 |
| Inner City Unit | 'Solitary Ashtray'/ 'SO T RY AS id' 7" | September 1979 |
| Motörhead | *On Parole* | 8 December 1979 |
| Inner City Unit | *Pass Out* | January 1980 |
| Hawkwind | *Hawkwind* (Rock File reissue) | February 1980 |
| Sonic Assassins/ Dave Brock | *s/t* (Weird Tape 101) | March 1980 |
| Hawkwind | 'Shot Down In The Night'/ 'Urban Guerilla' 7" | 27 June 1980 |
| Inner City Unit | 'Paradise Beach'/'Amyl Nitrate' 7" | July 1980 |
| Hawkwind | *Live Seventy Nine* | 21 July 1980 |
| Hawkwind | *Repeat Performance* (compilation) | September 1980 |

| Artist | Title | Released |
|--------|-------|----------|
| Hawkwind/ Hawklords | *Hawkwind* (Live)/*Hawklords* (Weird Tape 102) | October 1980 |
| Hawkwind | *Free Festivals* (Weird Tape 103) | October 1980 |
| Hawkwind | *Levitation* | 27 October 1980 |
| Hawkwind | 'Who's Gonna Win The War?'/ 'Nuclear Toy' 7" | 7 November 1980 |
| Michael Moorcock & The Deep Fix | 'Dodgem Dude'/'Starcruiser' | December 1980 |
| Del Dettmar & Gerald Toon | *Synthesis* (cassette) | – 1980 |

◇◇◇◇◇◇◇◇◇◇◇◇◇◇◇◇◇◇◇◇◇◇◇◇◇◇◇◇◇◇◇◇◇◇◇◇◇◇◇◇◇◇◇◇◇◇◇◇◇◇◇◇◇◇◇◇◇◇◇◇◇◇◇◇◇

1    A United Artists sampler compiled by Andrew Lauder which includes a 5.45 version – "An Excerpt" – of 'Be Yourself'.

# BBC Sessions In The 1970s

## 1970

### John Peel's *Top Gear*

'Hurry On Sundown'/'Seeing It As You Really Are'/'Some Of That Stuff'

| | |
|---|---|
| *Recorded:* | Maida Vale Studio 4, London – 18 August 1970 |
| *Broadcast:* | 19 September 1970; repeated 12 December 1970 |
| *First released:* | 'Hurry On Sundown' on *The Text Of Festival* (Illuminated) – July 1983; 'Some Of That Stuff (aka 'Came Home') on *Anthology Volume 3* (Samurai) – June 1986 |
| *Current availability:* | YouTube, 2015. *HAWKWIND (John Peel Session 1970)* (recording of 12 December repeat session) |

[For more information, see p31 and endnotes 6 & 7, p36]

### John Peel's *Sunday Concert*

'Paranoia' / 'Seeing It As You Really Are' / 'Untitled' (aka 'We Do It')

| | |
|---|---|
| *Recorded:* | Paris Theatre, London – 5 November 1970 |
| *Broadcast:* | 15 November 1970; repeated 18 November 1970 on *Sounds Of The Seventies* (John Peel) |
| *First released:* | *The Text Of Festival* |
| *Current availability:* | YouTube, 2017. *Hawkwind on John Peel's Sunday Show, 15th November 1970* (full concert, different recording from *Text*) |

[For more information, see p32-33 and endnote 10, p36]

# 1971

## John Peel's *Top Gear*

'Inwards Out' (aka 'Master Of The Universe') / '(You Know You're Only) Dreaming' / 'You Shouldn't Do That'

| | |
|---|---|
| *Recorded:* | Playhouse Theatre, London – 19 April 1971 |
| *Broadcast:* | 24 April 1971 |
| *First released:* | *The Text Of Festival* |
| *Current availability:* | YouTube, 2018. *Hawkwind live studio sessions* (different recordings from *Text*) |

[For more information, see p47-48 and endnotes 5-7, p50-51]

## Sounds Of The Seventies

'Master of the Universe' / 'You Know You're Only Dreaming'
/ 'You Shouldn't Do That'

| | |
|---|---|
| *Recorded:* | Maida Vale Studio 4, London – 19 May 1971 |
| *Broadcast:* | 27 May 1971 (Stuart Henry); repeated 24 June 1971 (Pete Drummond) |
| *First released:* | N/A |
| *Current availability:* | N/A |

[For more information, see p48 and endnote 9, p51]

# 1972

## Johnnie Walker

'Brainstorm'/'Silver Machine'

| | |
|---|---|
| *Recorded:* | Maida Vale Studio 5, London – 2 August 1972 |
| *Broadcast:* | 14 August 1972 |
| *First released:* | *At The BBC – 1972* (EMI) – March 2010 |
| *Current availability:* | As above |

[For more information, see p82 & 85 and endnote 17, p92]

## *In Concert*

'Countdown' / 'Born To Go' / 'The Black Corridor' / 'Seven By Seven' / 'Brainstorm' / 'Electronic No. 1' / 'Master Of The Universe' / 'Paranoia' / 'Earth Calling' / 'Silver Machine' / 'Welcome To The Future'

| | |
|---|---|
| *Recorded:* | Paris Theatre, London, 28 September 1972 |
| *Broadcast:* | 14 October 1972; repeated 4 August 1973 |
| | |
| *First released:* | *BBC Radio 1 In Concert* (Windsong) – October 1991 (mono version) |
| *Current availability:* | *At The BBC – 1972* (mono and stereo versions) |

[For more information, see p85-86]

# A Miscellany Of 70s Songs Released Post-1980

## 1969

### 'Kiss Of The Velvet Whip' (demo)

| | |
|---|---|
| *Recorded:* | EMI Studios – late 1969 |
| *First released:* | Hawkwind Zoo EP (Flicknife) – May 1981 |
| *Current availability:* | *Hawkwind* (EMI) – 2001 reissue |

A very English take on the Velvet Underground's 'Venus In Furs', showing another, more melodic, side to early Hawkwind. The band re-recorded it as a space rock track during the *ISOS* sessions in May 1971 (possibly where it was renamed '**Sweet Mistress Of Pain**'), but its lyrics seem mismatched in this context, with Brock adding a salacious "You like it like that!" refrain (available: *Parallel Universe – A Liberty/UA Years Anthology 1970-1974* (EMI) – 2011).

## 1970

### 'You Know You're Only Dreaming' (alternative version)

| | |
|---|---|
| *Recorded:* | Trident Studios – 9 March 1970 |
| *First released:* | *Parallel Universe* |
| *Current availability:* | As above |

Of all the unreleased songs and versions on *Parallel Universe*, this is the most striking, a radically different take of the track that later appears on *ISOS*, recorded during sessions for the first album. Driven by a fast acoustic riff and breakneck drumming, Brock's vocal is much more strident here. The middle section sounds like the Muppets on bad acid, but there's some surprisingly cogent harmonising between Lloyd-Langton and Turner. It's another insight into the band's early sound, and confirms once again that the direction they took had nothing to do with an inability to write more conventional songs.

(The other noteworthy unreleased tracks on *Parallel Universe* are '**Hog Farm**' from the May 1971 *ISOS* sessions – which sounds like it was inspired by Pink Floyd's 'Let There Be More Light'– and '**Take What You Can**' from the September/October 1972 *Doremi* sessions – a slightly pedestrian West Coast-ish singalong, Brock even sounding a little transatlantic…)

## 'Hurry On Sundown' (Peel session version)

| | |
|---|---|
| *Recorded:* | Maida Vale Studio 4 – 18 August 1970 |
| *First released:* | The Text Of Festival (Illuminated) – July 1983 |
| *Current availability:* | YouTube, 2018. Hawkwind live studio sessions |

Notable as a more dynamic, full band version of the song, it features some stinging playing from Lloyd-Langton and rampaging, effects-drenched sax from Turner.

## 'Untitled' aka 'We Do It' (live Peel session)

| | |
|---|---|
| *Recorded:* | Paris Theatre – 5 November 1970 |
| *First released:* | Friends & Relations – Twice Upon A Time |

(Flicknife) - April 1983 (edited version) /
*The Text Of Festival* (full version)

*Current availability:*      YouTube, 2017. *Hawkwind on John Peel's Sunday Show, 15th November 1970*
(this version is the correct speed - all previously released versions are faster)

Hawkwind's first major space rock recording. Built around a series of cyclical bass riffs, it positions Thomas Crimble as an unsung architect of their early, Krautrock-paralleling sound. Referred to as 'I Do It' on *Text*, but as 'We Do It' on most other releases.

# 1971

## 'Inwards Out' aka 'Master Of The Universe' (Peel session version)

*Recorded:*               Playhouse Theatre - 19 April 1971
*First released:*         *The Text Of Festival*
*Current availability:*   YouTube, 2018. *Hawkwind live studio sessions*

An early version of this classic song, charged with both cosmic energy and the urgency of a freshly-written track. Brock's guitar coming in after the first verse is a real lose-your-mind moment, as is the return of Dave Anderson's bass following the instrumental section. Plus some spoken words by Turner unique to this version.

# 1972

## 'Time We Left This World Today' (extended live version)

*Recorded:*               Brixton Sundown - 30 December 1972
*First released:*         *Space Ritual Volume 2* (American Phonograph) -

May 1985

*Current availability:*    *Space Ritual* (EMI) - 2013 reissue

Edited down to under six minutes on the original *Space Ritual*, 'Time We Left' sprawls to over 13 minutes in its original form. This version lacks overdubs and Turner's sax is noticeably more prominent in the mix. Also features a brief section of 'Paranoia'.

# 1973

**'Wage War'** (live spoken word)

*Recorded:*    Wembley Empire Pool - 27 May 1973
*First released:*    *Bring Me The Head Of Yuri Gagarin* (Demi Monde) - January 1985
*Current availability:*    As above (on Plastic Head) - 2008

Despite coming from a poor quality and much repackaged recording of the band's Wembley show, 'Wage War' nevertheless catches Calvert at his most possessed, spitting out Jerzy Kosiński's words with a furious passion. This performance also features his similarly animated recitation of Günter Grass's 'In The Egg'.

There are a number of other Calvert spoken word pieces that were never officially released, but can be found on bootlegs from this period. They include: **'Technicians Of Spaceship Earth', 'Angels Of Space', 'The Beast Of Chaos', 'Shores Of Paradise', 'The Starfarer's Despatch', 'Ode To A Time Flower',** and **'Ode To A Crystal Set'**

## 'It's So Easy' (studio version)

| | |
|---|---|
| *Recorded:* | Olympic Studios – 28 May 1973 |
| *First released:* | *Parallel Universe* |
| *Current availability:* | As above |

Recorded during the 'Urban Guerilla' sessions, this is an earlier version of the track that eventually appeared as the live B-side to the 'Psychedelic Warlords' single in August 1974. It misses the ethereal keyboard intro, and the emphasis in the chorus is slightly different, but once again, with a decent mix and edit, this could have made a great single.

# 1974

## 'The Watcher' (live version)

| | |
|---|---|
| *Recorded:* | Chicago Auditorium – 21 March 1974 |
| *First released:* | *The '1999' Party* (EMI) – November 1997 |
| *Current availability:* | as above (2019 vinyl reissue) and *This Is Your Captain Speaking…* (EMI) – 2015 |

Resurrected as a full band version, and recorded here on the band's second US tour, 'The Watcher' is transformed into a Stooges-esque groover. It's a little ragged, but there's some crashing Mellotron, and it grows into a powerful number by the final verse.

## 'Kings Of Speed' (Deep Fix version)

| | |
|---|---|
| *Recorded:* | Jackson's Studio, Rickmansworth, 1974 |
| *First released:* | *The New Worlds Fair* (Esoteric) – 2008 reissue |
| *Current availability:* | as above |

Not a Hawkwind recording, but a fine version nonetheless. Essentially a different song with the same words, this has a pulsating rhythm track and Moorcock semi-improvising the lyric melody in a way that actually suits his voice. A shame this direction wasn't pursued on the Deep Fix album.

# 1975

### 'Motorhead' (alternative version)

| | |
|---|---|
| *Recorded:* | Olympic Studios - January 1975 |
| *First released:* | 'Motorhead' / 'Valium 10' 7" & 12" single (Flicknife) - August 1981 |
| *Current availability:* | Warrior On The Edge Of Time (Atomhenge) - 2013 reissue |

Recorded during the 'Kings Of Speed' session, this version features just the power trio of Brock, Lemmy and Powell, and is a good deal rawer and ballsier than the 'KOS' B-side – ironically, Brock's vocal is more wired than Lemmy's. (N.B. there is some speculation that Brock's vocal (and synth part) was overdubbed after the Olympic session, possibly years later). In addition, the Atomhenge reissue of *Warrior* includes an instrumental version of 'Motorhead', which pumps and grinds nicely.

(The Atomhenge *Warrior* reissue is also notable for including the unreleased track '**Dawn**' – starting with a lovely extended section of symphonic Mellotron, this turns into a chug-driven jam, the band trying to will a song into existence without success.)

# 1976

## 'Time For Sale' (live track)

*Recorded:*             Colston Hall, Bristol – 27 September 1976

*First released:*       Atomhenge 76 (Voiceprint) – October 2000

*Current availability:*  as above

Hawkwind get (relatively) funky as Calvert raps about Helen of Troy and immortality. Presumably no studio version exists, the song swept aside and forgotten after the Powell/Turner/Rudolph split.

# 1977

## 'Fable Of A Failed Race' (extended version)

*Recorded:*             Rockfield Studios – January 1977

*First released:*       Quark, Strangeness And Charm (Atomhenge) – 2009 reissue

*Current availability:*  as above

Basically the same track, but with a longer fade-up and fade-down, making it double the length of the *Quark* original. Those wordless backing vocals sound more stacked and oceanic than ever, and Brock delivers one of his most fluid solos.

## 'Uncle Sam's On Mars' (studio version)

*Recorded:*             Rockfield Studios – January 1977

*First released:*       Quark, Strangeness And Charm (Atomhenge)

*Current availability:*  as above

Featured in the band's live set since mid-1976, this is

a fascinating staging post in its development, and a much airier take than the one that eventually appears on *PXR5*. In fact, this might well be Hawkwind's most Krautrock-indebted track– with its *motorik* beat, ambient keys and mellow guitar, it could almost be Neu! Great opening lines from Calvert: "The first man to set foot on Mars / Before the highways arrived with their cars / Got its last remaining lifeform stuck / To the sole of his boot. He said, 'Oh fuck!'"

## 'Robot' (alternative live version)

| | |
|---|---|
| *Recorded:* | Hammersmith Odeon, London – 5 October 1977 |
| *First released:* | *Friends & Relations* (Flicknife) – March 1982 |
| *Current availability:* | *The Flicknife Years 1981–1988* (Atomhenge) – 2014 (edited version). Full original version here: YouTube, 2015. *Hawkwind Robot F+R1 Vinyl* |

A tremendous version of one of Hawkwind's spikier songs, Calvert telling us, "We could all end up like robots…" There are some very high backing vocals from Adrian Shaw in the chorus, and House's distorted violin is unearthly, like being attacked by *Forbidden Planet*'s Monster From The Id. And it builds to a hell of a climax… which makes it all the more mysterious that the version currently available is edited a good two minutes before the end.

## 'Over The Top' (Sonic Assassins live improvisation)

| | |
|---|---|
| *Recorded:* | Queens Hall, Barnstable – 23 December 1977 |
| *First released:* | Sonic Assassins 12" EP (Flicknife) – December 1981 |

*Current availability:*   *Hawklords/25 Years On* (Atomhenge) - 2009 reissue

An edited and overdubbed portion of the Sonic Assassins gig – including this track – had been made available on the first *Weird Tape*, but 'Over The Top' was first released on vinyl in 1981 as part of a three track EP (alongside early versions of 'Free Fall' and 'Death Trap'). All of the Sonic Assassins set is essential listening – the other officially available tracks are 'Magnu', 'Angels Of Life' and 'The Golden Void' (all tracks available on the *Hawklords* reissue, except 'TGV', available on *The Flicknife Years 1981-1988*) – but 'Over The Top' is something special, a compelling insight into Calvert's quicksilver thought processes, while the band invent trance techno in the background.

# 1978

## 'We Like To Be Frightened' (unreleased track)

*Recorded:*            Rockfield Studios - 12 February 1978
*First released:*       *PXR5* (Atomhenge) - 2009 reissue
*Current availability:*  as above

Driven along by a staccato electric piano, with lots of horror film imagery and "woo woo"s in the chorus, this is a miniature gem of a track, which would later appear (in re-recorded form) on Calvert's 1981 *Hype* album. It had previously been demoed in 1977 – this version is a properly arranged and recorded song, so its excision from *PXR5* is another mystery. Perhaps it was judged to be too poppy? Or perhaps Brock didn't want a Calvert solo track on the album, the singer having left acrimoniously a few months before *PXR5*'s eventual release?

### 'Drug Cabinet Key' (live version of 'Flying Doctor')

| | |
|---|---|
| *Recorded:* | unknown venue – October 1978 |
| *First released:* | *Friends & Relations Vol. 3* (Flicknife) – April 1985 |
| *Current availability:* | *The Flicknife Years 1981-1988* |

Recorded during Hawklords' Heavy Street-Punk Show tour, this version is notable for starting with Calvert's Russian roulette routine: "To find the bullet is to win. I am going to find the bullet – and I'm going to win!" Cue drum roll and the clicking of a gun. Whereas the album version has an air of novelty about it, this take – with its rubbery bassline and slashing guitar – sounds positively deranged.

# 1979

### 'Valium 10' (Hawklords track)

| | |
|---|---|
| *Recorded:* | Rockfield Studios – early 1979 |
| *First released:* | 'Motorhead'/'Valium 10' 7" & 12" single |
| *Current availability:* | *The Flicknife Years 1981-1988* |

One of Hawkwind's most joyous songs, it gets straight in your face and just keeps on driving – in fact, it sounds like it could go on forever.

### 'Who's Gonna Win The War?' (Hawklords version)

| | |
|---|---|
| *Recorded:* | Rockfield Studios – early 1979 |
| *First released:* | *Friends & Relations* |
| *Current availability:* | *The Flicknife Years 1981-1988* |

A harder and angrier song than the *Levitation* version, this is a chilling musical evocation of Cold War nuclear terror. The bleak interplay between Swindells' deliberately colourless soloing and Brock's ragged guitar is just brilliant.

# A 70s Filmography

## 1970

### Atomic Sunrise Festival
'Hurry On Sundown' / 'The Reason Is?' / 'Be Yourself'

*Recorded:* The Roundhouse, London – 13 March 1970
*Availability:* Adrian Everett, who owns this footage, is hoping to release an Atomic Sunrise film in 2020. A short clip can be viewed online: YouTube, 2010, *Atomic Sunrise Festival 1970*\* [See endnote 7, p21 for further details]

## 1972

### *ATV Today*

*Recorded:* 5 January 1972
*Broadcast:* January 1972
*Availability:* Unknown

Dave Brock was interviewed by *ATV Today*, a popular Midlands-based news/current affairs programme. Hawkfan Phill Jones recalls, "*ATV Today* did a feature on album covers and spoke to Hawkwind about the *In Search of Space* cover." The feature was presumably broadcast a few days later.

### *Callan*: 'Charlie Says It's Goodbye'
'You Shouldn't Do That'

*Broadcast:* 12 April 1972
*Availability:* *Callan - The Colour Years* DVD (Network)

Not an appearance, but a minute-long blast of 'YSDT' features in this episode of the popular Edward

Woodward-starring spy drama. It plays over a scene of a foppish ne'er-do-well reading the *Financial Times*, before a sinister heavy tells him, "Turn off that ridiculous music."

## 'Silver Machine' promo film

| | |
|---|---|
| *Recorded:* | Queensway Hall, Dunstable – 7 July 1972 |
| *Broadcast:* | *Top Of The Pops* – 13 & 27 July, and 10 August 1972 |
| *Availability:* | *Space Ritual* Collector's Edition DVD (2007) |

Dave Brock has said that the BBC film crew "recorded about half an hour of the show" ('Hawkwind Solo' – Mark Paytress, *Record Collector*, February 1993), but it remains unknown if additional footage exists.

# 1973

## The Final Programme

| | |
|---|---|
| *Recorded:* | Elstree Studios, Borehamwood. Early 1973. Directed by Robert Fuest. |
| *Released:* | 4 October 1973 |
| *Availability:* | Network DVD (2013) |

Adaptation of the Michael Moorcock novel, featuring a very brief appearance by Hawkwind.
[See p331 & 333 for further details]

## 'Urban Guerilla' promo film

| | |
|---|---|
| *Recorded:* | Unknown venue – possibly 24 Frames studio, Wardour Street, London, mid-1973. Directed by Cynthia Beatt. Edited by Gary Weis. |
| *Availability:* | *Space Ritual* Collectors Edition DVD (2007) |

A further 23 minutes of film exists from this performance. The accompanying tape boxes featured a recording from *Space Ritual* – sides 1 & 2, plus 'Orgone Accumulator', 'Master Of The Universe' & 'Welcome To The Future' – but it is currently unknown which of these tracks were performed. The film is being restored, with a view to it being released in the near future.

[See endnote 11, p131 for further details]

## PopFestival 73

'Master Of The Universe'

| | |
|---|---|
| *Recorded:* | Scandinavium Gothenburg, Sweden – 15 September 1973 |
| *Broadcast:* | The band's performance was filmed, and 'MOTU' was broadcast on Swedish TV the following year. |
| *Availability:* | Unknown – a copy does not exist in the channel archives. |

# 1975

## Watchfield Festival

| | |
|---|---|
| *Recorded:* | Watchfield Free Festival, Oxfordshire – 23 August 1975 |
| *Broadcast:* | *Time Shift*: 'New Age Travellers', BBC Four, 21 October 2004. |
| *Availability:* | YouTube, 2011. *New Age Travellers documentary**\* |

Features five seconds of Hawkwind's performance at Watchfield.

# 1976

## *Astounding Sounds, Amazing Music* tour

| | |
|---|---|
| *Recorded:* | Newcastle City Hall, 19 September 1976. Fan footage – silent 8mm film. |
| *Availability:* | YouTube, 2018, *Hawkwind 1976 1977 Atom henge** |

# 1977

## *Marc*

'Quark, Strangeness And Charm'

| | |
|---|---|
| *Recorded:* | Granada Studios, Manchester – early September 1977? |
| *Broadcast:* | 7 September 1977 |
| *Availability:* | YouTube, 2012. *Marc Bolan's MARC, Episode Three** |

## Spirit Of The Age tour

| | |
|---|---|
| *Recorded:* | Newcastle City Hall, 20 September 1977. Fan footage – silent 8mm film. |
| *Availability:* | YouTube, 2018. *Hawkwind 1976 1977 Atom henge** |

# 1978

## Pan Transcendental Industries

| | |
|---|---|
| *Recorded:* | 1978. Directed by Barney Bubbles & Chris Gabrin. |
| *Running Time:* | 15 minutes |
| *Availability:* | Held in the Arts Council Collection, South Bank Centre, London. |

This is the introductory film played before each show of the Hawklords tour. The Arts Council describes it as follows: "In addition to the video, the work consists of an installation of four chipboard panels showing four photographs. A milk bottle containing earth,

rags, air and water is centred on the floor in front of
each panel on top of record covers."
[See endnote 5, p316 for further details]

### *Hawklords* tour/Heavy Street-Punk Show

'Automoton' / '25 Years' / 'High Rise' / 'Death Trap' / 'The Age Of The
Micro Man' / 'Spirit Of The Age' / 'Urban Guerilla' / 'Sonic Attack'
/ 'Psi Power' / 'Brainstorm' (track listing taken from Atomhenge *Live
78* album, though fewer songs may have been filmed)

| | |
|---|---|
| *Recorded:* | Brunel University, Uxbridge – 24 November 1978 |
| *Broadcast:* | *Night Moves*, Channel 7, Australia, mid-1979 |
| | ('25 Years', possibly more) |
| *Availability:* | Release pre-announced by Cherry Red in 2017, |
| | but has yet to appear. Ten seconds of the band |
| | performing 'Psi Power' can be seen on YouTube, 2017. |
| | *Top Ten Progressive Rock (British TV Documentary)** |
| | [See endnote 7, p316-17 for further details] |

# 1979

### Silicon Teens: 'Memphis Tennessee' video

| | |
|---|---|
| *Availability:* | YouTube, 2007, *Silicon Teens - Memphis Tennessee** |

Robert Calvert appears as the captain of the Titanic
[See endnote 6, p379 for further details]

### Masters Of The Universe tour

'Lighthouse'

| | |
|---|---|
| *Availability:* | YouTube, 2014, *Hawkwind Live 79-82** |

Grainy footage of the laser show accompanying the
first few minutes of this track, originally released on
the *Hawkwind Live 1979-82* video.

# 1980

## *Levitation* promos

'Levitation' / 'Who's Gonna Win The War?' / 'World Of Tiers'

| | |
|---|---|
| *Recorded:* | Ewart Studios, Wandsworth – November or December 1980 |
| *Availability:* | YouTube, 2012, *Hawkwind - Levitation (promo).flv*\* |
| | YouTube, 2008, *Hawkwind - Who's Gonna Win The War? (Promo)*\* |
| | YouTube, 2007, Hawkwind - *World Of Tiers (Promo)*\* |

## Miscellaneous items

Hawkwind played various festivals that were professionally filmed, including the Isle Of Wight (1970), Glastonbury (1971) and Bickershaw (1972), so it's possible that footage exists from at least one of their performances.

Possible animated promos made for Australian TV, for tracks including 'Space Is Deep', circa 1974?

Doug Smith has some 8mm black & white footage taken at the Steins Academy of Music, New York, 25 November 1973. He also organised the filming of Hawkwind's performance at Futurama, Leeds, 9 September 1979 – this footage remains unedited and in storage.

Brian Tawn recalls seeing a late night documentary about monks and beekeeping on Anglia TV in the late 70s which featured 'Goat Willow' as background music.

\* Video online at date of publication

# Further Listening

## Parallels, Precursors & Influences

Pink Floyd
  *The Piper At The Gates Of Dawn* (1967) / *A Saucerful Of Secrets* (1968) / *More* (1969) / *Ummagumma* (1969)
Soft Machine
  *The Soft Machine* (1968)
The Moody Blues
  *Days Of Future Passed* (1967) / *In Search Of The Lost Chord* (1968) / *To Our Children's Children's Children* (1969)
The Rolling Stones
  '2000 Light Years From Home' (1967)
Pretty Things
  *S. F. Sorrow* (1968)
The Deviants
  *Ptooff!* (1967) / *Disposable* (1968) / *3* (1969)
The Jimi Hendrix Experience
  *Are You Experienced* (1967) / *Axis: Bold As Love* (1968) / *Electric Ladyland* (1969)
The Doors
  *The Doors* (1967)
13th Floor Elevators
  *The 13th Floor Elevators* (1966) / *Easter Everywhere* (1967)
The Byrds
  'Mr Spaceman' (1966) / 'Eight Miles High' (1966) / 'Space Odyssey' (1968)
Grateful Dead
  *Live/Dead* (1969)
Quicksilver Messenger Service
  *Happy Trails* (1969)
Steve Miller Band
  *Sailor* (1968) / *Number 5* (1970)
The Velvet Underground
  *The Velvet Underground and Nico* (1967) / *White Light / White Heat* (1968)

The Stooges
*The Stooges* (1969) / *Funhouse* (1970)
MC5
*Kick Out The Jams* (1969)
Silver Apples
*Silver Apples* (1969) / *Contact* (1970)
Fifty Foot Hose
*Cauldron* (1968)
The United States Of America
*The United States Of America* (1968)
White Noise
*An Electric Storm* (1969)
Pärson Sound
*Pärson Sound* (archival – 2001)
International Harvester
*Sov Gott Rose-Marie* (1968)

## Fellow Travellers & Related Contemporaries

High Tide
*Sea Shanties* (1969) / *High Tide* (1970)
Edgar Broughton Band
*Wasa Wasa* (1969) / *Edgar Broughton Band* (1971) / *Keep Them Freaks A Rollin'*
*– Live At Abbey Road* (archival – 2004)
Pink Fairies
*Never Never Land* (1971) / *What A Bunch Of Sweeties* (1972) / *Kings Of
Oblivion* (1973)
Arthur Brown/Kingdom Come
*Galactic Zoo Dossier* (1971) / *Kingdom Come* (1972) / *Journey* (1973)
Amon Düül II
*Phallus Dei* (1969) / *Yeti* (1970) / *Wolf City* (1972)
Can
*Monster Movie* (1969) / *Soundtracks* (1970) / *Tago Mago* (1971)
Neu!
*Neu!* (1972) / *Neu! 2* (1973) / *Neu! 75* (1975)

Nektar
*Journey To The Centre Of The Eye* (1971) / *A Tab In The Ocean* (1972) / *Down To Earth* (1974)

David Bowie
'Space Oddity' (1969) / *The Man Who Sold The World* (1970) / 'Starman' (1972) / *Diamond Dogs* (1974) / 'Station To Station' (1976) / *Low* (1977) / *Stage* (1978) / *Lodger* (1979)

Roxy Music
*Roxy Music* (1972) / *For Your Pleasure* (1973) / *Country Life* (1974)

Brian Eno
*Here Come The Warm Jets* (1974) / *Taking Tiger Mountain (By Strategy)* (1974) / *Another Green World* (1975)

Black Sabbath
*Paranoid* (1970) / *Master Of Reality* (1971)

Magic Muscle
*The Pipe The Roar The Grid* (archival – 1988)

Ark
*VA – Made In Cornwall* (1976)

Gong
*Flying Teapot* (1973) / *Angel's Egg* (1973) / *You* (1974)

Tim Blake
*Crystal Machine* (1977) / *Blake's New Jerusalem* (1978)

Planet Gong
*Live Floating Anarchy* (1977)

Here & Now
*Give And Take* (1978) / *All Over The Show* (1979)

Melodic Energy Commission
*Stranger In Mystery* (1979) / *Migration Of The Snails* (1980)

Adrian Wagner
*Distances Between Us* (1974) / *Disco Dream And The Androids* (1979)

Steve Swindells
*Fresh Blood* (1980)

## Sci-Fi Connectors

The Liverpool Scene
'Universes' (1968) / 'We'll All Be Spacemen Before We Die' (1969)
Julian's Treatment
*A Time Before This* (1970)
Van Der Graaf Generator
'Pioneers Over 'C'' (1970) / 'Still Life' (1976)
Genesis
'Watcher Of The Skies' / 'Get 'Em Out By Friday' (both 1972)
Ramases
*Space Hymns* (1971)
Paul Kantner & Jefferson Starship
*Blows Against The Empire* (1970)
Magma
*Magma* (1970) / *1001° Centigrades* (1971) / *Mëkanïk Dëstruktïẁ Kömmandöh* (1973)
Sun Ra
*The Heliocentric Worlds of Sun Ra Vol. 1* (1965) / *Space Is The Place* (1972) / *Astro Black* (1973)
Parliament
*Mothership Connection* (1975) / *The Clones Of Dr. Funkenstein* (1976) / *Funkentelechy Vs. The Placebo Syndrome* (1977)
Rush
'2112' (1976) / 'Cygnus X-1' (1977)
Heldon
*Electronique Guérilla* (1974) / *Un Rêve Sans Conséquence Spéciale* (1976) / *Interface* (1977)
Zolar X
*Timeless* (archival – 2004)

## Post-Punk Descendants

Joy Division
  *Unknown Pleasures* (1979) / *Closer* (1980)
Public Image Ltd
  *First Issue* (1978) / *Metal Box* (1979)
Wire
  *Pink Flag* (1977) / *Chairs Missing* (1978) / *154* (1979)
Cabaret Voltaire
  *Mix-Up* (1979) / *The Voice of America* (1980) / *Red Mecca* (1981)
Killing Joke
  *Killing Joke* (1980)
Jimmy Pursey
  *Imagination Camouflage* (1980)
The Normal
  'TV OD'/'Warm Leatherette' (1978)
Fast Breeder & The Radio Actors
  'Nuclear Waste'/'Digital Love' (1978)
Tanz Der Youth
  'I'm Sorry, I'm Sorry'/'Delay' (1978)
Blood Donor
  'Rubber Revolution'/'Chemical Babies' (1979)
Chrome
  *Alien Soundtracks* (1977) / *Half-Machine Lip Moves* (1979) / *3rd From The Sun* (1982)
Pere Ubu
  *Datapanik In The Year Zero* (1978)
Dead Kennedys
  'Holiday In Cambodia' (1978)
Wipers
  *Youth Of America* (1981)
Simply Saucer
  *Cyborgs Revisited* (archival – 1989)

# Selected Bibliography/ Further Reading

Abrahams, Ian, 2004. *Hawkwind: Sonic Assassins*. SAF Publishing. Revised edition, CreateSpace 2017.

Andrews, Stephen E. & Rennison, Nick, 2006. *100 Must-Read Science Fiction Novels*. A & C Black.

Ash, Brian (ed.), 1977. *The Visual Encyclopedia Of Science Fiction*. Pan.

Beckett, Andy, 2010. *When The Lights Went Out: What Really Happened to Britain in the Seventies*. Faber & Faber.

Brotherstone, Stephen & Lawrence, Dave, 2017. *Scarred For Life: The 1970s*. Lulu.

Chapman, Rob, 2015. *Psychedelia And Other Colours*. Faber & Faber.

Clerk, Carol, revised edition 2006. *The Saga Of Hawkwind*. Omnibus Press.

Deakin, Rich, 2008. *Keep It Together: Cosmic Boogie with the Deviants and the Pink Fairies*. Headpress.

Diski, Jenny, 2010. *The Sixties*. Profile Books.

Doggett, Peter, 2011. *The Man Who Sold The World: David Bowie and the 1970s*. Bodley Head.

Farren, Mick, 2001. *Give The Anarchist A Cigarette*. Jonathan Cape.

Gorman, Paul, revised edition 2010. *Reasons To Be Cheerful: The Life and Work of Barney Bubbles*. Adelita.

Green, Jonathon, 1989. *Days In the Life: Voices from the English Underground, 1961-71*. Minerva.

Greenland, Colin, 1983. *The Entropy Exhibition: Michael Moorcock and the British New Wave in Science Fiction*. Routledge & Kegan Paul.

Heller, Jason, 2018. *Strange Stars: David Bowie, Pop Music, and the Decade Sci-Fi Exploded*. Melville House.

Kent, Nick, 2010. *Apathy For The Devil: A 1970s Memoir*. Faber & Faber.

Lemmy with Garza, Janiss, 2002. *White Line Fever – Lemmy: The Autobiography*. Simon & Schuster.

Luckhurst, Roger, 2005. *Science Fiction*. Polity.

MacDonald, Ian, 1995. *Revolution In The Head: The Beatles Records and the Sixties*. Pimlico.

Matthews, Austin (ed.), 2014. *Interstellar Overdrive: The Shindig! Guide to Spacerock.* Volcano.

Moorcock, Michael (ed.), 1983. *New Worlds: An Anthology.* Flamingo.

Reynolds, Simon, 2016. *Shock And Awe: Glam Rock and Its Legacy.* Faber & Faber.

Stubbs, David, 2014. *Future Days: Krautrock and the Building of Modern Germany.* Faber & Faber.

Sandbrook, Dominic, 2011. *State Of Emergency – The Way We Were: Britain, 1970-1974.* Penguin.

Savage, Jon, 1991. *England's Dreaming: The Sex Pistols and Punk Rock.* Faber & Faber.

Sladek, John, 1974. *The New Apocrypha: A Guide to Strange Sciences and Occult Beliefs.* Hart-Davis, McGibbon.

Strick, Philip, 1976. *Science Fiction Movies.* Octopus.

Turner, Alwyn W., revised edition 2013. *Crisis? What Crisis? – Britain in the 1970s.* Aurum Press.

Turner, Nik & Thompson, Dave, 2015. *The Spirit Of Hawkwind 1969-1976.* Cleopatra.

Wheen, Francis, 2009. *Strange Days Indeed: The Golden Age of Paranoia.* Fourth Estate.

Young, Rob & Schmidt, Irmin, 2018. *All Gates Open: The Story of Can.* Faber & Faber.

## Online Sources

*The Archive: UK Rock Festivals 1960-1990 & UK Free Festivals 1969-1990.* ukrockfestivals.com

Cross, Nigel, 2007. *Cries From The Midnight Circus: Ladbroke Grove 1967-78.* (sleeve notes to the Castle Music compilation, 2007) terrascope.co.uk/Features/LadbrokeGrove.htm

Dunthorne, Stephen. *The Plastic Fragment Of A Child's Toy.* plasticfragment.com/

Gerwers, Knut. *Spirit Of The P/age.* aural-innovations.com/robertcalvert/news/calvertnews.htm

*International Times* archive. internationaltimes.it/archive/

Johnson, Chuck. *Hawklord.com.* hawklord.com/hw/

Law, Dave. *The Hawkwind Museum.* web.archive.org/web/20071126060452/http://www.hawkwindmuseum.co.uk/

*OZ* archive. ro.uow.edu.au/ozlondon/

Skinner, Jim. *Group X: In Search Of Hawkwind.* faojc.com/media/1009/
    hawkwalk.pdf

Sneyd, Steve & Jones, David. *Gnawing Medusa's Flesh: The Science Fiction Poetry
    Of Robert Calvert.* aural-innovations.com/issues/issue18/medusa.html

Youles, Steve. *Starfarer's Hawkwind Page.* web.archive.org/
    web/20170427224959/http://starfarer.net/

## The Hawkwind Mythos

Butterworth, Michael, 1976. *The Time Of The Hawklords.* Star.

Butterworth, Michael, 1977. *Queens Of Deliria.* Star.

Butterworth, Michael & Walker, Bob, 1994. *Ledge Of Darkness.* Included with *25
    Years On*, a Griffin Music boxset compilation (not the Hawklords album).

Calvert, Robert, 1972. Fly As A Kite, *Frendz.* 14/7/72.

Calvert, Robert, 1972. Commentary On The Saga Of Doremi Fasol Latido, back
    cover and inner sleeve of *Doremi Fasol Latido.*

Calvert, Robert, 1972. An Extract From The Saga Of Doremi Fasol Latido,
    Space Ritual programme.

Calvert, Robert & Bubbles, Barney, 1971. *The Hawkwind Log.* Included with *In
    Search Of Space.*

Calvert, Robert & Bubbles, Barney, 1971. Galactic Tarot, *IT*, 18/11/71.

Moorcock, Michael & Cawthorn, James, 1971. Codename: 'Hawkwind' – The Sonic
    Assassins, *Frendz,* 29/11/71.

## Lyrical Inspirations

Asimov, Isaac, 1950. *I, Robot.* Doubleday.

Ballard, J. G., 1962 [2006], The Garden Of Time, in *The Complete Short Stories.*
    HarperCollins.

Ballard, J. G., 1975. *High-Rise.* Jonathan Cape.

Bradbury, Ray, 1950. *The Martian Chronicles.* Doubleday.

Bradbury, Ray, 1953. *Fahrenheit 451.* Ballantine.

Burroughs, William, 1964. *Nova Express.* Grove Press.

Farmer, Philip José, 1965-91. *World Of Tiers* series. Ace Books.

Hesse, Herman, 1927. *Steppenwolf.* Fischer.

McCaffrey, Anne, 1967- . *The Dragonriders Of Pern* series. Ballatine.

Moorcock, Michael, 1968-77. *The Cornelius Quartet.* Allison & Busby.

Moorcock, Michael, 1969. *The Black Corridor.* Mayflower.

Moorcock, Michael, 1970. *The Eternal Champion.* Mayflower.

Russell, Eric Frank; Aldiss, Brian (ed.), 1956 [2007]. Sole Solution, in: *A Science Fiction Omnibus.* Penguin.

Spinrad, Norman, 1972. *The Iron Dream.* Avon.

Zelazny, Roger, 1967. *Lord Of Light.* Doubleday.

Zelazny, Roger, 1969. *Damnation Alley.* G.P. Putnam.

Zelazny, Roger, 1971. *Jack Of Shadows.* Walker.

# Index

Henri, Adrian: 344 (4)

Henry Kiel Auditorium, St Louis: 152

Henry Cow: 194

Henry, Stuart: 48

Herbert, Frank: 324, 346 (10)

*Dune*: 324, 327, 346 (9)

Here & Now: 397, 397 (6)

Hermann, Bernard: 39

Herzog, Werner: 157

High Tide: 71, 74 (2), 150, 190 (7), 193, 208, 266, 303 (1)

*Sea Shanties*: 71

Hipgnosis: 256, 263 (3)

Hitchcock, Alfred: 39

Hitler, Adolf: 155, 160 (15), 253, 276, 335, 336

Hoban, Russell: 342

*Riddley Walker*: 342

Holy Modal Rounders: 193

Hodgson, Brian: 39

Hook, Peter: 374, 376, 380 (13)

Hopkins, John ('Hoppy'): 65, 69, 70, 72

Hopkins, Sonny: 43 (11)

Horn, Paul: 304 (5)

*Hot Hits XIII* (album): 104 (6)

**House, Simon:** 40, 150, 152, 157, 159 (7), 171, *178*, *191*, 190 (7), 192, 195, 201, 205, 208, 216, 221 (10), 225 (1), *227*, *245*, *249*, *255*, 256, 267, 269, 287, 295 (29), 301, 302, 303 (2), 307, 365 (5)

Quoted in press: 170

Style of playing: 164-166, 169, 181, 186-190, 193, 195, 218, 219, 223-225, 250-253, 309, 310, 357-360

*Also played with:*

High Tide: 72, 266, 303 (1)

Michael Moorcock & The Deep Fix: 197

David Bowie: 208, 301, 303 (2), 304 (10), 353

Housham, David: 312

Howard, Tony: 216, 256, 263 (5), 268, 304 (4)

Howe, Ashley: 397 (2)

Howlett, Mike: 304 (6)

Hubbard, L. Ron: 276, 292 (12)

Hughes, Bob (Robert): 283, 289, 294 (24), 310 (4)

*The Shock Of The New*: 294 (24)

Hughes, Trevor: 290

Hull, Rod: 308

Hüsker Dü: 375

Huxley, Aldous: 28 (4), 328

*Brave New World*: 328, 335

*The Doors Of Perception*: 28 (4)

Hyde, Tony: 228, 231 (3)

Hyman, Dick: 42 (6)

*Moog: The Electric Eclectics of Dick Hyman*: 42 (6)

## I

Ian Dury and The Blockheads: 263 (2), 316 (1)

*Do It Yourself*: 316 (1)

Implosion (club): 19, 70, 216, 368

Inner City Unit: see Turner, Nik

International Harvester: 43 (9)

*Sov Gott Rose-Marie*: 43 (9)

*International Times*: see IT

*Invaders From Mars* (film): 322

*Invasion Of The Body Snatchers* (film): 293 (16), 322, 334

Iommi, Tony: 210, 211, 213 (12)

IRA: 128, 143, 157, 283, 388

Iron Maiden: 388, 392

Isle Of Wight Festival: 18, 20 (1), 31, 32, 67, 73,

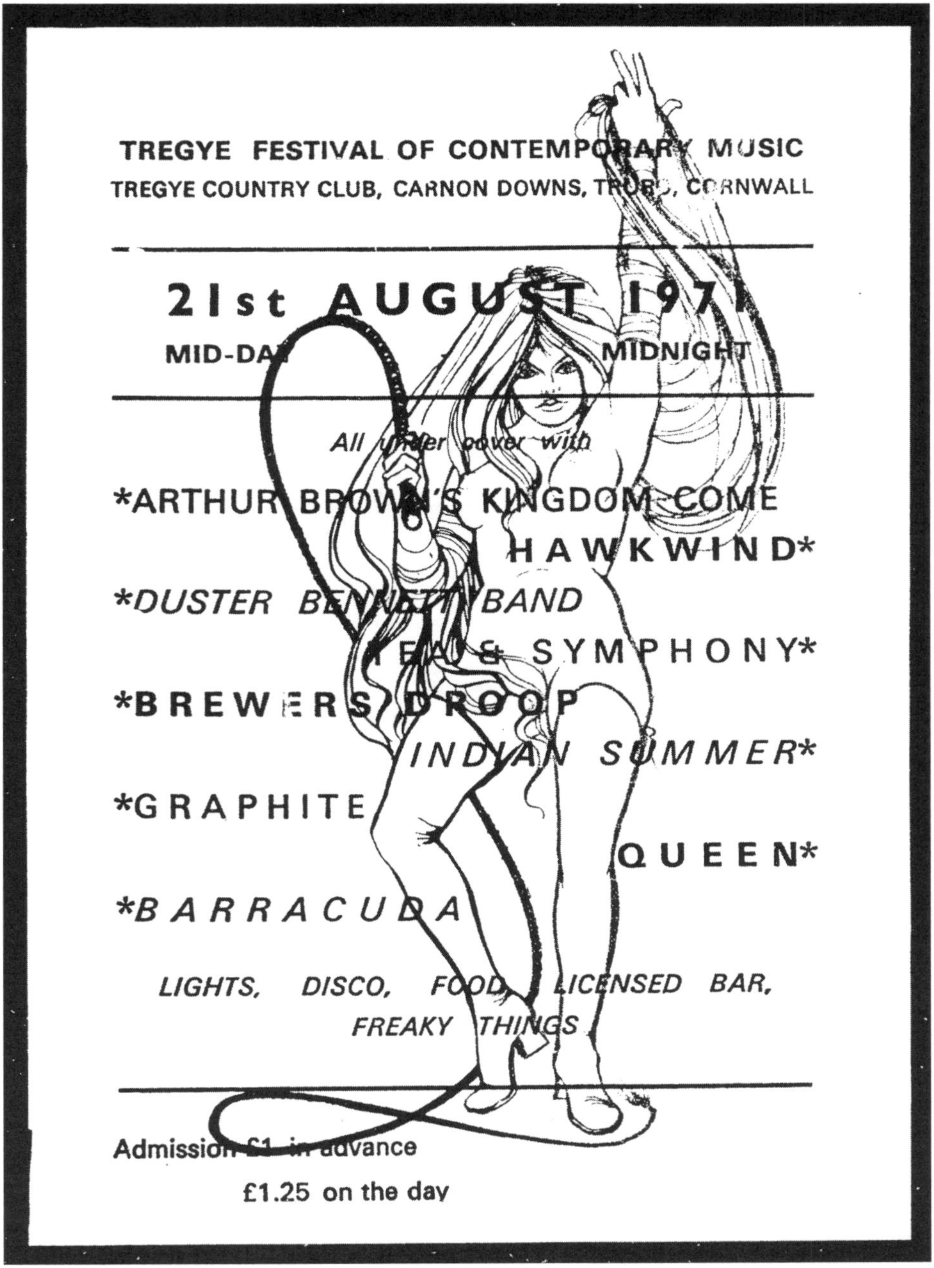

**TREGYE FESTIVAL OF CONTEMPORARY MUSIC**

TREGYE COUNTRY CLUB, CARNON DOWNS, TRURO, CORNWALL

# 21st AUGUST 1971

**MID-DAY** — **MIDNIGHT**

*All under cover with*

*ARTHUR BROWN'S KINGDOM COME

HAWKWIND*

*DUSTER BENNETT BAND

TEA & SYMPHONY*

*BREWERS DROOP

INDIAN SUMMER*

*GRAPHITE

QUEEN*

*BARRACUDA

*LIGHTS, DISCO, FOOD, LICENSED BAR, FREAKY THINGS*

Admission £1 in advance

£1.25 on the day

# HAWKWIND

## HAVE FLOWN

Bookings, loons and good clean fun
Phone **Angie, 636 1655, ext. 334**

Clearwater ads by
Alan Tanner (1970)

**PEACE FESTIVAL EASTER MON. 3RD APRIL**
12 NOON—6 P.M.
ADMISSION FREE
COME EARLY

**JOHN PEEL** INTRODUCES
**HAWKWIND**
**ROY HARPER**
GRAHAM **BOND** AND PETE **BROWN**
**ADRIAN HENRI**
**ADRIAN MITCHELL**
**STEVE TOOK**
AND SURPRISE GUESTS
**ARMADA**
ORGANISED BY C N D   01-242-3872
ON FALCONFIELD · TADLEY
**ALDERMASTON**
READING 12 miles   NEWBURY 11 miles   BASINGSTOKE 7 miles
Buses from Reading General (British Rail) to the Falcon Inn

March from London to a
**FREE PEACE FESTIVAL**
**at ALDERMASTON**
Monday, 3 April, from noon till 6 p.m.

**HAWKWIND,   ROY HARPER**
**STEVE TOOK** (ex-T. REX)
**GRAHAM BOND & PETE BROWN**
**ARMADA,   ADRIAN HENRI**
**ADRIAN MITCHELL**

Info · CND (M), 14 Gray's Inn Road, W.C.1   Tel. 01-242 3873

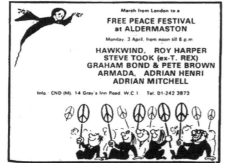

**FEB 13   3-12**
**GREASY TRUCKERS**
GRAND OPENING PARTY
*at the*
**ROUNDHOUSE**
**HAWKWIND**
**BRINSLEY SCHWARZ**
DJ · ANDY DUNKLEY   **MAN**   LIGHTS · CLEARLIGHT
**★ BYZANTIUM ★**
**MAGIC MICHAEL + FRIENDS**
**BLACK DEATH AND FOOTMEN**
50P   **LADY JUNE + BAND**   50P
**MIKE GRIGGS**
**LIGHTING BY DAVE COHEN**
★ ★ SUPPORT THE TRUCKERS ★ ★

**HIPPODROME - BRISTOL**
7.30 — MONDAY, 3rd OCTOBER — 7.30
PRICES: £2.50  £2.00  £1.50   Box Office open 10.00 a.m. - 8.30 p.m.

Kennedy Street Enterprises Ltd. present
**Spirit of the age**
FEATURING
**Hawkwind**
**LIQUID LEN and the LENSMEN**
**ATOM HENGE**

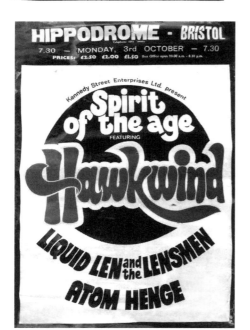

**THE HAWKLORDS**

**HAWKWIND LIVE AT**
Malvern Winter Gardens   Thursday 2nd November 1978
£2.00 Adv.  £2.50 Dr.  8pm   Presented by Cherry Red

European tour stage pass 1975

SILVER MACHINE. YOU KNOW WHAT I MEAN. IT WON'T EVER BE SEEN. SILVER MACHINE. A SINGLE. JUNE NINTH **HAWKWIND.**

'Silver Machine' ad from *OZ 43*, July 1972

# Thank You

Major thanks to everybody I interviewed for this book: DikMik, Nik Turner, Michael Moorcock, Stacia Blake, Alan Powell, Paul Rudolph, Adrian Shaw, Paul Hayles, Harvey Bainbridge, Andrew Lauder, Doug Smith, Jeff Dexter, Alex 'Higgy' Higgins, Gerry Fitzgerald, Mike Hart, Arthur Rhodes, Jonathan Smeeton, Renée Berg, David Hardy, Philip Tonkyn, Anton Matthews, Richard Ogden, Michael Butterworth, Ashley Howe, Léonie Scott-Matthews, Pamela Townley, Tony Vesely, Chris Gabrin, Gail Colson, Tony Davies, Chris Carter, Cosey Fanni Tutti, Colin Newman, Daniel Miller, Jah Wobble, Jello Biafra, Jon Savage, Paul Gorman, Richard H. Kirk, Stephen Morris, Youth, and James Riley. Special shout-out to Doug and Nik for services above and beyond.

A big thank you to Mark Pilkington and Jamie Sutcliffe at Strange Attractor for commissioning this book – I'm pretty sure that nobody else would have let me write it this way! To Mark Sinker, for the heroic edit. To John Coulthart, for the wonderful cover. To Maia Gaffney-Hyde, for saintly perseverance. To Richard Bancroft for his superhuman proofing and indexing skills. And to Andrew McGrory, for endless discussion, the title, and long-term loan of materials.

Thank you to the following people for kindly providing visual material and insight: Brian Tawn, Nick Calvert, Mica Davies, Laurie Lewis, Pennie Smith, Pedro Bellavista, Wolfie Smith, Cynthia Beatt, George Galitzine, Keith Kniveton, Michael Scott, Jim Skinner, Johan Edlundh, Paul Windle, Steve Readhead, Oz Hardwick, Peter Zabulis, Sandy Cameron, Stephen Dunthorne, Sam Kirwan, Mark Kennedy, Ian Abrahams, John Kilbride, Pete Knifton, and Steve Lines. And thanks to Steve R, Paul Eaton-Jones and Tom Stone for their memories.

Thanks to the following people for assistance/support along the way: Dave & Kris Brock, Mick Slattery, Dave Anderson, Simon King, Simon House, Steve Swindells, Gabi Nasemann, Alan Warner, Andy Sharp, Stephen E. Andrews, Mr. Dibs, Tom Kirkham, Eleri Stedman, Bryan Pitkin, Mick Ouen, Tim Cumming, Adrian Everett, Chris Purdon, Ken Garner, Rebecca & Mike, Chris Shearer, Zoe Miller, Lailah O'Donnell, Dante Bonutto, Nazar Ali Khan, Jerry Richards, Kate Price, Andy Fraser, Daryl Easlea, Stefan Granados, Paul Trynka, Jonathan Muller, Greg Healey, Michael Hann, John Doran & Luke Turner at *The Quietus*, Jerry Ewing & Jo Kendall at *Prog*, Jon Mills & Andy Morten at *Shindig!*, Ian

Harrison & Danny Eccleston at *MOJO*, Philippe Manoeuvre at *Rock & Folk*, Nigel Reeve at Warner Music, and Matt Ingham at Cherry Red.

And not forgetting everybody online who's taken the time to respond to my questions and requests, particularly those denizens of the following Facebook groups: Hawkwind And Related Album History; Brian Tawn's SCRIBE; Robert Calvert; The Hawkwind Bootleg Emporium.

Strange Attractor Press

2020